Growth and Development From an Evolutionary Perspective

T0340130

Growth and Development From an Evolutionary Perspective

JOHN C. H. FEI AND GUSTAV RANIS

BLACKWELL
Publishers

First published 1997

First published in paperback 1999
2 4 6 8 10 9 7 5 3 1

Blackwell Publishers Inc.
350 Main Street
Malden, MA 02148
USA

Blackwell Publishers Ltd
108 Cowley Road
Oxford OX4 1JF
UK

Library of Congress Cataloging in Publication Data
Fei, John C. H.
    Growth and development from an evolutionary perspective / John
C.H. Fei and Gustav Ranis.
        p.   cm.
    Includes bibliographical references and index.
    ISBN 1–55786–079–3 (alk. paper)—ISBN 0–631–21889–0 (pbk: alk. paper)
    1. Economic development.   I. Ranis, Gustav.   II. Title.
HD82.F378   1997
338.9—dc21   96–45155
                                                  CIP

ISBN 1557860793

British Library Cataloguing in Publication Data

A CIP catalogue record for this book is available from the British Library.

Contents

PART III THE ANALYTICS OF GROWTH AND DEVELOPMENT

List of Figures

List of Tables

Preface

Work on this volume began some years ago, with the original intent of responding to a request from Blackwell Publishers to prepare a revised edition of our out-of-print 1964 book *Development of the Labor Surplus Economy: Theory and Policy*. With the passage of time, however, that original purpose has undergone radical change. While the basic dual economy model first presented there has by no means been abandoned, the present volume represents a major departure from that earlier work in a number of directions.

Most importantly, the book takes an evolutionary approach, endeavoring to analyze the development process from its physiocratic, agrarian origins to the ultimate "promised land" of modern economic growth. In modeling this transition process, complete with epochs, graduations and sub-phases, it relies in part on the tool-kit found in the history of economic thought, and in part on the application of a system of growth equations derived from the general neoclassical production function. We also seized the opportunity to respond to the microeconomically-based neoclassical criticism of the "surplus labor" concept which we share with Arthur Lewis. The previously closed economy has now been opened to trade, factor mobility and technology, and the emerging critical issues of equity, poverty and human development as they relate to growth are addressed within the same evolutionary perspective. Finally, the volume concludes with a major section dealing with the empirical, policy and political economy implications of our view of development for the comparative experience of Asia, Latin America, and Africa.

Thanks are due to the editors of the *American Economic Review*, the *International Economic Review*, the *Journal of Development Economics*, the *Quarterly Journal of Economics*, and *World Development* for permitting the use of selective materials appearing in previous work by the authors. Thanks are due also to Gary Fields, Yujiro Hayami, Shirley Kuo, Gary Saxonhouse and Frances Stewart for their comments, contributions and insights; to Ryan Schneider and Michael Wang for research assistance;

to Glenna Ames for help with the figures; and to Megan Weiler and Lora LeMosy for their typing and their fortitude.

Tragically, John C. H. Fei, my long-time personal friend and professional partner, passed away suddenly in July 1996, just as this work was making its way through the final editing stages. This volume is dedicated to his memory.

Gustav Ranis

PART I

Introduction

1
Growth and Development: An Overview

1.1 Introduction

1.1.1 The age of growth consciousness in the developing world

It is generally accepted that the Third World's efforts to join the ranks of the so-called "mature industrial countries" represents one of the major social, economic and political phenomena of the second half of the twentieth century. This attempted transition to modern growth will rank with the taming of the atom as the most important event of this period. With more and more time having elapsed since achieving political independence, and thus the possibility of blaming their unsatisfactory state of development on pre-existing colonial relations, the world's developing countries have increasingly focused on the need to act decisively to reach the charmed circle of the developed countries – and as quickly as possible. Neither oil crisis nor debt crisis are likely to be seen as more than blips when the history of this era is definitively written.

This period is characterized by the effort to promote growth through the exercise of political force. For their part, the rich countries, anxious to "do the right thing", especially in the early years of the post-war era, have become increasingly aware of the importance of this Third World development effort from the point of view of their own enlightened self-interest. As some of the poor countries have with surprising suddenness turned into major players on the international economic scene, in fact attracting the newly coined label of NICs (newly industrialized countries), North–South relations have begun to occupy one of the front burners of international political as well as economic concern. Especially now that the world has emerged from the Cold War and managed to avoid a nuclear holocaust, this effort, and the extent to which it ultimately proves successful for two-thirds of humanity, will be seen as **the** major event of the second half of the twentieth century.

1.1.2 Revival of growth theory

This change in the political configuration of the globe over the past four decades has found its reflection increasingly in the concern of academic economists focusing on problems of growth or, better, a more broadly defined development process in the Third World. Although this endeavor has long and distinguished antecedents, especially in the physiocratic and classical traditions, it is only after the termination of World War II that we have witnessed a marked revival of the sub-discipline called development economics which has focused its attention fully on this problem.

Undoubtedly, a major difficulty encountered in this renewed effort to obtain a better understanding of the development process is the increasingly marked diversity among developing countries. The reasons for successful development in some parts of the Third World, specifically in the NICs of East Asia (Taiwan, South Korea, Hong Kong, and Singapore), and its relative absence elsewhere, (for example, in Latin America, South Asia, and Sub-Saharan Africa) remains something of a mystery; and surprisingly few comprehensive attempts have been made to generalize from the abundance of the inductive evidence from the post-war experience now before us. In the early post-war era a substantial number of useful, if ad hoc, theoretical insights and policy-related constructs had been deployed (for example, the "big push," the "critical minimum effort," the "takeoff," "balanced growth") but there has been a glaring absence of any more generally accepted macro-theoretical framework to systematically tackle the totality of the development phenomenon in a comparative setting.

Admittedly, in the early post-war era, given the relatively few years of decent data and experience, we were all severely handicapped by the need to either restrict our laboratory to cross-sectional analysis or to an examination of the long-run historical pattern of a group of now developed countries which had earlier effected a successful transition. This latter group prominently includes the so-called "latecomer countries", that is, Japan and Germany, though the UK, the USA, Canada, Australia, etc., with very different original endowment conditions, are sometimes added. Today, in sharp contrast, we have at our disposal the historical record of more than 40 years of post-war economic growth in more than 100 developing countries, based on both national sources and the records accumulated by such international bodies as the International Monetary Fund, the World Bank, and the United Nations agencies. Yet even now, with four decades of post-war economic data available to permit the fuller exploration of this historical laboratory, there still exists a widespread feeling in parts of the profession that the Third World's terrain remains too forbidding, its heterogeneity too pronounced, and the available inductive evidence too meager or lacking in quality, to permit the search for general formulations to go forward successfully. In juxtaposition to this, especially in the wake of the post-1982 Less Developed Country (LDC) debt crisis, is an increasingly vociferous mainstream view which has accepted the so-called "Washington Consensus" and proposes to treat the development problem as just another branch of applied macroeconomics as deployed to analyze growth issues in the mature industrialized countries. Finally, there is a growing branch of the profession which applies sophisticated micro-economic tools to the development problems very much as it would in any setting. Accordingly, development economics has become the object of a substantial number of funereal orations in recent years emanating from both the extreme neoclassical (Lal) and structuralist (Hirschman) wings of the profession (see Lal, 1985).

In our own view, neither the simple application of post-Keynesian or monetarist macroeconomic growth models, with all their additional micro-analytic refinements, nor the ad hoc, country-specific and institutionally laden efforts associated with much of early post-war development eco-nomics, is appropriate for fruitful progress in understanding the develop-ment process. On the one hand, we do not believe that the same neoclassical analytical tool kit applied to the Developed Countries (DCs) (for example, USA, UK, Japan) can necessarily always be applied success-fully to the macroeconomic development problems of LDCs in which the very change in the rules of operation is likely to represent the essential issue. On the other hand, we do not share the timidity of some with respect to the ability to generalize beyond individual "case studies" (that is, stressing what is relevant only to a particular developing country at a particular point in time) even as we fully recognize the marked hetero-geneity in initial conditions, endowments, institutional frameworks, etc. among the many countries bearing the Third World label.

The retention of a general equilibrium macroeconomic framework of analysis proposed here has the strength of analyzing the relatedness of economic events in a holistic operational perspective and is an essential component of our intellectual inheritance as demonstrated by the classical growth theories of Smith, Malthus and Ricardo. However, to be really fruitful, such a "new classical" system must be embedded in a larger con-ceptual framework that is both typologically sensitive (that is, sensitive to the existence of different types of LDCs engaged in the transition growth effort) and characterized by the existence of sub-phases within that long-term historical perspective (inclusive of the interaction between initial conditions and the political process of development policy formation over time). No effort will be made in this volume to put forward one integrated general theory of development; we are admittedly not quite ready for that. Instead, we shall be content with proposing our own definition of what the transition growth process is all about and demonstrating an approach we have found useful for analyzing the efforts of typologically different LDCs to reach the charmed circle of the developed industrial countries. This chapter will hopefully serve as an introduction to this proposed way of looking at the development problem – both in relation to the tool kit left to us by development economists of different vintages and the full exploration of the post-war laboratory of actual development experience.

1.2 Epochal and Transition Growth

We find it useful to distinguish between epochal and transition growth, where epochs are defined as long period growth eras characterized by the unity of a set of essential growth phenomena and the relative stability of the rules of the game. Growth under agrarianism and under mature mixed economy rules are examples. Transition growth, on the other hand, occurs when a system is shifting from one epoch to another and thus constitutes a more short-run phenomenon, even though it may, of course, take many decades to accomplish. The industrial revolution in England between 1780 and 1820 would constitute a leading example of such a transition growth process (see figure 1.1a). It was in this period that the classical growth theory of Smith, Malthus and Ricardo was born. The post-World War II period (1950–90) represents another example of transition growth, with contemporary LDCs attempting to move out of their pre-war heritage of agrarian colonialism (see figure 1.1b). It was in this period that inherited development theory has been revised and modernized. It is concerned especially with the transition growth process – just as today's neoclassical economists tend to be relatively insensitive to the disequilibrium conditions implied.

In conclusion, we believe it not only helpful but essential to think of the development problem itself as one of transition between two major epochs, agrarianism and modern growth, navigated by the now mature countries at an earlier stage and attempted by the less developed countries mainly in the post-World War II era. The juxtaposition in figure 1.1 of these two transition growth experiences in historical perspective suggests both the historical spread of modern growth within the North as well as the latter day imitation efforts by the contemporary LDCs in the South.

It is convenient to first describe the epoch of modern growth by briefly outlining the contours of the "promised land" to which developing countries are aspiring; and, second, to examine the epoch of agrarianism which

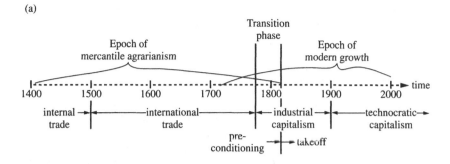

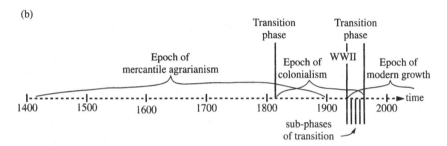

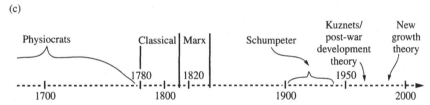

Figure 1.1 (a) Northern epochal sequence (b) Southern epochal sequence (c) Growth theoretic ideas

many LDCs have by now left behind, but which still holds some Third World countries, for example, in Africa, at least partially in its grip.

1.3 The Epoch of Modern Economic Growth

Simon Kuznets (1966), more than anyone else, has provided us with the stylized facts of modern economic growth which can be summarized in the form of a number of more or less clearly identifiable statistical characteristics.

These six stylized facts attending modern growth, referred to by Kuznets, include indicators of the rapidity with which growth takes place, structural change indicators, and the spread of the modern growth phenomenon across regions and countries.

1.3.1   The stylized facts: science, technology and the demographic transition

The modern growth epoch (MGE) represents an era during which the primary growth promotion force is the systematic exploration of the frontiers of science and technology and the systematic application of that knowledge to the industrial art of production. For the first time savings and capital accumulation, carrying the results of scientific inquiry and new technology, lie at the heart of economic endeavor. The primary rapidity indicators of modern growth thus include an acceleration of labor productivity and of GNP growth.

A second indicator of "speed" is the process of demographic transition manifested in an initial increase and then decline in population growth. Increases in labor productivity and in per capita income occur in part because increases in the rate of capital accumulation overwhelm the population growth rate, thus leading to the phenomenon of secular capital deepening; the rest is due to technology change.

This completion of the demographic transition with the eventual decline in the population growth rate signifies a basic change in societal values. Population growth declines only when physical survival is assured by scientific breakthroughs and human beings opt for sustained increases in the quality of life. While Adam Smith believed that the most reliable index of "prosperity" was population growth, a large population was already regarded as a curse by Malthus.

1.3.2   The stylized facts: structural change

Another set of stylized characteristics associated with modern growth centers on structural changes within the population. A major type is represented by what might be called dualistic structural change. During the long agrarian epoch, the coexistence of agricultural and non-agricultural activities was characterized by stability or intersectoral proportionality as can be seen from the fact that agricultural populations were maintained at 70–80 percent of the total over centuries. With the arrival of the modern epoch, dualistic structural change can be seen from the sustained and continued shift of the population from agricultural to non-agricultural activities, or similarly, in terms of value added, as in the A (agricultural) to M (manufacturing) to S (services) sectoral shifts preferred by Kuznets.

A second type of structural change may be referred to as the rapid metabolism (that is, the birth of new industries and products and the death of others) within the non-agricultural sector. That such rapid metabolism is a key structural characteristic of MGE can be readily seen by a comparative examination of a Sears catalogue over any recent 30-year period. Dualistic structural change and a vigorous metabolic process within non-agriculture are the direct consequence of rapid technology change and income growth that combine to continuously expand the consumption horizons of citizens in the mature industrial society.

In summary, the stylized characteristics of modern economic growth include persistent increases in per capita income and accompanying structural changes among the component sectors. During the transition, the economy shifts from its preponderantly agricultural origins to a preponderantly non-agricultural system, with capital intensity and per capita incomes rising consistently as a result of the routinized exploration of the frontiers of science and technology.

1.3.3 The stylized facts: the geographic spread of MGE

The modern growth epoch represents a new way of economic life initiated in England by the industrial revolution slightly more than 200 years ago. That new life style proved irresistible as it spread geographically from England to the Continent and thence to the other so-called "latecomer countries" in the course of the nineteenth century. As illustrated in figure 1.1, in the UK that transition was probably completed between 1780 and 1820; it then spread to Western Europe and North America. In Germany, the MGE began around 1860 and in Japan not until the period between 1880 and 1920. It should also be noted that this geographic spread also had its limits, that is, it did not naturally spill over to the so-called "overseas territories" – the world's developing countries. Indeed, in long-run historical perspective, the post-war transition growth of contemporary LDCs represents a resumption of the attempt at a geographic spread of MGE.

This brief sketch of the geographic spread of MGE suggests not only its eventual irresistibility as a way of life (that is, its growing acceptability and desirability) but also the obstacles that need to be overcome (that is, its much later spread to some regions of the globe). It is generally acknowledged that the desirability of accomplishing a similar successful transition, if much later, in the Third World has proven irresistible because the MGE promises improvements in material well-being for the majority of the population. Moreover, what lies behind the assurance of sustained increases in per capita income and consumption standards is a way of life dedicated to the ceaseless exploration of the full potential of the human being. In the Northern historical context, such secularization of culture centered almost entirely on the exploration of man's virtually unlimited human potential as he used reason and science to pave the way for modern growth. During MGE, the realization of this capacity via the exploration of science and technology occurs as individual agents gain the requisite confidence that they can overcome nature and control their own destinies. This constitutes perhaps the strongest reason for the demonstrated irresistibility of the MGE.

Referring to the cultural and political traditions of the North, Professor Kuznets stated that a number of values amenable to the spirit of MGE should be emphasized. One is secularism, that is, belief in the devotion of human energy to objectives achieved in this world – art, science and economic welfare – rather than other-worldly objectives (as in medieval Europe). Another is egalitarianism, the belief in the equalization of opportunity for human endeavor, with commensurate rewards for the vast majority, associated with the appearance of constitutional democracy. A third is nationalism, the broadening of people's faith in human contact as they move from feudalistic particularism and localism to a larger national community which shares the same standardized behavioral norms – for example, language, transportation, communication, the measurement system, monetary standards, contractual forms, etc. – making it feasible for the enforcement of a standard legal code essential for economic exchange and the division of labor "between strangers." These various politico/cultural values have led to a particular model of economic institutions – that of industrial capitalism which has accommodated the MGE. Inferentially, the MGE has spread more readily to regions where these values are shared and not inhibited by colonial obstacles.

In this regard it is useful to remind ourselves that the classical economists (for example, Smith) glorified a particular type of government–society relations, sloganized as *laissez faire* under industrial capitalism. Beyond the protection of property rights and contract enforcement, Smith's government was seen as having to do little to promote growth. While this is an overstatement, we must also acknowledge that there is in evidence a marked contrast between the relatively low levels of interference during the British transition growth process (1780–1820), the more substantial extent of government interventions on the Continent, especially in the latecomer countries, and the transition growth process in most contemporary LDCs (1950 onward) which has been characterized by marked across-the-board political interference in its early stage. In the typical LDC "mixed economy," that is, one that represents some mixture of market and direct controls, that choice results from the combined effects of a system's particular colonial heritage, postponing the earlier "natural" spread of the MGE and eroding some of the politico/cultural values previously referred to, as well as the importance of the "initial" endowment at its disposal when the curtain rises.

1.4 The Epoch of Agrarianism

In contrast to the relatively brief period, spanning less than two centuries, during which the world has witnessed the phenomenon of modern economic growth, agrarianism has been the central characteristic of economic behavior over many centuries in Western Europe prior to the industrial revolution and in the overseas territories which now constitute the bulk of the Third World with which we are concerned here. Its beginnings should probably be dated from the time traditional societies shifted from nomadic hunting patterns to a pastoral way of life anchored in sedentary agriculture. Transition growth in the North (1780–1820) as well as in the contemporary South (1950–?) represents but a relatively short phase between the much longer epoch of agrarianism and the hopefully long epoch of modern growth.

While in both cases the transition growth effort aims at achieving MGE, there is an important difference in that contemporary LDCs were typically forced to start from a heritage of open agrarianism or colonialism characterized by political domination within a colonial empire. The relations between Great Britain and Malaya, between Holland and Indonesia, or between Japan and Taiwan served to initially embed the overseas territory within a particular agrarian economic structure. Such political domination may occur in covert form (for example, in Thailand or mainland China which were never really "occupied" by foreigners) or more overtly (for example, in India or Egypt) but exhibited essentially common characteristics in terms of empire–colony economic relations. The essential characteristics of these relations centered on a colonial trade pattern and a colonial investment pattern. Primary product exports from the colonies were exchanged for the import of factory produced goods that are the product of modern science and technology (for example, textiles); and profit seeking international capital movements occurred in the form of direct investments under which the mother country supplied capital, entrepreneurship, plus marketing and managerial ability.

As we shall show in greater detail below, growth of the overseas territories in this context served the needs of the North but did not necessarily advance the cause of MGE in the South. In this sense the transition growth effort in the contemporary developing countries – essentially in the post-World War II era, but starting somewhat earlier in Latin America – represents an attempt to replicate the earlier Northern transition by clearing away and restructuring colonial economic and political relationships and thus permit the geographic spread of MGE to be resumed. The exercise of political force by the newly independent nation state in order to promote such "catch-up" growth is very much a key instrumentality of this effort and something we shall examine in this volume.

We may therefore think of the industrially advanced countries as those which reached modern growth earlier, and of the developing countries as those which are now trying to achieve essentially the same goal – if under somewhat different circumstances, that is, of colonialism, or open agrarianism. The *modus operandi* of a primary production export economy based on the specificity of its natural resource endowment (for example, minerals and cash crops), rather than on its human capital and human ingenuity, had been characteristic of many parts of the developing world prior to the political changes associated with World War II. That the latecomers (today's LDCs) are today trying desperately to catch up testifies to the fact that what is essential about the modern growth epoch is that it encompasses the development of the full human potential (human capital and ingenuity) essential for our modern science and technology sensitive era.

There can be little doubt that the search for colonies and the establishment of mercantilist relations with the overseas territories was part and parcel of the extension of the modern growth process in the North – and just as little doubt about the importance of the largely post-war political event granting developing countries the political right to run their own affairs. Consequently, their effort to achieve modern growth must be seen as an attempt to duplicate on the economic front what had already happened on the political front. The so-called "post-World War II decolonization effort" ushered in a crescendo of actions in the South to move quickly and make up for lost time, a phenomenon which can be expected to last well into the twenty-first century.

1.4.1 Closed agrarianism

Let us return to a simple description of the workings of a closed agrarian economy. Europe, before the mercantilist period (that is, before 1400), Japan before the Meiji Restoration, and China before the Opium War, essentially represent agrarian systems in which international economic relations can be de-emphasized as a first approximation. Our interest in the closed agrarian system is due primarily to the structural and locationally dualistic characteristics of such agrarian economies.

1.4.2 Structural dualism

Closed agrarianism was characterized by the coexistence of agricultural and non-agricultural production, but with settled agriculture providing the main engine of growth and non-agriculture devoted mainly to the production of handicrafts, services and "cultural goods," often historically defined as "non-productive." In such a society economic life centered on the extraction of a fraction of the agricultural product in the form of a surplus, that is, after sustaining those working in agriculture, to have something left over for the non-agricultural labor force to produce cultural or other luxury goods for the elite, as well as some collectively consumed services, such as law and order, communication, transportation, etc.

The attempt to describe the operational perspective of the functional dualism of closed agrarianism was a major contribution of the French physiocrats. Quesnay's *tableau economique* (see Kuczynski and Meek, 1972) represented the first attempt to treat the economic system in an analytical and holistic perspective more than 250 years ago. It remains important to this day as a point of departure for any analytical approach to economic development in societies that inherit a dualistic structure.

1.4.3 The spatial or locational dimension

An agrarian system, in addition to its dualistic structural features, has an important spatial dimension much neglected in the economics literature. Such spatial (or locational) dualism is shown in figure 1.2; it is characterized by the coexistence of a spatially concentrated urban population, located at the urban center, and a much larger spatially dispersed rural population, functionally specialized in the production of agricultural products and/or rural handicrafts or Z-goods. This rural–urban dichotomy basically reflects a spatial (or locational) specification with important economic implications quite aside from the functional. It occurs early in the history of settled agriculture because the population must live close to the land in order to economize on daily transportation costs. Under this arrangement the nearby urban center becomes the focal point for human contact among the tillers of the soil for economic, political as well as cultural purposes. Due to the usually primitive means of transport, spatial dualism customarily takes on a partitioned form (see figure 1.2) under which the urban center and its adjacent rural population form independent

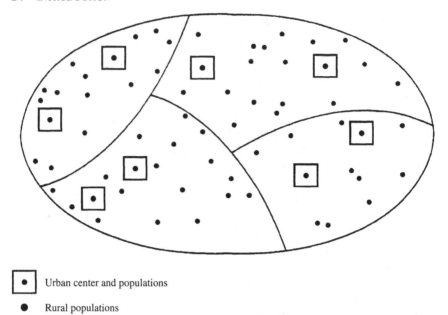

•	Urban center and populations

●   Rural populations

Figure 1.2 Spatial dualism

localized "dualistic communities" that cover the land space. In Europe before 1500 this was referred to as feudalistic localism primarily because of the partitioned characteristic of agrarian dualism.

1.4.4 Nationally integrated spatial dualism and transition growth

In the North, the historical origins of the emergence of nationalism (after 1500) can be traced to the breaking down of a feudalistic particularism as the entire economy took on a more integrated outlook, with the urban centers becoming linked to each other by a transportation network (roads and rivers) that facilitated human contact for social, political and economic reasons. The economic system became much more efficient as a division of labor developed among strangers living under conditions of an increasingly heterogeneous factor endowment.

The extent (or absence) of such spatial integration provides an essential ingredient (or obstacle) for successful transition growth in contemporary less developed countries. Modern science and technology destined for industry as well as for the agricultural sector (for example, factory produced fertilizer, seeds, farm equipment) represent, almost without exception, the product of urban centers that can be "extended" to spatially dispersed rural populations via increased human contact, made possible by improving transportation networks. It is indeed mainly through the possibility of such enhanced physical contact with the nearby urban center that the rural economy, both agricultural and non-agricultural, is likely to be modernized in a sustained fashion.

1.4.5 Spatial perspectives in open dualistic economies

Some of the urban centers (that is, the coastal as well as the inland cities which can be reached by sea-going vessels) are in turn linked, mainly via ocean transport, to the outside world – especially the industrially advanced countries. Historically, agrarian colonialism has a special characteristic in that economic enclaves (see figure 1.3) are carved out of the land space of the colonies, to be integrated, via trade and investment, with the mother country. Consequently, as a result of the operation of colonialism, the land

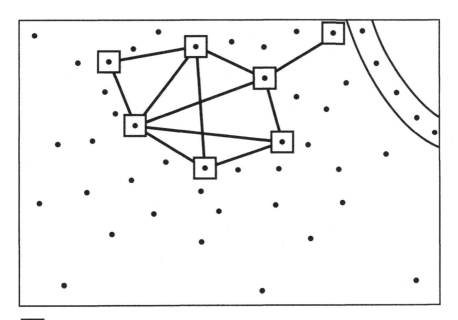

☐• Urban center and populations
• Rural populations

Figure 1.3 Linked dualism and colonialism

space of the LDC is partitioned into a relatively modern outward-looking enclave that coexists with a vast and relatively backward hinterland. Given this spatial perspective, the transition growth of LDCs can be seen as a process of the adaptation and spread of modern technology, much of it originated abroad, to the domestic urban production sectors and from there to the system's rural production sectors.

In summary, once closed agrarianism gives way to open agrarianism, what we encounter, at least from the viewpoint of the overseas territories, is a form of colonialism which, in a spatial perspective, means that the developing country is divided into roughly two parts: (1) an export-oriented production enclave, plus the ancillary services required for that activity, inter-phased with the advanced country world by means of a relatively modern transportation network and focused in large part on the ability to satisfy the raw material import needs of the mother country's economy; and (2) a traditional, usually staple food-producing and domestically-oriented hinterland, representing the relatively untouched agricultural production activities described by the physiocrats. Even a pre-existing closed agrarian dualism with its very limited dynamic potential may be set back by the advent of colonialism (see the Z-goods story analyzed below).

1.5 Colonial Heritage and Typological Sensitivity

This open agrarian or colonial epoch may be described by reference to three characteristics: (1) a sharp contrast between the export and traditional sector technologies, with the former augmented by a "modern" service sector concentrated in the ports, banks, transport network and other import/export-facilitating institutions, while the latter remains domestically oriented and both organizationally and technologically backward; (2) the enclave and its growth prospects are dependent on the colonial mother country's evaluation of the future market prospects of the specific raw material or colonial export in question, which determines whether or not there is long-run capital movement into or out of the enclave; (3) there usually results a compartmentalization of the growth process in the sense that what goes on in terms of the routine export/import operations of the system, the technology that is being imported and the institutions which are being perfected, all penetrates minimally into the food-producing hinterland.

It should, of course, be added that the specific nature of the commodity or mix of commodities which is exported under the colonial system –

whether it is coffee and/or cocoa, which usually involve relatively large numbers of small producers, or copper and/or oil, which do not – is likely to make a great deal of difference with respect to the extent of compartmentalization and the existence of any "spillover" or spread effects. Similarly, we should keep in mind that the precise nature of a colonial relationship will also differ with the particular mother country's own characteristics and needs. Both the colonial background and the export commodity mix affect the overseas territory's later chances for successful transition by determining some of the important initial conditions governing the attempt. Independent development must necessarily be based, *inter alia*, on whatever colonial heritage has been left "in the sand."

1.5.1 Typological sensitivity

Differences in colonial antecedents represent, of course, only one dimension of what has increasingly been recognized in recent years as the overwhelming heterogeneity of the Third World as it tries to move in transition to modern growth. One can consider this in terms of distinguishing between geographic regions, such as Latin America, South Asia, East Asia, Southeast Asia and sub-Saharan Africa, or by the differing levels of per capita income and the categorization into poor, middle income, oil exporting, or non-oil exporting subsets as deployed by the World Bank and now widely used in the profession. Alternatively, a typological approach to economic development may be based on the initial conditions defined for each country type, for example, transition growth in a labor surplus dualistic economy must be differentiated from one faced with unlimited supplies of land; ditto for the size of countries, which must clearly affect the importance of the open economy dimensions of growth; similarly the relative abundance of human versus natural resources evidently makes an important difference for a system's potential as well as, as we shall see below, the political economy obstacles to policy change along the way. Ideally, one should seek means of segmenting the LDC population by all the major significant differences in initial conditions, including size, initial income per capita, natural versus human resource endowments, as well as the organizational and/or institutional features derived from one's colonial heritage.

The basic point to be made here is that the transition growth effort represents a relatively short period in a society's history, perhaps thirty to fifty years, during which the typological characteristics of various subfamilies of countries, in terms of their differing economic, geographic and colonial backgrounds, make a good deal of difference. In this respect we are taking a position somewhat intermediate between the old view that "a developing country is a developing country" and can be analyzed in a more or less standard fashion, and the equally frequent assertion that every developing society is *sui generis* and indeed so different that the basic transition phenomenon can only be studied on an individual country basis. Needless to add, we reject the simple-minded assertion that there is no "special case," that is, that the straightforward extension of neoclassical equilibrium analysis will do equally well for Afghanistan and Argentina. Instead, in this volume we adhere to the notion that the basic phenomenon to be understood is that of an historical transition from agrarianism to modern growth and that this process will differ in different "types" of developing countries.

1.6 The Evolution of Relevant Development Theory

Economists have sometimes been accused, like generals, of conceptualizing the "last war," in this case a bygone epoch. Whether or not that complaint is valid, it must be acknowledged that the tool-kit left behind by the physiocrats, the classical school, Marx, Schumpeter and the post-Keynesians all contained something of analytical value for post-war development economists to build upon, that is, to help us analyze the two epochs that we have been dealing with as well as the crucial transition between them. In this section we hope to demonstrate this point.

In figure 1.1(c) above, on the same time axis previously used to trace the Northern transition, we can also place various growth theoretic ideas in sequential historical order. Accordingly, in the pre-modern or agrarian epoch, that is, before approximately 1780, we encounter the work of the French physiocrats whose writings were mainly concerned with depicting the mode of operation as well as the structural stability of the closed agrarian dualism of an earlier day. The classical writers who followed, Smith, Ricardo, Mill and Malthus, lived at a time when England was already engaged in the process of transition from traditional agrarianism to modern growth. But their major contribution can be said to reside in the construction of the outlines of economics as a separate area of scientific inquiry concerned not only with what a modern economist would refer to as "microeconomics" but also with a more aggregative type of "growth theory." Within "microeconomics" the classical writers emphasized the notion of the productive efficiency of a market economy characterized by the division of labor and rules governing the distribution of income. In fact, it was their income distribution theory based on the modern notion of "marginalism" which represented the essential component of their basically pessimistic view of the prospects for growth, dominated by diminishing returns and reflecting their unawareness of the imminent arrival of the modern scientific epoch.

The years which followed (from approximately 1830 to 1950) represent a relatively "dry period" as far as development theory is concerned. Economists generally turned their attention to two other types of problems, that is, microeconomics (concerned with efficiency) in the late nineteenth century neoclassical tradition and the aggregative analysis of the economics of instability as it came to the fore in the inter-war period. The two major exceptions during this dry spell are represented by the evolutionary theory of Marx and the Schumpeterian analysis of growth and instability within the capitalist system. Marx attempted to formulate an evolutionary theory of human society over the long run, that is, through five stages – primitive communism, feudalism, capitalism, socialism and communism – from the beginning of civilization into its indefinite future. His contribution is significant in that it aimed to explain the transformation of the entire social, political and economic system within one common framework of analysis based on the idea that changes in the art of production necessitate accommodating changes in other institutions, that is, his "dialectic materialism." The ultimate inevitability of the transition of the capitalist society into one in which all private property rights are abolished represents an important theoretical conclusion of his system. The theory of Schumpeter, on the other hand, was significant in that it attempted to explain instability within the capitalist system while giving full recognition to the importance of science and technology. Let us now turn to a brief summary of the relevance of each of these strands of thought for contemporary development theory.

1.6.1 The physiocrats

The *tableau economique* of the French physiocrats is of special interest to the modern economist because it signifies the initiation of a general analytical approach which can be applied to modern development economics. In spite of important differences with respect to the very meaning or even existence of "growth" their contribution to today's tool-kit was enormous. By emphasizing, really for the first time, a quantitative operational approach to the working of the economic system as a whole they, in effect, managed to lay the groundwork for virtually all the analytical macroeconomic approaches which followed.

The physiocrats' holistic perspective in analyzing all of the essential economic phenomena within one framework of reasoning is illustrated in figure 1.4. In this version of their *tableau economique* there exists a double

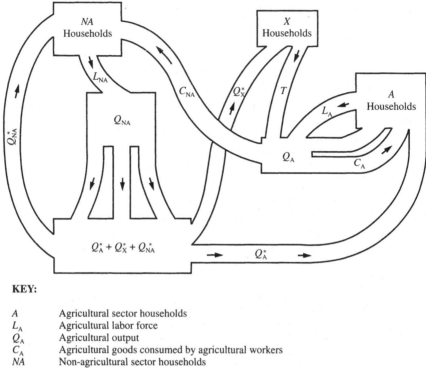

KEY:

A	Agricultural sector households
L_A	Agricultural labor force
Q_A	Agricultural output
C_A	Agricultural goods consumed by agricultural workers
NA	Non-agricultural sector households
L_{NA}	Non-agricultural labor force
Q_{NA}	Non-agricultural output
C_{NA}	Agricultural goods consumed by non-agricultural workers
Q_A^*	Non-agricultural goods consumed by agricultural workers
Q_X^*	Non-agricultural goods consumed by landholders
Q_{NA}^*	Non-agricultural goods consumed by non-agricultural workers
T	Land
X	Landlords

Figure 1.4 Physiocratic tableau economique *(real flows)*

dichotomy in the classification of "sectors" at the bottom of the figure, that is, under agrarian dualism these sectors are classified into an agricultural sector and a non-agricultural sector. Each sector contains decision-making agents as households and production units, with agricultural households further sub-classified into working families and land owning families. The operational significance of these sectors is described in terms of the flow of real goods and services, the direction of which is indicated by arrows in the figure. The non-agricultural labor force L_{NA} flows into the non-agricultural production sector while the services of land T and of the agricultural labor force L_A flow into the agricultural production sector. The total agricultural output Q_A is allocated as consumer goods for the farmers C_A or for the non-agricultural labor force C_{NA}, while the total output of the non-agricultural sector Q_{NA} is consumed by the farmers Q_A^* the land holding class Q_X^*, or the non-agricultural workers Q_{NA}^*.

The physiocrats made use of this *tableau economique* to describe the outlines of the operations of the whole economy as a continuous process through time. Figure 1.4 can be seen to be composed of three circular flows. With L_A labor service supplied for the production of agricultural goods, a portion of Q_A is "returned" to the farmers for consumption C_A. Another portion of the agricultural output, C_{NA}, is used to sustain the non-agricultural labor force which, in turn, produces goods and services destined in part for consumption by the farmers, Q_A^*. With land T also supplied as an input into agricultural production, a part of agricultural output becomes rental income to the landlord class. This rental income, however, is spent mainly on the consumption of "nonproductive" non-agricultural goods and services, Q_X^*, with the consumption of food by landlords so trivial that it can be ignored. The existence of an agricultural surplus, the famous *produit net* of the physiocrats, is indicated by the flow of C_{NA}, agricultural goods in excess of what is required to feed the agricultural workers, which can be deployed to feed non-agricultural workers as well as, indirectly, to provide for the consumption of non-agricultural goods by agricultural workers Q_A^*, non-agricultural workers, Q_{NA}^* and landlords, Q_X^*. The physiocratic system can thus be seen to touch on almost all the essential phenomena of development economics at the aggregate level: production, consumption, income distribution, allocation of inputs and outputs, and even the exchange of agricultural for non-agricultural output in the intersectoral commodity market and the existence of an agricultural surplus. All these aggregate flows are treated in a related fashion, that is, the holistic operational perspective presented is very modern in that it really lays the groundwork for our modern national income accounting framework within which "growth" (or its absence) is viewed as the result of the continuous operation of an inter-related economic system.

Given the specification of the quantifiable variables A, NA, L_A, L_{NA}, Q_A, Q_{NA}, X, and T, the performance of the whole economy over a particular period of time can be registered. The physiocrats themselves were quite sensitive to the need for such quantification as they believed that the total output of agricultural goods was being divided roughly into three equal parts – one-third consumed by the agricultural labor force, one-third the rental share of output consumed by landlords in the form of non-agricultural luxury goods, and one-third consumed by the non-agricultural labor force. Today's quantification of the growth phenomenon was thus clearly anticipated by the physiocrats more than 250 years ago, but with the important difference that they were describing what was essentially a circular flow or stagnant economy.

Indeed, the stylized facts of modern economic growth as emphasized by Kuznets – the acceleration of population growth, sustained increases in per capita income and structural changes in labor allocation and output – are not yet relevant here. Since the notion of asset accumulation is absent in the basic physiocratic framework, "growth" in the modern sense is not possible. Given the two types of capital for non-agricultural production that can be distinguished, that is, fixed capital K_f, which embodies technology in the modern economic growth context, and commercial or variable capital K_v, which represents changes in the inventory or stock of food to accommodate trade, both are virtually absent in the physiocratic system. What is present is so-called *avances annuelles* to provide for annual expenses, including wages, that is, a given stock of working capital representing the *produit net* or agricultural surplus. While the *tableau* listed the flow of services, the physiocrats really had in mind primarily an agent or class point of view in the specification of their household sector. Their households primarily represent different classes, with the operational purpose of the system being that of sustaining the cultural life of the landlord class. This societal purpose is in marked contrast to the value attached to the improvement of the material well-being of the population as a whole in the context of the transition growth effort in contemporary LDCs.

What is important for our purposes, however, is the primacy accorded to agricultural production and the agricultural surplus. Productive activity outside of agriculture (for example, artisan industry, trade and services) is labeled as "non-productive" by the physiocrats. Since what differentiates agricultural from non-agricultural production is that land is conspicuous as the essential input only in the former, they held the view that land, rather than labor, is the creator of all basic economic values. This notion of the primacy of agriculture can be traced to the fact that, if the society is to be able to "afford" the existence of non-agricultural households, the agricultural sector must produce an agricultural surplus – delivered to the non-agricultural households through an "intersectoral exchange process" as depicted in figure 1.4.

In modern dualistic growth theories, the focal point of analysis stresses very much such interactions between the agricultural and non-agricultural sectors, and the existence of an agricultural surplus represents a point of departure for many theoretical formulations. In fact, as we shall see below, the failure to modernize one's agricultural sector must still be regarded as the basic development bottleneck in many contemporary LDCs. The determination of "equilibrium" magnitudes in the context of an abstract model represents the *sine qua non* of modern analytical economics. Although the variables and the model structure of the *tableau economique* are reminiscent of such a structure, the *tableau* was, in fact, used by the physiocrats primarily as a descriptive device to indicate the outlines of the operation of agrarian dualism, rather than as a conceptual tool for deterministic modeling. Such analytical determinants, including the introduction of capital accumulation and production functions involving a tripartite division of labor, was left to be introduced by the classical school which followed.

1.6.2 The classical school

The classical economists were concerned with the "microeconomics" of production efficiency achievable via an enhanced division of labor as well as the "macroeconomics" of capital accumulation and growth. Their writings roughly coincided with the transition growth period in England – even though their analysis was still focused heavily on its agricultural antecedents. In sum, they accepted the holistic operational perspective of the physiocrats and postulated the juxtaposition of an aggregative agricultural production sector and a tripartite division of the household sector – corresponding to land T, labor L and capital K – to represent a tripartite division of labor. While the classical school recognized industrial activity and endeavored to describe what was essentially a two-sector agrarian world, their analytical focus was almost entirely on agriculture.

For the modern development economist the classical contribution of greatest significance is the treatment of the household sector at three levels: the definition of three classes of families, their assets, and the services rendered. Since the services of T, L, and K are supplied to the production sector as primary factor inputs, there is a corresponding tripartite division of agricultural output A into the rent share ϕ_T, the wage share ϕ_w and the profit share ϕ_K. Indeed, a major analytical contribution of the classical school is their deterministic theory of this functional distribution of income. When T and K are interpreted as productive assets, the introduction of K which accumulates through time introduced an important new dimension of the growth process not fully recognized by the physiocrats. Indeed, the classical growth theory can be said to rest on the foundation of their functional distribution of income theory plus their analysis of the capital accumulation process.

The classical economists thus inherited their sensitivity to the class structure of households from the physiocrats. Behind the productive assets T, K, and L are their owners, that is, the landlord class, the capitalist farmers and the landless working class. This class sensitivity, moreover, reflects a changing mode of organization for agricultural production in Britain in the eighteenth century in contrast to the feudalistic era which preceded it.

We now have a new class of profit seeking capitalist farmers renting land from the landlord class and hiring newly free workers.

In this respect, the classical writers may be said to really be analyzing an economy with the organizational features of commercial capitalism, namely a system that is characterized by the private ownership of the means of production (K and T) and by social relations typified by the voluntarism of wage and rental contracts. Commercial capitalism disposes over an inventory of liquid capital which differentiates it from the industrial capitalism which follows, sporting for the first time fixed capital capable of carrying technology. Indeed the preponderance of capital gradually shifts from the "liquid" to the "fixed" variety, especially in non-agriculture, during the transition to the modern growth epoch.

The contributions of the classical school were mainly focused on the emerging rules of commercial capitalism in which the capital stock is primarily of the aforementioned liquid capital – or inventory – type. Their non-agricultural labor force was mainly in light manufactures and especially in trade and commerce. Since all trade and commerce serve to overcome the natural resistance to exchange due to the alienation of distance and time, a stock of food is absolutely indispensable as a lubricator to bridge the gap between production (harvest) and consumption and to "set the non-agricultural labor force in motion". With the appearance of this liquid capital, the physiocratic notion that non-agricultural production is non-productive or sterile disappears since shipping a loaf of bread to the consumer is certainly no less essential than the production of wheat by farmers.

The classical saving rule states that the capitalist farmers are the only class which saves, while both the landlord and working classes devote their entire incomes to consumption. Since, under private capital ownership, it is only the savers (in this case, the capitalists) that will be rewarded with capital ownership, rigid immobility across classes is implied, that is, workers cannot become members of the capitalist or landlord class because they do not save. Once liquid capital gives way to the technology carrying "fixed capital" a little later (in the nineteenth century), the production conditions in the modern growth epoch can be said to be characterized by the efficiency of large scale production and by the appearance of specialized management to handle technologically complicated productive tasks. With the arrival of industrial capitalism we therefore witness an increased separation between capital ownership (receiving mostly interest income) and entrepreneurship (receiving mostly profit income associated with the uninsurable risk derived from technology change). As a consequence, the tripartite distribution of the shares of the classical school becomes quadripartite – wages, rent, interest and profit – as recognized by the modern economist.

This modern view implies that everyone with income can save if they choose to, even the vast majority of families who possess no managerial or entrepreneurial ability. For this reason, with the arrival of industrial capitalism the saving base is broadened as it is accommodated by increasingly complex financial arrangements (for example, banking, financial institutions and stock markets) to separate ownership from control. This, in turn, brings about a softening of the class oriented specificity of both the physiocrats and the classical school, given the now higher degree of inter-class mobility.

In summary, we see that the classical writers were really concerned with an agrarian society organized on a commercial basis. In this context some families appeared as capital owning enterprises subject to rigid inter-class mobility. But now labor, rather than land supplemented by commercial capital, was regarded as the creator of all value.

Turning to the use of these tools for development theory, it should be recalled that at the time of the industrial revolution, as England became the factory of the world many new industries grew up in its coastal urban centers accompanied by the flourishing of trade-related activities. The classical economists consequently speculated on the long-run tendency towards industrialization but, while they differed a bit amongst themselves, they generally came to the pessimistic conclusion that these new urban centered industrial activities would only be a temporary and transitory phenomenon and that, sooner or later, England would be forced to revert to the stagnant agrarianism portrayed by the physiocrats. They arrived at this conclusion via a deductive reasoning process based on assumptions about the continued primacy of agriculture, the initial conditions in that sector, plus arguments concerning demographic behavior and the way income distribution is determined and savings take place. Their predictions proved way off the mark because they were indeed looking over their shoulders and thus failed to realize that they were themselves living at a time of transition in which science and technology, essentially ignored by them, would have an increasing role to play in both agriculture and non-agriculture.

For our purposes, however, the major analytical contribution of the classical economists remains their deterministic theory of the functional distribution of income based on their analysis of the working of the market under the assumption of profit-seeking behavior. Their point of departure here is the specification of the production conditions prevailing in the agricultural sector based on the joint input of K, L, and T and subject to the law of diminishing returns on the land. With capital and labor viewed as one "bundled" factor input, each of the "two" factors (capital/labor and land) tends to be rewarded, under competitive conditions, by its productive contribution at the margin. The law of diminishing returns to land then implies that the rent share ϕ_T will increase as the result of population (cum capital) pressure on the land because land becomes a relatively ever scarcer factor. The shared income of labor ϕ_L and capital ϕ_K consequently declines. But as between these two "bundled" inputs the income distribution determination results from a bargaining rather than a competitive process; since the wage rate cannot be permitted to fall below some floor level related to subsistence – a phenomenon referred to as the "iron law of wages" – it is the profit share ϕ_K which ultimately declines towards zero. Given the classical savings rule, the volume of savings and the rate of capital accumulation will accordingly also decline towards zero, resulting in the prediction of long-run stagnation.

The contemporary development economist can, no doubt, detect many loopholes in these basic classical arguments, for example, with respect to the explicit or implicit acceptance of the Malthusian theory of population growth, the neglect of technology change and indeed the absence of any analysis of the interaction between agricultural and non-agricultural activities. Nevertheless, classical growth theory remains most significant for our current purposes in terms of its initiation of a methodology focusing on agriculture and stressing analytical determinism within a holistic operational framework.

This classical pessimism indeed was not shared by Adam Smith, who saw increasing returns in non-agriculture possibly overwhelming diminishing returns in agriculture. But inevitably, within the only sector that was carefully analyzed, the predicted exhaustion of capital accumulation was due primarily to the fact that the classical economists were quite unaware of the unlimited technology potential being opened up by the arrival of the modern growth epoch, sufficient to overwhelm the limitations traced to the law of diminishing returns. For most modern writers, whether "old" or "new" growth theory adherents, the combination of technology change and the law of diminishing returns indeed represents the point of departure for growth theoretic reasoning.

In fact, there are really two distinct types of labor productivity gains to be distinguished, a "Kuznets type" associated with the modern growth epoch when fixed capital "carries" science and technology, and an earlier "Smithian type" prevailing during the transition when commercial capital, owned and managed by a capitalistic entrepreneurial class, brings about productivity gains via an enhanced division of labor. This enhanced division of labor has a special spatial dimension related to the interaction of dispersed economic actors gradually forming an integrated national economic system.

In sharp contrast to their ignorance of the importance of productivity gains of the Kuznets type, the classical economists were indeed familiar with productivity gains of the Smithian type. In fact, they believed so fervently in the efficiency of commercial agrarianism, characterized by the voluntary interaction among private agents as a way to realize the advantages of an enhanced division of labor, that they focused their policy recommendations on *laissez faire*, that is, government restraint in direct interference in the economy. These recommendations emerging out of the classical model, if properly interpreted, may still rank among the more important for many growth conscious contemporary LDCs engaged in the transition growth process, as we shall see below.

1.6.3 Marx

Marx, the economist, was a many-faceted contributor whose growth theoretic contributions were embedded within a larger political and social framework. We will only touch on that small portion of his output which appears to us to be relevant to the development of modern development theory. As is well known, Marx borrowed heavily from the classical school, in terms of his acceptance of the "labor theory of value," his pessimism about the prospects for capital accumulation and, above all, his sensitivity to the dichotomy between social classes, that is, the coexistence of a property owning capitalist class with a property-less laboring class traceable to the absence of inter-class social mobility resulting from the previously analyzed classical savings rule. Marx, however, in sharp contrast to the classicists, while he concerned himself with the prognosis for the economic system as a whole, focused analytically only on the non-agricultural sector.

The theory of Marx differed from the classical theory in one other major respect. While the classical school recognized the significance of the accumulation of commercial capital (the food stock, or wages fund, that sets labor in motion), the Marxian framework represents a hybrid accumulation theory because of its attempt, if not very successful, to provide an integrated treatment of both commercial and fixed capital. Theoretical developments after Marx indeed gradually purged all reference to commercial capital from the literature and, instead, concentrated on fixed capital carrying technology as is evident in the work of Schumpeter and virtually all the post-war contributors.

What is really significant about Marx is that he was the first economist to formally treat the accumulation of fixed capital as the central phenomenon of modern economic growth. The impact of the increasing "bundles" of labor and commercial capital on the fixed land that was crucial for the classical agricultural stagnation thesis was only slightly relieved by Ricardo's preliminary discussion of variable fixed capital in relation to labor in non-agriculture. But Marx made the issue of variable proportions between the two primary factors of production, that is, capital and labor, central to his dynamic analysis.

The reader need not be reminded that, while the present volume is concerned with the transition growth process of an agrarian society *en route* to modern growth, the theory of Marx really represents a completely different type of theorizing – it is concerned with the prognosis of long-run stagnation in the mature industrial economy based on the application of the law of diminishing returns, the conceptual tool invented by the classical economists. Given the capitalist's drive for accumulation, Marx posits an inherent tendency toward capital deepening in mature industrial capitalism, that is, for the capital-labor ratio to rise and for distribution therefore to turn against the capitalist class. Hence, unless accompanied by "labor saving technology change," we have the ever present tendency toward a fall in the profit rate, or the rate of return to capital.

These notions of Marx were later formulated quite rigorously in the hands of modern growth theorists (Hicks, Harrod, Fellner), in which the joint impact of capital accumulation, labor force growth and technology change on the functional distribution of income – the impact on the profit and/or the wage rate – is formulated symmetrically. While the modern treatment of the functional distribution of income will be discussed below, we should emphasize that such symmetrical treatment in the determination of wages and profits in the growth process is independent of all reference to social classes (for example, of the physiocrats, the classicists and Marx). All factors are rewarded according to their respective productive contributions (that is, their marginal productivities) at the margin.

In Marxian theory, however, the tendency towards capital deepening and a decline in the profit rate causes mature capitalists to face the perpetual threat of the crisis of unemployment accompanied by political unrest due to the mounting protests of the working class. The only possible outcome ultimately is that the central organizational feature of industrial capitalism – profit-seeking under a system of private capital ownership – has to be abandoned since it proves to be incompatible with the production reality of the modern epoch. Whether the Marxian prediction is valid is largely an empirical matter turning once again on the potential for science and technology. Technology change can overcome any slowdown in the accumulation of capital due to declining profits. Indeed, the long period of post-war prosperity even past 1973 has demonstrated quite conclusively that capitalist societies are far from a state in which science and technology are exhausted. Industrial capitalism may indeed suffer from the long-term impact of changes in the tempo of innovative activity which is the central thesis of Schumpeter (see below); but the stagnation theorists of the 1930s, stimulated by Marx, have certainly been proven radically wrong to this date.

Of course, no discussion of Marx is complete without some reference to the political dimension. His theory of the inevitability of the decline of capitalism has inspired popular movements that have profoundly affected the lives of a third of the human race in the twentieth century. In the final analysis, it was undoubtedly his humanistic concern with distributional justice that accounted for the emotional appeal of his theory. Marx was fundamentally right in believing that, with the arrival of the epoch of modern growth, industrial society entered a phase in which distributional rules are characterized by the rewards for successful capital accumulation. His view of the accumulation drive as unsatiable has proven close to the mark, since it is indeed rewarded by material affluence, social status and (often) political power. Where he was wrong was with respect to the simultaneous declining rewards to labor in the presence of technology change and, most importantly, with respect to the maintained classical hypothesis of immobility between the classes.

Contemporary economists may have a different view of the "equity" (or fairness) of the principles of income distribution under capitalism. While Marx and the classical economists believed in inter-class social immobility imposed by the classical savings rule, such rigidity has since been abandoned and, with it, the whole notion of "class" in economic literature has been downgraded if not abandoned. Given the broadening of the saving base, that is, with everyone potentially a participant saver, the size distribution of income has replaced the functional distribution of income as the more meaningful indicator of equity in a society, as we shall see below.

In mature capitalism the accumulation drive is, indeed, characterized by an unusually high degree of "rationality," in other words, sensitivity to the rate of return to capital, as recognized by Marx. However, such profit sensitivity in a technologically complex MGE has led to the further differentiation of the roles of the "capitalist class," with the owners and managers of the fixed capital separated, leading to the quadripartite division of the functional distributive shares (that is, profit as differentiated from interest, plus wages and rent). The basis of savings is further broadened since everyone can now be a saver without necessarily being a manager, with a whole network of financial intermediation arrangements appearing, over time, to accommodate this separation. It is such institutional developments which provide part of the background for the theory of secular capitalist instability which was advanced by Schumpeter after the turn of the century.

1.6.4 Schumpeter

The fundamental contribution of Schumpeter relates to the impact of technology change on the development process. Although there exist many theories of the "business cycle" in mature capitalism, the theory of Schumpeter (1942) deserves special emphasis here because the instability he focuses on is directly traceable to some of the crucial growth relevant phenomena characteristic of the modern growth epoch as analyzed above.

For Schumpeter, invention resulting from scientific research and the application of such invention to the industrial art of production "carried" by capital accumulation, that is, innovation, are two different things. Long before the MGE the world had experienced two centuries of enlightenment, with scientific discoveries routinely made but without significant application. Schumpeter recognized the importance of an environment conducive to the continued flow of scientific activity but focused most of his attention on innovation, the application of these scientific discoveries as carried by additions to the capital stock. His growth theory is modern in the sense that the notion of commercial capital is completely overtaken by fixed capital and both the capacity to invent and the capacity to innovate become institutionalized and are taken for granted.

To stress the importance of science and technology, Schumpeter employed the concept of an "imaginary" state of growth (known in the literature as the "Schumpeterian state") characterized by stationary technology. One may visualize the existence of multiple production sectors $(1, 2, \ldots n)$ receiving inputs of labor $(L_1, L_2, \ldots L_n)$ and capital $(K_1, K_2, \ldots K_n)$ and producing output $(Q_1, Q_2, \ldots Q_n)$, where the proportionality of these variables is determined by technology at any moment in time.

A growth process characterized by stationary technology implies that population growth and capital accumulation through investment $(I_1, I_2, \ldots I_n)$ proceeds at rates such that the proportionality of K_i, Q_i, and L_i remains essentially unchanged. A Schumpeterian state is then described as a type of growth whereby the economy is getting larger without changes in its "organic" or structural composition. The well-known stylized facts of MGE emphasized by Kuznets focusing on various types of structural change should remind us that such a Schumpeterian state is almost completely fictitious. But it is a convenient device for him to relate observed structural changes to the disturbance of a stationary production structure by innovations which appear in wave-like fashion as a consequence of entrepreneurial action.

This notion of a Schumpeterian state, though fictitious, represents an important idea that provoked a more rigorous formulation in mathematical growth models (for example, by von Neumann and Solow). Such models have shown that, in the absence of technology change, the growth of an economy will transitionally approach the Schumpeterian state in the long run regardless of the arbitrariness of the "initial" capital and output structure. Such modern theoretical conclusions suggest that the stability of the structure of a Schumpeterian state reflects a viable pattern warranted by stationary technology.

For Schumpeter, the instability of capital accumulation in the mature capitalist society is due primarily to the "bunching" of innovations. The argument is that, even given the continuous discovery of new technological ideas, innovations will not occur continuously or smoothly over time. Instead, innovations tend to occur in "clusters" and "spurts" depending on the rather mysterious appearance or absence of swarms of entrepreneurs. An upturn occurs when an increase in innovations induces rapid structural changes which destroy the Schumpeter equilibrium. This is followed by a downturn during which the pace of innovation slackens and the economic structure brings us to a new Schumpeterian state at a higher level of per capita income.

As societies enter the modern growth epoch, the exploration of new frontiers of science and technology implies that they will forever face an uncertain and volatile future. Investment, in particular, is full of uncertainty and risks. In a multi-sectoral context, whether or not a particular product (or particular firms) created by past innovative investments are viable in the long run can only be "tested" experimentally through consumer choice. Viewed in this light, the existence of a depression phase that corrects the imbalance, by weeding out those products and firms left behind by the new technology, is completely reasonable. The transition to a new Schumpeterian state thus serves a "housecleaning" purpose.

The critical theoretical issue that must be faced in Schumpeter's theory is the causation of the mysterious "clustering" of innovative investments. This issue is central to his notion of "finance" in an industrial world in which savers and investors are separated.

During modern economic growth, investment finance – the channelization of the saving fund to meet the monetary demand for investment – assumes a crucial role. While it was not an essential issue in the classical or the Marxian view of the world, it is important for the clustering thesis of Schumpeter. By the early twentieth century, industrial capitalism had matured sufficiently for the separation of the ownership and management of real assets to occur. The decisions to save and to invest were accordingly separated and investment finance took on a new and complex form as a result of the coming into prominence of various types of financial institutions that "intermediate" between savers and investors.

An important type of financial intermediary is the commercial bank which differs from all other financial institutions in that it can create purchasing power to meet the needs of investment finance. The arbitrariness of the creation of such artificial monetary power constitutes a disturbance of the market clearing interest rate resulting from the interaction of the demand for loanable funds I by investors and the supply of loanable funds S by savers. The classical saving rule is now violated as voluntary S is no longer the sum of savings out of property income S_K and/or wage income S_w but is augmented by the monetary expansion of commercial banks (dM/dt) to allow total investment I to command additional goods in the commodity markets.

An understanding of such financial arrangements is essential for the Schumpeterian thesis concerning the intrinsic instability of capital accumulation. Innovations tend to occur in "clusters" primarily due to the fact that, once a new entrepreneurial swarm appears, the expansion phase is characterized by rapid monetary expansion (dM/dt) due to the accelerated pace of lending by commercial banks. The profit expectations of all investors are raised, not only because a potentially market clearing interest rate was artificially suppressed by dM/dt, but also because a snowballing effect is attached to monetary expansion. When monetary purchasing power is created for some entrepreneurs, it induces others, Schumpeterian "follower" entrepreneurs, to increase their investment as well, with increasing proportions generated out of newly created purchasing power. As commodity markets become exhausted and/or inflation results from the financial excesses of follower entrepreneurs a recession follows and we approach a new Schumpeterian steady state. In the modern development theory context (see below) this notion of development finance has other, longer term, consequences.

1.6.5 The post-war planning school of development

For the early post-war period we may distinguish between two main approaches or "schools of thought" – a planning oriented school associated with such names as Tinbergen, Mahalanobis, and Chenery, and a behavior oriented school associated with such names as Simon Kuznets and Arthur Lewis. The so-called "planning school" became very popular in the early part of the post-war period. Political independence in the ex-colonies became associated with a faith that rapid growth via industrialization could be promoted via the application of political power by government. While the market system and private property rights were generally accepted as instruments, at least by the non-socialist LDCs, pervasive government interference in that market was tolerated. Almost all mixed economy LDCs consequently set up planning commissions to blueprint and co-ordinate the national development effort via the formulation of five year plans; in this atmosphere a system of detailed microeconomic interventions to promote industrialization was created.

The planning school may be characterized by the relative formalism of its methodology, usually envisioning a multi-sectoral production function with multiple inputs K_i, L_i, and outputs Q_i allocated for consumption C_i and investment I_i, quite similar to the Schumpeter model. However, the planning model in this multi-sectoral set-up was rendered more complicated for three additional reasons. First, the heavy influence of the input–output table was clearly apparent since a part of the total output of each sector was assumed to be used as a current input into the other production sectors. Second, the model was formally or informally dynamic, as it envisioned a time horizon of, for example, five consecutive years (with all the planning variables such as K_i, L_i and Q_i dated to indicate their projected values into the future). Third, some variables relating to the open economy, for example exports, were usually exogenously postulated. In this way, an economic plan could be seen to portray the operation and growth of an economy in a holistic perspective in which all sectors tended to be viewed as essentially homogeneous and "symmetrical."

A second methodological trait of the planning school was the systematic application of mathematical models in order to determine the magnitude of all the planning variables consistently through time. This involved not only the postulation of production conditions (such as input, output and import coefficients) and the separation of the exogenous variables (for example, population growth, export potential and the availability of foreign capital) from the endogenous variables, but also the use of mathematical techniques (for example, dynamic input–output or linear programming models) for their determination. The formalism of the planning methodology gave the school a strongly technocratic cast.

A third methodological trait of the planning school was its reliance on the use of numerical data to construct multi-year plans. The underlying idea was that once such a plan had been constructed, the government could give orders for it to be implemented; in the mixed economy context, this meant partially as a result of the government's own investment actions and partly via the exercise of a host of policy instruments to influence private sector actions.

Such "planning for resources" exercises represented, in part, a somewhat naive belief in the appropriateness of the policy rails on which the economy initially found itself. In part, it was also an understandable political response to the age of decolonization in which the very presence and visibility of a newly independent government, presumably at work on behalf of the common weal, for a time satisfied the psychological needs of the population. While such resources oriented planning probably did serve a constructive purpose by providing an overall, if crude, guide for political action, as well as attracting foreign aid, its usefulness for realistic "holistic" planning quickly wore off in the course of the 1960s. It became increasingly doubtful that forecasting resource changes over time for a given structure of the economy was really useful during a period of transition growth, when it is changes in that very structure which lie at the heart of the process. Moreover, forecasting and publishing the details of a resources oriented plan five years down the road inevitably led to the early creation of political albatrosses around the necks of governments, as the inevitable exogenous shocks occurred and post mortem re-evaluations just as inevitably followed. While macroeconomic projections, of course, continue to be made to this day by LDC governments they are more frequently kept on a rolling basis, in the drawers of policy-makers' desks, and couched for general consumption in terms of high, low and medium ranges for the major performance variables – while the real focus of planning has notably shifted to devising strategies for policy change to accommodate the transition process, a subject to which we shall return at some length.

1.6.6 Post-war development theory

The post-war years (1950–90) also witnessed a revival of interest in development theory which, with the notable exceptions of Schumpeter and Marx, had been practically out of the mainstream of professional economics for almost a century and a half. The ideas that were being revived and developed during this period fall into two categories: the transfer of growth theory initially applied to the DCs and development theory devised specifically for the LDCs. Post-war DCs, with the Great Depression fresh in memory, were initially largely preoccupied with the problem of income instability, that is, unemployment and the potential inflation problem related to its cure. The key message conveyed by "Keynesianism" was that such instability is mainly caused by the deficiency of demand for absorbing the super-abundance of savings at full employment levels. The policy implications of Keynesian macroeconomic analysis focused on aggregate demand management to compensate for the deficiency of *ex ante* private demand by the exercise of monetary and fiscal policies. More recently, monetarism has been in the ascendancy. Its key message has been a greater belief in the natural flexibility of the economy and a diminished need for government intervention to overcome structural defects. Indeed even post-Keynesian economists are now ready to accept the notion that full employment (at some natural rate of unemployment) is not likely to be in conflict with price stability in the long run.

While macroeconomic theory and policy were largely directed at the short-run issue of economic stabilization, early DC sensitivity to unemployment led directly to an inquiry into the inevitability or persistence of instability even in the long run. The threat of long-run stagnation recurring in the theses of the classical school, Schumpeter and Marx was revived in the form of the Harrod–Domar growth model. This, however, originated as a direct outgrowth of the short-run instability Keynesian thesis, with the analytical focus now shifted towards the impact of capital accumulation and technology change on the profit rate. The inevitability of a decline in the profit rate in the course of the capital accumulation process was at the heart of the theoretical arguments predicting long-run stagnation in a mature economy characterized by an overabundance of savings.

In contrast, as far as the post-war LDCs were concerned, their problem was different, focused on the secular problem of catching up with those who had already completed their transition process. In pursuing that goal, the vast majority of contemporary LDCs opted for the adoption of a mixed economy with vigorous growth promotion policies put in place via the exercise of power by newly independent sovereign states.

Given such a political climate, in addition to the resources-planning-oriented planning school there also emerged a school of development theory emphasizing the holistic behavior of an economy in which the totality of growth-related tasks (for example, output growth, labor mobility, international trade) were to be co-ordinated by a mixture of market forces and government interventions of various types. The policy implications of this school differ from those of the planning school in that, instead of planning for resources, the focus here is on "planning for policy change," that is, on the art of mobilizing macro and microeconomic policy change for purposes of development.

Planning for resources as well as planning for policy change was substantially aided by methodological advances in the form of abstract economic modeling complete with econometric implementation. The dynamic modeling of economic growth by the so-called "Harrod–Domar model" and its derivatives (see below) represents only one illustration of this methodology. Such models were closely related to both the LDC planning school as well as to some of the behavioral growth theories primarily intended for the DCs but adapted to LDC use.

1.6.7 The Harrod–Domar model

The post-World War II revival of interest in growth yielded quantifiable dynamic models in which all the economic variables are dated. The conspicuous advantage of such dynamic formalism is that it allowed us to investigate the sequential order of events over time with logical precision. However, it also meant that many of the non-quantifiable attributes of economic relations had to be de-emphasized, or even entirely neglected, as a first approximation. The methodological conflict implied is well illustrated by the Harrod–Domar model which dominated growth-related thinking in the early post-war years.

The Harrod–Domar model accepted an aggregative national income accounting framework in which labor L and capital K are jointly supplied to the production sector to yield total output Q, which is used either for current consumption C or investment I leading to additional capital accumulation. The five dated variables (K,L,Q,I,C) are related by the following equations:

$$Q = C + I \quad \text{(output allocation, an accounting equation)} \tag{1.1a}$$
$$I = sQ \quad \text{(saving function, where } 0 < s < 1) \tag{1.1b}$$
$$Q = (1/k)K \quad \text{(production function, where } k = K/Q > 0) \tag{1.1c}$$
$$I = dK/dt \quad \text{(capital accumulation, an accounting equation)} \tag{1.1d}$$

Equation 1.1a is a static accounting equation which accounts for the allocation of output while 1.1d is a dynamic accounting equation which accounts for the accumulation of capital through time. Equation 1.1b is a saving function that specifies that a certain fraction s of Q is always invested. Equation 1.1c is a simple production function where k, the capital–output ratio, is the simple reciprocal of the productivity of capital. While s (the average propensity to save) is a parameter which measures the degree of national austerity, the parameter k indicates how productive or unproductive capital is as an input. Using $\eta_x = (dx/dt)/x$ to denote the growth rate of any dated variable x, equation 1.1 leads directly to:

$$\eta_K = s/k \quad \text{implying} \tag{1.2a}$$
$$\eta_Q = \eta_I = \eta_K = \eta_C = s/k \tag{1.2b}$$

Thus, given constant s and k, the capital stock grows at a constant rate (s/k) which is related positively to the degree of austerity s and negatively to the productivity of capital k. Since C, I, and Q are all proportional to K, these variables also grow at the same constant rate through time (equation 1.2b). In this equation system the labor force is not even involved. Hence, to determine the system completely, the labor force can be treated as an exogenous variable, for example, postulated to grow at a constant rate r:

$$\eta_L = r \quad \text{(constant population growth rate), implying} \tag{1.3a}$$
$$\eta_c = \eta_C - \eta_L = s/k - r, \text{ where } c = C/L$$
$$\text{(growth rate of per capita consumption)} \tag{1.3b}$$
$$\eta_p = \eta_Q - \eta_L = s/k - r, \text{ where } p = Q/L$$
$$\text{(growth rate of per capita income)} \tag{1.3c}$$

The growth rates of the per capita consumption standard (equation 1.3b) and of per capita income (equation 1.3c) are seen to be the difference between the growth rate of capital s/k and the population growth rate r. Thus, we can readily see that statements on the relatedness of Q, L, K, C, and I through time, by logical deduction, lie at the heart of the formalism of post-war growth modeling. Indeed, the Harrod–Domar formulation, initially intended for cyclical purposes, simultaneously provided the basic underpinnings for long term growth-related modeling in both the capitalist DC setting and the LDC planning school context.

1.6.8 Extensions of the Harrod–Domar model

The applicability of the Harrod–Domar model to the dominant post-war LDC planning school rests on three of its main methodological properties: its power of prediction, its amenability to statistical implementation, and its feasibility for theoretical extension. Its power of prediction relates to its statements about the rapidity of growth over time (for example, in terms of the growth rate of capital, of GNP, and/or of consumer welfare). Thus Q and K grow at a faster rate, given a larger austerity effort (larger s) and/or higher capital productivity (smaller k). The consumption standard grows at a faster rate when population growth is "under control" (lower r).

These theoretical predictions can be quantified when, via implementation by statistical data, the parameter values s, k, and r are estimated. The popularity of the planning school in the early post-war years was due primarily to the fact that "conditional policy advice" could be given to government in numerical terms. (For example, if $r = 1.5$ percent and $k = 5$, then, when the per capita income growth rate is targeted at 2.4 percent, the average propensity to save must be sustained at 19.5 percent of GNP in the closed economy.)

The simple Harrod–Domar model deployed for such a "planning for resources" purpose was extended in several directions. One was to the open economy, with the addition of imports, M, exports, E, and foreign capital, A, to finance an import gap ($A = M - E$). When equation 1.1a is modified to include exports and when the import function is added we obtain

$Q = E + C + I$ (modification of equation 1.1a to include an export component E) (1.4a)

$A = M - E$ (including the use of foreign capital A to close the trade gap $M - E$) (1.4b)

$M = mQ$ (including an import function with import coefficient m) (1.4c)

The specification of foreign capital A or of exports E as an exogenous variable determines the entire system dynamically. Thus, numerical policy advice can be given to the effect that if exports E are growing at a certain rate, the country will **need** to negotiate for foreign aid and/or private foreign capital inflows at a certain rate. Conversely, if the amount of foreign aid is politically predetermined, the country may **have to** reduce its import coefficient m and/or increase its exports E in order to close the trade gap. Similar statements could be made with respect to the need, alternatively, to increase the productivity of capital and thus reduce the saving requirement on the domestic side, or to reduce the target rate of per capita income growth.

The popularity of the planning school during the early post-war years was a phenomenon closely related to the popularity of LDC planning commissions and five-year plans. Both rested on rather dubious foundations. On the one hand, there was in evidence an unwarranted faith in growth promotion by means of political force. On the other hand, the usefulness of dynamic resource-oriented modeling with the help of econometrics was exaggerated. The models and targets of the planning school, when embodied in the ubiquitous five-year plans, proved to be little more than a statement of political intentions. Knowledge on the need to raise the saving rate and/or the export rate by a certain percentage if certain targets are to be achieved is spurious when more specific policy advice as to just how this was to be accomplished is not provided simultaneously. The need to put the economy on different rails rather than move more quickly on the old ones was gradually recognized as the key issue. Consequently, as we shall see below, the influence of the "planning for resources" approach was gradually replaced by "planning for policy change."

The above simple version of the Harrod–Domar model has also constituted a point of departure for the mature capitalist economy. This is due primarily to the fact that the notions embodied in the model – that is, fixed capital as a productive input, savings pushed capital accumulation and population expansion – go a long way towards depicting the growth process during the modern growth epoch. For this reason, modified versions of the basic Harrod–Domar approach have been applied to the analysis of the long-run growth process in the mature capitalist society.

One such modification of the Harrod–Domar model begins with the recognition that labor (L) and capital (K) are joint inputs in a variable proportions production process, each subject to the law of diminishing returns. When the production function of equation 1.1c (in which labor is not involved) is replaced by the neoclassical production function of equation 1.5c, we have the following basic model of Solow:

$$Q = C + I \tag{1.5a}$$
$$I = sQ \tag{1.5b}$$
$$Q = f(K,L) \text{ (neoclassical production function)} \tag{1.5c}$$
$$\eta_L = r \tag{1.5d}$$

This model is a straightforward extension of the Harrod–Domar model as defined in equations 1.1a, 1.1b, 1.1c and 1.3a and provides us with the tools to analyze and compare the alternative equilibrium paths which an economy – developing or mature – may follow.

The above equation system (1.5) defines the structure of the basic Solow model with a given static technology and per capita consumption standard. In application to the poor developing economy case, progress depends on the rate of capital accumulation exceeding the exogenous rate of population growth. On the other hand, the continued absence of technological change can lead to another type of difficulty. With the saving capacity too high relative to the population growth rate, the return to capital (that is, the profit rate) will ultimately be depressed as increasing levels of capital intensity cause the profit rate to decline due to the operation of the law of diminishing returns.

The most substantial modification of the Harrod–Domar framework therefore deals with the admission of technological change, either of the exogenous type as incorporated in neoclassical growth theory or of the endogenous type as incorporated in the "new" theory of growth. The realistic modeling of technological change continues to present substantial conceptual as well as empirical difficulties.

Solow himself incorporated technological change by postulating a Hicks-neutral technology parameter (J) with an exponential trend:

$$J(t) = J(0)e^{gt} \qquad (1.5e)$$

where

$$Q = J*f(K,L) \qquad (1.5c')$$

replaces equation 1.5c. This yields a Pareto optimal equilibrium in which all variables grow at the exogenous rate of total factor productivity growth (g). Empirically, more than 50 percent of US output growth between 1874 and 1975 has been found to be attributable to such technological progress, with capital accumulation accounting for most of the remainder.

The importance of technological progress for explaining the stylized growth facts in the empirical work of Solow has spawned a huge literature focused on measuring and quantifying the effects of technological change on economic growth. Griliches and Jorgenson (1967) were among the first to attempt this, with the later work of Denison (1985) and Hendrick and Grossman (1980), who disaggregated the primary inputs more finely, especially worthy of note. Denison, for example, found that US per capita output growth, largely attributable to total factor productivity, was composed primarily of advances in technology (64 percent) and increases in worker education (30 percent).

Solow thus provided a new point of departure for neoclassical growth theory via the acceptance of exogenous technological progress plus the effort to whittle down this "residual" as much as possible. In the 1980s a new branch of growth theory came into vogue which, based on some well-accepted earlier notions in the literature, sought to endogenize changes in technology through credible models of market externalities to explain the stylized growth-related facts in both developing and mature economies. This literature, led by Romer, Lucas, Grossman and Helpman, shares the Solowian result of technological progress as the driving force of output growth while allowing the analysis of non-steady state equilibrium paths that are not Pareto optimal for the economy.

Romer (1986), for example, revived the concept of endogenous growth based on the learning-by-doing model initially employed by Arrow (1962). Using a dynamic production function as in the second Solow model, Romer postulates constant returns to scale (CRTS) at the firm level but increasing returns to scale (IRTS) at the economy level:

$Y = F(K, L, A)$　(Cobb-Douglas production function)　(1.6a)

A = societal capital stock = X^λ　where individuals solve　(1.6b)

$$\text{Max} \int_{t=0}^{\infty} e^{-\rho t} \frac{c^{(1-\theta)} - 1}{1-\theta}$$　subject to　(1.6c)

$dk/dt = k^B X^\lambda - c$　where $y = k^B X^\lambda$ is per capita output　(1.6d)

with individuals taking society's capital stock (X) as fixed. Equation 1.6c represents a constant intertemporal elasticity of substitution utility function where ρ is the rate of time preference and θ is the rate of consumption smoothing. Lowercase letters denote per capita variables.

The source of aggregate IRTS is the positive externality to capital investment (X^λ), not recognized by individual firms, which increases the productivity of the whole economy by raising the productivity of the aggregate capital stock. The positive externality to capital investment must be external to the firm to assure a set of competitive prices that support an equilibrium. Solving the model for steady-state values, Romer shows that the competitive equilibrium need not be Pareto optimal (since individuals do not recognize the positive externality to private capital investment), with endogenous growth driven by unintentional capital accumulation.

Lucas (1988) presents another variant of the Solow model in which technology and endogenous growth are modeled through the existence of two distinct CRTS inputs to the production process: physical capital (k) and human capital (h). Lucas postulates a positive social externality to human capital accumulation, as the productivity of any individual in the economy is an increasing function of the aggregate stock of human capital.

Lucas (1993) subsequently shows that this externality predominantly takes the form of on-the-job learning. His basic individual production function may be stated as follows:

$$y = F(k,h,l) = Ak^{B}(uhl)^{1-B} \qquad (1.7a)$$

where h is the individual level of human capital, l is labor input, and $0 < u \leq 1$ is the proportion of time devoted to work, such that uhl is the quality-adjusted labor input. Given a positive social externality to human capital accumulation, the actual individual production function is:

$$Y = Ak^{B}(uhl)^{1-B}H \qquad (1.7a')$$

where H is the aggregate stock of human capital in the economy.
This model implies the existence of two dynamically accumulated assets at the individual level:

$$dk/dt = Ak^{B}(uhl)^{1-B}H - c \qquad (1.7b)$$

$$dh/dt = \gamma h(1 - u) \qquad (1.7c)$$

where γ is a parameter and $(1 - u)$ is time devoted to human capital accumulation. The actual Lucas model is the individual maximization of equation 1.6c subject to the dynamic constraints equation 1.7b and c.

While Romer needs a private capital investment externality coupled with IRTS at the macro level to generate endogenous growth via technological progress, the Lucas model – with a more precise concept of capital – needs only CRTS, with the crucial difference that in the Lucas model **all** inputs to the production process can be accumulated. This model produces constant growth rates for all economic indicators and sustained per capita income growth arising from the intentional accumulation of human capital, while growth in the Romer model is driven by unintentional accumulation alone. The Lucas model also yields permanently different growth rates between nations based on differing initial endowments – an economy with low levels of human and physical capital will remain permanently below a better-endowed economy.

A third descendant of the Solow model is a set of models formulated by Grossman and Helpman (1989a–d, 1991) analyzing the open economy implications of endogenous growth based on research and development (R&D). Investment in R&D serves two functions. First, it accelerates the introduction of new capital goods of higher productivity. Second, it provides spillovers onto the aggregate stock of knowledge, reducing the costs both of producing manufactured goods and of further investment. Grossman and Helpman model the spillover effects of R&D investment as the positive externality driving endogenous growth.

The formal process of R&D is usually associated with mature capitalist economies and not with those immersed in the transition to modern growth. However, R&D-based growth models are also applicable to LDCs. Even though LDCs undertake relatively little R&D in the formal sense, the transition to industrialization in the developing world involves technological change by gaining competence with new processes and ideas. Pack and Westphal (1986) argue that "the minor role of invention in LDC industrialization means technical change consists of assimilating and adapting foreign technology." This learning process requires, like R&D in mature economies, the allocation of resources away from current production processes, where the size of LDC investments in mastering foreign technology should respond to the same market incentives as does R&D investment in mature economies.

There is a heterogeneity among the various R&D growth models where firms develop new consumption goods, generate new production goods, or increase the quality of a fixed set of goods (Grossman and Helpman, 1989a–e). All feature a positive production knowledge externality to R&D investment and the same result: growth can be endogenously driven by knowledge accumulation from R&D investment alone in a CRTS world. However, the private return to investment is below the social return and the steady-state growth rate is below the socially optimal rate. The economy does not reach a Pareto optimal allocation due to the unrecognized externality from R&D investments.

These Solowian-based theoretical models of the 1980s yielded important insights on the heterogeneity of the possible sources of growth during the transition to the modern growth epoch based on endogenous technological change. The models treat the externalities caused by technological progress as public goods that are privately and costlessly provided. More recent "new growth theory" models have expanded these earlier efforts to more accurately capture the stylized growth facts observed in both developing and mature capitalist economies. The literature of the 1990s thus proceeds in two directions, delving deeper into the existing ideas about growth and expanding the set in order to provide a more holistic perspective on growth theory, especially its relation to earlier work.

Romer (1992) recognizes that technology transfer and adaptation are far from costless for LDCs. He departs from his original growth model and focuses on ideas-based models in which innovations generate new investment opportunities. In this model, however, the ideas and innovations leading to technological progress are not pure public goods. "Ideas" are considered a separate input in a CRTS neoclassical production function, unrelated to either human or physical capital. Ideas, by producing technological innovations, drive both output growth and capital accumulation. Romer's framework departs from the traditional focus on different capital accumulation rates (Romer, 1989) since the latter "misses opportunities via the creation of new ideas."

Pack (1992) empirically analyzes the propositions of Solowian-type growth models. He dismisses the convergence hypothesis as time-series analysis of growth and emphasizes that total factor productivity shows "poorer nations ... grow slower, not faster, than wealthy nations and ... benefits to relative backwardness do not exist." Average annual growth rates for poor (high-income) nations were 0.3 percent (1.8 percent) from 1960 to 1985. Pack finds that technological change is initially not the main engine of growth in the developing world, as almost two thirds of growth in per capita income in LDCs is driven by the sectoral reallocation of labor from agriculture to industry as explored in this volume. Empirically, the shift of labor from agriculture to industry explains 68 percent (55 percent) [1 percent] of the growth in low (middle) [high] income nations from 1960 to 1980. Net of labor reallocation, growth rates are highest for high-income countries and negative for low-income countries. This rejects the convergence hypothesis across all countries and the presumed benefits to relative backwardness.

As an alternative to Solowian growth models, we can thus envision a multi-stage growth process for LDCs. The first is highlighted by productivity gains achieved via the reallocation of labor from agriculture to industry. Later on, the transfer of technology from rich to poor countries and its adaptation to local conditions shifts the aggregate production function and drives economic growth in a manner consistent with Solowian growth models. Still later, it is technological leadership at home, consistent with the new growth theory, which dominates.

While Romer and Pack expand and explore the implications of existing growth models, other authors have focused on the methodological approaches to economic growth by taking a somewhat different perspective. For example, Scott (1989, 1992) develops an alternative theory by defining "investment" to include all manner of technological change, including production externalities, labor reallocation, scientific discovery, and invention, in a model that provides a bridge between Solow and the endogenous growth literature – encompassing both exogenous and endogenous growth sources and implications. Scott's model differs from orthodox growth models by explaining economic growth as a function of the growth of the quality-adjusted labor force (human capital investment), the rate of (material) investment, and the efficiency of this investment. In this model continuous investment does not depress its return, but instead has a positive externality by creating further investment opportunities and generating faster economic growth. While this analysis is quite different from the other growth models, it is not in direct conflict with them. Instead, it focuses on growth from the same sources (all grouped as "investment") but from a different perspective which pinpoints the role of capital in the actual growth process and avoids forcing distinctions between endogenous versus exogenous growth.

With a similar goal of relating existing growth theory to earlier developments in economics, Krugman (1992) argues for a "counter-counter-revolution" in development theory to relate Solowian growth models to the ideas of development economists in the 1940s and 1950s. Early development theory stressed both IRTS and externalities. Given recent advances in growth theory, these early development ideas look much more applicable today and are easier to model. In this sense the new growth theory has made a useful contribution by introducing welcome rigor into some useful old concepts lying around in the attic of development economics. Moreover, it has become one of the most active areas of development-related research in recent years and attracted considerable new talent into this general area of inquiry.

Our work in this volume focuses heavily on the importance of technology change, especially in non-agricultural activities. But we continue to rely on the neoclassical CRTS production function which combines economies of scale, externalities, etc. under "technology change." The Inada conditions do not hold. We focus instead on the decomposition of exogenous technology change into its intensity and factor bias which permits us (see below) to derive what we believe to be a very useful and realistic set of growth equations. Adherence to the new growth theory emphasis on endogenous technological advances would complicate but not fundamentally affect our findings.

A second – and more significant – methodological difference is that our analysis focuses on the historical phenomenon of transition growth, while the new growth theory is mainly concerned with the analysis of steady states within a given growth epoch. Our focus is on the changing behavior of a dualistic developing economy as it moves through various sub-phases, from agrarianism via dualism to modern growth. The new growth theory analyzes the qualities of a homogeneous one-sector world at the end of that process.

We of course acknowledge that we are still not ready to present a general theory of development applicable to all contemporary LDCs. While the relatively sophisticated formulations of the new growth theory clearly represent distinct and valuable additions to our inventory of ideas, the particular theory of development to which we adhere may be characterized as based substantially on a revival of classical growth theoretic ideas (1750–1820), combined with the basic neoclassical production function.

Although both the "classical" and "contemporary" theories of development are confronting similar problems, their visions differ markedly. Modern development economists, benefiting from historical hindsight, do not subscribe to the pessimistic thesis of the inevitability of long-run stagnation as the classical economists did. Explicitly or implicitly, they believe that the contemporary Third World is indeed engaged in a successful transition effort the feasibility of which has been demonstrated both by the historical experience of such contemporary DCs as Japan and the more recent experience of the newly industrialized countries. Compared to the classical economists, we have consequently become much more convinced of the unlimited potential of science and technology to ultimately lift all the boats in the developing world.

It is fair to say that it was Kuznets, though concerned mainly with describing the modern growth epoch rather than analyzing the transition process in getting there, who stimulated much of the thinking of post-war development economists. The basic problem he posed was that of understanding why some countries were successful, others not. Chenery and his associates took their cue from Kuznets and used regression analysis in order to depict various dimensions of "average" LDC structural change, first via the use of cross-sections and, later, via increasing resort to LDC time series analysis and pooled regressions (see Chenery, 1960; Chenery and Taylor, 1968). The basic question consistently being addressed was how productivity gains and increments in domestic and foreign demand are allocated among sectors as income per capita rises, and how one explains deviations from the "average" pattern. Eventually, an effort was made to stratify the sample, not only by country size, but also by identifiable development strategies, for example, of primary specialization, "balanced development," etc.

Chenery's inclusion of differences in policy among his typological categories raises difficult methodological issues; Kuznets, on the other hand, always insisted that his structural changes result from the interaction of underlying modifications in final demand and capacity conditions, with deviations from any "normal" pattern largely attributable to differences in the state of nature. His view was that "if established groups attached to large economic sectors suffer or foresee contraction of their share or base in economic society ... they are likely to resist by using political pressure to slow down the process," (Kuznets, 1980) and he ultimately viewed the emerging policy compromises as either basically more accommodative or more obstructive of the play of underlying economic forces. He avoided the risk of circular reasoning by not permitting policy to be a defining exogenous variable.

Our own approach to development theory, as presented in this volume, may be characterized more as comparative analytical economic history in the classical/neoclassical tradition. In this sense we are most comfortable in the company of W. Arthur Lewis, along with many others, including Little, Scitovsky and Scott, Kelley, Williamson, and Cheatham, Bhagwati and Krueger, in addition to more recent efforts organized by the World Bank, all of which have taken the comparative longitudinal route. Aside from our greater willingness (than many of these authors) to accept and model asymmetric and non-equilibrium behavior across sectors, for example, the existence of dualism, we also make more of an effort to render policy considerations as endogenous as possible in terms of relating them to different systems' typologically distinct initial conditions.

1.7 Road Map to the Volume

We accept the "transition to modern economic growth," previously defined, as our basic analytical framework. Developing countries initially find themselves in an agrarian epoch, as analyzed by the physiocrats, and the initial historical task facing such a society is to be able to graduate into a classical/neoclassical type of dynamic dualism. Chapter 2 accordingly presents agrarianism in the light of modern theory, emphasizing both the importance of the strength or weakness of linkages between agricultural and non-agricultural rural activities and the conditions affecting the chances for graduation when the forces of population pressure on the scarce land are pitted against modest rates of technology change.

In chapter 3 we present a development model which we believe to be applicable to the predominant labor surplus economies of the Third World, for which the termination of that disequilibrium condition represents a major landmark of developmental success. This model of the labor surplus dualistic economy essentially focuses on the analysis of intersectoral interactions – that is, of goods, labor and finance – between the agricultural and non-agricultural sectors at the aggregative (or macroscopic) level.

Since transition growth itself represents a relatively short run, that is, 20–50 year phenomenon, rather than an epochal process, we further explicitly abandon at this point the notion of its uniformity across LDC situations. Instead, we opt for a typological approach, recognizing that the process is bound to be substantially different in countries varying in size, in the extent of their unskilled labor surplus, in their human versus natural resource endowments, as well as in the nature of their colonial heritage.

The actual contemporary LDC world, abstracting from its socialist members, is composed of more than 100 countries scattered over five major geographic regions: (1) the four "dragons" of East Asia (Taiwan, Hong Kong, Singapore, South Korea); (2) South and Southeast Asia; (3) Latin America; (4) the Arab world; and (5) sub-Saharan Africa. Since any typological approach to development must necessarily be somewhat selective in its scope, the important types of LDCs that can readily be identified from their initial conditions must include, at a minimum, the relatively large (closed) labor surplus dualistic economy (for example, India, China), the small (open) dualistic economy (such as Taiwan, South Korea), as well as the natural resources rich open economies of Southeast Asia and Latin America.

In order to provide the full technical underpinnings underlying our analysis of development, we derive, in chapters 4 and 5, a set of general growth equations based on the neoclassical production function, focusing attention on the impact of technology change and the accumulation of capital on productivity and the functional distribution of income. The usefulness of this system for the analysis of modern economic growth in the industrially advanced countries is explored in chapter 6; its important application to the "special case" of the labor surplus developing economy and to an investigation of the factors underlying its successful graduation into modern growth is reserved for chapter 7.

Chapter 8 introduces hitherto neglected "open economy" dimensions of the transition growth process. Chapter 9 broadens the analysis by focusing on the relationship between growth and distribution as part of our typological/historical approach to development. The Gini decomposition analysis introduced, when combined with further applications of the growth equations of chapters 4 and 5, permits us to relate the technology dimensions of growth to the question of what it takes for LDCs to avoid the inverse U-shaped (Kuznets curve) conflict between growth and equity during the transition. This chapter also deals with the absolute poverty and human development-related dimensions of development.

Finally, in chapter 10 we turn to country experience and policies. Consistent with our notion that typology matters, we differentiate between the experience of the open dualistic economy which is natural resources rich (for example, the Latin American and Southeast Asian cases) and human resources rich (such as the East Asian cases). These two sub-types performed quite differently in the course of the transition growth process, and it was differences in their initial conditions – along with partly induced differences in policy choice over time – which yielded different paths of sequential sub-phases of transition.

The policy implications of development theory as presented here are quite different from those attempted by the planning school. Instead of a planning for resources orientation, our policy analysis focuses on planning for a change in macroeconomic as well as microeconomic or structural policies. Moreover, our treatment of policy is characterized by two conditions. On the one hand, the totality of all the growth promotion policies of the government are treated as facets of the operations of the economy in the same holistic perspective as adhered to earlier. Furthermore, the evolution of policy over time is treated in a way consistent with our historical perspective based on tracing the impact of differing initial conditions on the sequential order of sub-phases chosen. Our investigation of development policies in different parts of the developing world, accordingly, hopefully permits us to achieve a better understanding of the endogeneity of some of the policy choices made in different typological contexts and to focus on those areas in which enhanced understanding permits an improved selection of policy and its sequencing in the future.

PART II

Agrarianism and Dualism

2

From Closed and Open Agrarianism to Modern Dualism

2.1 Graduation from Closed Agrarianism

The basic notion of the eighteenth-century physiocrats was a circular-flow mechanism operating between a preponderant agricultural sector and a smaller non-agricultural sector. Neglecting the quantitatively insignificant consumption of the landlord class, the total output of the agricultural sector serves as consumption for farm families and for families that have moved into non-agricultural activities. In turn, the output of these non-agricultural activities either flows back to the agricultural sector in the form of consumer goods or subsidiary productive services to sustain agricultural productivity or is "consumed" by the nobility, the church, and the aristocracy to sustain cultural, religious and/or military activities. While, to the credit of the physiocrats, the regularity and stability of such a circular flow system was identified, it was left to the classicists to provide a causal explanation of the same phenomenon when population growth and land scarcity are added ingredients.

A crucial role is assigned to the level of agricultural labor productivity (p) over time in the agrarian schema. If p stagnates, then there is little chance of "success." If it is rising, then the dynamic question becomes whether or not the increase is sufficient to overcome the forces "on the other side" – population growth and diminishing returns to scarce land.

Under these conditions, increases in agricultural productivity generating an agricultural surplus to sustain the workers in the non-agricultural sector is a prerequisite for the emergence of a non-agricultural sector and the expansion of its size. The physiocratic idea of an agricultural surplus is a powerful tool for the analysis of growth dynamics in all economies with an initially sizeable agricultural base.

The basic arithmetic surrounding the existence and deployment of an agricultural surplus can be summarized with the help of three indicators: θ, p, and c. $\theta = B/L$ is the fraction of the total population or labor force (L)

already allocated to non-agriculture (B); $p = Q/V = Q/L(1 - \theta)$ is the remaining farmers' average productivity and $c = Q/L$ is the per capita consumption standard for the population as a whole. This yields:

$$1 - \theta = c/p \qquad (2.1)$$

demonstrating that the agricultural population V as a fraction of the total, $1 - \theta$, equals the consumption standard as a fraction of agricultural labor productivity (c/p).

The dynamic relationship among θ, p, and c is summarized in figure 2.1(a), in which the vertical (horizontal) axis measures p and c (θ). Since θ cannot exceed 1, if the initial value of θ is given by point "m", then $o'm$ is $1 - \theta$. p_0 and c_0 (with $c_0 < p_0$) are indicated on the vertical axis. q_0 is the point of intersection of the straight lines $o'p_0$ and c_0c. The distance q_0c_0 is the equilibrium θ, that is, θ_0, and $c_0/p_0 = 1 - \theta_0$ (from equation 2.1).

Figure 2.1(a) traces the dynamics of an increase in agricultural labor productivity p. If p increases ($p_0, p', p'', p_e \ldots$) the value of θ also increases ($q_0, z', z'', z_e \ldots$) **if c remains constant** at c_0. We call this full "allocation adjustment." On the other hand, the value of c increases ($q_0, q', q'', q_e \ldots$) **if θ remains constant** at θ_0. We call this full "consumption adjustment." It is common sense that a higher level of agricultural productivity p leads to either a higher fraction of the population allocated to the non-agricultural sector θ or a higher consumption standard c. More realistically, it is likely that increases in agricultural productivity are used to permit both the allocation of more workers to non-agricultural activity (higher θ) and additional consumption of agricultural goods (higher c). Such a path is traced out by the "propensity to consume" curve in figure 2.1(a).

The use of an emerging agricultural surplus to finance non-agricultural activities is the starting point for our analysis of whether or not a mercantile agrarian system – with p rising – can escape from stagnation. First, the phenomenon of agrarian stagnation must be defined in terms of the long-run stability of the triplet θ, p, and c. Using a Cobb–Douglas production function as an example with fixed land (N), the rate of technological change i (the intensity of agricultural innovation) and the growth rate of agricultural population are related:[1]

$$Q = e^{it}V^\alpha N^{1-\alpha} \qquad \text{(V is the agricultural population)} \qquad (2.2a)$$
$$\eta_p = i - (1 - \alpha)\eta_V \quad \text{where} \qquad (2.2b)$$
$$p = Q/V \qquad (2.2c)$$

Equation 2.2b is represented by one of the parallel negatively sloped straight lines labeled Ω in figure 2.1(c) in which η_p (η_V) is measured on the vertical (horizontal) axis. These lines may be called the "agricultural progress function" and reflect the struggle between innovation intensity i and the law of diminishing returns α. Thus, for any innovational intensity i (the vertical

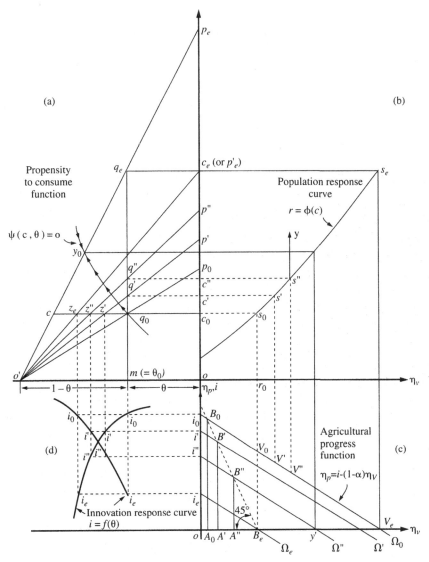

Figure 2.1 Closed agrarianism: comparative dynamics

intercept) we can determine the agricultural population growth rate η_V (the horizontal intercept) which represents a steady state. In other words, given i_0 and any initial η_{V_0}, $\eta_V = V_e$ represents the point of "long-run stagnation" as p and V take on stationary values ($\eta_p = 0$ along the horizontal axis). Any thesis of long-run stagnation must explain how such an equilibrium point is reached and maintained in the long run.

It is frequently argued that initial productivity gains in agriculture lead to upward revisions of the consumption standard or wage. If the gains are used entirely for consumption adjustment, then the Jorgenson classical thesis of stagnation applies.[2] For this thesis a positively shaped population response curve is shown in figure 2.1(b):

$$r = \phi(c) \quad \text{(population response)} \tag{2.3a}$$

where

$$r = \eta_L \quad \text{(rate of growth of population)} \tag{2.3b}$$

This relation simply states that the population growth rate is "controlled" by the consumption standard c, and that complete consumption adjustment as c rises along the vertical axis may drive up the population growth until stagnation is reached, that is, at s_e in figure 2.1(b) and V_e in figure 2.1(c).

To illustrate this, initial values p_0, c_0, and θ_0 in figure 2.1(a) generate the initial population growth rate r_0 or V_0 in figure 2.1(c). If continuously positive (if diminishing) η_p leads to continuous consumption adjustments, the system moves down along Ω_0, from V_0 to V' to V'' etc.[3] For example, since η_p is positive (and large) at V_0, p increases to, say, p' (figure 2.1(a)) and c increases to c'. This, via s' (figure 2.1(b)) and V' (figure 2.1(c)), depresses the rate of increase of p from V_0 to V'. Nevertheless, since v' is still positive, p continues to increase following the sequence p_0, p', p''. The long-run stagnation equilibrium position is ultimately reached at the triplet p_e, c_e, and θ_0 corresponding to the point s_e on the population response curve and V_e on the agricultural progress function.[4] Thus, according to the Jorgenson classical mechanism, the long-run stability of p_e, c_e, r, and θ_0 is due to the fact that the population growth rate is controlled in crude Malthusian fashion by the consumption standard.

This represents the Jorgenson classical "trap" case. Jorgenson, unlike the classicists, also presents a "take-off" case according to which the population growth rate[5] at some point does not respond to further increases in the consumption standard. For example, if the population response curve in figure 2.1(b) turns inelastic – that is, has the shape $s_0 s'' y$ – the rate of growth of productivity η_p stabilizes at V'' (figure 2.1(c)) and continued growth in p (and c) occurs.

Another way the system can be rescued from stagnation is, of course, for the rate of exogenous technological change, i, to rise. At some point, if not at s'' then beyond s_e, the population response curve is bound to become inelastic or even backward bending, as per capita consumption continues to rise, socio-economic change occurs, and/or fecundity limits are reached.

Another realistic way to model changes in i is to admit the possibility, counter to Jorgenson,[6] that some allocation adjustment takes place along with consumption adjustment, that is, the economy moves along the propensity to consume function in figure 2.1(a), and that the rate of technological change is related to changes in θ:

$$i = f(\theta) \text{ with } f'(\theta) < 0, \quad \text{or} \quad f'(\theta) > 0 \qquad (2.4)$$

The first alternative is represented by the negatively sloped "innovation response" curve (figure 2.1(d)). A justification for this relation would be that part of the labor force in the agricultural sector is engaged in the maintenance of overhead capital and that its presence is necessary to sustain technological progress. This involves long-term improvements in crop practices, many of which are barely perceptible over time. Such progress is possible only where terracing, irrigation, and drainage networks, for example, are kept from falling into disrepair. Some observers, especially those impressed with African conditions, have noted that,

> besides revenue, they [feudal landlords and kings] need servants, bodyguards and soldiers, and these requirements set an upper limit to the investment activity they are willing to organize ... Feudal landlords and government are likely to reduce the village population too much in their desire for soldiers, servants and luxuries.[7]

If relatively too much labor is drawn out of the farm sector, the intensity of innovation in agriculture may decline. On the other hand it may be more realistic to consider i as a positive function of θ, that is, a relative decline in the size of the agricultural labor force permits the required reorganization in agriculture. Thus the innovation response curve in figure 2.1(d) may be positively sloped, representing a more optimistic scenario. However, this is an empirical matter – heavily dependent on the initial extent of population pressure on the land.

Finally, in the more realistic case of simultaneous consumption and allocation adjustment following consumer preferences for some non-agricultural goods,[8] the demographic response curve is more likely to shift to the left and/or become inelastic earlier as socioeconomic change overcomes the single-minded Malthusian link between food consumption and fertility. This method of escape from closed agrarian stagnation permits the utilization of modern microeconomic tools of analysis, but is not attempted here. For present purposes it is sufficient to demonstrate the forces that tend to lock closed agrarian systems into long-run stagnation, as well as those which may permit them to escape. It is probably more realistic and useful to extend our analysis to the agrarian economy open to international trade.

2.2 Graduation from Open Agrarianism

2.2.1 Introduction

In the previous section, the economy was able to escape its low-level equilibrium trap and yield continuous increases in productivity because the population response curve turned inelastic "early enough," innovational intensity shifted up sufficiently – either exogenously or endogenously – or the allocation adjustment mechanism eventually weakened the Malthusian response to productivity increases. The initial conditions – the extent of population pressure on the land, the strength of the law of diminishing returns, the strength of technological change, and the rate of population growth relative to the critical population growth rate V_e in figure 2.1(c) – represented an important determinant of the final outcome.

We can thus distinguish between the trap (continued stagnation) and non-trap (graduation) cases in the closed agrarian economy. Nonetheless, an analysis of the conditions which permit an economy to graduate from agrarianism to dualism requires more than a purely resource-oriented approach. It must incorporate the interaction between the economy's human agents, the institutional framework within which they organize themselves, and the economic functions proper. To illustrate the challenge, we must understand the differences in the causation of agricultural innovations between an agrarian or modern dualistic situation, the most critical issue in determining whether or not a successful graduation takes place.

As Schultz and others have emphasized, the motivation for an increase in the flow of agricultural innovations is directly tied to opportunities perceived on the part of the decision-making units in the traditional agrarian society – to consume non-agricultural goods and to acquire ownership of the industrial capital stock. The incentive to increase agricultural productivity is enhanced if the proceeds from such increases can be utilized to obtain non-agricultural assets. Once the relationship between these objectives and the human effort involved becomes clear, marked change in agricultural productivity can be realized. In this connection, the contiguity between agricultural and non-agricultural activities is of great importance – a subject which has been relatively neglected in the literature. The experience of Japan during the Tokugawa Period (its mercantile agrarian epoch) indicates that increased inter-sectoral connectedness enhanced both agricultural productivity and the growth of rural industry and services (or Z-goods). The essence of graduation from agrarianism thus represents the activation of an innovation inducement mechanism, the coming into play of an entrepreneurial group sensitive to surplus-generating opportunities within and outside of agriculture. This class associates its personal well-being in a direct fashion with the continuous improvement of agricultural practices and makes it possible for capitalistic dualism to replace the agrarian situation tending towards long-term stagnation.

Decentralized rural-oriented industrialization or the existence of vigorous Z-goods activities is extremely helpful not only for success in the dualistic period which follows, but also for the initial graduation effort itself. Thus, the routinization of agricultural productivity increase well before the advent of Kuznetsian technology change in the modern growth context is critical. However, there is also the critical dimension of openness to consider, and how it affects the interactions between domestic agriculture and rural non-agricultural activity.

Before tackling this it is helpful first to analyze the case of open agrarianism without Z-goods, where non-agricultural activity resides exclusively in a service sector which exists to facilitate the exporting of raw materials to the rest of the world. This is the way the typical overseas territory would look as the closed agrarian system is penetrated by a new economic agent, the foreigner. Making his debut typically as a trader, this foreigner takes on successively more important economic functions. He is instrumental in creating a new sector in the agrarian society – the export production sector. This implies three domestic production sectors (figure 2.2): agriculture, services, and raw material exports. The export production sector relies on the exploitation of cheap labor and/or natural resources. Inputs flowing into this sector are food (R') produced by the agricultural sector and services (K) produced by the service sector T. The output of the export sector Q_E is assumed to flow entirely abroad. The economic functions of the service sector differs drastically from those encountered in closed mercantile agrarianism. Instead of serving the interests of the landed aristocracy, it serves the interests of export-oriented foreigners and their domestic commercial allies.

Once the new economic order of the open colonial economy is established, the importation of consumer goods introduces a different way of life into the traditional agrarian economy. Non-agricultural activities focus exclusively on export processing and the facilitating services sector which becomes a "port city," an economic and cultural enclave within the agrarian system. Another imported input, K', represents additions to the commercial capital stock – warehouses, transportation equipment, etc. – to facilitate the export trade. The foreigners thus utilize the export proceeds Q_E in part for the importation of consumer goods directed at agricultural households and in part to support additions to the capital stock in the export enclave. Export goods Q_E are converted into foreign exchange M which is disposed of either as two kinds of current expenses B or as profits π.

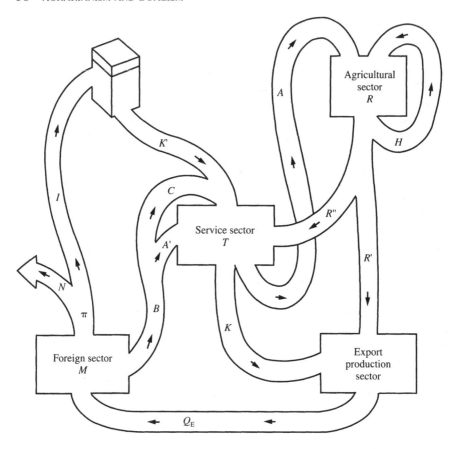

KEY: (Real Flows)

A = Imported consumer goods for agricultural workers
A' = Imported consumer goods for service sector workers
B = Current expenses
C = Imported luxury consumer goods
H = Factor services of agricultural labor
I = Reinvestment finance
K = Services facilitating exports
K' = Imported commercial capital
N = Repatriated profits
R' = Agricultural output consumed by export sector workers
R'' = Agricultural output consumed by service sector workers
π = Reinvested commercial profits
Q_E = Export sector output

Figure 2.2 Open agrarianism in the absence of Z-goods

The establishment of the new service sector introduces new agents (resident foreigners and a new domestic commercial class), new factors of production (commercial capital K'), new production activities (exports), and new consumer goods (A) into the agrarian economy. Most important is the introduction and acceptance of a new mode of rational economic behavior. The new life is characterized by an appetite for economic acquisition which, although taken for granted in contemporary analysis, represents a radically different value system from the feudal relationships that preceded it.

Commercial profits π, the immediate objective of all of this activity, can be reinvested (I, leading to additions to the commercial capital stock) or repatriated (N). Profit repatriation ensures that not all savings generated by the export activity are used for capital accumulation within the system. If continuously profitable export opportunities are anticipated, profits are likely to be reinvested in the service or export sector or both. If prospects are dim or uncertain, profits will be repatriated and capital accumulation will decline. Thus, profit repatriation can be blamed – and often has been – as the primary economic evil of colonialism because it signifies that the foreigner regards the developing economy as an enclave and refuses to invest beyond what is necessary to augment future repatriable profits. The calculus of whether or not there is net investment ($N > 0$) or repatriation ($N < 0$) of foreign capital depends on factors substantially "outside" the system, and frustration of the overseas territory's own development effort is the norm of performance. But this is for reasons quite separate from the phenomenon of insufficient reinvestment. Important as "profit repatriation" may be as a contributing factor, given the vagaries of exogenous forces such as discovery, conditions in other international markets, conditions in the "mother" country's home market, and the exhaustion of raw material and mineral deposits, it is not **the** primary cause of long-run stagnation. The prognosis of likely long-run stagnation in such a system holds, even if all profits were reinvested. For this reason we assume that $\pi = I$ (or $N = 0$) – all profits are reinvested in the open agrarian system.

2.2.2 The anatomy of open agrarianism

The organization just sketched carries out certain essential economic functions in the open agrarian society: (1) acquisition of the necessary labor force; (2) production of exportable goods; (3) successful sale of the good in the export market; and (4) accumulation of commercial capital. These correspond to the four components of figure 2.2, each of which is briefly analyzed to elicit the appropriate analytical assumptions for the successful performance of the four functions.

Acquisition of the labor force   The concepts of allocated labor – labor no longer employed in the agricultural sector – and of agricultural surplus – the food consumed by that labor – are crucial to the analysis of the open agrarian economy. Let θL be the allocated labor, with θ the fraction of the total labor force L employed in the service sector **or** the export production sector. The total agricultural surplus R in figure 2.2 consists of food flowing to the service sector R'' and to the export production sector R'. Regardless of the physical location of employment, such allocated labor is used to promote exports, and there is no need to distinguish between labor in the service sector and in the export production sector proper. It is evident that θL and R – the allocated labor and the agricultural surplus – represent the primary means of export production, and that export-oriented entrepreneurs are vitally interested in a steady supply of these factors. The major instrument at the disposal of these entrepreneurs in their effort to induce the desired movement out of agriculture is the delivery of imported consumer goods (A in figure 2.2) not previously consumed by the cultivators. The following equation expresses a ratio

$$w = A/L \qquad (2.5)$$

which is the "inducement ratio" – A is used to "induce" the delivery of labor and food for export production. The inducement ratio is the volume of imported consumer goods per unit of population L.

The earlier prognosis of the possibility of reaching long-run stationary equilibrium – in the sense of a constant per capita consumption standard c and a constant agricultural labor productivity p – continues to be valid for the open agrarian economy. In other words, the stand-off between the forces of population growth and technological change in the Malthusian trap case continues to hold. Figure 2.3(a) is a reproduction of figure 2.1 in which the long-run stagnation point is q_0 – corresponding to the stationary triplet θ_0, p_0, and c_0. The question is whether stagnation can be broken by the importation of goods from abroad. For example, suppose food grains are imported in the amount ($\bar{w}$) per unit of total population as indicated in figure 2.3(a). Then, with fixed values of p_0 and c_0, the equilibrium allocation point shifts from q_0 to q_0'', signifying an increase in θ.[9] This corresponds to what we intuitively expect: "food imports" substitute for "domestic productivity increase" as a factor causing the reallocation of a larger fraction of labor θ. We then have:

$$\theta = \theta(w) = (1 + (w - c)/p) \quad \text{with } \theta' > 0 \qquad (2.6)$$

stating that the allocated labor ratio θ is an increasing function of the inducement ratio.

In the more general case where the consumption standard c_0 is above the caloric minimum, a larger non-agricultural allocation ratio χ is induced

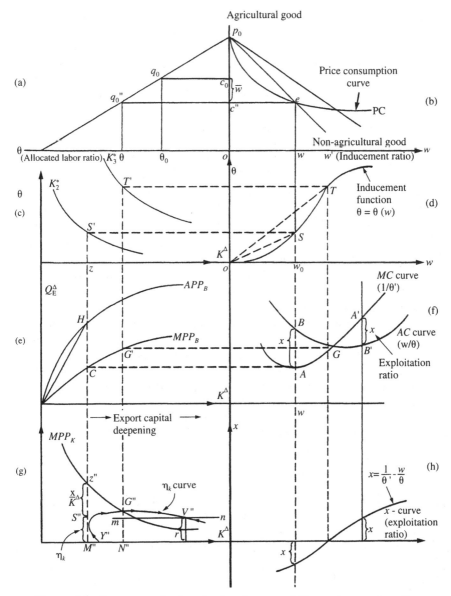

Figure 2.3 Open agrarianism in the absence of Z-goods: comparative dynamics

through the delivery of industrial consumer goods – rather than food – to the agricultural sector. In figure 2.3(b), assume an indifference map (not shown) of a typical peasant as a consumer. With productivity (and hence his total income in terms of food) at p_0, a price-consumption curve (PC curve) can be drawn. Suppose then that the inducement ratio is w units of goods as marked on the horizontal axis. Then the equilibrium consumption point is at e with c'' units of food consumed. Returning to figure 2.3(a), the new equilibrium allocation point is established at q_0'', signifying an increase of θ. In this way the allocated labor ratio remains an increasing function of the inducement ratio (w) as postulated in equation 2.6 when the inducement takes the form of imported industrial goods.

In general, the ratio in equation 2.6 is the labor reallocation inducement function presented in figure 2.3(d). This function predicts the manner in which surplus labor (and agricultural surplus) can be induced to leave the rural sector through the delivery of imported consumer goods. On the basis of the above, the inducement curve is positively sloped and new goods appearing on the taste horizon has its strongest cumulative effects initially, both in terms of the choice between food and industrial goods and between leisure and industrial goods. Finally, a "law of diminishing returns to the seduction process" ultimately sets in after some point S.

Thus θ measures the relative "availability" of labor to the export sector and w measures the cost to the entrepreneurs in the export production sector. This inducement function generates two equations. The first defines the average cost of labor (in terms of imported goods per unit of labor allocated):

$$u = w/\theta \; (= wL/\theta L) \tag{2.7a}$$

The second defines the marginal cost of such labor:

$$m = dw/d\theta \; (= 1/\theta') \tag{2.7b}$$

From the point of view of the export-oriented entrepreneur, the **total** cost of labor is simply the total volume of imported goods used to induce the flow of labor to non-agricultural activity.

This inducement is strictly a "market phenomenon." If w represents units of imported industrial consumer goods per unit of L, the terms of trade between imported industrial and domestic agricultural goods established in the market is represented by the slope of $p_0 e$ (figure 2.3(b)). The total value of consumption (w units of industrial goods and c units of food) of a typical worker at the established terms of trade has the same market value as p_0 units of food. Moreover, the total value of imported goods is equivalent to $*c''p_0 L$ units of food, which, since p_0 is equivalent to the real wage, enables the trading entrepreneur to buy $*c''p_0 L/p_0$ units of labor or, as a fraction of L, $\theta = *c''p_0/p_0$. This can be measured horizontally in figure

2.3(a) as $c''q_0''$, or vertically in figure 2.3(d) as w_0S. Thus under open agrarianism, labor becomes a fully marketable commodity. The relevance of this new maximizing calculus to the labor market is shown more directly by representing varying levels of u and m – the average and marginal cost of allocated labor – by an AC (average cost) and an MC (marginal cost) curve in figure 2.3(e). Comparing figures 2.3(d) and 2.3(f), the MC curve reaches a minimum point at A as the law of diminishing returns sets in at S, and the MC curve crosses the AC curve at the minimum point of the latter at G when the inducement curve has unit elasticity at T. Intuitively, the profit-maximizing entrepreneur carries out his "labor seduction" according to a marginal principle. For this reason, define the vertical gap between the MC curve and the AC curve:

$$x = MC - AC \qquad (2.8)$$

as the "exploitation ratio." This is an important concept in the open agrarian society. As a function of w, the exploitation ratio is plotted in figure 2.3(h) as the x-curve and is positive (negative) if the inducement curve is inelastic (elastic).

Production of exported goods   Surplus labor is induced to leave agriculture to provide the necessary overheads and direct inputs into the production of exportable commodities. As Fisk put it,

> where external factors, such as the development of European commercial enterprise ... have brought marketing facilities within reasonable reach of the subsistence units, the labor surplus has been used first to complete the linkage with the markets, and then to increase agricultural production for sale.[10]

It is possible to classify sub-types of open agrarian economies by differentiating among the production conditions prevailing in specific export activities. For example, in the

> export-dominated economies of South-East Asia, two rather distinct sub-types can be identified for the historical pre-World War II period ... For one type, export production continued to emphasize traditional, labor-intensive methods applied to an indigenous if commercialized or cash crop – rice being the outstanding example. For the other type, export production was associated with modern capital-intensive methods introduced from abroad. Most commonly these were applied to products which were also implanted from abroad – rubber and sugar representing two important examples ... Exploitation of mineral rather than agricultural resources for export (for example, tin and petroleum) may be considered as a variant of the second case.[11]

Further sub-classification of the export production sector also has general significance in terms of dynamic linkage of "spill-over effects."[12] The initial contact of the traditional economy is afforded by, and the growth-promoting force of the open agrarian economy is expressed through, the production of agricultural goods for export.

Distinctions among crop types and organizational configurations are important and must be dealt with in any analysis of the transition from open agrarianism to dualism. However, these distinctions need not distract from the basic fact of export production – that it is through the joint effort of allocated labor and capital K that output for export Q_E is generated. Thus we can apply a production function:

$$Q_E = f(K,B) \quad \text{(export production function)} \tag{2.9a}$$
$$B = \theta L \tag{2.9b}$$

If the exportable item is derived from an exhaustible source, the production function is subject to the condition of long-run decreasing returns and stagnation is likely to occur. Under the neutral assumption of constant returns to scale, the productivity of allocated labor $Q_E^\Delta \equiv Q_E/B$ is an increasing (and convex) function of capital-per-unit of labor, $K^\Delta \equiv K/B$. This production function is expressed by the equations:

$$Q_E^\Delta = f(K^\Delta,1) \quad \text{where} \tag{2.10a}$$
$$Q_E^\Delta \equiv Q_E/B \quad \text{and} \tag{2.10b}$$
$$K^\Delta \equiv K/B \tag{2.10c}$$

The function is represented by the APP_B curve in figure 2.3(e). In the same diagram, the marginal product of allocated labor is represented by the MPP_B curve. The marginal product of capital as a function of K^Δ is shown in figure 2.3(g). When K^Δ increases, export sector capital intensity increases – this is export capital deepening. The average product curve in figure 2.3(e) shows how the law of diminishing returns to capital operates to further the process of export capital deepening.

Selling in the export market   All exported goods are destined for the foreign market. If the terms of trade are t, then the total amount of exported goods Q_E sell for $M = tQ_E$ units of "foreign goods" – the revenue in real units of foreign exchange:

$$M = tQ_E \tag{2.11}$$

A whole set of factors may affect the terms of trade conditions in foreign markets. If the exporting open agrarian economy is a major supplier of a commodity (for example, cocoa for Ghana), t is a decreasing function of Q_E. If the economy is a price taker, t takes on a constant value in the short run. However, in either case the terms of trade are likely to change in the long run according to world demand and a variety of other considerations discussed at length in the Prebisch versus Kindleberger literature. It is rather difficult, and not necessary here, to come up with a satisfactory generalization about the behavior of t over time. Purely to emphasize the internal logic of open agrarianism and independent of the admittedly important exogenous considerations, assume the constancy of t. This permits, by redefining the unit of measurement of imports, t to be 1.

Accumulation of commercial capital   As is evident from the flow chart in figure 2.2, the proceeds from the export sale, on the assumption of no capital repatriation, may be used in three different ways: investment I; luxury consumption C by the export-related entrepreneurs; and the importation of incentive consumer goods designed for rural consumption. It is reasonable to assume that C is proportional to K (that is, $C = gK$), because the luxury consumption of entrepreneurs tends to be proportional to the stock of commercial capital managed by them. Finally, since investment leads to capital accumulation, we can summarize these relations as:

$$I = M - A - C \tag{2.12a}$$
$$C = gK \tag{2.12b}$$
$$dK/dt \equiv I \tag{2.12c}$$
$$\eta_K = I/K = (dK/dt)/K \tag{2.12d}$$

where equation 2.12d is the growth rate of capital.

We should recall that in performing the four economic functions just outlined, the open agrarian economy must face certain conditions inherited from the closed agrarian system. One of the most important is the persistence of population pressures. Assume that population continues to grow at a constant rate:[13]

$$\eta_L = r \tag{2.13}$$

The long-run stagnation thesis of closed agrarianism provided the ultimate stability of the population growth rate r, the consumption standard c, and labor productivity p. As evident from the discussion, these conditions ensure that a steady supply of labor and surplus food flow into the export sector in the open agrarian setting. In other words, demographic factors inherited by open agrarianism are such that they are "right" for the open economy in which labor is induced to move into the export market. The extent of population pressure can be weighed in terms of the factor endowment of the economy measured by capital per head K^* ($=K/L$):

$$K^\Delta = K^*/\theta \quad \text{where} \tag{2.14a}$$
$$K^* = K/L \quad \text{(by equation 2.9b and 2.10c)} \tag{2.14b}$$

These equations show a simple relation between the overall factor endowment K^*, export capital intensity K^Δ, and the allocated labor ratio θ. At any point in time, the economy's overall factor endowment K^* is fixed. Therefore, as equation 2.14a shows, K^Δ is inversely related to θ in the export sector. This relationship is shown in figure 2.3(c) by the system of rectangular hyperbolas, where a rectangular hyperbola represents a fixed value of K^* in 2.14a.

Figure 2.3 may now be used to summarize the open agrarian economy up to this point. To begin with, let the total stock of capital and the labor force be fixed at any point in time. Using the inducement ratio w as an instrument to acquire surplus labor, entrepreneurs set a "trial" value of w as indicated on the horizontal axis (figure 2.3(d)). This determines the values of the allocated labor ratio ($w_0 S$ in figure 2.3(d)), the level of export capital intensity (z in figure 2.3(e)), and the marginal and average product of allocated labor (C and H in figure 2.3(e)). This enables the entrepreneur to calculate total revenue ($M = tAPP_B B$) in terms of foreign exchange. On the other hand, when w is chosen, the entrepreneur can also calculate the total labor cost (wL) in terms of the foreign exchange expended on imported consumer goods. Thus profits, the difference between total cost and total revenue, are determined by the inducement ratio w.

The most conspicuous new institutional aspect of open agrarianism is that the society is dominated by the insatiable acquisitive commercial spirit of the entrepreneurial class. This spirit translates itself concretely into the desire to maximize total profits or, since at any point in time the capital stock is fixed, the desire to maximize profits per unit of capital. Thus entrepreneurs, either through calculation or through trial and error experimentation, tend to set w at the level maximizing total profits at each point in time.

Investment I in equation 2.12a is precisely the definition of profits and "the rate of growth of capital" η_K in equation 2.12d is the definition of the profit rate – profits per unit of capital. The profit rate can be written as:

$$\eta_K = \frac{tf(K^*, \theta(w)) - w}{K^*} - g \qquad (2.15)^{14}$$

Thus, for a fixed K^* (t,g), the profit rate is a function of w. To maximize the profit rate with respect to w by setting $d\eta_K/dw = 0$:

$$tf_B = 1/\theta, \quad \text{or} \qquad (2.16a)$$
$$tMPP_B = MC \quad \text{and} \quad MPP_B = MC \text{ (if } t = 1) \qquad (2.16b)$$

These equations illustrate the condition for the maximization of profits at equality between $MPP_B t$ (the marginal product of allocated labor in export production) and MC (the marginal cost of allocated labor in terms of imported consumer goods).

Any such equilibrium condition is relative to a fixed value of K^*, the factor endowment of the economy. Under our assumption that K^*_2 (figure 2.3(c)) represents the current value of K^*, the equilibrium condition 2.16 is represented by the "equilibrium rectangle" $S'SAC$, signifying the equality between MPP_B (at point C in figure 2.3(e)) and MC (at point A in figure 2.3(f)).

2.2.3 The operation of open agrarianism

An understanding of the origin of profits – inducement to capital accumulation and the source of investment finance – throws considerable light on the internal logic of open agrarianism. The optimum profit rate can be written as:

$$\eta_K + g = MPP_K + \frac{x}{K^\Delta} \tag{2.17}^{15}$$

The exploitation ratio, x, introduced in equation 2.8 is equivalent to the definition of labor exploitation given by Joan Robinson: "the deviation of the actual wage from the competitive level of the real wage." This can be verified as follows: $wL/B = w/\theta = AC$ (the distance wB in figure 2.3(f)) is the actual average wage cost per unit of allocated labor, while the competitive wage cost is $MPP_B = MC$ (the distance wA in figure 2.3(f)). Hence x represents the tax on (or subsidy of) allocated labor, and the term $x/K^\Delta = xB/K$ is the "exploitation" per unit of capital. x can be negative as well as positive since labor can be subsidized as well as taxed. Referring to figures 2.3(d) and (f), when the inducement function is elastic $MC < AC$ and both x and x/K^Δ are positive since there is a tax on labor to the right of point G.

We can attempt an economic interpretation of equation 2.17. The term $MPP_K + x/K^\Delta$ is the "gross income" per unit of capital – the sum of the competitive income per unit of capital (MPP_K) and the "exploitation" per unit of capital. The term $\eta_K + g$ is the "disposition of capitalist income." In the case of the equilibrium rectangle $S'SAC$, x is negative – labor is subsidized – and the profit rate η_K indicated by distance $S''M''$ (in figure 2.3(g)) falls short of the MPP_K by the amount $S''Z''$ – the sum of consumption g and the subsidy per unit of capital x/K^Δ.[16]

Now suppose that the factor endowment of the economy as a whole changes so that K^* increases from K^*_2 to K^*_3, represented by the upward shift of the corresponding rectangular hyperbola. The new optimal solution is the equilibrium rectangle $T'TGG'$ and the new rate of return to capital is the vertical distance $N''G''$ (figure 2.3(g)). This is the special case when the inducement function is of unitary elasticity and the exploitation ratio is zero ($x = 0$ in figure 2.3(h)). For this special case the profit rate is $MPP_K - g$. However, since $g = 0$ by assumption, the profit rate η_K coincides with the MPP_K in figure 2.3(g). In similar fashion, as increasing values of K^* are postulated by a system of rectangular hyperbolas in figure 2.3(c), the equilibrium values of the profit rates H_K generate a locus of points such as the curve η_K in figure 2.3(g) passing through the points Y'', S'', G'', V'' as K^* increases.

There obviously exist many subcases of open agrarian economy in the real world, both on the contemporary scene and in an historical context. Other colonial differentiations could focus on different needs by the mother country and on different, including non-economic, objectives. We leave this to the imagination of the reader. Nevertheless, it is our hope that the general analysis of section 2.2.2, through the identification of the four economic functions required for execution in one type of open agrarian economy, makes possible the elucidation of other subcases by (hopefully empirical) reference to how such functions are performed. In accordance with the special characteristics of each subtype, open agrarianism may exhibit a wide variety of behavior patterns during the growth process. Specifically, changes in essential observable characteristics that take place as the factor endowment of the economy changes (as K^* increases) may be in different directions. Our model (and figure 2.3) has been designed to answer only some of the problems that can arise – for example, the impact of a change in K^* on other observable characteristics. We briefly indicate some of the comparative static results of our analysis.

Referring to figure 2.3, the two equilibrium rectangles indicated earlier – $S'SAC$ and $T'TGG'$ – correspond to two special cases: where the point of inflexion of the inducement function falls (S) and where the inducement function is unit-elastic (T). Corresponding to these two special "landmark" cases, S and G divide the η_K curve (in figure 2.3(g)) into three segments: $Y''S''$ (corresponding to the falling portion of the MC curve in figure 2.3(f)), $S''G''$ (the portion of the rising MC curve that lies below the AC curve), and the segment $G''V''$ (the portion of the MC curve that lies above the AC curve). Keeping these points in mind, the comparative static conclusions can be summarized:

1   As K^* increases, the value of w increases. This means that in case of overall capital deepening, the w set to maximize profits and the inducement ratio always increase. Thus, if the inducement function is positively sloped, then the allocated labor proportion (θ) also increases. Figure 2.3(b) shows that the terms of trade tend to move against the entrepreneurs in the export sector.

2   As K^* increases, the value of K^Δ decreases (increases) if the inducement function is elastic (inelastic) before (after) point S. This is shown in figure 2.3(g) by the fact that the η_K curve moves left before and right after S''. The economic interpretation is that there is capital shallowing in the export sector as long as surplus labor can be pried loose

from the subsistence agricultural sector. This turns to capital deepening once the inducement function becomes inelastic. As the law of diminishing returns takes effect in the labor acquisition process – making it increasingly difficult to acquire labor – capitalists are forced to use less labor per unit of capital in the export production sector.

3   As K^* increases, η_K increases (decreases) if $x < 0$ ($x > 0$). This is indicated in figure 2.3(g) by the fact that the curve η_K reaches a maximum value at the point crossing the MPP_K curve, signifying that the profit rate increases when labor is subsidized and decreases when labor is taxed. This is further illustrated by the fact that the vertical gap between the MPP_K curve and the η_K curve shrinks to zero before G'', signifying that in the process of increasing export capital intensity, the diminishing need to subsidize labor more than compensates for the unfavorable effect of a lower MPP_K produced by the operation of the law of diminishing returns to capital. Conversely, when labor is taxed the profit rate declines after G''.

In the above, a reasonable behavioristic pattern for the inducement function illustrated the flexibility of our framework of analysis. Clearly other *a priori* hypotheses as to the slope of the inducement function are admissible and would lead to different conclusions. Moreover, other applications of our framework of analysis are possible – we could identify the behavioral characteristics of the production functions more fully or make "richer" assumptions in connection with the terms of trade or the value of g.

2.2.4 *Prognosis for open agrarianism*

We can inquire about the long-run prospects for the open agrarian or colonial system depicted here. To facilitate this, a horizontal line *mn* is drawn in figure 2.3(g) at the height of the population growth rate r in equation 2.13. Suppose the point of intersection of that curve with the η_K curve is V''. Then there must be eventual capital deepening to the left of V'' because the rate of growth of capital η_K exceeds the rate of growth of labor r. Similarly, there must be capital shallowing to the right of V''. With a stable equilibrium prevailing at V'', the long-run stationary value of K^* implies long-run stationary values for all essential economic magnitudes (for example, K^Δ, MPP_K, MPP_L, θ and w).

This conclusion is valid irrespective of the detailed framework presented earlier. In other words, the prospect for long-run stagnation or graduation is independent of the precise transitional stages through which the economy passes. For ultimate stagnation, all that is essential is that the η_K curve declines over the long run, a phenomenon which can be traced to an inelastic inducement function for higher values of w. The inelasticity of the inducement function at large values of w is compellingly reasonable since $\partial\theta$ cannot exceed one. In other words, the attempt by foreign-oriented entrepreneurs to take advantage of the existing labor surplus in the open agrarian economy ultimately runs up against physical limitations. If a stagnant p and c are inherited from the closed agrarian system, they cannot be shaken off. The growth that does take place may be substantial, but as long as it is restricted to the export production sector, the prospects are for ultimate stagnation. This conclusion can be avoided only when the opening of the closed agrarian system occurs under conditions where "take-off" is already indicated or when it brings with it additional dynamic benefits relating to a boost in the rate of technological change. The ability or inability to successfully implement such technological dynamics is what distinguishes stagnant open agrarianism from vigorous dualism. A possible reverse side of that coin results if the new condition of openness interferes with the process of closed mercantile agrarianism *en route* to graduation. Such interference could take the form of destroying a vigorously growing Z-goods sector.

In summary, there are a number of reasons why the structure of open agrarianism is likely to be closer to dualism than that of the closed variety. First and foremost among these is the advent of profit maximization as the propellant force. As Georgescu-Roegen put it,

> from the middle of the nineteenth century, if not before, these [agrarian] countries began ... to receive the impact of Western capitalism. Increasing trade with the West revealed the existence of other economic patterns and at the same time opened up new desires for the landlords and new ambitions for the bureaucracy. Under this influence the feudal *contrat social* began to weaken.[17]

Second, while surplus labor may have been employed to satisfy cultural or religious values in the closed economy, open agrarianism is likely to make productive use of such labor in the modern sense, commercializing it by mobilization via the price mechanism instead of by feudal edict. As enhanced labor mobility results in changes in commodity flows, the foundations are laid for what eventually develops into intersectoral labor and commodity markets in a dualistic setting.

Third, physical capital formation makes its appearance for the first time via the creation of social and economic overheads serving the export sector. Finally, a new class of economic agents – acquisitive foreign entrepreneurs and their local counterparts with whom they form flexible alliances – gradually replaces a reluctant landed aristocracy in positions of economic and political power.

The environment has changed markedly under the impact of foreign trade and the profit-maximizing calculus. There nevertheless remains a considerable gap between the operations of open agrarianism and the workings of a vigorous dualistic system. We have no more than to look about us to see a considerable number of less developed countries, especially in Sub-Saharan Africa, trapped in an essentially open agrarian situation. The advent of openness on the mercantile agrarian scene is thus not a simple matter. In a closed system which was trapped – given its parameters governing agricultural productivity change, the strength of the law of diminishing returns, and population growth – the chances for transition into dualism are clearly and substantially enhanced. In another closed system which, given its parameters, was heading for graduation, the wrong kind of colonial intrusion could frustrate that effort.

Even in the optimistic scenario in which openness makes a positive difference, there remain a number of crucial factors that are likely to keep the less developed economy in the grip of stagnation over the long term. Dominant is the failure of development in the export enclave to touch the life of the agricultural production sector in a meaningful or pervasive fashion. Industrial capital formation in the sense of a dualistic economy has not as yet put in an appearance, and in this context the required interaction between a small but expanding industrial sector and a large but shrinking agricultural sector has no chance to take hold. As a direct consequence, the ability to count on a dependable innovation-inducement mechanism in both sectors is missing. This mechanism represents the most important link in the chain of successful dualistic growth. In the dual agrarian economy there is no dualistic entrepreneur in place with one foot in each sector, making his profit maximizing investment and innovative decisions to ensure balanced progress. As one observer has aptly put it,

> technological change is, itself, one of the more difficult products for a country in the early stages of economic development to produce. In fact, it sometimes appears that an industrial economy is a prerequisite for technological change in the agricultural sector.[18]

We have tried to shed light on the functioning of an open agrarian system and the reasons why continued stagnation might result, as well as why openness might permit departure from that norm. In addition to initial conditions governing the scarcity of land, the rate of technological change in agriculture, and the force of population growth, a critical element is the extent to which openness brings enhanced opportunities in terms of a boost to technological change or why the inhibition to an organically growing domestic interaction between agriculture and the Z-goods sector may cause a delay of the graduation effort. The relevance of such a pre-existing Z-goods sector for our prognosis is treated more fully in the next section.

2.3 Open Agrarianism with Z-goods

2.3.1 Introduction

We now examine the case of open agrarianism in a self-sufficient economy when the overseas territory affected by foreigners already has an existing Z-goods industry. A formal model of an agrarian economy incorporating the production of food and Z-goods utilizing only labor was first presented by Hymer and Resnick.[19] The Z-goods model focuses on two types of productive activity in the agrarian economy: food production and the output of non-agricultural activities – including services, handicrafts, and food processing, all for village consumption.

However, as growth and development link the rural economy with the world economy, two related developments occur. First, the economy is opened to foreigners interested in raw materials and cash crop production and export. As in the case of the open agrarian model, imported consumer goods offer an alternative use for rural labor by inducing workers to shift into the production of raw materials for export, in this case labor is induced to move from Z-goods production into export activities. In other words, external trade provides the basis for the replacement of traditional industry in homes and villages by the output of similar goods imported from the mother country as export activities expand. The imported non-durable consumer goods – often of higher quality and fulfilling a wider range of needs than the domestically produced goods – are purchased using foreign exchange generated by the new export-oriented sector producing raw materials and cash crops desired by foreigners within the open agrarian or colonial system. These raw materials and cash crops for export (A_E) are assumed to not be consumed domestically. The foreign exchange earned from A_E goods permits the purchase of imported manufactures which substitute for Z-goods production and allows further expansion of A_E activities. As a consequence, there is a decline in the Z-goods sector and an expansion of both exports and imports. The production of food for domestic consumption is assumed to be broadly unaffected by these developments.

The Hymer–Resnick model with relaxed assumptions has important implications in the post-colonial case. However, that is an issue of open dualism, to be addressed later, while here we are concerned with the colonial case under open agrarianism. With a constant terms of trade, there are two possible scenarios illustrating the Z-goods displacement hinted at above. We explore both the favorable and unfavorable colonial archetypes in turn.

2.3.2 Unfavorable colonial archetype

The unfavorable archetype is the basic Hymer–Resnick model in which colonial policies inhibit the development of domestic industry through mercantilist restrictions by the mother country on the pattern of trade and investment. This is coupled with the relative neglect of food producing agriculture, where the focus of government attention is on the export of minerals/cash crops and the services required to bring them to market. Little attention is paid to agriculture for domestic consumption and exports (A_E) are concentrated in the hands of a few. These large landholdings yield an unequal distribution of income and wealth, both of which contribute to weak linkages with the non-agricultural sector since now few individuals have sufficient income to purchase non-agricultural goods. When the primary export consists largely of minerals the resulting rural income distribution is even more unequal and the rural linkages even weaker. In this situation Z-goods production is concentrated in traditional household activities and is gradually displaced by imported consumer goods while domestic agriculture stagnates.

This basic archetype of Hymer–Resnick Z-goods displacement – the unfavorable colonial case – is illustrated in figure 2.4. $A_{E0}Z^0$ in quadrant I represents the production possibilities curve as the fixed supply of labor (all rural labor after the society's food needs have been met) is allowed to shift between the production of non-traded Z-goods and the production of non-domestically consumed A_E goods. Cash crop exports (A_E) are exchanged for imports (M) at some terms of trade p^0 in quadrant IV. Using a 45° line to project OM^0 imports onto the horizontal axis in quadrant II, Z^0M^0 represents the consumption possibilities curve corresponding to the original production possibilities curve given terms of trade p^0. A price-consumption (PC) curve can be constructed in quadrant II representing the locus of all tangencies between the consumer indifference map of Z and M goods for alternative terms of trade. Given terms of trade p^0, equilibrium at time zero is established at (1) for consumption and (1') for production. Production of A_E is the given by $Oa*$ and that of Z-goods by $OZ*$, representing Z displacement of Z^0Z* compared with a no-trade position.

If the terms of trade improve to p' (that is, as agricultural productivity increases), the consumption possibilities curve shifts out to Z^0M' and the consumption [production] equilibrium becomes (2) [(2')], showing further Z-goods displacement by M-goods as the substitution effect overcomes the income effect and shifts consumption towards M. If Z is assumed to be an inferior good, both the price and income effects are negative and there is substantial Z displacement in response to further improvements in the terms of trade. But, as Bautista[20] has pointed out, the decline of Z-good

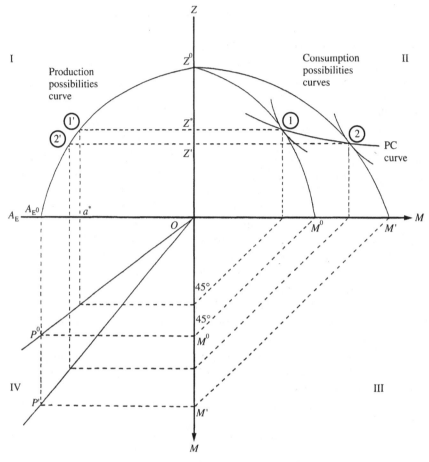

Figure 2.4 Unfavorable colonial case

activities does not depend on the inferiority of Z-goods. However, if Z is not an inferior good, at some point the income effect overcomes the substitution effect and the price-consumption curve turns up as Z-displacement ceases.

2.3.3 Favorable colonial archetype

While the basic Hymer–Resnick model illustrated the unfavorable colonial situation, it is quite possible that developing nations will foster circumstances more favorable for rural development, especially when the colonial government focuses attention on food producing agriculture and land reform. It is illustrative to compare this situation with the basic Hymer–Resnick model outlined above.

Under favorable development circumstances, the agricultural sector is composed of a large number of individual landholders with a similar income distribution instead of a plantation system concentrating wealth in the hands of the few. The more equally distributed agricultural income yields stronger linkages with the non-agricultural sector as a much higher percentage of the population can afford to purchase non-agricultural goods. In this favorable case, the colonial government is less restrictive with respect to local entrepreneurs, permitting indigenous industrial development to progress naturally as a consequence of the various linkages.

Under these assumptions, figure 2.5 illustrates the favorable colonial

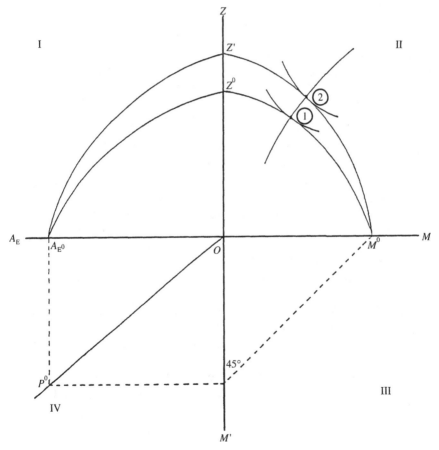

Figure 2.5 Favorable colonial case

archetype. As agricultural productivity increases, more labor and land are released, permitting an outward shift of the production possibilities curve from $A_{E^0}Z^0$ to $A_{E^0}Z'$ and leading to an outward shift in the consumption possibilities curve Z^0M^0 to $Z'M^0$ in the second quadrant. Z-goods production now increasingly takes the form of modern goods that are more dynamic and innovative in character than the traditional goods produced. As a consequence of both these qualitative and quantitative shifts, the displacement of Z-goods by M-goods predicted by Hymer–Resnick is considerably weakened and may not even occur if modernizing rural industries can compete with imported goods. Both the substitution and income effects are likely to be positive, leading to a new equilibrium position at (2) in quadrant II. Consequently, Z-goods production increases, especially relative to the pessimistic Hymer–Resnick case illustrated in the previous section.

It is an historical fact in many overseas territories that the variety and quantity of Z-goods produced prior to the mid-nineteenth century declined as foreign manufactures displaced them in many parts of the developing world.[21] Yet evidence from East Asia suggests that there exists a strong positive relationship between the achievement of dynamic balanced rural growth and success in the overall development effort for a system as a whole. All three East Asian countries examined by Resnick experienced a rapid expansion of growth and trade while reallocating resources away from Z-goods. Such penetration of imported goods and destruction of Z-goods production is likely to be more important in relatively small countries. In the larger overseas territories such as India and China, and even in countries like the Philippines which has many islands and thus limited internal transportation, Z-goods enjoy a measure of natural protection. While imported goods can penetrate the enclaves in exchange for the raw materials which customarily originate in more remote regions, the hinterland is less likely to be similarly affected.

It is no accident that once dualistic growth begins in earnest in newly independent overseas territories, now termed the developing countries, there is a much larger heritage of rural industry to build on in some cases than in others. While this is partly due to differences in size and topography, it also depends on the colonial policy pursued, including the level of transportation and other infrastructural investments left behind. Such spatial considerations are particularly relevant in the case of the open agrarian economy which does not have a land constraint. In the final section of this chapter we turn our attention to an analysis of the land surplus model in the open agrarian context.

2.4 Open Agrarianism with Abundant Supplies of Land

There are some overseas territories in which the fixity of land assumption does not apply or applies with less force than in the majority of cases. Africa is usually cited as a possible exception, with the endowment more reminiscent of what the physiocrats were describing than what the classical school and its successors focused on. Gerald Helleiner, Bent Hansen, and Ester Boserup have concerned themselves with this type of economy.[22] In what follows we explore the Helleiner "land-surplus" model.

In this type of economy the contention is that the relative factor endowments of land and labor are such that land is in surplus due to a relatively low labor endowment. At the heart of this issue is the possibility that labor may voluntarily refrain from work so that a difference appears between man-hours available and man-hours offered. In this sense the issue of leisure becomes relevant for the first time. Figure 2.6(a) represents a conventional two-factor production function with land on the vertical axis and labor in terms of available man-hours on the horizontal axis. The usual assumptions regarding constant returns to scale, homogeneity of factor inputs, and fixed technology are employed. The production contours are marked off by two ridge lines OB and OC showing the limits beyond which further additions of only one factor contributed nothing to total output. One, OB, delineates the region of an unlimited supply of land – where land approaches a zero marginal product – and the other, OC, indicates an unlimited supply of labor, where labor approaches a zero marginal product. The completely vertical and/or horizontal lines represent extreme cases and are only shown for illustrative purposes. For example, given N as the fixed quantity of land in the economy, the segment MP_5 represents the extreme classical labor surplus economy along which further increases in labor supply have no effect on output.

However, while this classical paradigm has received the lion's share of attention in the literature, there exists the possibility that the converse exists: surplus land, represented when labor quantity falls in the region OQ such that the segment NP is to the left of the OB curve. In this region part of the land supply available for cultivation contributes zero to total output. The development problem in economies of this type cannot be dealt with by exploiting underemployed labor, but must be accomplished by increasing labor productivity.

This situation is also represented in figure 2.6(b), which is "lined up" vertically with figure 2.6(a) with labor measured on the horizontal axis and output on the vertical axis showing the production function with OFQ as the total physical product curve. There are constant returns to scale between O and E, diminishing returns to scale between E and F, and a horizontal (or zero marginal product of labor) portion to the right of *F*. In other words, as we move to *OE* in figure 2.6(b) (or to point *P* along *OB* in figure 2.6(a)) there are constant returns to scale since land is redundant. Between *E* and *F* there are variable proportions, and to the right of *F* is the extreme labor surplus condition.

In the land surplus economy there exists a considerable agricultural surplus consisting not only of unutilized land but also of unutilized labor which could be mobilized to expand material output. However, this unutilized labor in a land surplus economy has a positive marginal product in agriculture, being underemployed as a matter of choice for leisure over additional output at the given price and technology level. This unemployment is a result not of their inability to raise material output with further increases in labor inputs, but of deficient demand for the physical output.

The system can initially be assumed to make use of the most land-intensive available technique known – slash and burn agriculture – along *OB*. The labor actually available is equal to *OR* units in figure 2.6(a), with the endowment in land shown as *ON*. At this point, with the supply of labor available at less than *OQ*, *ST* amount of land is redundant – an unlimited supply of land condition. The agrarian story is that as population rises and falls due to positive and negative Malthusian effects, the economy moves up and down *OB* between *S* and *P* indicating different amounts of land surplus in any given period.

A second type of surplus is a matter of preference, not technology. It relates to a situation where food is plentiful and the population is satiated quickly. This is more true in the African type of LDC, or at least in the African case in the 1950s and 1960s observed by Helleiner, Boserup and Hansen. Such a situation exhibits itself by actual labor hours offered and production falling below the production possibility curve – the actual production function in figure 2.6(b) is described by *OG* rather than *OFQ*. This means that the food demanded by the average worker is only *JA/OA* rather than *EA/OA*. *EJ* therefore represents a mobilizable surplus in output terms, while *KJ* represents a labor surplus in labor terms. This "labor surplus" has a positive marginal product and is caused by a demand-side preference for leisure rather than a supply-side technology constraint. The economy produces below its potential via the withholding of labor services on the given land which happens also to be in surplus.

We can now relate this situation to the typical open mercantile agrarian system. In the absence of *Z*-goods, satiation with food causes the voluntary withdrawal from work. To avoid this phenomenon, productivity per person must increase via the provision of additional non-agricultural incentive goods. In figure 2.6(b) this is indicated by a "swivel" that can be explained by a substitution of work for leisure as long as the total labor supply remains at a level less than *OA*. In other words, an output increase

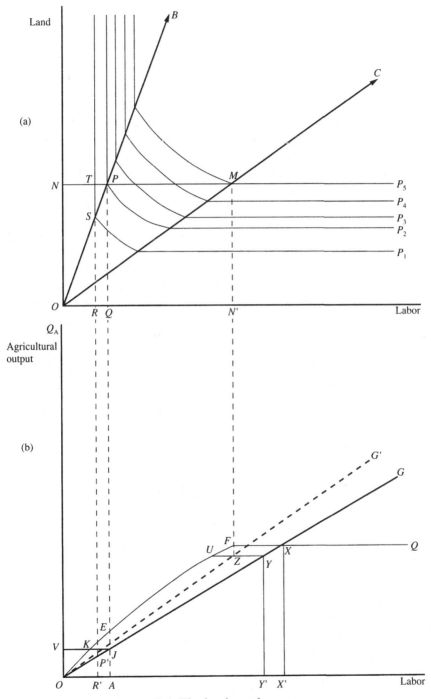

Figure 2.6 The land surplus economy

under a fixed labor force requires a reduction of the opportunity cost of leisure relative to work.

This individual trade-off can be illustrated with the help of figure 2.7, in which man-hours are pictured on the horizontal axis, physical output and the total physical product curve on the vertical axis (upward) and the value of output on the vertical axis (downward). For simplicity all farmers have an equal land share so that the total product curve for the individual is shaped the same as for the economy. Assume that the typical farmer has OC_1 man hours after the minimum required leisure, and that the maximum output in the constant returns range of figure 2.6(a) is Q_A on a per capita basis if all labor is applied. How much labor the typical farmer does apply depends on his indifference map between leisure and the value attached to the output indicated in the lower quadrant in figure 2.7. C_1V_1 is the transformation curve – and a unique one exists for every different level of technology and prices – representing the trade-off between leisure and the value of output. Equilibrium results at T_1 where C_1E_1 man-hours would be offered in agricultural production, with OE_1 units left as leisure (at given prices and technology) and physical output of E_1F_1 units per head. E_1F_1 equals the slope of OG in figure 2.6(b) – as a consequence of satiation with food, the value of output is such that it does not interest the typical peasant to work more than C_1E_1 man-hours. A price rise, a new kind of importable good, or external markets developing are represented by the transformation slope shifting from C_1V_1 to C_1V_2. The new equilibrium – T_2 in this case – depends on the indifference map chosen. Here the substitution effect of increasing labor input wins out over the income effect of increasing leisure. E_2F_2 units of output are produced and the slope of the new total production curve in figure 2.6(b) shifts to OG'. In this way the system obtains greater labor participation as a consequence of the introduction of new Z-type goods, either domestic or foreign in origin. As OG swivels left, the voluntary labor surplus KJ is reduced and land used in production moves along the ridge line from S towards P in figure 2.6(a), leaving less excess **land**. This assumes increases in labor inputs are matched by increases in land inputs without changing constant production techniques away from the land-intensive ones. Once all available labor is productively applied – OA units of labor producing AE units of output – both the labor and land surplus have been eliminated.[23]

If the economy experiences population growth driving the labor force to the right from point A, it eventually enters the diminishing returns region of the production function. This exhibits itself by departure from pure slash and burn cultivation with a gradual reduction in fallow time, since further increases in cultivation can only be obtained by decreasing fallow periods. This change in technology is the next step in the land-surplus model subject to population pressure. If this process continues

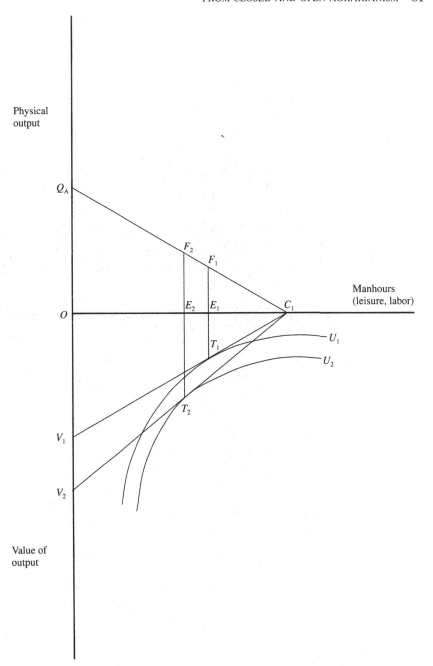

Figure 2.7 Voluntary labor surplus under land surplus conditions

under a constant supply of land, now no longer in surplus, the economy is ultimately driven to the right of M in figure 2.6(a) as the power of diminishing returns pushes the system toward labor-intensive farming techniques as the economy enters the labor surplus region.[24] Once ON in figure 2.6(a) is reached, additions to the supply of labor have no effects on output and the labor-surplus stage is achieved. The labor surplus economy is the final stage of a process of population growth and increasing labor participation with a fixed supply of land and initial land surplus.

It is not unreasonable to assume that overseas territories found themselves in this situation in the early stage of their development. It is equally likely that some newly independent developing countries, particularly in Africa, continued in this open agrarian land surplus condition after independence. This certainly seems to be the world Ester Boserup describes when she rejects labor surplus and Malthusian pressures. Boserup views population growth as a favorable event, which

> can set off a genuine process of economic growth, with rising output per man hour ... The intensification of agriculture may compel cultivators and agricultural laborers to work harder and more regularly ... The increasing population density facilitates a division of labor and a spread of communications and education ... Contemporary observers would not fail to notice this increased activity and might well describe the period of rapidly rising population as a period of agricultural revolution ... The agricultural revolution in 18th century Western Europe seems to have been of this type ... Future historians will perhaps describe the decades after 1950 as those of the Indian agrarian revolution.[25]

We seriously doubt that this particular model applies to post-1950 India and, in fact, there is considerable question whether it even applies to contemporary sub-Saharan Africa. Nevertheless, it may be relevant to some parts of the developing world which have a low population density and free land available where increasing population pressure on the land might permit economies of scale to come into operation. In our own view, buttressed by empirical observation, if this situation existed in substantial parts of the Third World in the past, it is rapidly receding from view. The fallow period in East and West Africa, for example, has fallen from seven to four years over the past few decades, illustrating the move towards the labor surplus condition implied by the land surplus model under population pressure. The image of free land available for slash and burn agriculture has given way to desertification and land shortage, while good soil calling for fertilizer inputs is reminiscent of the more "normal" conditions of Asia and Latin America. Some regions of every developing country, of course, still have land surpluses – the Amazon in Brazil, parts of Kenya, etc. – and land supply is always somewhat elastic since the fixity of land is only a convenient approximation. But it is more likely that land surpluses have given way to the range of variable proportions of land and labor and that many developing countries are approaching the labor surplus condition of the variety accepted in much of the literature.

Ultimately, this is an empirical rather than a theoretical matter. The point to stress here is that if there is a trade-off between work and leisure, it is likely to occur when there exists a relative abundance of land and people are satiated. In this sense the destruction of Z-goods in overseas territories during the colonial era can be left at the doorstep of imported colonial goods or by the growth of domestic consumer goods industries producing a similar type of product. It may well be that the typologically distinct set of land surplus has become a historical curiosum, especially given the rapid rates of population growth and the reduction in cultivation in some African countries.

In some ways the agrarian or colonial economy is basically under alien policy control, with the drive for commercial profits the motivating force where growth is compartmentalized, focuses heavily on the enclave, is directed by the outside, and where relatively little attention is paid to the domestic interaction between agriculture and non-agriculture in the commercial agrarian world. Its essential economic function is the acquisition of labor and management of raw materials to serve the needs of production, exports to foreign markets, and the reinvestment and repatriation of profits. The prognosis in the long term depends, as before, on the struggle between agricultural productivity increases and diminishing returns combined with population growth, especially once the shortage of land has reestablished it as a major concern. Successful graduation means transition into a condition of modern dualism.

APPENDIX

Our model for the open agrarian economy in the absence of Z-goods may be summarized by the following six equations presented in the text:

$$\theta = \theta(w) \qquad \text{equation 2.6} \qquad \text{(A2.1a)}$$

$$m = 1/\theta'(w) \qquad \text{equation 2.7b} \qquad \text{(A2.1b)}$$

$$Q_E^{\Delta} = f(K^{\Delta},1) - g \qquad \text{equation 2.10a} \qquad \text{(A2.1c)}$$

$$K^{\Delta} = K^*/\theta \qquad \text{equation 2.14a} \qquad \text{(A2.1d)}$$

$$\eta_K = \frac{tf(K^*,\theta(w)) - w}{K^*} - g \qquad \text{equations 2.15} \qquad \text{(A2.1e)}$$

$$m = tf_B(K^{\Delta},1) \qquad \text{equation 2.16a} \qquad \text{(A2.1f)}$$

which solve for six unknowns: θ, w, m, Q_E^{Δ}, K^{Δ}, and η_K, when K^* is given. Thus for any fixed value of K^*, the optimum values can be written as

$$\bar{\theta} = \bar{\theta}(K^*); \bar{m} = \bar{m}(K^*); \bar{w} = \bar{w}(K^*); \bar{Q}_E^\Delta = \bar{Q}_E^\Delta(K^*);$$

$$\bar{K}^\Delta = \bar{K}^\Delta(K^*); \bar{\eta}_K = \bar{\eta}_K(K^*) \qquad (A2.2)$$

This merely shows that the optimum values (indicated by the upper bar) are all functions of K^*. The comparative static conclusions relevant to open agrarianism and referred to in the paper are obtained by investigating the signs of the derivatives of the functions in equation A2.2. For the dynamic aspect of our model we have:

$$\eta K^* = \bar{\eta} - r = \phi(K^*) \quad \text{(by equation 2.13)} \qquad (A2.3)$$

The notation $\phi(K^*)$ states that the rate of growth of K^* is a function of K^*. Thus equation A2.3 is a differential equation in K^*, the solution of which is the time path of K^*. When this is substituted in equation A2.2, the time paths of all variables are determined. This theorem of long-run stagnation is dynamic and refers to the properties of these times paths. In equations A2.1, A2.2, and A2.3, the problem is stated in such a way that only "ratios" are involved and that the absolute magnitudes of $K, L, Q_E, I, M, \dots$ are all dispensed with via the constant-returns-to-scale property of our model.[26]

CHAPTER 2   FROM CLOSED AND OPEN AGRARIANISM TO MODERN DUALISM

NOTES

1   Where $\eta_x = \mathrm{d}x/\mathrm{d}t/x$, i.e. the time rate of growth of x.
2   See Jorgenson (1961, 1966).
3   For convenience we assume all population growth initially takes place in the agricultural sector, thus $\eta_V = 0$.
4   Conversely, starting from an initial value of p greater than p_e, p decreases to p_e in the long run.
5   Starting from the same initial level v_0.
6   See Fei and Ranis (1966).
7   Boserup (1965, p. 96).
8   Jorgenson (1961) makes unnecessarily restrictive assumptions by assuming that only consumption adjustment takes place initially and only allocation adjustment after a time, abruptly creating an industrial sector from one day to the next. This turning point occurs when people are satiated with agricultural goods, which happens at precisely the same moment when population growth becomes non-responsive to further increases in the per capita consumption of agricultural goods. The ultimate evolution of a non-agricultural sector, in other

words, occurs for reasons of the sudden emergence of a demand for non-agricultural goods at the margin. The rate of technological change in agriculture is fixed and constant, which certainly rules out important and realistic alternatives to the pure consumption-population adjustment mechanism found in his analysis of an agrarian economy's graduation prospects.

9 Due to the fact that the consumption demand for domestically produced food is lowered to c'' on the vertical axis of figure 2.3(b).

10 Fisk (1962).

11 Paauw and Fei (1965, pp. 204–5).

12 For example, with special reference to Africa, see Baldwin (1956).

13 A more sophisticated endogenous population theory could easily be substituted.

14 Proof: $\eta_K = \dfrac{M-A-C}{K} = \dfrac{tQ_E-wL-gK}{K}$ (by equations 2.12ab, 2.5, 2.11)

$\qquad = \dfrac{tQ_E^\Delta-w/\theta}{K^\Delta} - g$ (by equations 2.10bc, 2.9b)

$\qquad = \dfrac{t\theta f(K^*/\theta,\, 1)-w}{K^*} - g$ (by equations 2.10a, 2.14a, 2.6)

$\qquad = \dfrac{tf(K^*,\, \theta) - w}{K^*} - g$ (by CRTS property of equation 2.9a)

15 Proof: $\eta_K = \dfrac{f_K K^*+f_B\theta - w}{K^*} - g$ (by equation 2.15, CRTS)

$\qquad = f_K + \dfrac{f_B - w/\theta}{K^*/\theta} - g$

$\qquad = f_K + \dfrac{1/\theta' - w/\theta}{K^\Delta} - g$ (by equation 2.16a)

$\qquad = f_K + \dfrac{x}{K^\Delta} - g$ (by equation 2.8)

16 $g = 0$ in figure 2.3(g). If $g > 0$, point S'' shifts down by the constant amount g and our entire analysis below holds after suitable (easily accomplished) modification. We assume for convenience that $g = 0$.

17 Georgescu-Roegen (1960, p. 33).

18 Ruttan (1991). See also the contributions of Nicholls and Tang on this subject, including Nicholls (1961), and Nicholls and Tang (1958).

19 Hymer and Resnick (1969). See also Ranis and Stewart (1993).

20 Bautista (1971).

21 See Resnick (1970).

22 Helleiner (1966); Hansen (1969); and Boserup (1965).

23 The diagrammatic coincidence of the two points is merely for convenience.

24 Such a situation would be worsened if there were a reduction in the supply of land, e.g., due to desertification.

25 Boserup (1965, pp. 62-4, 118).
26 The model structure defined above is similar, at least from a purely mathematical point of view, to the socialist type "maximum speed" development model presented in Fei and Chiang (1966).

3
Development of the Closed Dualistic Economy: A Bird's Eye View

3.1 Introduction

Within our typological perspective, one important type of transition growth experience during the post-World War II era is development in so-called "labor surplus dualistic" economies. The adjectives "dualistic" and "labor surplus" will be treated analytically in sections 3.2 and 3.3. But the notion of "dualism" suggests a production dualism marked by the coexistence of non-homogeneous agricultural and non-agricultural production sectors, while "labor surplus" suggests that the relative abundance of population or labor force on the land represents a crucial element that gives this growth type its unique characteristic. As we saw earlier, virtually all contemporary LDCs began their transition growth process within an economic heritage of "agrarian dualism" as emphasized by the *tableau economique* of the physiocrats. However, their labor surplus characteristics were very much related to the subsequent population explosion that occurred in the context of a demographic transition process as developing economies sought to enter the epoch of modern growth.

The analysis of the growth process in a labor surplus dualistic economy experiencing population pressure at the margin must be centered on the key issue of the reallocation of its labor force from agriculture to industry (or non-agriculture), representing a critical component of the "structural change" accompanying the transition to modern growth. This labor reallocation process has a labor absorption aspect (section 3.4) as well as a labor release aspect (section 3.5). While the latter stresses the role of the traditional agricultural sector (that is, to produce an adequate food surplus to feed the new urban population "released" by the agricultural sector), the former puts the spotlight on the industrial sector which "absorbs" that labor by providing it with employment opportunities through capital accumulation and/or technology change. The interaction of these two aspects is treated in the last section of this chapter (section 3.6).

3.2 The Operation of a Dualistic Economy

3.2.1 Production sectors and the primary factors of production

For a dualistic economy, the required holistic operational perspective is provided by the national income accounting framework of figure 3.1(a) which may be viewed as a straightforward extension of the *tableau economique* of the physiocrats. In this framework there is a double dichotomy, as the agricultural sector (on the right-hand side) and the industrial sector (on the left-hand side) are further subdivided into a production sector (on top) and a household sector (at the bottom). The operations of the closed dualistic economy are regulated by three intersectoral markets: the intersectoral commodity market, the intersectoral financial market and the intersectoral labor market, as shown by the three circles in the center of the diagram.

One basic structural asymmetry of the dualistic economy that we assume, mainly for convenience, is that while labor is used as a primary input in both sectors, capital (K) is used only in the industrial sector and land (T) only in the agricultural sector. This choice of input asymmetry is made only for the sake of convenience and guided by problem sensitivity. During the transition growth process, the issue of population pressure is definable in terms of the ratio of agricultural population to land, while with the arrival of the modern epoch the growth phenomenon is centered on the generation of new technology carried by fixed capital K "absorbing" agricultural labor into the industrial sector.

3.2.2 Production and allocation in the dualistic economy

In figure 3.1 the direction of all flows is indicated by arrows. Labor and land flow into the agricultural production sector to produce total agricultural output A. A part of A (denoted by A_a) is consumed by the farmers while the remainder, that is, the total agricultural surplus (TAS), flows through the intersectoral commodity market to the industrial sector to feed the industrial labor force (W). The notion of TAS, which can also be traced back to the *tableau economique* of the physiocrats, plays a crucial role in the analysis of the "labor release aspect" of growth in the dualistic economy.

In the non-agricultural or industrial sector, the services of labor (W) and capital (K) flow to the production sector as inputs. Total industrial output (Q) has three components: the first component Q_i is industrial goods consumed by the industrial labor force, while the second component

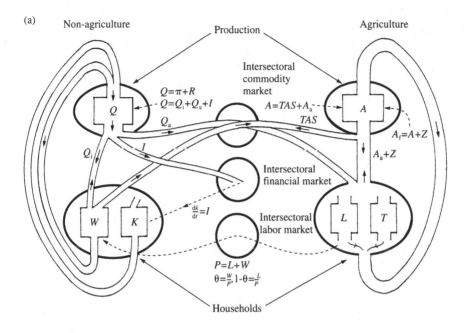

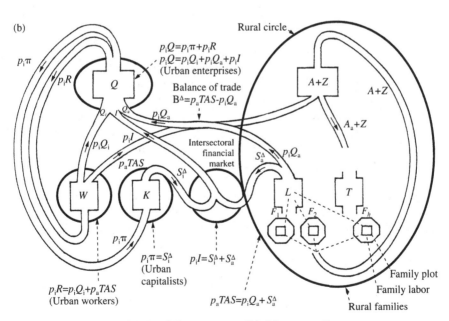

Figure 3.1 (a) Real flow system; (b) Monetary flow system

Q_a flows through the intersectoral commodity market to the agricultural households. This second component contains both consumer goods (such as, textiles) and modern inputs (such as, inorganic fertilizer). The latter are essential for the increase of agricultural productivity, the first from an "incentive" perspective, the second from an "input" perspective.[1] The third component is investment goods I leading to changes in the non-agricultural capital stock K.[2] The allocation of the outputs of the two sectors can be summarized in the following equations:

$$Q = Q_i + Q_a + I \tag{3.1a}$$
$$A = A_a + TAS \tag{3.1b}$$
$$A_f = A + Z \qquad \text{(a modification of equation 3.1b to be explained below)} \tag{3.1c}$$

At this point, we should note the existence of an "organizational asymmetry" between the industrial sector (with its spatially concentrated labor force $W(t)$ located mainly in the urban centers) and the agricultural sector (with its spatially dispersed rural labor force $L(i)$). The agricultural sector is characterized by a "traditional" rather than a "commercialized" outlook. This traditionalism of the agricultural sector has many dimensions, with an operational significance that will be identified in this section.

The production manifestation of traditionalism is that farmers produce with an orientation towards self-sufficiency. Aside from the growth of a commercialized cash crop which farmers may either consume within the family (A_a) or sell in the market (TAS), the traditional farmers also grow a non-cash "crop" Z (subsidiary food and such items as chickens and pigs) in their spare time, strictly for the survival of the members of their own families. These Z-goods may actually also include non-agricultural goods (baskets, artisan and other hand-loomed cloth products) that share, with the non-cash crop, the common property that they have survival value and the production of which does not require modern inputs or modern knowledge. Thus the "full income" of the farmers (A_f), in terms of agricultural plus rural non-agricultural goods, is the sum $A + Z$ (as indicated in equation 3.1c).

The urban labor force, clearly denied the opportunity of growing its own food, must (in the closed economy) rely on TAS as the exclusive source of caloric intake acquired through exchange in the market. Because of the existence of the non-cash crop Z, the farmer can also manage to increase his consumption.

3.2.3 Income distribution in the dualistic economy

In a production process characterized by the joint input of primary factors of production, there is always the problem of the functional distribution of income which helps us partition total output into distributive shares. In the industrial sector, the distribution of Q into the wage share R and the capital income share π may be denoted as follows:

$$Q = R + \pi \tag{3.2a}$$
$$R = \phi_L Q \tag{3.2b}$$
$$\pi = \phi_K Q \tag{3.2c}$$
$$\phi_l + \phi_K = 1 \tag{3.2d}$$

In these equations ϕ_L and ϕ_K are positive fractions that add up to one so that the total output Q is partitioned into the two shares R and π. In historical perspective, a long-run observable fact for the industrially advanced countries is the long-run stability of the distributive shares ϕ_L and ϕ_K.[3] In the perspective of transition growth, we shall assume that the principle of income distribution in the industrial sector is already the commercialized version (much as in an industrially advanced country), so that the real wage rate, as well as the relative shares, are determined competitively in the urban labor market (see below).

In the agricultural sector, the principle of income distribution is, however, different. In a traditional sector which is not yet fully commercialized, the "real wage" w_a is A_a per unit of the agricultural labor force L, that is, $w_a = A_a/L$ as defined in equation 3.3a below. This wage is called the institutional real wage (IRW) to suggest the notion that it is determined by the non-commercialized kinship (or bargaining) relations in the traditional rural society of an LDC at a level likely to be related to the caloric minimum food requirements.[4] The rural families will not let some workers starve by ensuring that every family member is fed at the IRW before the surplus food TAS is delivered to the cities (see equation 3.3d below).

Since the farmers can also produce a non-cash crop Z, the full rural wage w_f is thus the sum of IRW and $Z/L = z$, the output of Z-goods per farmer.

$$w_a = A_a/L \; (= IRW) \tag{3.3a}$$
$$w_f = A_f/L = w_a + z \text{ where} \tag{3.3b}$$
$$z = Z/L \tag{3.3c}$$
$$A = L \cdot IRW + TAS \text{ (by 3.1b and 3.3a)} \tag{3.3d}$$

This initial asymmetry of the principle of income distribution represents an important manifestation of the rural traditionalism relative to which the thesis of a "turning point" en route to economic maturity will be developed.

3.2.4 Population, structural change, and capital accumulation

When a country with an agrarian background enters into the epoch of modern economic growth, the three major aspects of growth, as emphasized by Simon Kuznets, are population acceleration accompanied by per capita income growth, structural change, and rapid capital accumulation carrying modern science and technology. Let $P(t)$ be the time path of total population, with $W(t)$ and $L(t)$, the industrial and agricultural populations, respectively. We then have:

$$P = W + L \tag{3.4a}$$
$$\theta = W/P \tag{3.4b}$$
$$1 - \theta = L/P \tag{3.4c}$$
$$W/L = \theta/(1 - \theta) \tag{3.4d}$$

In equations 3.4b and 3.4c, θ is the fraction of the population allocated to the non-agricultural or industrial sector, and $(1 - \theta)$ is the fraction remaining in the agricultural sector. Continued labor reallocation from agriculture to industry, under conditions of population pressure, is proxied by a sustained increase in θ through time. The analysis of the labor reallocation process may thus be viewed as the central phenomenon of development in a dualistic economy. The ratio W/L really represents the number of industrial workers "supported by" a typical farmer. When θ increases, the number of workers supported by a typical farmer will increase.

Next, we have:

$$dK/dt = I \tag{3.5}$$

which states that investment leads to an increase in the capital stock at each time point in the industrial sector. The dynamics of the development of the industrial sector is therefore traced primarily to population expansion and capital accumulation which carries technology change. In contrast, in the more traditional agricultural sector productivity gains are traced to the infusion of modern inputs, as well as to such non-quantifiable causes as the incentive effects of greater market participation and the enhanced commercialism of farmers, as we shall observe below.

3.2.5 Consumption standard and survival

In the analysis of this chapter, the focus is on the transition growth process within an economy whose agricultural sector is still sizeable and poor. With the help of Z-goods, the traditional farmer can usually manage to eke out a living. However, the problem of the consumption standard is a particularly sensitive issue for the urban working class. For this reason, we define the consumption standard of a typical industrial worker by:

$$c_a = TAS/W \, (= AAS) \tag{3.6a}$$
$$c_i = Q_i/W \tag{3.6b}$$
$$w_i = R/W \tag{3.6c}$$
$$c_a = w_a \, (\text{or } AAS = IRW) \tag{3.6d}$$

In equation 3.6a the per capita consumption of food c_a is determined at the level corresponding to "TAS per unit of industrial labor" and is referred to as the AAS, that is, the average agricultural surplus. In equation 3.6b, c_i is the per capita consumption of industrial goods by industrial workers. In equation 3.6c, w_i is the real wage of a typical urban worker in terms of industrial goods obtained by dividing the wage share R (of 3.2b) by the number of industrial workers. In the transition growth process an important historical mission of agricultural workers is to produce a large enough TAS to feed the urban working force at the minimum consumption standard specified as IRW (equation 3.3a). This idea can be traced back to the physiocrats who believed that a prosperous agricultural sector is the precondition for the prosperity of the non-agricultural sector.

Notice that we have defined two per capita consumption standards for food: $w_a = A_a/L \, (=IRW)$ for the agricultural labor force and $c_a = TAS/W$ (equation 3.6a) for the industrial labor force. It is intuitively obvious that these two consumption standards for food (a basic commodity required for survival) can be expected to be nearly the same in any poor LDC that is struggling for survival at or near the caloric minimum level. Thus we assume that the two food consumption standards are equalized (that is, $AAS = IRW$) as stated in equation 3.6d.

Such an equalization of the per capita food consumption standards has many shades of meaning in the dualistic economy as can be stated in Lemma 1:

Lemma 1 The following set of conditions are equivalent:
(a) $c_a = w_a$ (equation 3.6d)
(b) $A = P \cdot IRW$
(c) $\theta = TAS/A$; $1 - \theta = A_a/A$
(d) $1 - \theta = IRW/p$ (where $p = A/L$)

Condition (b) states that total food output A is just adequate to feed the entire population of the IRW level. Condition (c) states that there exists equality between the population allocation fraction θ and the food allocation fraction TAS/A. Condition (d) states that the proportion of the population still in agriculture $(1 - \theta)$ is the same as the institutional real wage to agricultural labor productivity parity. The proof is obvious.

In summary, we have introduced a system of economic magnitudes into the holistic operational framework of figure 3.1(a). The system is a real system that, according to the language of economics, involves neither money nor prices. The next step is to broaden our framework to introduce these concepts.

3.2.6 Organizational dualism and monetization

A contemporary LDC with an agrarian heritage is a dualistic economy not only in the production (or commodity) sense (that is, agricultural versus industrial products) but also in the organizational sense, manifested by the coexistence of a commercialized urban sector and a traditional rural sector, with different degrees of monetization (that is, money-usingness).

In the literature on LDCs, the notion of market participation (for example, the traditional farmer may be more or less willing to participate in the intersectoral commodity market via the production of a commercialized cash crop and thus move away from self-sufficiency) is a concept applicable only in the rural sector. The population in the commercialized urban centers has no choice but to participate in the market to earn a monetary income and to fulfill its payments obligations in monetary terms. Thus, another basic manifestation of agricultural traditionalism is with respect to the relatively lower degree of monetization.

To pursue this organizational duality in an operational perspective, the framework for the analysis of the real (that is, non-monetary) flows in figure 3.1(a) is reproduced in figure 3.1(b) to show the direction of all monetary payments (indicated by single arrows). There are five "circles" in this diagram. For the industrial sector, the circles around the production sector, workers' households and capitalists' households, suggest that for these a meticulous accounting of indebtedness covering the highly impersonal transactions of an urban industrial society must be adhered to at all times, using money as a unit of account. Monetary payments into and out of each sector must be exactly the same.

For the agricultural sector there is a coincidence between farm and household management under the so-called "family farming system." Money is less needed as a medium of exchange (because of a high degree of production for self-sufficiency) or as a unit of account (due to the fact that the need for a meticulous accounting of indebtedness is obviated by kinship or community-oriented relations) or as a standard of value (due to the existence of non-commercialized crops or Z-goods) within the rural sector. The household and production sectors in figure 3.1(b) are jointly circled to show that what is important about money relates strictly to the aggregative payments into or out of one merged agricultural household and production sector.

Let p_a and p_i denote the prices of the agricultural and non-agricultural products, respectively. The price ratio

$$d = p_a/p_i \qquad (3.7)$$

is the (intersectoral) terms of trade which is the most significant commodity price ratio in the dualistic economy. Monetary flows (that is, the flow of monetary payments) between the four sectors, as indicated in figure 3.1(b), may be summarized by the following equations to show the equality of inflows and outflows for each sector:

	Sum of inflows	=	Sum of outflows	
Industrial production:	$p_iQ_i + p_iQ_a + p_iI =$		$p_i\pi + p_iR$	(3.8a)
	(by equations 3.1a and 3.2a)			
Industrial workers:	p_iR	=	$p_iQ_i + p_aTAS$	(3.8b)
Industrial capitalists:	$p_i\pi$	=	S_i^Δ	(3.8c)
Rural households:	p_aTAS	=	$p_iQ_a + S_a^\Delta$	(3.8d)

In all these equations, what the sector earns is shown on the left-hand side and what it spends is shown on the right-hand side, the equality sign indicating the fulfillment of monetary obligations. The equality of equation 3.8a within the urban production sector follows directly from the real allocation equation (equation 3.1a) and the functional distribution of income equation (equation 3.2a) – that is, from the fact that the total output is exhaustively distributed as the wage share R and the property or rent share π.

The equality of equation 3.8b shows that what industrial workers earn (p_iR) is spent entirely on the consumption of food (p_aTAS) and industrial consumer goods (p_iQ_i). Equation 3.8c shows that the monetary income of the urban entrepreneurial class ($p_i\pi$) is disposed of as S_i^Δ, that is, as urban monetary savings (or monetary savings in the industrial sector) that flow into the intersectoral finance market (see figure 3.1(b)). These two equations (3.8b and 3.8c) portray what is known in the literature as the "classical saving rule," that is, while the workers spend all their income on consumption, capitalists save all their income as part of their insatiable drive for capital accumulation. (Equation 3.8b can be converted into the budget equation for industrial workers that will play an important role in our analysis.) Equation 3.8d shows that the rural sector spent all its monetary income (p_aTAS) acquired by selling the surplus food TAS in the intersectoral commodity market on the purchase of manufactured goods Q_a or S_a^Δ, the monetary savings of the rural (or agricultural) sector. This equation is later converted into a monetized budget equation that involves the term of trade for the rural families. Peasants are likely to be very sensitive to these terms of trade d which represent the only monetary linkage between the spatially dispersed rural community and the urban sector.

3.2.7 Intersectoral trade and finance

In the dualistic economy, the monetary investment p_iI is financed by monetary savings from the rural sector S_a^Δ or the urban sector S_i^Δ. The monetary balancing equations in 3.8 lead immediately to:

$$p_iI = S_i^\Delta + S_a^\Delta \qquad (3.9)$$

Proof: add equations 3.8a, 3.8b, 3.8c, and 3.8d.   Q.E.D.

showing the equality of savings and investment in the dualistic economy in monetary terms. (This is emphasized in figure 3.1(b) by the linkage of the three "pipes" in the intersectoral financial market.) This equality is brought about when all sectors fulfill their payment obligations, including the monetary payment obligations of farmers toward the "outside world." This financial equation can also be converted into real (non-monetary) terms:

$$I = S_i + S_a \text{ where} \qquad (3.10a)$$
$$S_i \equiv S_i^\Delta/p_i \qquad (3.10b)$$
$$S_a \equiv S_a^\Delta/p_i \qquad (3.10c)$$

Proof: divide equation 3.9 by p_i.   Q.E.D.

where S_i and S_a are now defined in terms of physical units of industrial goods. Since all the investment I is intended to form capital in the industrial sector K, by the hypothesis of asymmetry, S_i is the intrasectoral finance while S_a is the intersectoral finance, that is, the use of the saving of the agricultural sector to finance capital accumulation in the industrial sector. Intersectoral finance may be viewed as the financial contribution of the agricultural sector to fuel the expansion of the non-agricultural sector via the intersectoral financial market.

From the intersectoral commodity market we can define a balance of trade:

$$B^\Delta = p_aTAS - p_iQ_a \qquad (3.11a)$$
$$B = B^\Delta/p_i = dTAS - Q_a \qquad (3.11b)$$

As an analogy to international trade, B^Δ represents the monetary "export surplus" of the agricultural sector on current account. Thus B^Δ can be interpreted as the "net commodity contribution" of the agricultural sector to the industrial sector – it is the difference in the values of the commodity shipments from (p_aTAS) and the shipments into (p_iQ_a) the agricultural sector. In equation 3.11b, B is the agricultural sector's export surplus measured in terms of industrial goods.

The agricultural sector thus appears to make two distinct contributions to the industrial sector, that is, a financial contribution as well as a commodity contribution. This is, however, an illusion. For we have:

$$B^\Delta = S_a^\Delta \qquad (3.12a)$$
$$S_a = B = dTAS - Q_a \qquad (3.12b)$$

Proof   Equation 3.12a follows from equation 3.8d; equation 3.12b follows from equation 3.11b.   Q.E.D.

Equation 3.12a states that agricultural monetary savings S_a^Δ have exactly the same magnitude as the "export surplus." Hence the real agricultural savings S_a (the financial contribution) is precisely the same as the net commodity contribution (equation 3.2b). The two contributions are really the two sides of the same coin, as in international trade, by the truism that an export surplus in the current account is always accommodated by a surplus on capital account.

The essence of intersectoral and intrasectoral finance, however, has a deeper significance. For we have:

$$I = \pi + B \qquad (3.13a)$$
$$S_i = \pi \qquad (3.13b)$$
$$S_a = B \qquad (3.13c)$$

Thus, intrasectoral finance S_i really represents the reinvestment of the profits of the urban entrepreneurial class (equation 3.13b), while the intersectoral finance represents the net commodity exports B of agriculture.

In the course of the transition growth process, intersectoral finance S_a is extremely important not only for the industrial sector but also for the agricultural sector. Since the agricultural sector is initially large and the industrial sector relatively small, the former initially has to provide the lion's share of the total saving fund. While this role of the agricultural sector can be readily appreciated, it should be emphasized that the existence of an intersectoral financial market also provides an opportunity for savers in the agricultural sector to acquire title to industrial assets. In a traditional society the main productive assets farmers can own is land providing the owners with a sense of security. But in the transition process, rural savers begin to have the opportunity to own a part of the growing capital assets, especially in the industrial sector. When this occurs, the income sources of the rural population are diversified as farmers begin to have non-agricultural incomes and assets.

With the acquisition of productive non-agricultural assets, farmers can now acquire an accumulation orientation and become just as acquisitive as industrial entrepreneurs. The ownership of industrial capital contributes to what may be referred to as the commercialization of the peasants, an important factor contributing to agricultural modernization. Finally, to stress the notion of population pressure on the land in the labor surplus economy, we shall assume that the quantity of land is approximately fixed:

$$T = \bar{T} \tag{3.14}$$

3.2.8 The dynamic growth process[5]

A rough count shows that some 30–40 variables have been introduced so far in this chapter describing the operations of the economic system. As shown in figure 3.1(a) and (b), they convey an impression that the growth process is the result of the operation of the entire economic system in which many related tasks, that is, production, allocation, income distribution, consumption, savings, investment, as well as technology change in both sectors of the dualistic economy, are simultaneously performed. Since all the variables are dated time series, it is our purpose to show the causal order of their determination in a dynamic context.

While this task is complex enough, we also must not lose sight of the institutional aspects in view of the existence of organizational dualism signifying the coexistence of a commercialized industrial sector with a traditional agricultural sector which provides the basis for the system's expansion. That family farms are non-monetized, self-sufficient and survival-oriented, that real wages are initially institutionally supported by sharing and kinship relations, and that peasants become commercialized through market participation are all components of "institutional economics" well known to anthropologists which cannot simply be brushed aside in this age of neoclassical equilibrium theory. Kenneth Arrow, one of the high priests of neoclassical economics, recognizes this reality.[6] Indeed, the growth process is "transitional" primarily because of the organizational dualism that the economy has inherited from its agrarian past. Let us now proceed to a discussion of an economy which is dualistic and of the labor surplus type.

3.3 Underlying Behavior Patterns in the Dualistic Economy

3.3.1 Connotations of the labor surplus condition

The notion of surplus labor may be traced to three historical background factors. First, as an LDC inherits agrarian dualism from its past, a lion's share (for example, upward of $1 - \theta = 80$ percent) of the population is rural and engaged in agricultural production. Second, as an LDC initiates its transition towards modern economic growth, it normally encounters a demographic transition or population explosion (increasing η_P). Third, with sustained population pressure on the fixed land, the supply of labor is likely to be extremely abundant, some of it even completely redundant, from the production standpoint. The related notion of disguised unemployment is taken up below. Let the time path of total population $P(t)$ and agricultural population $L(t)$ be as shown in figure 3.2(a). The vertical gap

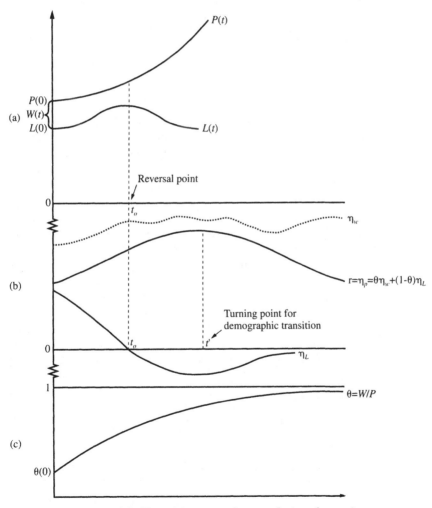

Figure 3.2 Transition growth: population dynamics

between them is $W(t)$, the time path of the industrial labor force (see equation 3.4a). The time path of $\theta = W/P$ is shown in figure 3.2(c) where the initial value $\theta(0)$ (for example, $\theta = 20$ percent) is indicated. Let the population growth rate be denoted by $\eta_P = r$. The demographic transition phenomenon is described by the postulation of the inverse U-shaped time path of r in figure 3.2(b) satisfying:

$$\eta_r = \eta_{\eta_p} > 0 \text{ for } t < t' \tag{3.15a}$$
$$\eta_r = \eta_{\eta_p} < 0 \text{ for } t' < t \tag{3.15b}$$

Thus before (after) t' there is population acceleration (deceleration) as the population growth rate $r = \eta_P$ increases (decreases) through time.

The time path of $\theta(t)$ shows a sustained increasing trend from $\theta(0)$ toward 1. Transforming equation 3.4b we have:

$$\eta_\theta = \eta_W - \eta_P \tag{3.16a}$$
$$\eta_\theta > 0 \text{ if and only if} \tag{3.16b}$$
$$\eta_W > \eta_P \tag{3.16c}$$

Thus the necessary and sufficient condition for θ to increase through time is that the growth rate of the industrial labor force $W(t)$ is higher than the growth rate of the total population. This condition is the condition for "successful" transition growth over time. In the successful case the curve of η_W must consistently lie above the curve $r = \eta_P$ (see the dotted curve in figure 3.2(b)).

The fact that "increasing θ" is referred to as a sign of success can be justified on both empirical and theoretical grounds. Empirically, with the arrival of the epoch of modern economic growth the historical evidence is that the demographic transition in the industrially advanced countries has produced such a pattern (see Kuznets, 1966). Theoretically, the shifting of the economic "center of gravity" from the agricultural to the non-agricultural sector – referred to as Engel's law – is traced to the fact that, with gains in labor productivity in both the agricultural and non-agricultural sectors, labor is reallocated to non-agriculture because the population, with higher income, prefers to consume relatively more industrial products (that is, the income elasticity of demand for non-agricultural goods is higher). Define:

$$a_w = c_a d/w_i = p_a c_a/p_i w_i \ (0 < a_w < 1) \tag{3.17}$$
$$\text{(see equations 3.6a and 3.7)}$$

as the coefficient indicating the fraction of the real wage income (w_i) that a typical urban worker spends on food. In a poor LDC, a_w can be as high as 60 percent, much higher than that for a typical worker in the industrially advanced countries. Finally, by equation 3.4a, we have:

$$r = \eta_P = \theta\eta_W + (1 - \theta)\eta_L \qquad (3.18a)$$
$$\eta_W \to r \text{ when } \theta \to 1 \qquad (3.18b)$$

Thus, the population growth rate (r) is the weighted average of η_W and η_L in figure 3.2(b). In case of "success" we encounter a "reversal point" in the transition growth process when the agricultural population declines absolutely (that is, when η_L becomes negative). This reversal phenomenon is significant because, when the agricultural population declines absolutely, the historical population pressure on land in the agricultural sector is finally reversed. In the long run, as $\theta(t)$ approaches 1 (for example, approaches 97 percent in the USA), η_W approaches r (equation 3.18b). In other words, the total population growth rate is governed almost completely by the increase of the industrial population as the agricultural sector is reduced merely to an "appendage".

Thus, to put our analysis in the right historical perspective, the transition growth process usually begins in the early phase of demographic transition when the country inherits an initially high percentage of its population in the agricultural sector (that is, low θ). It is in this sense, of the initial preponderance of population and economic activities in agriculture, that this sector may be viewed as the "base" to fuel the expansion of the rest of the economy in the course of the development process.

3.3.2 Labor release and labor absorption

When the emphasis of "successful" transition growth is put squarely on labor reallocation, the analysis of the growth process in a labor surplus dualistic economy can be divided into two facets: a labor release aspect and a labor absorption aspect. The former centers on the analysis of the role of the agricultural sector, in particular on the generation of an agricultural surplus (TAS in figure 3.1(a)) to feed the non-agricultural population W that is being released. The latter is concerned with the analysis of the role of the industrial sector that must expand its capital stock in order to provide employment opportunities for the labor thus released. These two aspects are analyzed in sections 3.4 and 3.5, while the simultaneous interaction between the two sectors is examined in section 3.6. First, certain additional concepts need to be clarified.

3.3.3 Significance of the intersectoral terms of trade (d)

In the interaction between the agricultural and non-agricultural sectors of the dualistic economy, the terms of trade $d = p_a/p_i$ (equation 3.7) play a particularly crucial role in all three intersectoral markets. The intersectoral terms of trade regulate labor reallocation through the intersectoral labor market, peasant participation in both the commodity and financial markets, and consumption choices for the urban working class.

Regulation of Labor Migration   First, d regulates labor reallocation in the intersectoral labor market. Under the condition of perfect labor mobility (that is, the equality of w_f (equation 3.3b) for the rural labor force in terms of agricultural goods, with w_i (equation 3.6c) for the industrial labor force in terms of industrial goods):

$$p_a w_f = p_i w_i \text{ or} \tag{3.19a}$$
$$w_i = d w_f \tag{3.19b}$$

In other words, the rural labor force seeks employment in the urban centers as long as there is a gap between the two wage rates ($p_i w_i > p_a w_f$). Labor will not migrate to the cities when the urban money wage $p_i w_i$ is less than the full income of the rural labor force $p_a w_f$. Equation 3.19b also suggests that the real wage prevailing in the industrial sector w_i is causally determined by the w_f prevailing in agriculture adjusted (that is, multiplied) by the terms of trade d. This is traced to the fact that a lion's share of labor $(1 - \theta)$ is initially accounted for by the agricultural labor force. The industrial real wage rises if the terms of trade move against the industrial sector (for example, when d increases during an agricultural shortfall) and/or if w_f increases at its "base".

Referring to equation 3.3b, we see that the full wage rate w_f in agriculture is higher than the $IRW = w_a$ by a margin corresponding to z (the Z-goods production per farmer) that often eludes official statistical detection, although, in principle, it can be "imputed." Thus, when equation 3.19 is satisfied, reliance on official statistical data usually shows the illusion of a wage gap in favor of industrial labor (that is, $w_i > d w_a$). Through time, this nominal wage gap gradually narrows and finally disappears (that is, $w_i = w_a$).[7] Such a "narrowing of the wage gap" means a commercialization of the peasants in the sense of abandoning non-cash rural production Z, as analyzed in the last section (3.6.7) of this chapter.

Farmer's Market Participation Benefit (MPB) and the Propensity to Invest (s)   The terms of trade also provide guidance for market participation on the part of the farmers in the intersectoral commodity market. Figure 3.1(b) indicated that what the peasants bring to market is TAS. In return, they obtain Q_a and S_a from the industrial sector. Using equation 3.12b, we have

$$d = (S_a + Q_a)/TAS = p_a/p_i \text{ (rural budget equation)} \tag{3.20a}$$
$$N = S_a + Q_a \text{ (MPB)} \tag{3.20b}$$
$$d = N/TAS \tag{3.20c}$$

Equation 3.20a is the "monetized budget equation" for the rural families derived directly from equation 3.8d. In delivering TAS to the industrial sector, the rural families receive two types of real goods in return: modern goods Q_a (factory produced modern agricultural inputs and consumer goods) and S_a (the title to industrial capital wealth).[8] Thus, the terms of trade d represents the benefit to the farmer per unit of agricultural goods delivered to the cities. T.W. Schultz believes that the maintenance of favorable terms of trade d is essential to provide the incentive for market participation on the part of the peasants, based on rational cost/price calculations. The rural budget equation shows that what lies behind the cost/price parity is the real modernizing benefit per unit of TAS. Spatially dispersed farmers are, therefore, very sensitive to the level of d.

In equation 3.20b the benefit to the peasants is denoted by N and is labeled the (market) participation benefit (MPB) to the farmers. Since N has two components, the farmer must decide how to divide his monetary income between them. Rewriting equation 3.12b, we have:

$$N = S_a + Q_a = TASd \tag{3.21a}$$
$$s = S_a/N, s_q = Q_a/N, s + s_q = 1 \quad \text{implying} \tag{3.21b}$$
$$S_a = s(TASd) = s(S_a + Q_a) = sN \tag{3.21c}$$
$$Q_a = s_q TASd = s_q(S_a + Q_a) = s_q N \tag{3.21d}$$

Thus, the monetized income of the farmer in terms of industrial goods ($TASd$) can be used to buy consumer goods or fertilizer (Q_a) to raise agricultural productivity and/or to acquire title to industrial capital (S_a) (equation 3.21a). From the viewpoint of the whole society, the farmers' decision in this respect represents a crucial aspect of balanced growth between the two sectors of the dualistic economy – they provide more intersectoral finance only when they decide to allocate a larger fraction of their monetized income to S_a.

Equation 3.21b defines the propensity to invest (s) of the peasants as the fraction of their monetized income ($N = dTAS$), which they allocate to the purchase of investment goods (S_a) to provide for intersectoral finance, and s_q as the "propensity to buy modern inputs" (Q_a) that are conducive to the increase of agricultural productivity. Thus an improvement in the terms of trade not only benefits the farmers but also induces them to raise agricultural productivity by increasing s_q. These notions are crucial for our analysis of "balanced growth" below.

Urban Worker Consumer Preference   The terms of trade are also crucial for guiding the consumption choice of the urban labor force for agricultural goods c_a and industrial goods c_i. Equation 3.8b implies:

$$p_i w_i = p_i c_i + p_a AAS \quad \text{implying, in turn,} \tag{3.22a}$$
$$w_i = c_i + dAAS \tag{3.22b}$$

Proof: Equation 3.22a is derived by dividing equation 3.8b by W and applying equation 3.6. Equation 3.22b is derived by dividing equation 3.22a by p_i.   Q.E.D.

This shows that a typical industrial worker spends all his real wage income on $c_a = AAS$ or c_i. This is, in fact, his "budget equation" which involves the terms of trade d. The determination of d involves both urban consumer preference and the average agricultural surplus and is analyzed below.

Finally, the terms of trade are also involved in the intersectoral finance market. To see this:

$$Q = Q_i + Q_a + S_a + S_i \text{ (by equations 3.1a and 3.10)} \qquad (3.23a)$$
$$Q = Q_i + S_i + N \text{ (by equation 3.20b)} \qquad (3.23b)$$

Thus, the total output of the industrial sector Q can take on four forms. It can take on the form of (1) manufactured consumer goods destined for the urban labor force (Q_i); (2) modern inputs (for example, fertilizer) or incentive consumer goods (for example, textiles) destined for the farmers (Q_a); (3) "new factories" (that is, investment goods) destined for urban entrepreneurs who save (S_i); and (4) "new factories" owned by rural savers (S_a). Equation 3.23b shows that Q can also be conceived of as divided into participation benefits ($N = Q_a + S_a$) for farmers and benefits for urban actors ($Q_i + S_i$). Equations 3.2a and 3.13 imply:

$$Q = R + \pi \text{ (equation 3.2a)} \qquad (3.24a)$$
$$S_i = \pi \text{ (equation 3.13b)} \qquad (3.24b)$$
$$R = Q_i + N \qquad (3.24c)$$

Thus, the functional income distribution in the industrial sector implies that the industrial working class W is provided with industrial wage goods Q_i (which they consume themselves) as well as the N-goods they spend on agricultural goods to purchase TAS at the terms of trade d (see equation 3.20c). In such an exchange process, N reaches farmers as participation benefits channeled through the intersectoral finance and/or commodity markets. When R (equation 3.24c) is divided by W (the industrial labor force), the industrial real wage rate w_i for a typical worker can be decomposed as:

$$w_i = c_i + N^0 \text{ where} \qquad (3.25a)$$
$$N^0 = N/W = S_a^0 + Q_a^0 \text{ and} \qquad (3.25b)$$
$$S_a^0 = S_a/W \qquad (3.25c)$$
$$Q_a^0 = Q_a/W \qquad (3.25d)$$

Thus, the industrial real wage w_i is the sum of c_i – consumption of industrial goods per worker – and N^0 – the participation benefit per industrial worker which can be subdivided into two components (S_a^0 and Q_a^0) on a per industrial worker basis.

In summary, the three types of "agent families" – urban workers W, urban entrepreneurs (owners of K), and rural agricultural households L – behave quite differently in the dualistic economy. The urban workers and entrepreneurs are modern in that their activities are "functionally specialized." After the income of the industrial sector is distributed by impartial market forces into the wage R and profit π shares, the workers W maximize their consumption welfare and the entrepreneurs accumulate capital K with a single-minded simplicity quite familiar to readers of a modern economics textbook. In contrast, the activities of the spatially dispersed rural families are anything but familiar. The "household" and "farm" are amalgamated into one paternalistic family farm that has to make production, consumption and investment decisions. Given a high degree of initial self-sufficiency through the production and consumption of Z-goods, the acquisition of Q_a (that is, incentive consumer goods and modern agricultural inputs) and S (the title to industrial wealth) through market participation and the provision of family labor for off-farm employment in the industrial sector may be quite limited at first. This modernization of agriculture via increases in agricultural productivity is very much related to the evolutionary modification of the traditional behavior pattern of rural families in an evolutionary perspective. While a rigorous analytical formulation of this process is difficult, the effort must be nevertheless made.[9]

3.3.4 Modernization of the agricultural sector

Agriculture is "traditional" primarily because its actors are spatially dispersed and alienated by "distance" from the forces of modernization in the urban centers. While economists have recently gained a better perspective on the idealized historical mission of that sector – to provide a savings fund S_a or export surplus $B = S_a$, as well as a dependable supply of cheap labor – precisely how to modernize it has remained something of a mystery.

The participation benefit ($N = S_a + Q_a = dTAS$, from equation 3.20b) provides us with some clues to help solve this mystery. The benefit of market participation provides farmers not only with modern inputs (fertilizer and seeds required for technology change, that is, the "green revolution") but also with incentive consumer goods (such as textiles) that are quantifiable (Q_a), as well as with the title to industrial capital (S_a) that contributes to the commercialization of traditional farmers via the diversification of their incomes and the ability to accumulate assets. Heuristically, let us define two indices:

$$N^* = N/L \ (= dTAS/L) \ \text{(AMPB)} \tag{3.26a}$$
$$\psi = TAS/A \qquad \text{(DMP)} \tag{3.26b}$$

The first index, N^*, represents the participation benefit **per unit of the agricultural labor force** and may be referred to as the average market participation benefit (AMPB). It measures the benefit experienced by a typical farmer. Whatever benefits accrue to the farm sector must be gauged on a per farmer basis. The second index, ψ, (the marketed agricultural surplus as a fraction of total agricultural output A) may be referred to as the degree of market participation (DMP) and provides a quantitative measurement of the degree of commercialization of the traditional farm sector. With respect to N^*, the number of industrial workers W supported by a typical farmer is W/L, while the expenditure of a typical industrial worker on food c_a has an exchange value of $c_a d = c_a p_a/p_i$ in terms of industrial goods. Thus N^* is the product of these two numbers:

$$N^* = c_a d \cdot \theta/(1 - \theta) = TASd/L \tag{3.27}$$

Proof: $N^* = c_a d \cdot \theta/(1 - \theta) = (Wc_a d)/L$ (by equation 3.4)
$= TASd/L$ by equation 3.6a. Q.E.D

When the value of $c_a d$ is fixed, N^* as a function of θ is shown in figure 3.3(a), with θ measured on the horizontal axis (pointing to the left). In the course of a successful transition growth process, as θ increases monotonically through time, two conclusions are apparent:

First, N^* **increases monotonically (from zero to infinity) as θ moves from zero toward one.** Since N^* can be taken as a "proxy" for contact with modernization that is conducive to agricultural productivity gain, this conclusion implies that the modernization of the agricultural sector becomes increasingly easy at a later stage of transition growth when θ becomes larger. In figure 3.3(a), for each θ, N^* is partitioned into sN^* and $s_q N^*$ by the propensity to invest s and the propensity to buy modern inputs s_q. Such a contact-related notion means that each component can contribute to agricultural modernization.

Notice that $\theta N^* = c_a d$ when $\theta = 0.5$. Thus, at an early stage of transition growth (that is, for θ less than 50 percent), N^* is less than $c_a d$. Since N^* is the result of monetized transactions as a result of farmer market participation, we see that the extent of monetization of a typical farmer is far below the level $c_a d$ which is only a part of the monetized transition of a typical worker in the industrial sector. (For, according to equation 3.17, the real wage of the industrial sector is $w_i = c_a d/a_w > c_a d$, which, for urban workers, is presumably entirely monetized.)

The participation benefit N^* contributes to an increase of labor productivity $p = A/L$ in the agricultural sector via a "backward linkage effect." Indeed, recalling Lemma 1, since $\theta = 1 - IRW/p$ and IRW is assumed to be constant, θ can only increase when p rises. The common sense of this is that the mystery of agricultural modernization can only be solved by a full understanding of contact between the two sectors. If labor is successfully reallocated, the benefits to farmers increase; but these benefits in turn must increase p to allow θ to rise in the first place. In this fashion vicious circles can become virtuous circles.

In the particular case of an equalization of consumption standards ($c_a = IRW$), the value of N/A can be defined as:

$$N/A = (c_a d\theta/(1 - \theta)/(IRW + c_a\theta/(1 - \theta) - d\theta \text{ or}$$
$$\text{(when } c_a = IRW) \tag{3.28a}$$
$$\theta = p_i N/p_a A \tag{3.28b}$$
$$N/A \to d \text{ as } \theta \to 1 \tag{3.28c}$$

Turning next to the market participation rate defined in equation 3.26b, Lemma 1 of section 3.2.5 immediately shows us that:

$$\psi = TAS/A = \theta \text{ if } IRW = c_a \tag{3.29}$$

These conclusions (equations 3.28 and 3.29) may be summarized as follows:

Theorem 3.1:   If the consumption standards for food of the two sectors are equalized and constant ($IRW = c_a$) then $\theta = \psi = p_i N/p_a A = TAS/A$.

The condition of the equalization of the consumption standards at a constant level ($IRW = c_a = $ a constant) is assumed in section 3.5, implying that a particular type of agricultural technology change is associated with the sustained increase of agricultural productivity depicted in figure 3.3(b).

The modernization of the agricultural sector is less mysterious because N^* and ψ are seen as both cause and effect. They must accompany an increasing θ. But they also represent "causes" of agricultural labor productivity gain because their occurrence contributes to the development of the farmer as a "human resource" as he is provided with modern inputs as well as modern incentive consumer and capital goods.

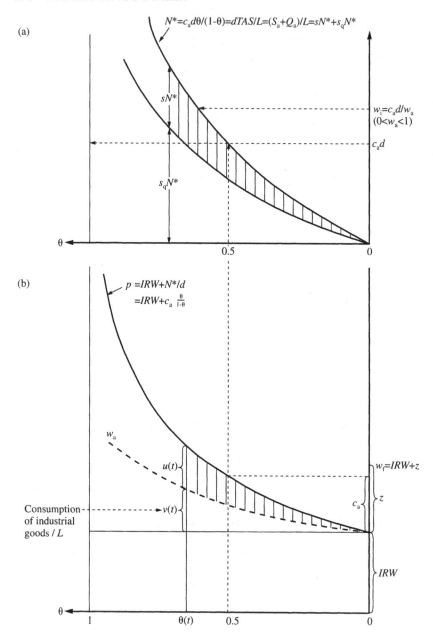

Figure 3.3 Modernization of agricultural sector

3.4 Labor Absorption Analysis

In this section we analyze the labor absorption process from the viewpoint of the industrial sector of the dualistic economy. As a point of departure let us examine some historical evidence.

3.4.1 Historical evidence of labor absorption

Referring to the time path of the industrial real wage during the 40-year period (1780–1820) when England was in the process of transition, we see considerable real wage stability (see figure 3.4). The classical economists, obviously impressed, referred to this stability of the real wage as the "iron law of wages," believing it to be ordained. They were obviously wrong. For barely after the age of classical writing was over, a turning point was reached when the real wage increased sharply, a permanent feature of modern economic growth. By the time the "turning point" arrived, a full 45 percent of the labor force was absorbed into the industrial sector in England. The British experience was repeated almost exactly 100 years later in Japan, when real wages turned up sharply (around 1917) after

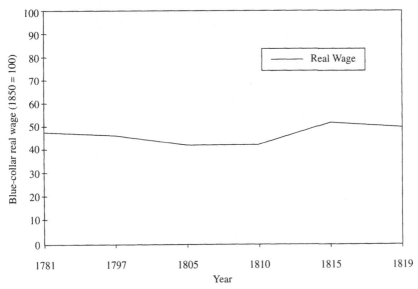

Figure 3.4 "Blue collar" industrial real wage: Great Britain, 1781–1819
Source: Lindert and Williamson (1983).

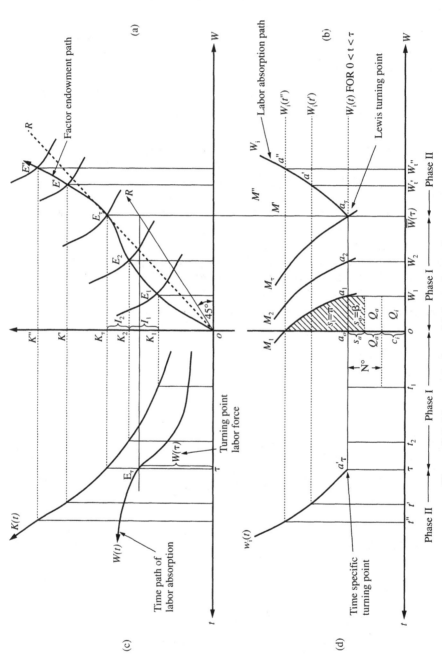

Figure 3.5 Non-agricultural labor absorption process

nearly 40 years of "relative" real wage stability. The arrival of the turning point is obviously a most significant landmark of transition growth because the economic welfare of the working class which constitutes the vast majority of the population increases steadily thereafter.

Motivated by this historical evidence, we refer to the length of time (for example, $\tau = 40$ years in the cases of England and Japan) during which the real wage is relatively stable, as the duration τ of wage constancy and refer to $W(\tau)$, $L(\tau)$ and $\theta(\tau)$ as their turning point values. A major purpose of this chapter is to investigate what determines the value of $\theta(\tau)$ and the duration τ.

For the analysis of the labor absorption process in this section, we take the constancy of real wage in the first phase as given and postulate that w_i turns up sharply after the size of the industrial labor force has reached its turning point value $W(\tau)$. Thus we shall assume approximately that:

$$w_i(t) = \bar{w}_i \text{ for } \theta < \theta(\tau) \text{ — phase I} \tag{3.30a}$$
$$w_i(t) = w_i(t) \text{ with } dw_i/dt > 0 \text{ for } \theta(\tau) \le \theta \text{ — phase II} \tag{3.30b}$$

In this equation, the turning point value of $\theta(\tau)$ is a fixed number that marks off two phases (I and II) of transition growth. The behavior of w_i as postulated in equation 3.30 is an assumption that is defended when the labor release problem is analyzed. In view of the fact that the lion's share of the labor force is initially in the agricultural sector, it is intuitively obvious that the level of the real wage as well as the size of the labor force at the turning point $(W(\tau), L(\tau))$ are determined by the performance of the agricultural sector. Purely for expositional convenience, we assume that the total population is constant:

$$P(t) = P(0) \tag{3.31}$$

Under this (unrealistic) assumption, the turning point $W(\tau)$ is fixed, and equation 3.30 can be rewritten as a special case:

$$w_i(t) = \bar{w}_i \text{ for } W(t) < W(\tau) \text{ — phase I} \tag{3.32a}$$
$$w_i(t) = w_i \text{ for } W(\tau) \le W(t) \text{ — phase II} \tag{3.32b}$$

which states that the first phase comes to an end when the industrial labor force $W(t)$ has reached a definite size $W(\tau)$. We analyze the special case in this chapter while postponing the analysis of the general case (with population growth) to the next chapter.

In figure 3.5(b), the two phases (I and II) are marked off by $\bar{W}(\tau)$, the turning point labor force in the industrial sector. Over the first phase, w_i approaches constancy as is indicated by the horizontal line $a_o a_r$. In phase II, $w_i(t)$ increases over time. To show the time dimension, let the time path of $w_i(t)$ be shown in figure 3.5(d) where time t is measured on the horizontal axis (pointing to the left) and where the duration τ of the first phase (I) is indicated. Thus, w_i is constant before $t = \tau$ and increases over time after $t = \tau$. The horizontal (dotted) lines projected from figures 3.5(d) to indicate the competitive wage rate prevailing at each time.

3.4.2 Labor absorption with competitive income distribution

Let the production function prevailing at time t for the industrial sector be denoted by

$$Q = f(K,W,t) \tag{3.33}$$

At each time t, the production function is represented by a production contour map as shown in figure 3.5a, with labor W (capital K) measured on the horizontal (vertical) axis. The marginal productivity of labor M_l (capital M_k) at each time are given by:

$$M_l = \partial Q/\partial L = f_L(K,W,t) \tag{3.34a}$$
$$M_k = \partial Q/\partial K = f_K(K,W,t) \tag{3.34b}$$

Since the competitive principle of income distribution is assumed to hold in the industrial sector, the real wage $w_i(t)$ is equated to M_l in equation 3.35a:

$$M_l = f_L(K,W,t) = w_i(t) \quad \text{implying} \tag{3.35a}$$
$$W(t) \equiv y(K,t) \quad \text{(labor absorption path)} \tag{3.35b}$$

Since the real wage is given for each t (by equation 3.32), we can determine the amount of labor $W(t)$ absorbed into the industrial sector when the size of the capital stock $K(t)$ at time t is given. This is shown in equation 3.35b and is referred to as the labor absorption path.

This determination of labor absorption is illustrated diagrammatically in figure 3.5(a) and (b). Suppose at $t = t_1$ the size of the capital stock is K_1 which, with the production function at $t = t_1$, determines M_1, the demand curve for labor in figure 3.5(b). Where M_1 intersects the real wage line at a_1, the amount of labor absorbed into the industrial sector W_1 is indicated on the horizontal axis. In this fashion, the labor absorption path over time is described by a_0, a_1, a_τ, a', a'' in figure 3.5(b). Thus, the amount of labor absorbed into the industrial sector is completely determined if we know the time path of capital $K(t)$ and the state of technology at time t.

3.4.3 Rapidity of capital accumulation and duration of the first phase

Since under our assumptions investment I, which leads to non-agricultural sector capital accumulation (dK/dt), is financed by S_i (intrasectoral finance) and S_a (intersectoral finance), the rapidity of capital accumulation is:

$$dK/dt = I = S_a + S_i \quad \text{(from equations 3.5 and 3.10)} \tag{3.36a}$$
$$S_i = \pi = M_k K \quad \text{(from equations 3.13b and 3.34b)} \tag{3.36b}$$
$$S_a = sTASd \quad \text{(from equation 3.21c)} \tag{3.36c}$$

Thus, under the classical savings rule S_i is the industrial sector's profit share determined by the competitive principles of income distribution (equation 3.34b). In the dualistic economy, S_a is the value of $TASd$ multiplied by the farmers' propensity to invest s. The propensities in both sectors to acquire title to industrial assets determines the rapidity of capital accumulation.

In figure 3.5(b), for the demand curve M_1 at time $t = t_1$ (that is, for $K = K(1)$) the total output of industrial goods Q is partitioned into four types of goods according to equations 3.23 and 3.25. The two shaded portions $(S_i + S_a = B + \pi)$ are investment goods I, with titles claimed respectively by urban savers $(S_i = \pi)$ and rural savers $(S_a = B = sTASd)$.[10] In the next period $K(2) = K(1) + I$. In this way the time path of capital $K(t)$ is determined recursively, as shown by the time path of $K(t)$ in figure 3.5(c).

For each $K(t)$, the factor endowment path of figure 3.5(a) shows the amount of labor $W(t)$ absorbed by the industrial sector. With the aid of the 45° line OR in figure 3.5(a) the amount of labor absorbed is projected onto figure 3.5(c) to become the time path of labor absorption $W(t)$. When this time path reaches the turning-point labor force, $W(\tau)$, at the point E_τ, the time required to reach turning point τ is indicated. Thus $K(t)$, $W(t)$ and τ are all determined endogenously in the course of the labor absorption process.

Thus when the turning point labor force $W(\tau)$ is given, the duration τ of the first phase (I) is determined by the rapidity of labor absorption. The rapidity of labor absorption in turn depends on capital accumulation and the nature of technology change – both its strength and bias. The more powerful technology change and the more powerful and biased in a labor using direction, the more labor will be absorbed per unit of capital accumulation. This important dimension of the forces determining the rapidity of the labor absorption process is analyzed in chapter 7.

3.4.4   The quantitative importance of intersectoral finance

In the dualistic economy, the savings of the agricultural sector (S_a) are initially expected to provide the lion's share of investment finance. Taking the ratio of S_a to S_i as a measure of the relative importance of agricultural savings, that is, intersectoral relative to intrasectoral finance:

$$S_a/S_i = a_w sq \qquad \text{where} \tag{3.37a}$$
$$a_w = c_a d/w_i \qquad \text{(equation 3.17)} \tag{3.37b}$$
$$s = S_a/N \qquad \text{(equation 3.21b)} \tag{3.37c}$$
$$q \equiv \phi_W/\phi_K = R/\pi \quad \text{(equations 3.2b and 3.2c)} \tag{3.37d}$$

Proof: by equation 3.36c, $S_a = sTASd = sd(TAS/W)W = sdc_a W$
(by equation 3.6a) $= sdc_a Ww_i/w_i = sa_w R$ by equations 3.6c and 3.17.
Thus, $S_a/S_i = sa_w R/\pi$.   Q.E.D.

The relative importance of intersectoral finance (S_a/S_i) is a product of a_w, s, and q. a_w, the fraction of expenditures of urban workers on food, usually takes on an order of magnitude of, say, 0.5. In the Cobb–Douglas case, q, the ratio of the relative shares, usually takes on an order of magnitude of, say, two (for $\phi_W = 2/3$). In that case, the ratio S_a/S_i would be close to the farmer's propensity to save and invest, s – if the farmers should devote 60 percent of their monetary income to investment, S_a is 60 percent of S_i.[11] Notice that $a_w sq$ is a "pure number" which does not depend on θ, the fraction of the labor force allocated to the industrial sector. This implies that, in spite of the fact that θ increases through time (that is, as more urban workers are supported by a typical farmer), the farm sector will, for a long stretch of time, provide 60 percent of S_i. In historical perspective, intersectoral finance will decline in importance only over time when a_w declines (because of Engel's Law), or when s declines once farmers devote more of their income to consumption and/or to the purchase of farm inputs, such as fertilizer.

3.4.5 Distributional significance of the turning point

A major element of organizational dualism is traced to the fact that the commercialized principle of income distribution postulated for the industrial sector (equation 3.35a) does **not** initially apply to the traditional agricultural sector. Let the production function for the agricultural sector, with inputs of L (agricultural labor force) and T (land), be:

$$A = A(L,T,t) \tag{3.38a}$$
$$f_L = \partial A/\partial L = A_L(L,T,t) \tag{3.38b}$$
$$f_T = \partial A/\partial T = A_T(L,T,t) \tag{3.38c}$$
$$\phi_L = f_L L/A \tag{3.38d}$$
$$\phi_T = f_T T/A \tag{3.38e}$$
$$\phi_L + \phi_T = 1 \tag{3.38f}$$

f_L and f_T are the marginal productivity of L and T, and ϕ_L and ϕ_T are the economic wage share and the economic rent share in the agricultural sector. While this commercialized principle does not initially prevail in the agricultural sector, a major thesis developed in the next section is that it will prevail once the "turning point" arrives. Denote the wage and rent share at the turning point by:

$$\phi_L(\tau) = L(\tau)f_L(\tau)/A(\tau) \tag{3.39a}$$
$$\phi_T(\tau) = 1 - \phi_L(\tau) \tag{3.39b}$$

Then:

$$\theta(\tau) = W(\tau)/P(\tau) = \phi_T(\tau) \tag{3.40a}$$
$$1 - \theta(\tau) = L(\tau)/P(\tau) = \phi_L(\tau) \tag{3.40b}$$

Equation 3.40 states that when the turning point arrives, the fraction of the labor force absorbed by the industrial sector $\theta(\tau)$, for example, $\theta(\tau) = 45$ percent, is precisely equal to the rent share ($\phi_T(\tau)$) in the agricultural sector. Thus, when the population structure has reached the turning point value ($\theta(\tau)$) the country loses its labor surplus characteristic as the determination of income distribution in both production sectors is unified by the commercialized or neoclassical principle. Before that point the income distribution in agriculture is still governed by a sharing or non-commercialized principle in the presence of a constant agricultural real wage.

3.4.6 A remark on the "unlimited supply of labor"

While the classical economists referred to the constancy of the real wage in the first phase as governed by an "iron law," W. Arthur Lewis refers to this phase as characterized by an "unlimited supply of labor." In fact, figure 3.5(b) is a reproduction of a diagrammatic device first used by Professor Lewis. Hence, the turning point a_τ may be labeled as the "Lewis turning point."

The choice of the term "unlimited supply" of labor has, however, turned out to be somewhat misleading. For with the wage rate measured on the vertical axis of figure 3.5(b), it has led to the unwarranted interpretation that the labor absorption path shown there depicts the supply of labor by rural families in response to changes in the wage rate. This unwarranted interpretation has led to the formulation of hypotheses concerning household behavior with respect to the sensitivity of labor supply in response to changes in the wage rate that can be verified econometrically and seem to contradict the Arthur Lewis hypothesis. The contribution of such "micro-modeling," while certainly valuable in its own right, has little relevance to the issue of wage behavior over time – the basic proposition underlying the time path of the wage rate depicted in figure 3.5(d). The fact is that the relative constancy of the real wage over a long stretch of time (for example, 40 years in England and Japan) is a long-run phenomenon crucially related to population growth, labor migration, the dynamics of agricultural technology change, as well as the process of commercialization of the agricultural sector as stated in equation 3.40. The phenomenon of long-run real wage constancy has little to do with short-run household labor supply behavior.

Lewis's path-breaking model focused on the role of the non-agricultural sector in absorbing labor out of agriculture. Urban–rural interactions in the commodity, finance, and labor markets were really not addressed. Our work analyzes the two sectors separately and focuses on their interaction. What underlies the pattern of real wage behavior through time (for example, as characterized by the existence of two phases in equation 3.30 or 3.32), is investigated in the analysis of the agricultural sector which follows.

3.5 The Release of Labor from the Agricultural Sector

3.5.1 The family oriented consumption and income distribution principle of traditional rural households

In the analysis of the labor release aspect of labor reallocation, our attention shifts from the commercialized industrial sector to the "traditional" rural sector. In a traditional rural economy there can be a wide variety of arrangements (for example, owner-cultivator, landlord-tenant, or share-cropping arrangements with or without hired farm hands on a contractual basis) under which plots of land are cultivated. In the microscopic literature on rural households, the unequal size of households and the unequal ownership of land are recognized. In that case the renting out of land and labor (as well as the special case of landless labor) make an appearance. We abstract from this issue since we want to retain the simplest micro-foundations for our holistic approach to the operation to dualism.

To indicate what might be called a profile of traditionalism as an abstraction of these complexities, we can imagine that at the beginning of the transition growth process there are h owner-cultivating families without hired farmhands. A typical rural family cultivates a plot of T^f acres, supporting a family size of L^f units of labor:

$$T^f = T/h \text{ (family plot size)} \tag{3.41a}$$
$$L^f = L/h \text{ (family size)} \tag{3.41b}$$

The h families of $F_1, F_2, \ldots, F_h$ that are "collective" economic decision-making units grounded on kinship affinity are indicated by the hexagons in figure 3.1(b) with family plot size and family size indicated. For these families, we can define the family cash crop income, non-cash crop income and full income:

$$A^f = A/h = pL^f \qquad \text{(family cash crop income)} \qquad (3.42a)$$
$$Z^f = Z/h = zL^f \qquad \text{(family non-cash crop income)} \qquad (3.42b)$$
$$F^f = A^f + Z^f = (p + z)L^f \quad \text{(family full income)} \qquad (3.42c)$$

In all cases family-related income is obtained from the individual labor related income (that is, the labor productivity, p, and the per labor Z-goods, z) by the family size L^f. For these "paternalistic" families, we make the simplifying intra-family behavioral assumption of equal sharing of consumption. For example, the average market participation benefit $N^* = N/L$ (equation 3.26a) – the per agricultural worker volume of industrial goods that the family acquires by selling the TAS in the market – can be split into its two components S_a/L (the title to industrial wealth per worker) and Q_a/L (the modern inputs and consumption goods per worker) (equation 3.20b). Rigorously, the computation of an average (per worker) value from the family-related magnitudes (S_a, Q_a) may be quite misleading because the paternalistic family may not entertain the idea of a partition of family fortunes to the individual member. Q_a can be split further into Q'_a (modern agricultural inputs) and Q''_a (incentive consumer goods):

$$N = S_a + Q_a = S_a + Q'_a + Q''_a \qquad (3.43)$$

The principle of the equal sharing of consumption implies that only the last component of the participation benefits is equally shared. Given this principle, the "profile of consumption" of a typical rural labor has three components representing per worker consumption of food (IRW), modern industrial goods valued in terms of agricultural goods ($v = (Q''_a/L)d$) and non-monetized Z-goods.

One direct consequence of the principle of equal sharing of consumption is that the per labor consumption of food (IRW) that is close to a caloric minimum level may be greater than the marginal productivity of labor:

$$MPP_L < IRW = \bar{w}_a \text{ (existence of disguised employment)} \quad (3.44)$$

This condition defines the existence of disguised unemployment and implies that the commercialized principle of income distribution does not apply, given the sharing oriented family relations. The existence of disguised unemployment need not imply that farm workers are not working, as they are likely to be handicapped by lack of sufficient land to co-operate with and can engage in Z-goods production within the household. The commercialization of income distribution is likely to be closely related to the atrophy of traditional Z-goods (production and consumption) during the transition process as the behavior of the traditional rural families is "modernized."

3.5.2 Production conditions and initial factor endowment

The production function of the agricultural sector at $t = 0$ is denoted by the production contour map (that is, the production isoquants) in figure 3.6(a), with land T (labor force L) measured on the vertical (horizontal) axis. In agricultural production we postulate that the production function is CRTS. In figure 3.6(a) we also postulate the existence of a ridge line OR and partition the input space into two regions: the labor non-redundant region (above OR) and the labor redundant region (below OR) where all production contours become horizontal. In the latter region, total output will not increase measurably with further additions of labor to a fixed amount of land.[12]

To stress this notion of a "labor surplus condition," we can visualize that land $T = \bar{T}$ is fixed ($\bar{T}T'$ in figure 3.6(a)) and that the land/labor ratio T/L is so low that the **initial** factor endowment point (for example, at T') falls into the labor redundant region. These assumptions are justified by the long history of population pressure on the land in many developing countries before the arrival of the modern epoch.

For a fixed amount of land $\bar{T}$ the TPP_L and the MPP_L are shown by curves in figures 3.6(c) and (b). Over the labor redundant region the TPP_L curve approaches the horizontal, while the MPP_L curve tends to coincide with the horizontal axis.

3.5.3 Institutional real wage (IRW)

To simplify the exposition in this chapter, assume that the total population is fixed (equation 3.31) and that the entire population (ON in figure 3.6(b)) initially resides in the agricultural sector:

$$P = P(0) \tag{3.45a}$$
$$W(0) = 0 \tag{3.45b}$$

These restrictive assumptions are relaxed in the next chapter.

Heuristically, the labor absorption path $W(t)$ is reproduced in figure 3.6(d), with time (t) measured on the vertical axis. $W(0) = 0$ by equation 3.45b. Through time $t_1, t_2, \ldots$ the industrial labor force $W(1), W(2), \ldots$ is indicated on the horizontal axis. A typical $W(t)$ partitions the (constant) total population $P(0)$ into the industrial labor force $W(t)$ – those absorbed by the industrial sector – and $L(t) = \bar{P} - W(t)$ – those who remain in the

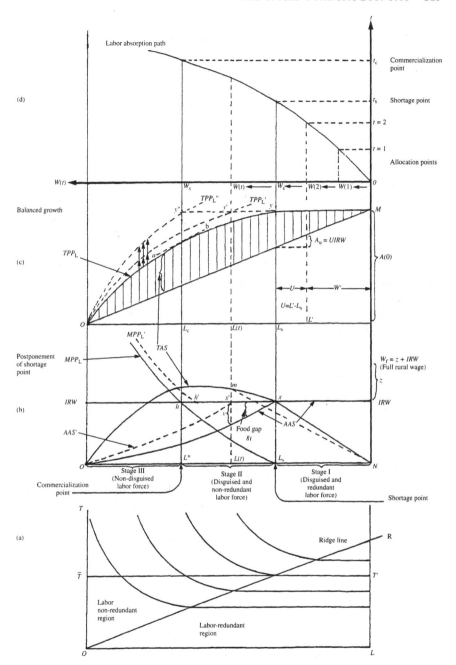

Figure 3.6 Agricultural sector dynamics

agricultural sector. Each $W(t)$ is an "allocation point" which moves toward the left as laborers are **released** by the agricultural sector. We first assume, for convenience, that the IRW is determined at a level corresponding to the initial level of agricultural labor productivity:

$$IRW = A(0)/L(0) \ (=A(0)/P(0) \ ) \qquad (3.46)$$

which is the same as the initial per capita consumption for the entire population (by equation 3.45a). The IRW is represented by the slope of the radial line OM (in figure 3.6(c)) or the height of the horizontal IRW line (in figure 3.6(b)).

Thus, rural families are initially "traditional" in that the degree of participation (ψ in equation 3.26b) and AMPB (N^* in equation 3.26a) are zero while the rural wage $w_f = IRW + z$, defined in equation 3.3b, is represented on the vertical axis of figure 3.6(b) by a point w_f exceeding the IRW by z (per worker output of non-cash crop activities). The typical agricultural family is not yet overcome by the forces of commercialization, as there still exists disguised unemployment (equation 3.44). We analyze the labor release aspect in two steps. First, we (unrealistically) assume a stationary technology (equations 3.44 and 3.45) and subsequently that balanced (or unbalanced) technology change occurs.

3.5.4 Stages of labor reallocation under stationary technology

In figure 3.6(b) the MPP_L curve intersects the horizontal IRW line at h and determines a portion of the agricultural labor force L^* defined by

$$A_L(L^*,T,0) = IRW \qquad (3.47)$$

L^* is the size of the agricultural labor force that equates the MPP_L with the IRW if there is no change in agricultural technology. Disguised unemployment exists as long as the agricultural labor force is larger than L^* (that is, as long as the MPP_L curve lies below the horizontal IRW line).

L_s is the agricultural labor force corresponding to labor redundancy. Since

$$L^* < L_s \qquad (3.48)$$

the vertical lines erected over L^* and L_s partition $P(0)$ into three stages:

$$\text{Stage I:} \quad MPP_L = 0 < IRW \qquad (3.49a)$$
$$\text{Stage II:} \quad 0 < MPP_L < IRW \qquad (3.49b)$$
$$\text{Stage III:} \quad 0 < IRW < MPP_L \qquad (3.49c)$$

In Stage I there exists disguised unemployment with labor redundancy; in Stage II there exists disguised unemployment with labor non-redundancy;

and in Stage III the disguised unemployment has disappeared completely. As the allocation point moves to the left through time, labor release proceeds through the three stages in the given order. However, as long as agricultural technology is stationary, food shortage problems arise in the closed economy. We now investigate the economic significance of these stages.

To facilitate the exposition, we refer to L^* as the labor force at the commercialization point and to L_s as the labor force at the shortage point. The economic significance of these points will become evident in the discussion which follows.

3.5.5 Total agricultural surplus (TAS) and average agricultural surplus (AAS)

Rewriting equation 3.3d as:

$$TAS = A - L \cdot IRW \qquad (3.50)$$

we see that the total agricultural surplus (TAS) is the cash crop that the farmers supply to the urban sector (through the intersectoral commodity market) after the caloric minimum food requirements of all the agricultural workers $(L \cdot IRW)$ have been taken care of. In figure 3.6(c), the TAS is the vertical gap (shaded) between TPP_L and the straight line OM. The value of TAS is maximized when the marginal productivity of agricultural labor A_L is equal to the IRW – at the point of tangency between ab (parallel to OM) and the TPP_L curve in figure 3.6(c). Thus the TAS curve is inverse U-shaped and takes on a maximum value at the commercialization point L^*, as shown in figure 3.6(b).

Under our simplifying assumption the TAS curve is linear during Stage I. Once the commercialization point arrives the TAS declines absolutely. The average agricultural surplus (AAS) was defined in equation 3.6a and is reproduced here:

$$AAS = TAS/W = c_a \qquad (3.51a)$$
$$AAS = IRW \qquad \text{(Stage I)} \qquad (3.51b)$$
$$d(AAS)/dW < 0 \qquad \text{(Stages II and III)} \qquad (3.51c)$$

Thus AAS is the amount of food (c_a) consumed by a typical allocated worker in the industrial sector. AAS is a constant $(=IRW)$ over Stage I because the total output of food A as well as the total population $W+L$ are constant and, in the absence of any real wage gap between the two sectors, the entire population can be fed at the constant consumption standard IRW. Thus in Stage I the consumption standards can be equalized at the level of IRW. However, after the shortage point is reached, if the agricultural labor force is further reduced (beyond L_s) the total agricultural output A declines as the labor force is no longer "redundant." If the agricultural labor force maintains a constant consumption standard, there will be a food shortage in the urban sector and the caloric minimum consumption standard cannot be sustained. The AAS is represented by the AAS curve in figure 3.6(b) which coincides with the IRW line during Stage I and declines from point x onward, with more labor allocated out of the agricultural sector. The food gap (that is, the food deficiency) per unit of industrial worker is

$$g_f = IRW - AAS = IRW - c_a \qquad (3.52)$$

At a typical point $L(t)$ in Stage II (figure 3.6(b)) the food gap is represented by the vertical distance between the IRW and the AAS curve. With the emergence of such a food gap, the consumption standard can no longer be maintained at the IRW level.

3.5.6 Food shortage

Consider the agricultural labor force L' at a typical point in Stage I (figure 3.6(c)) indicating that while W' units of workers are absorbed by the industrial sector, there are still U-units ($U = L' - L_s$) of agricultural workers (who consume $U \cdot IRW$ units of food) which are redundant. It is quite likely that some workers migrate temporarily to the urban areas to become part of the unemployed urban labor force. In the early post-war period, the existence of such transient rural migrants in the large urban centers was observable in almost all countries of Latin America, Africa, and South and Southeast Asia.

When the labor reallocation process reaches the shortage point (L_s), Stage II occurs. It takes only a very slight food gap (g_f) to produce a food crisis because c_a is often close to the caloric minimum. Such food crises were, indeed, quite common in the early post-war years – in India and Communist China during 1959–62 – when tens of millions of the rural population starved to death. Our phases of growth thesis predicts that when the agricultural sector is neglected, a food crisis not only appears but can appear without warning at some such "shortage point."

For successful transition growth to occur (that is, one in which θ increases persistently through time), agricultural technology cannot be stationary after the shortage point has arrived. Success is necessarily associated with balanced growth where continuous agricultural technology change must accompany the labor release process.

3.5.7 Growth with balanced technology change

If the agricultural labor force is reduced to $L(t) < L_s$, technology change in the agricultural sector must occur so that the entire population can be fed at the minimum consumption standard level IRW:

$$A(L(t),T,t) = P(t)\cdot c_a(t) \text{ (general case, when population expands)} \quad (3.53a)$$
$$A(L(t),T,t) = P(0)\cdot IRW \text{ (special case, when population is} \quad (3.53b)$$
$$\text{constant)}$$

Equations 3.53a and b provide a general definition of balanced agricultural technology change (BATC) that may be formally stated as follows:

> *Definition* Balanced agricultural technology change (BATC) occurs through time if, at any time t, the agricultural labor force $L(t)$ is able to produce enough food to feed the entire population $P(t)$ at a prescribed per capita consumption standard $c_a(t)$.

The BATC is definable only after the triplet of time series, $P(t)$, $L(t)$, and $c_a(t)$, are arbitrarily given. A numerical example is presented below to show the determination of BATC after $P(t)$, $L(t)$, and $c_a(t)$ are given. When the actual technology change is not BATC, total output is different from the prescribed time path of $P(t)c_a(t)$. There are two possibilities as implied by the following definition:

> *Definition* For the prescribed time series $(P(t), L(t), c_a(t))$, agricultural technology change is adequate (or inadequate) relative to BATC over any interval of time $(t' < t < t'')$ if $A(t) > P(t)c_a(t)$ (or $A(t) < P(t)c_a(t)$) for $t' < t < t''$.

Thus, at any point in time, technology change can be either adequate or inadequate (if it is not BATC). In case $c_a(t)$ is prescribed at a level $c_a(t) = IRW$ – close to the caloric minimum level – the BATC represents a "critical minimum" agricultural technology change, a yardstick that differentiates the adequate from the inadequate. Thus as the economy enters Stage II, further releases of labor ($L < L_s$) imply that the stagnant agricultural technology is inadequate and the food crisis halts the process of labor reallocation.

In figure 3.6(b), at time t, $L(t)$ is represented by a point in Stage II. In order to eliminate the food gap, the TPP_L curve must be raised to TPP_L' so that the same total output $A(0)$ can be produced. If the agricultural labor force is reduced to L^*, the TPP_L curve must be raised to TPP_L''.

Thus BATC implies that the consumption standard is equated to the *IRW* level at all times.

When BATC occurs continuously, the shortage point is postponed from *x* to *x'* (that is, a larger labor force can be released by the agricultural sector as compared with L_s). The horizontal portion of the *AAS* curve is "elongated" and the upward shift of the TPP_L curve causes the MPP_L curve to shift upward to MPP_L' – provided technology change in non-agriculture is "not very labor saving" (see chapter 4). The higher MPP_L' curve intersects the *IRW* line at *h'*, which lies to the right of *h*. Thus when BATC occurs there is not only a postponement of the shortage point (*x* to *x'*) but also a hastening of the arrival of the commercialization point (*h* to *h'*).

3.5.8 Turning point of transition growth under BATC

When BATC occurs through time, the persistent "postponement of the shortage" point $(L_s(1) > L_s(2) > L_s(3) > ...)$ and "hastening of the commercialization point" $(L^*(1) < L^*(2) < L^*(3) < ...)$ is illustrated in figure 3.7(a). If the allocation point moves toward *P*(0) without an upper bound, time $t = \tau$ is determined when $L^*(\tau) = L_s(\tau)$. Thus, the value of τ is determined when the following pair of conditions is simultaneously satisfied:

$$A(L(\tau),T,\tau) = P(0)IRW \quad \text{(by equation 3.53b) and} \tag{3.54a}$$
$$A_L(L(\tau),T,\tau) = IRW \quad \text{(by equation 3.47)} \tag{3.54b}$$

The remaining agricultural labor force at the turning point $L(\tau)$ is consistent with the equality of MPP_L with *IRW* (equation 3.54b) and produces enough food to feed everyone at the caloric minimum consumption standard *IRW* (equation 3.54a).

Given BATC, if and when such a coincidence of the commercialization point and the shortage point is achieved, the three stages (I, II, III defined in equation 3.49 for stagnant technology) are telescoped into just two phases marked off by a turning point labor force $L(\tau)$ (rigorously defined in equation 3.54). The turning point in time $t = \tau$ (that is, the duration of the first phase), is indicated on the vertical time axis in figure 3.7c. In the first phase the real wage in the agricultural sector is constant ($w_a = IRW$) as long as there is disguised unemployment (equation 3.43). However, with the arrival of the turning point disguised unemployment disappears. Further releases of labor by the agricultural sector in phase II (for example, at the point $L(t)$ in figure 3.7(a)) raises the MPP_L to levels higher than the *IRW* for two reasons. The absolute decline of $L(t)$ from $L(\tau)$ raises MPP_L (for example, to the point *j*) in the absence of technology change. Agricultural technology change would raise it further (to *j'*). Thus, if we

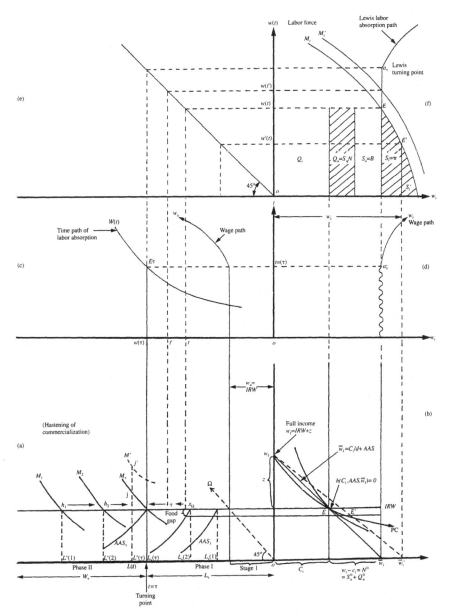

Figure 3.7 Balanced agricultural technology change

assume that the agricultural real wage is equal to the MPP_L once disguised unemployment has disappeared:

$$w_a(t) = A_L(L(t),T,t) \text{ when } L(t) < L(\tau) \qquad (3.55)$$

we can establish a two phases thesis for the behavior of the real wage (w_a) in the agricultural sector:

$$w_a = \overline{IRW} \text{ when } L(\tau) < L(t) \text{ by equations 3.43 and 3.49a} \qquad (3.56a)$$
$$w_a = MPP_L \text{ when } L(t) < L(\tau) \text{ by equation 3.55} \qquad (3.56b)$$

marked off by a turning point $L(\tau)$. Let us examine the significance of this turning point thesis from an historical perspective.

3.5.9 The turning point in historical perspective

The arrival of the turning point represents a significant landmark in the development of a labor surplus dualistic economy since it marks the advent of the functional distribution of income by the usual commercialized or neoclassical principle which is stated formally in the two-phase thesis, equations 3.56a and b. This implies that "traditionalism" in the economy's preponderant rural sector is terminated as the turning point approaches. Looking beyond it, sustained increases in the real wage in the agricultural sector signify that, for the first time in its life cycle, the agricultural labor force has acquired a scarcity value commensurate with its production contribution to the society at large, as its services are valued by impersonal market forces.

The relationship between rural workers and their families after the arrival of the turning point is divorced from paternalistic or sharing antecedents and approaches that of the commercialized urban labor force. Given such a societal reorientation, reallocated individuals are guided by impersonal market forces and the flexibility essential for the realization of the potential of modern science and technology.

Before the turning point the rural labor force could not have been compensated according to commercialized principles because of the very existence of disguised unemployment. For the typical rural family, the economic rent share ϕ_T (in equation 3.38) has no operational significance since part of it was shared among the family members to support their consumption. Thus, the kinship-oriented income distribution rule amounts to a subsidization of family members because a portion of the economic rent was transferred to them. The TAS that the families supplied to the markets was less than the economic rent share. With the arrival of the turning point this "inequality" is converted into an "equality" ($TAS = Tf_T$). This may be formally stated as follows:

Lemma 2   When the turning point arrives, the market participation rate equals the economic rent share in the agricultural sector:

$$\psi(\tau) = TAS/A = \phi_T(\tau) \; (= f_T T/A) \tag{3.57}$$

Thus we see that while economic rent was operationally insignificant in the traditional rural society it becomes the monetized market participation rate once the turning point arrives. For the first time, the agricultural labor force, subsidized via kinship relations before the turning point, receives a scarcity price set by market forces; equivalently, land also receives its full market value.

While land has always been especially treasured by rural families for security reasons, it now becomes a commercialized asset that enters into market transactions and is used, for example, as collateral. Traditionalism is thus eroded by the commercialization of labor and landed assets in rural communities.

While we have postulated the owner-cultivating family as typical for the rural society, along with the overpayment of labor by kinship relations, similar overpayments occur on tenant-cultivated land (under sharecropping) and/or under fixed rent arrangements supported by a tradition of paternalism (or feudalism) between landlords and peasants. Historically observed fixed contractual rent shares paid to landlords (stabilized around 50 percent for many agrarian societies over the centuries) were often above the economic rent share which would have implied consumption levels not permitting the working population to survive. In return, tenants were expected to fulfill other obligations to the landlord. Historically, the non-commercialized sharing principle of income distribution in the agrarian society was formed in the course of an evolutionary process in order to accommodate a population expansion which, according to Adam Smith, represents the most important index of the prosperity of a society.

The competitive or commercialized principle of income distribution which emerges in the course of the relatively short, transition period (for example, $\tau = 40$ years for Japan, 20 years for post-war Taiwan) represents new arrangements which radically modify the sharing nexus a labor surplus economy has inherited from its agrarian past. This modification can be traced to the arrival of the epoch of science and technology that practically guarantees the survival of the species, including population growth over time.

3.5.10   Turning point labor force

When the condition of BATC prevails over time, the arrival of the turning point in τ years leads to the satisfaction of two conditions defined in equation 3.54. On the one hand, the marginal productivity of labor in the agricultural sector is equated with the consumption standard of the rural labor force (equation 3.54b). On the other hand, agricultural productivity has been raised so that the entire population can be fed at the same consumption standard (equation 3.54a). Lemma 2 states that, with the arrival of the turning point, the market participation rate (that is, the percentage of food A which is supplied as TAS to feed the urban labor force) is precisely the economic rent share (equation 3.57). It follows that the percentage of labor allocated to the industrial sector (θ) is exactly the same as the economic rent share $\phi_t(\tau)$ when the turning point occurs. In section 3.4.5 we pointed out that the upturn of the wage rate in the industrial sector (that is, what corresponds to the Lewis turning point in figure 3.5) occurs when θ is the economic rent share in the agricultural sector. In equation 3.56 we established a two-stage thesis for agricultural wage rates marked off by a turning point when the condition of BATC is sustained over time. It is intuitively obvious for the dualistic economy inheriting a preponderantly agricultural population (large $1 - \theta$) that the real wage in terms of industrial goods governs the real wage in the industrial sector. Thus, the Lewis turning point occurs when the fraction of the labor force in the industrial sector θ equals the economic rent. The fact that the industrial wage is governed by the agricultural wage depends on intersectoral labor mobility and the behavior of the intersectoral terms of trade, as is analyzed rigorously below.

3.5.11 Causation of agricultural modernization

The modernization of the agricultural sector represents a particularly important and difficult issue. It is an important issue because, unless agricultural labor productivity $p = A/L$ is raised persistently through time to satisfy the condition of BATC, labor cannot be reallocated out of the sector (that is, θ cannot be raised). It is a difficult issue because such an increase in agricultural productivity necessitates an understanding of the slow process of modernization of activities – market participation, acquisition of modern fertilizer, incentive goods, and title to industrial wealth – as well as the traditional "outlook" – that is, the commercialization of labor and landed assets and the gradual atrophy of Z-goods in rural households. It is obvious that this modernization of the agricultural sector cannot be divorced from its contact and linkage with the industrial sector from which the forces of modernization originate. Our analysis of the causation of the mysterious process of agricultural modernization in section 3.3.4 is now re-examined and integrated with the labor release aspects of transition growth.

For the agricultural labor force indicated at $L(t) = 1 - \theta(t)$, the productivity p of the labor force is represented by the slope of the straight line OR in figure 3.8(b). If the condition of BATC is sustained over time, p can be represented by a rectangular hyperbola (in figure 3.8(a)) that increases as $\theta(t)$ increases from $\theta(0) = 0$ (when $p = IRW$). This is the path of agricultural labor productivity (or cash crop per unit of labor) **if** the condition of BATC is fulfilled over time. The vertical gap between the p path and the horizontal IRW path is N^*/d – the average market participation benefit (AMPB) valued in units of agricultural goods. Since per capita consumption of food is the same for the entire population (that is, $IRW = c_a$):

$$p = IRW + N^*/d = IRW + c_a\theta/(1 - \theta) \tag{3.58a}$$
$$N^*/d = c_a\theta/(1 - \theta) = TAS/L \text{ (by equation 3.27a)} \tag{3.58b}$$
Proof $p = (A_a + TAS)/L = A_a/L + TAS/L = IRW +$
$(TAS/W)(W/L) = IRW + c_a\theta/(1 - \theta)$. Q.E.D.

The vertical gap N^*/d is per capita consumption of food (c_a) multiplied by $W/L = \theta/(1 - \theta)$, the number of urban workers supported by a typical rural worker. The value of N^*/d increases through time with θ. It is also obvious that when the condition of BATC is fulfilled (that is, if the per capita food supply is barely adequate), the terms of trade d will not change drastically. This, in turn, implies that the AMPB increases in a sustained fashion through time. If we interpret the BATC as a "critical minimum effort" for agricultural modernization, the fulfillment of this condition implies increasing contact with modernization by the typical rural actor, measured in terms of the "benefit" N^*.[13]

The vertical gap N^*/d can be decomposed into two additive components, as indicated in figure 3.8(a) according to equation 3.21b. One component (sN^*/d) corresponds to the propensity to invest in the industrial sector while the other component (s_qN^*/d) corresponds to the propensity to purchase modern current inputs.

These decisions by the agricultural households lie at the heart of the mystery of agricultural productivity increases referred to earlier. Given agricultural output at a given point in time, we assume (for now) that agricultural households continue to maintain their consumption of agricultural goods at the level of *CIW*. What is left over, the TAS ($= Q_a + S_a$), is subject to a complicated three-way allocative decision: first (with $Q_a = Q'_a + Q''_a$) an austerity decision between the consumption of non-agricultural consumer goods (Q'_a) and total investment ($Q''_a + S_a$) and second, within investment, a decision between current expenditures on the improvement of land (such as fertilizer) Q''_a and the acquisition of industrial capital goods S_a. The austerity decision is governed by the character of the linkages between the agricultural and non-agricultural sectors, with current

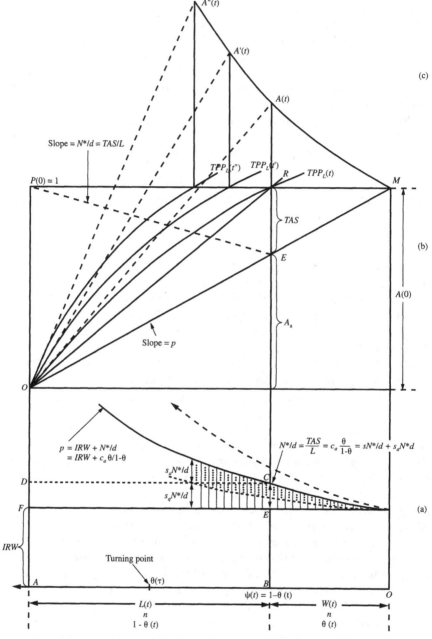

Figure 3.8 Dynamics of agricultural productivity change

consumption vying with future consumption as related to the gearing up of new investment opportunities. The investment decision between current expenditures on agriculture and capital investments in non-agriculture depends on the terms of trade d.

In figure 3.8(a) the value of θ at the turning point $\theta(\tau)$ is marked off to remind us of the fact that the transformation of the traditional rural sector in the direction of modernization (for example, increasing market participation and monetization via urban/rural contacts N^*) has proceeded imperceptibly long before the turning point is reached. The commercialization of the rural economy was a slow process during which farmers became price-sensitive as they acquired the commercial attitude of dealing comfortably with "strangers" in an arms' length environment.

While we have assumed that the population size is constant, it is obvious that the same analysis can be carried out when the population is growing. For example, when $P(t)$ is postulated to expand arbitrarily, for each $\theta(t)$ measured on the horizontal axis of figure 3.8 the required food output is increasing (as indicated by the path $A(t)$, $A'(t)$, $A''(t)$, ... in figure 3.8(c)) if the condition BATC is to be sustained. The p path of figure 3.8(a) also increases more rapidly as θ increases. It is intuitively obvious that the faster the population expansion, the critical minimum effort for the agricultural sector (measured in terms of the required productivity gain and therefore the necessity for urban/rural interaction) is greater if the condition of BATC is to be continuously sustained.

Rigorously, when the triplet $(P(t), W(t),$ and $c_a(t))$ is specified in the definition of BATC, we have, by $c_a/p = 1 - \theta$:

$$\eta_p = \eta_{c_a} + \eta_\theta \theta/(1 - \theta) \text{ when } \theta = W(t)/P(t) \text{ and} \qquad (3.59a)$$
$$\eta_p = \eta_\theta \theta/(1 - \theta) \text{ for } \eta_{c_a} = 0 \qquad (3.59b)$$

Proof   by $c_a/p(t) = 1 - \theta$ or $p(t) = c_a/1 - \theta$.   Q.E.D.

In equation 3.59a all terms on the right-hand side are specified by the triplet and η_p on the left-hand side is the "required" rate of increase of agricultural productivity for BATC to hold. Thus, η_p must be higher the higher the specified η_{c_a} and/or η_θ. Equation 3.59b is the special case when c_a is specified to be the constant IRW. Since θ can be expected to increase through time, $\theta/1 - \theta$ increases and η_p must accelerate even when η_θ is constant.

θ not increasing over time (that is, $\eta_\theta = 0$) is the case of stagnation in the dualistic economy. In that situation $\eta_p = \eta_L = \eta_W = r$ and (by equation 3.59) $\eta_p = 0$ – the economy is moving sideways with agricultural productivity levels just high enough to compensate for diminishing returns on the fixed land caused by continuously expanding population pressure.

Let the IRW curve of figure 3.7(b) be reproduced in figure 3.8(a). The total population $P(0)$, assumed to be constant for now, can be normalized to one and hence:

$$\theta = W(t)/P(t) = W(t) \text{ (for } P(0)=1) \qquad (3.60a)$$
$$1 - \theta = L(t)/P(t) = L(t) \qquad (3.60b)$$

as indicated on the horizontal axis (figure 3.8(a)). That BATC occurs through time is shown by the fact that, for any $\theta(t)$, the shifting $TPP_L(t)$ curve implies that a constant volume of total agricultural output $A(0)$ is maintained. This is just adequate to feed the entire population at the constant consumption standard IRW (shown in figure 3.8(b)).

3.6 Interactions between the Industrial and Agricultural Sectors

While we have studied the labor absorption process (section 3.4) and the labor release process (section 3.5) separately, we want to examine explicitly the simultaneous interaction between the two sectors of the dualistic economy. Since the intersectoral terms of trade $d = p_a/p_i$ regulate all three intersectoral markets, the determination of d is the point of departure for our analysis.

3.6.1 Consumer preference and the intersectoral terms of trade

In the urban sector consumer preference between agricultural goods A and industrial goods Q can be represented by a map of consumer indifference curves postulated for a typical worker in the industrial sector (see figure 3.9). Let p_a and p_i be the prices of the two commodities; then the budget line of the typical urban consumer is given by equation 3.22b which shows that the real wage w_i in terms of industrial goods is spent on the consumption of industrial goods c_i or agricultural goods AAS valued at the terms of trade ($d = p_a/p_i$). When the real wage of the typical urban worker is measured in terms of agricultural goods, the budget line becomes:

$$w_i/d = c_i/d + AAS \qquad (3.61)$$

If we assume no real wage gap between the two sectors (that is, $p_iw_i = p_aw_f$), the real wage of the urban worker in terms of agricultural goods (w_i/d) is regulated by the full real wage (that is, $w_f = w_i/d$) in the agricultural sector. The perfect labor mobility hypothesis (equation 3.19b) implies:

$$w_f = c_i/d + AAS \tag{3.62a}$$
$$AAS = 0 \text{ implies } c_i = dw_f = w_i \text{ (by equation 3.19b)} \tag{3.62b}$$

The budget line (equation 3.62a) is represented by a (negatively sloped) straight line passing through the point w_f shown on the vertical axis. The point of intersection of the budget line with the horizontal axis is w_i, the real wage of industrial workers in terms of industrial goods. When w_f is fixed, the improvement of the terms of trade for the agricultural sector (that is, an increasing d) leads to a system of budget lines "hinged" at the fixed point w_f as w_i increases (that is, $w_i < w_i' < w_i''$).

As the terms of trade vary, the consumption equilibrium points $E, E', E'', \ldots$, trace out a price–consumption curve defined for a fixed value of w_f:

$$h(c_i, AAS, w_f) = 0 \text{ (price–consumption curve)} \tag{3.63a}$$
$$\bar{w}_f = c_i/d + AAS \text{ (budget line)} \tag{3.63b}$$
$$w_i = d\bar{w}_f \text{ (perfect labor mobility)} \tag{3.63c}$$

The price–consumption curve takes on a fixed value $\bar{w}_f$ as a parameter. There are four variables (c_i, w_i, AAS, and d) related in three equations. When AAS is given, the other three variables are determined simultaneously.

In figure 3.9, in order to stress the fact that the country is poor, we have

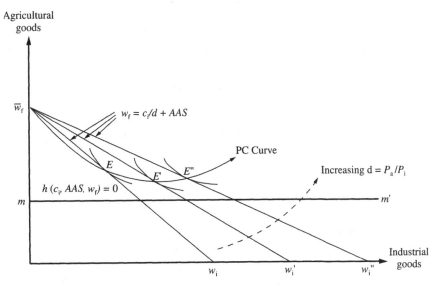

Figure 3.9 Consumer preferences in the two-sector world

postulated a caloric minimum consumption standard represented by the horizontal line mm'. The price–consumption line does not lie far above mm'. This implies that even a slight shortfall of AAS can send the price of food way up and severely worsen the terms of trade of the industrial sector.

3.6.2 Consumption equilibrium and the determination of the terms of trade

To see the impact of the performance of the agricultural sector on the terms of trade, let the price–consumption curve PC be reproduced in figure 3.7(b). This curve begins from the "fixed point" w_f corresponding to the full wage (that is, the sum of IRW and z of equations 3.3a and 3.3b) of a typical agricultural worker which determines the industrial real wage in terms of agricultural goods. Under our simplifying assumption w_f remains fixed as long as there is disguised unemployment (by equation 3.56). If the BATC is sustained through time (in other words, the entire population can always be fed at IRW), then:

$$AAS = IRW \text{ (implied by } c_a = IRW) \tag{3.64}$$

In other words, when the consumption standards are equalized, as ensured by BATC, $AAS = IRW$ (see Lemma 1).

Thus, when the horizontal IRW line of figure 3.7(a) is projected onto figure 3.7(b), the point of intersection with the price–consumption curve at E simultaneously determines the consumption equilibrium point E, the terms of trade d, and the real wage in terms of industrial goods w_i. For only at such a combination (d, w_i, and c_i) will the commodity market clear. The typical industrial worker buys c_i units of industrial goods while buying AAS units of agricultural goods, with the portion of his income ($w_i - c_i = N^0$) at the equilibrium terms of trade d.

Comparing equations 3.25a and 3.22b we see that the real wage in terms of industrial goods (w_i) of the typical industrial worker is partitioned into two types of consumption expenditures:

$$w_i = c_i + N^0 \text{ where} \tag{3.65a}$$
$$N^0 = S_a^0 + Q_a^0 = dAAS \text{ (equation 3.25b)} \tag{3.65b}$$
$$S_a^0 = S_a/W, Q_a^0 = Q_a/W \tag{3.65c}$$

where N^0 ($= dAAS = w_i - c_i$) is the "money" he spends for the purchases of AAS ($= IRW = c_a$) and sends claims against industrial capital stock S_a^0 and modern inputs Q_a^0 back to the agricultural families. The partitioning of N^0 into these components is indicated on the horizontal axis of figure 3.7(b).

3.6.3 Urban–rural interaction through time

The transition growth process of a dualistic economy represents a dynamic general equilibrium system in which outputs (Q, A), inputs $(K, W, T,$ and $L)$, savings (intersectoral S_a and intrasectoral S_i), output allocation $(Q_a$ and Q_i, including farm inputs and incentive consumer goods) and prices $(d = p_a/p_i, w_i,$ and $w_f)$ are determined simultaneously through time. Unlike the "general equilibrium theory" for the industrially advanced countries, however, the agricultural and industrial sectors are not symmetric. For this reason we have separately presented the "labor absorption facet" (Section 3.4) and the "labor release facet" (Section 3.5) of the story. The two facets are now integrated to show the general equilibrium process of interactions between the agricultural and industrial sectors.

To begin with, recall that when the time path of wage rate w_i (that is, the wage rate in terms of industrial goods shown in figure 3.5(d)) with a turning point (a'_τ) is given, we can determine the time path of the industrial labor force $W(t)$ absorbed into the industrial sector. The $W(t)$ time path is derivable from the unlimited supply curve of labor of Arthur Lewis (with a Lewis turning point a_τ in figure 3.5(b)) depicting the labor absorption process as capital accumulation takes place. The triplet of curves $(w_i(t), W(t),$ and the "Lewis supply curve") are reproduced in figures 3.7(d), (c), and (f), with their turning points $(a'_\tau, W_\tau,$ and $E_\tau)$ indicated. While the wage path w_i was postulated exogenously in section 3.4, we must now deduce it as a result of urban–rural interactions.

Referring to figures 3.7(a) and (b), when the condition of BATC is sustained the value of $IRW = AAS = c_a$ (supply of food per unit of labor in the industrial sector) is constant before the turning point is reached. Thus, in Stage I of the "labor release" process the terms of trade d as well as w_i are constant as indicated on the horizontal axis of figure 3.7b which is linked up with the point a'_τ in figure 3.7(d). Thus, the time path of w_i is determined by the time path of IRW and d in Stage I. (In figure 3.7(a), the constant value of IRW is projected by the 45° line or into a time path of $w_a = IRW$ in figure 3.7(c).) Thus, IRW regulates $w_i(t)$ under the assumption of the perfect labor mobility hypothesis (that is, the equality of $w_f d$ and w_i) and the constancy of w_i and the labor absorption analysis under this condition are based on BATC.

The intersectoral commodity market (shown in figure 3.7(b)) can be linked with the "financial aspect" of the labor absorption process shown in figure 3.7(f). At the constant w_i the labor absorbed into the industrial sector is $W(t)$. The partition of the output of the industrial goods into four shares $(Q_a, Q_i, S_a,$ and $S_i)$ is shown in figure 3.5(b). The distribution of total output Q into the profit share S_i and the labor share $(Q_i + Q_a + S_a)$ is determined by the competitive marginal productivity theory (as indicated above). However, the breakdown of the wage bill into its three components has yet to be determined.

The first partition is into Q_i (industrial workers' own consumption of industrial goods) and $Q_a + S_a = N$ (their expenditure on food in terms of industrial goods). On a per industrial worker basis, $Q_i/W = c_i$ and $(Q_a + S_a)/W = N^0$, as shown in figure 3.7(b). This represents an important aspect of the clearing of the intersectoral commodity market. The second partition between the two components of N depends on the choice of rural families with respect to the allocation of their "participation benefit" between Q_a, the two kinds of current expenditures, and S_a, the acquisition of industrial capital.

While the turning point labor force $W(\tau)$ is determined by BATC in the agricultural sector $L(\tau)$, the time required to reach the turning point τ is determined by the rapidity of labor absorption relative to population growth. A faster rate of capital accumulation and labor absorption or lower population growth produces a smaller τ, indicating that the turning point would have arrived earlier, at τ'. We have thus demonstrated the linkages among all three markets in the growth dynamics of a dualistic economy.

3.6.4 The real meaning of an unlimited supply of labor

When Arthur Lewis presented his "unlimited supply of labor curve" it conveyed the impression that it is grounded on the microscopically derived supply curves of labor offered by agricultural households to the non-agricultural sector. Consequently, many agricultural and labor economists have attacked this notion based on econometric investigations of rural household behavior in the Becker tradition.[14] As we hope to have shown, this is clearly a case of mistaken identity.

When the Lewis supply curve is examined in the context of figure 3.7(f) it becomes apparent that it is merely a facet of the operational interactions between the two sectors of the dualistic economy. The Lewis labor absorption path indicated there is derived from the time path of the industrial wage as indicated in figure 3.7(b). While Lewis refers to the labor absorption path as the unlimited supply curve of labor, this really constitutes the locus of various possible combinations of wage rates (w_i) and absorbed labor (W_i) associated with different levels of the industrial capital stock over time. The famous Lewis unlimited supply curve of labor is thus based on the time path of the industrial real wage (with a constant and a rising portion) which can be defended empirically and theoretically at a macro level and is quite irrelevant to the focus of timeless microscopic household studies.

Empirically, the near-constancy of the unskilled industrial real wage over time has been observed historically for England, Japan, etc. (see section 3.4) and was recognized by the classical economists in their discussion of the iron law of wages. The same can be established for contemporary LDCs during their post-World War II transition growth. It is such empirical evidence which sustains the "unlimited supply of labor" hypothesis.

Theoretically, real wage constancy is justified by the notion that the time path of w_i in terms of industrial goods is governed by the time path of w_f in terms of agricultural goods and the terms of trade d. The constancy of w_f is based on the postulation of a "shared" institutional real wage IRW and z near subsistence levels, while the near-constancy of d hinges upon the successful modernization of the agricultural sector – the maintenance of BATC. We see that the near-constancy of the industrial real wage observable through time when the per capita supply of food is nearly constant must be related to the gradual modernization of a traditional agricultural sector via its interactions with non-agriculture. This has little to do with micro models featuring already modern agricultural households maximizing utility when the wage is given.

3.6.5 The determination of the dynamic general equilibrium system

The formal determination of the dynamic general equilibrium system of the dualistic economy is given by the "causal order chart" (figure 3.10) containing two adjacent time points (t and $t + 1$). Let ten variables (K, S_i, N, d, A, w_f, w_i, P, W and L) at time t and the production functions $A = A(L,T,t)$ for agriculture and $Q = f(K,W,t)$ for non-agriculture be shown in Column I. Formally, we want to indicate the causal order for the determination of the same set of variables and functions at time $t + 1$. In this way, the entire system can be determined recursively for all future periods, which is the meaning of "dynamic determinism." (In this chart, the dotted lines and arrows indicate the "determinism" of a particular variable or function labeled 1, 2, ..., 11 to facilitate our discussion of the causal order.)

Intuitively, innovations in both the agricultural and non-agricultural sectors (proxied by changes in the production functions in the causal order chart), is the most difficult to "model" deterministically. Our treatment of innovations in the two sectors is different by deliberate theoretical choice. For the industrial sector we assume that the change of the production function $Q = f(W,K,t)$ is exogenous, implying the postulation of a certain strength (or intensity) and "degree of factor bias" of innovations at each time point.[15] For the agricultural sector, innovations are modeled endogenously and constitute an essential part of our reasoning about the growth process. This deliberate asymmetrical treatment of innovations allows us

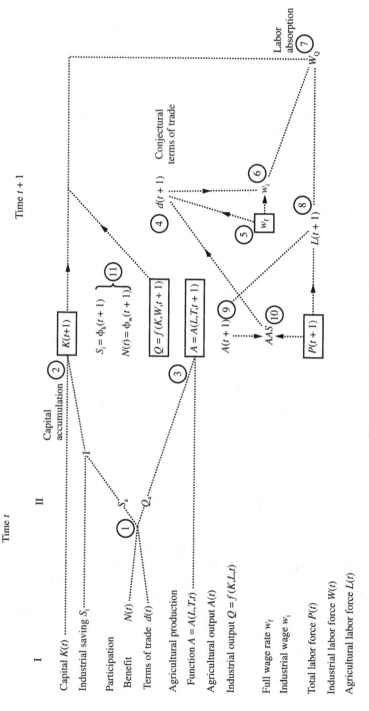

Figure 3.10 Causal order chart

to concentrate more fully on the process of agricultural modernization in the dualistic economy context.

The modernization of the agricultural sector hinges on two types of causative factors – the infusion of modern inputs and the incentive to invest – that raise agricultural labor productivity through time. Heuristically, these causative factors are modeled by two behavioral assumptions of the following type:

$$\partial A/\partial t = A_t(L,T,t) = A_t(L,T,Q_a(t)), \partial A(t)/\partial Q_a(t) > 0 \qquad (3.66a)$$
$$s(t) = s(d(t)) \text{ with } s'(d) < 0 \text{ implying} \qquad (3.66b)$$
$$S_a = s(d)N \text{ and } Q_a = (1 - s(d))N \qquad (3.66c)$$

Equation 3.66a states that "innovation intensity" in agriculture (that is, the extent total output A is increased through time) is determined by the quantity of modern inputs. Thus there is a "technological dimension" to agricultural modernization according to the linkages or contact school.[16] $s(t)$ is the percentage of $N(t)$ used by the agricultural household in the form of acquisition of title to industrial wealth (that is, $S_a = s(t)N$ and $Q_a = 1 - s(t)N$). Equation 3.66b states that $s(t)$ is determined by the intersectoral terms of trade $d = p_a/p_i$ such that the farmer has incentive to invest less via S_a (and spend more on Q_a) when the terms of trade are favorable to the agricultural sector. Thus there is an "incentive" aspect to agricultural modernization stipulated in terms of the spending behavior of the rural families. While there may be many ways to model the endogenous behavior of technology change, we have postulated a simple form in order to show the determination of the division of N into S_a and Q_a causally. As shown in equation 3.66c the pair (S_a, Q_a) are determined once the pair (N, d) are given in the causal chain (1), at time t in the causal order chart.

The determination of S_a (intersectoral finance) together with S_i (intrasectoral finance) leads to non-agricultural investment I and hence capital stock $K(t)$ in the next period. At the same time, the value of $Q_a(t)$ leads to the determination of the production function in the agricultural sector at $t + 1$. These are indicated as the causal chains 2 and 3 respectively for time $t + 1$. Thus, as the beginning of reasoning about the causal order of determination at $t + 1$, we take as given K, P, w_f as well as the two production functions (indicated by the boxes at $t + 1$ in figure 3.10).

Terms of trade $d(t + 1)$ is postulated conjecturally as indicated in causal order (4). When d is so postulated, the industrial real wage w_L is determined (that is, $w_i = dw_f$) as indicated in (6), based on the perfect labor mobility hypothesis (that is, based on the fact that the industrial wage rate w_i is "governed" by the agricultural real wage and the terms of trade). The industrial production function, the capital stock K and w_i serve to determine the industrial labor force W (indicated in (7)) as a result of the labor absorption analysis. With the size of total population P given, the agricultural labor force L that remains is then determined (indicated in (8)). Total agricultural output A is determined by the agricultural production function and L (indicated in (9)). We can determine the AAS by P and A (indicated in (10)). The value of AAS then determines the intersectoral terms of trade d as a result of clearance of the intersectoral commodity market. We see that only a correctly postulated d leads to a determination of its equilibrium value. This implies that the entire system of magnitudes (d, w_i, L, A, AAS) is determined simultaneously in $t + 1$.[17]

Since we have shown the causal determination of $K(t + 1)$ and $W(t + 1)$, the exogenously postulated industrial production function at $t + 1$ leads to the determination of the distributive share S_i (the industrial profit share) and the wage share R by the competitive principle of income distribution as an aspect of our labor absorption analysis. The consumption equilibrium of urban workers leads to the determination of the value of $N(t)$ (that is, the expenditures of industrial workers on food) as indicated in (11). The reader can check that all the values indicated in column (1) at time t are determined for time $t + 1$. Thus, the dynamic system is formally determined.

3.6.6 Comparative dynamics

We have shown that the growth path (containing a system of endogenous variables) can be formally determined once the exogenous variables – the population growth path $P(t)$ and the full wage rate w_f as well as exogenous innovation behavior (for the industrial sector) and the endogenous innovation behavior (for agriculture) – are postulated. There are many possible types of growth paths. Formally, comparative dynamic analysis is the classification of the growth path in respect to certain "essential characteristics" to show the impact of the variation in the exogenously postulated conditions. We may ask, for example, what happens to the growth path if the population growth rate is higher, if industrial technology change is weaker, or if agricultural output $A(t)$ fails to respond sensitively to the infusion of modern inputs.

We have taken η_θ (rapidity of increase of θ) as the most important "index of performance" of development in the dualistic economy. Figure 3.11 shows the alternative time paths of θ that may show cases of "failure" (θ decreases through time), "stagnation" ($\theta = \bar{\theta}$) or "success" (θ increases through time). In the case of success, θ may increase more (θ') or less rapidly (θ) so that the turning point (that is, when $1 - \theta(\tau) = \phi_T(\tau)$ – the rent share in the agricultural sector – may be reached sooner (τ') or later (τ). Thus, in the classification of growth paths, we may concentrate on the time profile of θ. In particular, we want some idea about the impact of

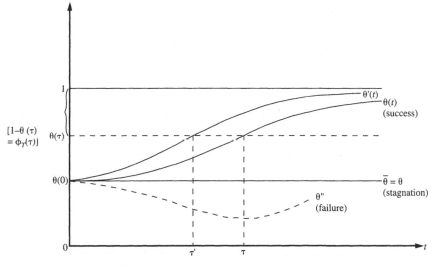

Figure 3.11 Comparative dynamics

variations in the exogenously postulated conditions on the rapidity and direction of changes in θ.

Heuristically, we first inquire what conditions must be fulfilled if the condition of BATC is to be met persistently through time in order to sustain an adequate and constant per capita consumption standard for food, $IRW = c_a$. From our causal order analysis we see that at each point in time, the agricultural production function (determined at causal order (3)) must be increased sufficiently so that the *AAS* (determined at causal order (10)) can be sustained at a constant level. To meet this condition, agricultural innovations must be sufficiently sensitive to the infusion of modern inputs and investment goods (discussed at causal order (1)). The strength of agricultural innovations must be greater the faster the population growth rate, because the value of *AAS* is determined by the population (indicated in causal order (10)). Thus, the faster the population growth rate, the higher the strength of agricultural innovation must be if BATC is to be met.

Meeting the BATC condition does not necessarily guarantee success in the sense of sustained increases in θ. θ can increase at a faster or slower pace (and may even decline) depending upon the rapidity of labor absorption. As analyzed in the causal order chain (7), when the industrial wage rate is constant the rate of labor absorption is faster when the capital stock $K(t+1)$ is larger and/or when the strength of innovation in the industrial sector and its labor-using bias are higher. The size of the capital stock $K(t+1)$, in turn, depends upon the intersectoral and intrasectoral finance that can be traced to the innovation intensity in the industrial sector that determines the absolute magnitudes of both S_a and Q_a. It follows that, even if BATC is met, θ can increase at a faster or slower rate (or not even increase at all) depending on the innovation intensity in the industrial sector.

There is the possibility that the growth path is characterized by a miserable performance in "agricultural innovation" such as that the per capita supply of food cannot even be sustained at a constant level. The appearance of a food gap (shown in figure 3.7(a)) implies that the per capita consumption standard cannot be sustained for the urban population. The consumption equilibrium point shifts from E to E' in figure 3.7(b), leading to a "drastic" worsening of the terms of trade for the industrial sector and an increase of the industrial real wage (from $\bar{w}_i$ to $\bar{w}'_i$ in figure 3.7(b)). This "food crisis" sets off chain reactions that slow down the labor absorption process for several reasons. First, less labor is absorbed because the industrial real wage is higher. Second, intrasectoral finance decreases because the profit share declines. Third, intersectoral finance decreases because the farmers spend relatively more on Q_a (and less on S_a) as induced by the more favorable terms of trade. The failure to maintain an adequate food supply on a per capita basis is a state of affairs that cannot be sustained very long if the consumption standard is close to the caloric minimum survival level. In a closed economy mass starvation may occur as skyrocketing food prices rule out continued even modest rates of labor absorption by the industrial sector.

Finally, it should be recognized that the constancy of the time path of w_i under BATC (in figure 3.7(b)) represents an idealized approximation in the trendal sense. In reality there are likely to be short-run fluctuations around that trend. For example, a temporary agricultural short-fall (food gap) would result in a temporary increase in d and w_i. This, in turn, would lead to a slowdown in θ. Conversely, a temporary glut in food (due to an above average monsoon) would have the opposite effect. Such deviation from "balance" in either direction would be self-correcting if the rural population is sensitive to changes in the terms of trade.

3.6.7 Market orientation and the atrophy of traditional Z-goods production

One manifestation of the modernization of the agricultural sector is the atrophy of traditional Z-goods production as non-cash crop and non-agricultural production is abandoned in the course of the transition growth process. With the disappearance of production for self-sufficiency, the rural sector becomes completely marketized and monetized. This trend is especially pronounced after the "reversal point" when the agricultural labor force declines absolutely (see figure 3.2) and continues as the system's disguised unemployed are absorbed. Traditional Z-goods activities are abandoned as peasants become more market-oriented and view the agricultural labor force as a scarce factor.

The abandonment of these traditional Z-goods activities implies that the consumption pattern of the rural population changes. While at the beginning of the process the per capita consumption of modern consumer goods (such as textiles) can be expected to be much lower in the rural than the urban sector, the former is likely to be urbanized as a consequence of increased contact and converges to the behavior of the industrial sector.

The abandonment of Z-goods by the rural families and their replacement by "modern textiles" is a family decision closely related to the non-commercialized principle of income distribution via the sharing nexus of the rural families. Refer to figure 3.8(a) in which the vertical gap between the p curve and the horizontal IRW line is the family cash income in terms of agricultural goods per unit of labor. It is partitioned into S_a and Q_a, or, on a per worker basis, in terms of agricultural goods into $S_a N^*/d$ and $S_q N^*/d$. The second component can be partitioned into $v(t)$, the per worker consumption of industrial goods valued in terms of agricultural goods, and $S_q N^*/d - v(t)$, the modern inputs into agriculture. We can define:

$$w_a' = IRW + v(t) \qquad (3.67)$$

representing the value of consumption in terms of agricultural goods of a typical rural worker. We refer to w_a' as the rural real wage. w_a' represents the "monetized value of consumption" because both IRW and $v(t)$ have a monetized value. In figure 3.12, the p curve of figure 3.8(a) is reproduced and the value of w_a' is represented by the mUE' curve. The value of $v(t)$ is then the vertical gap between the w_a' curve and the horizontal IRW line.

The fact that $v(t)$ increases through time is basically a family decision to allow its members to consume more modern textiles through time. This increased "consumption orientation" of the rural families has two elements of significance. On the one hand, it represents the "incentive effect" in operation, as it is the anticipation of such an increase in $v(t)$ that motivates the family to search for innovations to raise agricultural productivity. On the other hand, the increase of $v(t)$ means that Z-goods are replaced by modern consumer goods. In this diagram the atrophy of Z is indicated by the diminution of the shaded vertical gap until a point L_U is reached where a typical rural worker has the same consumption habits as a typical industrial worker. At such a point the "money wages" of both sectors are completely equalized.

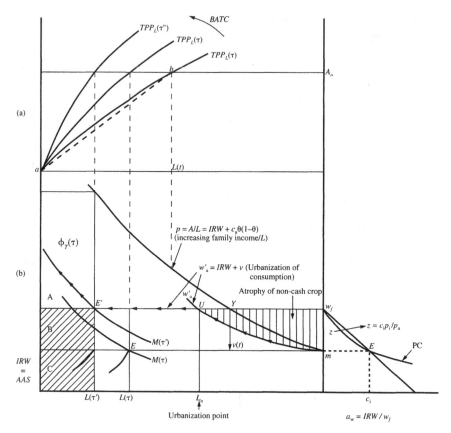

Figure 3.12 Urbanization of rural consumption patterns

There may still be disguised unemployment at such a point, where $w'_a = L_U$ is still greater than the marginal productivity of labor in the agricultural sector. Thus w'_a tends to be stable after the "urbanization point" is reached – as it is possible, but most unlikely, that the monetized real wage w'_a for rural labor increases significantly as long as disguised unemployment prevails. Thus, the real wage remains approximately constant until the turning point E' is reached where w'_a equals the marginal product of the agricultural labor force.

We have arrived at the conclusion in an earlier section that when the turning point arrives, the fraction of the total labor force allocated to the industrial sector $\theta(\tau)$ equals in magnitude the competitive rent share $\phi_T(\tau)$ in the agricultural sector. However, when we take into consideration the phenomenon of the urbanization of the consumption pattern, this conclusion must be slightly modified. When the turning point E' arrives, total agricultural output is partitioned into three parts, A, B, and C, represented by the various areas under the marginal productivity of labor curve $M(\tau)$. $A = \phi_T(\tau)$ is the economic rent share and $B + C = \phi_L(\tau)$ is the wage share of which C is the amount of food consumed by the agricultural labor force. Thus, the food consumed by the urban labor force is $A + B$. The ratio $u = B/(B + C)$ is the percentage of wage income of the typical worker that is being spent on industrial goods, and the turning point industrial labor force is $\theta(\tau) = (A + B)/(A + B + C)$ which is the same as the percentage of total agricultural goods consumed by the rural labor force. This is due to the fact that consumption patterns are completely equalized between the two sectors:

$$\theta(\tau) \qquad = \phi_T(\tau) + \phi_L(\tau)u \quad \text{where} \tag{3.68a}$$

$$u \qquad = B/(B + C) \qquad \text{(fraction of consumer} \tag{3.68a}$$
$$\text{expenditures on industrial goods)}$$

Proof: $\theta(\tau) = (A + B)/(A + B + C) = \phi_T(\tau) + B/(A + B + C)$
$\qquad\qquad = \phi_T + (B/(B + c))/(A + B + C) = \phi_T(\tau) + u\phi_L(\tau)$.

The turning point industrial labor force is larger than the economic rent share by the amount $\phi_L(\tau)u$. As a numerical example, $\phi_T(\tau) = 1/3$ and $\phi_L = 2/3$ are reasonable magnitudes. Moreover, u is usually a relatively small number, as the lion's share of household expenditures is on food. Suppose $u = 2$. Then the value of $\theta(0)$ takes on an order of magnitude of 0.46. In other words, the real wage increases once the labor allocation fraction reaches 46 percent, a fact which can be statistically verified.

When we take into consideration the phenomenon of the urbanization of the consumption pattern, we can soften the rigid constancy of the industrial real wage w_i assumption before the turning point is reached. In the real world the industrial real wage is likely to creep up slowly before the turning point, only to be followed by a more rapid increase when the turning point arrives. Since the industrial real wage w_i is governed by the agricultural real wage w'_a, the upward creep of w'_a is ultimately an institutional phenomenon traced in part to the urbanization of the consumption pattern. This transformation of the consumption pattern of rural families is an institutional phenomenon which defies spurious maximization calculations which become relevant only after commercialization.

Another reason why there may be an upward creep in w_i before the turning point is reached is the fact that families may allow their members to increase the consumption of food as agricultural productivity rises. At any point in time $w_f = IRW + Z + v(t)$. w_f may, therefore, increase over time for two reasons. While Z is likely to fall and $v(t)$ is likely to increase, the sharing consensus of families, especially if the initial IRW is near subsistence, may lead to a gradual rise in IRW over time. When an upwardly creeping exogenously postulated w_f is substituted for the constant version in the causal order of figure 3.10, the industrial real wage w_i increases (causal order (6)), leading *ceteris paribus* to a delay in the advent of the turning point.

APPENDIX
THE MICROECONOMICS OF "SURPLUS LABOR"

A3.1 Introduction

Chapter 3 raises the issue of the microeconomics of surplus labor, a question that remains unresolved in the development literature. With unskilled rural labor the abundant resource in almost all developing countries – especially at the early stages of development – what determines the price of labor has been a consistently controversial issue. Though the problem has been extensively analyzed, there is still no consensus. Economists in the classical tradition adhere to the notion of "surplus labor" – the presence of disguised unemployment – with wages determined institutionally in a bargaining context. In contrast, neoclassical economists accept the concept of competitive, well-functioning labor markets – they see labor markets clearing and labor supply decisions grounded in individuals' solution to the utility maximization problem based on a labor/leisure trade-off.

In this appendix, we examine these two views and try to determine whether they are mutually exclusive, as the neoclassical school claims, or if they can be reconciled. We focus on rural labor markets and real wages in the context of the model presented in chapter 3 (section A3.2). We then examine the neoclassical evidence brought to bear against the labor surplus model and evaluate their position as we understand it on its own merits (section A3.3). Section A3.4 presents our theoretical response to their critique. Section A3.5 contains empirical evidence to aid the evaluation of these two apparently contradictory views and defends the institutional wage hypothesis adhered to in this volume. Finally, in section A3.6 we attempt to reconcile some of the apparent differences.

A3.2 Our View

Our analysis of the labor surplus economy is based on the dualistic model of development presented in chapter 3. A main feature of that model is that there exists initial heterogeneity between commercialized (or modern) and non-commercialized (or traditional) sectors of the economy[18] in terms of both production and organization.[19] This heterogeneity manifests itself in a relative initial "overabundance" of the rural population given fixed land and leading to the absence of labor market clearance in the traditional sector; hence a labor surplus economy. The empirical reality is consistent with this theoretical construct since up to 80 percent of the labor force in developing nations is initially located in the traditional sector. Dualism is a dynamic concept, with technological change and non-agricultural capital accumulation the basic ingredients underlying a balanced growth process, and we are interested in the interaction of the two sectors over time in an (initially) closed economy context.

The defining characteristic of the traditional sector is that the output is jointly generated by the farm family, village, or commune. Given a large labor supply relative to the fixed available land, a neoclassical wage equal to the marginal product of labor is not able to satisfy subsistence or institutional requirements, a facet of traditional sharing arrangements. With labor inputs given at the outset – not fixed – an equilibrium or competitive wage is not realized. In other words, an institutional wage above the very low or even zero marginal product of labor may be necessary to meet subsistence requirements. This institutional real wage emphatically does not imply that labor is totally redundant (that is, of zero marginal product), only that some individuals receive a return in excess of their low marginal product. This wage, in a sector where household and production activities are fused and where individuals cannot be dismissed, is therefore not based on the normal tenets of economic analysis but on sharing conventions, social attitudes, subsistence requirements, and bargaining. It serves as a proxy for a consumption or income standard that determines the price of labor.

Since, by definition, an institutional wage cannot be derived analytically from first principles, it is not satisfying to most economists. However, historical evidence pointing to an only slightly rising real wage in the traditional sector over time, even during periods of rapidly increasing agricultural labor productivity, is a reality. There exists both economic and anthropological evidence supporting such an institutional wage. The neoclassical commercialized sector's wage is tied to the traditional sector's institutional wage as long as the labor surplus condition persists. As seen in the body of the chapter, a goal of development becomes achieving the end of that condition via the reallocation of labor over time. This implies the need for synchronized investment and innovative efforts in the two sectors to achieve balanced growth at a pace which exceeds the rate of population growth – which can be thought of as simultaneously adding to the labor surplus. In time, dualism consequently disappears as the traditional sector loses its characteristic labor surplus condition and converges toward the homogeneous one-sector neoclassical model.

The central issue we analyze in chapter 3 is the nature and speed of the convergence to the conventional one-sector neoclassical "equilibrium" when the initial conditions yield the dualistic system just described. The adjustment process is, at any rate, clearly not instantaneous because "surplus labor" from the traditional sector can only be gradually reallocated into alternative employment in the commercialized sector, where it is able to make a larger contribution to aggregate output. This stands in sharp contrast to the neoclassical instantaneous adjustment process with labor markets clearing in both sectors and wages moving in step with marginal productivity. As we show, the historical evidence is inconsistent with this neoclassical posture.

By definition, market clearing wages obtain in the commercialized sector, with the unskilled real wage tied to the traditional sector's institutional real wage at some premium reflecting the necessary inducement to move, possibly including an additional "gap" due to other government interventions (for example, minimum wage legislation) in the organized labor market.

Given this framework, figure A3.1 illustrates the basic labor reallocation process. Assuming an initial endowment L' of labor initially "in place" in agriculture at the institutional wage w with MP_L the marginal product of labor. The portion $(L'' - L')$ of the labor force whose marginal product is below the institutional wage is the underemployed or disguisedly unemployed. The so-called "unlimited" supply of labor to the commercialized sector is drawn from this segment and it is the reallocation of such labor to the commercialized sector over time that represents the ultimate transition to neoclassical equilibrium.

As more labor is demanded by the commercialized sector – due to the twin forces of capital accumulation and technological change – and as the productivity of workers remaining in the traditional sector rises – due primarily to technological change – the pool of individuals in the traditional sector paid a wage above their marginal product shrinks.[20] Agricultural productivity rises as the marginal product of labor curve shifts to the right $(MP_L$ to MP_L' to $MP_L'')$ as simultaneously labor demand by the commercialized sector shifts labor quantity still in place to the left $(ALS$ to ALS' to $ALS'')$ until all of the disguisedly unemployed are "squeezed out" (at A). Such a balanced growth process terminates when commercialization is achieved – when the wage equals the marginal product of labor – at A for a given population, indicating that the remaining agricultural workers (OL^*) are fully commercialized. The disguised unemployed have been fully "squeezed out" and labor markets in both sectors behave in a neoclassical fashion. Supply curves are upward-sloping as wages rise to induce

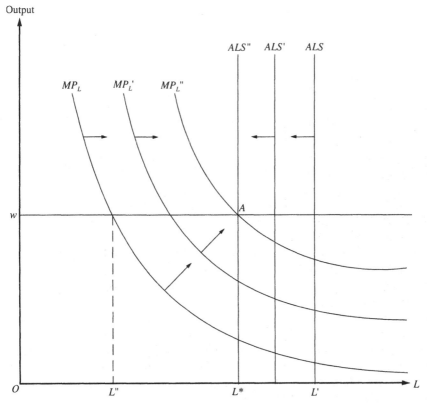

Figure A3.1 Transition process

individuals to change jobs or to offer additional hours, and the factor pay-ment/marginal product divergence noted above no longer exists.

The most important point to emphasize is that this story is not based on a static, timeless model focused on the microscopic labor supply curve depicting an individual family's response to variations in the real wage. Instead, it is a long-run, dynamic picture, with the demand for labor by the developing commercialized sector interacting with an exogenous – though not necessarily constant – unskilled wage to determine the rate of labor reallocation. As pointed out in chapter 3, whether or not labor surplus gives way to labor scarcity depends on the strength of the balanced growth process relative to the population growth rate. It is a process likely to play itself out over several decades of an LDC's transition growth effort.

A3.3 The Neoclassical Challenge

The neoclassical school, represented most ably by Rosenzweig (1988), finds it difficult to accept the notion of an institutional or bargaining wage. The theoretical objection is that, by definition, an institutional wage cannot be derived from axiomatic first principles employing the usual machinery of economics. Moreover, it is claimed that econometric evidence implementing the Becker tradition of household economics contradicts our conclusions. Such studies, however, are not focused on the aggregate supply of labor available to the commercialized sector over time. Instead, they focus on the comparative statistics of the individual rural household's consumption and production decisions, using the theory of rational choice and microeconomic data. By solving the utility maximization problem for each household under market-clearing assumptions, an equilibrium solution can be found which traces out individual or individual family labor supply, which can then be aggregated with that of others. This is a perfectly legitimate approach but, as we try to show, is addressed to a problem different from ours.

Rosenzweig presents the basic neoclassical model applicable to the analysis of LDC rural labor markets. He assumes individual households of n members, N of whom work, with a single family welfare function and a fixed amount of land from which the family realizes a return when it is worked. With family agricultural production (A) a function of labor hours (L) and land (T):[21]

$$A = \text{family agricultural output} = f(L,T) \ (F_L > 0, F_T > 0,$$
$$F_{LL} < 0, F_{TT} < 0) \tag{A3.1}$$

Each family maximizes a neoclassical utility function of consumption and leisure:

$$U = U(c,l) \quad \text{where } c = \text{consumption} = A/n \text{ and } l = \text{leisure.} \tag{A3.2}$$

Rosenzweig's empirical analysis of rural labor markets concludes that the usual assumptions on preferences and the marginal disutility of labor yield an upward-sloping (not a horizontal) labor supply curve. Given variations in the real wage, family labor supply can thus be expected to vary according to standard comparative static analysis and demonstrate the inelasticity of the agricultural labor supply curve. Rosenzweig (1988), Lau, Lin, and Yotopoulos (1978), and Adulavidhya et al. (1979) have found such a curve to be quite inelastic in a variety of developing countries – including India, Taiwan, and Thailand – based on a unitary elasticity between income and leisure. Barnum and Squire (1978) along with Straus (1983) also found an inelastic labor supply curve for countries in Africa and Asia even when the assumed income–leisure elasticity differed from one. It is such inelasticity of the individual labor supply curve yielded by microeconomic evidence that has led neoclassical economists to reject the institutional wage/surplus labor hypotheses. However, the existence of an inelastic microscopic labor supply curve within a labor surplus economy is quite plausible, as we shall see.

A3.4 Our Response

An inelastic labor supply response to a wage change at the individual family level at a point in time not only can be explained within the neoclassical paradigm but is not necessarily inconsistent with the classical position of an only slowly rising agricultural labor supply curve composed of a series of horizontal step functions over time. In order to reconcile these two apparently contradictory perceptions, we raise the question whether at an early stage of the development process, with a large percentage of the rural population living near subsistence levels, the concept of leisure via the application of the marginal disutility of labor as a labor supply determinant is likely to be a relevant criterion. As Booth and Sundrum (1985, p. 245) have pointed out, "most rural laborers in LDCs are desperately poor and are not inclined to reject any chance of extra employment in favor of leisure;" they are unlikely to exhibit the high preference for leisure necessary to account for the substantial unemployment documented in developing nations. The neoclassical mainstream recognize this for the case of landless workers, but maintain the existence of a positive income–leisure trade-off for landed families. In reality, even landed families near the subsistence level can be expected to supply close to the maximum number of labor hours possible to ensure survival.

With heterogeneous land ownership, the population of any LDC's traditional sector can be partitioned into three classes: large landowners who work their own land and hire labor, small landowners who work their own land and sell some of their labor, and landless workers who sell all of their labor in the rural labor market. Figure A3.2 illustrates individual family labor supply equilibria for each of the three classes of families with a given real wage. There are two distinct equilibria represented in figure A3.2: point E, the own-land production equilibria, and point J, the individual/family work-leisure equilibria. Landless families have only the J equilibrium to worry about. A change in these equilibria in response to a higher wage is depicted by the shift from line w to w' with a steeper slope. For a given total product curve (TP), a rise in the real wage from w to w' changes both equilibria to E' and J'. From this, the labor demand curve

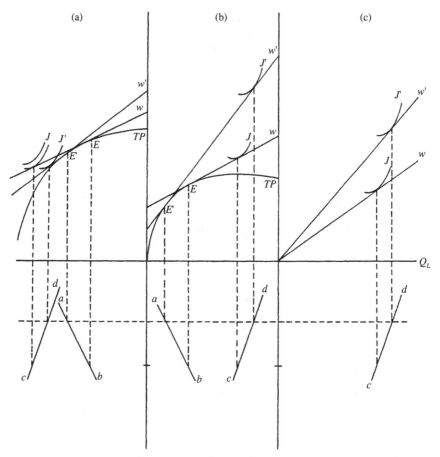

Figure A3.2 Household labor supply – fixed land

for own-land production (*ab*) in the lower deck and the individual/family labor supply curve to the market (*cd*) are generated for each type of family. Since individuals are assumed to be near their labor supply constraint, the increase in the quantity of labor supplied is slight and an econometrically measured labor supply response to a wage change across multiple individuals/families is likely to be inelastic. The point is most clear for landless workers who do not experience an income effect.

Figure A3.3 illustrates the own-land equilibrium labor demand in the converse situation: a constant wage and varying quantities of land affecting the *TP* curve. At the prevailing wage each tangency with the total product curve represents own-land labor deployment. The locus of

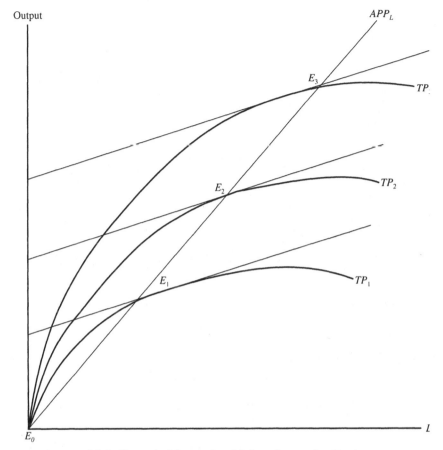

*Figure A3.3 Household own-land labor demand – fixed wage,
differing land*

tangencies in figure A3.3, depicting total product and quantity of labor combinations, traces out a constant average physical product of labor curve at the given wage.

Figure A3.4 combines both own-land demand and total labor supply at a given wage with heterogeneous-sized land ownership. More land implies both additional labor needed for own land cultivation and a higher rental income. Both the points E equilibria, the own-land production equilibrium, and the points J equilibria, the individual/family work-leisure equilibrium, are represented in this graph for households of different-sized land holdings. The locus of all work-leisure equilibria, comprising a cross-section of the agricultural population, traces out the aggregate income–consumption $(y-c)$ curve at the prevailing wage. Families who

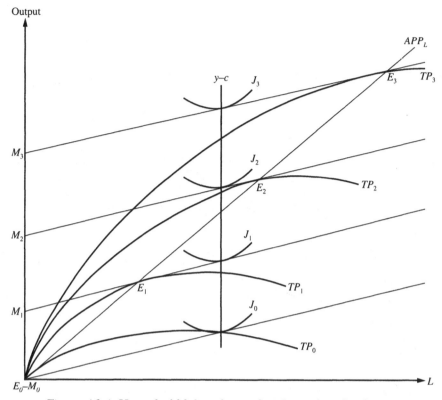

Figure A3.4 Household labor demand and supply – fixed wage, differing land size

demand additional labor to work their land have own-land labor supply equilibria positioned to the right of the $y - c$ curve, while families who sell their labor on the market have own-land labor supply equilibria located to the left of the $y{-}c$ curve.

If we now permit the wage rate to change, maintaining the heterogeneity of land ownership assumption, the APP_L curve, tracing out the E equilibria, shifts to the left and the $y{-}c$ curve, tracing out the J equilibria, shifts to the right, as illustrated in figure A3.4. In a relatively poor developing economy we assume that the $y{-}c$ curves have their origin near the subsistence level, where the labor/leisure indifference map is flat. For each wage, the intersection of the relevant APP_L curve with the relevant $y{-}c$ curve determines the actual quantity of labor supplied in rural labor markets. As demonstrated by the LS curve in figure A3.5, the locus of all such

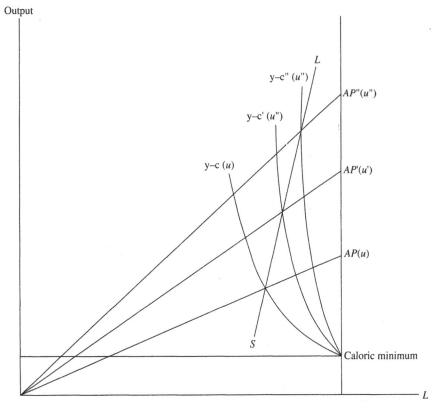

Figure A3.5 Aggregate labor supply curve

intersections, based on the own-land and work-leisure equilibria generated, traces the aggregate labor supply curve. This curve is likely to be
quite inelastic.

We should therefore not be surprised by Rosenzweig's India findings.
We expect inelastic individual family labor supply responses at a point in
time not only from landless families, as Rosenzweig himself acknowledges,
but from landed families as well. This by no means invalidates our labor
surplus hypothesis, which addresses a fundamentally different question.
The above neoclassical analysis is concerned with the comparative static
response of individual households to wage changes. Our problem is one of
tracing dynamic labor supply paths at the aggregate level. We hope to
show, moreover, that the empirical realities are consistent with our explanation of balanced growth in the successful dualistic economy context.

A3.5 Empirical Evidence

Before reviewing the historical evidence from some successful balanced growth cases, it is necessary to recall that our model implies neither a strictly constant real wage as has been asserted by Papanek (1990) nor a zero marginal product of labor as referred to by Rosenzweig (1988). As agricultural labor productivity rises over time, there is likely to be some upward creep in the institutional real wage. The time path of the agricultural real wage is more likely to approximate a step function, implying a statistically gently upward-sloping path until the Lewis turning-point is reached. The important point is that there exists an institutional wage above the very low marginal product of labor and that this wage rises only slowly via institutional wage adjustments and lags substantially behind the agricultural productivity increases.

If agricultural real wages and unskilled non-agricultural wages tied to them are found to lag markedly behind rising agricultural labor productivity change, then this pattern clearly supports the classical time-phased view. It certainly does not support the neoclassical position of continuous market clearance.

Figures A3.6 and A3.7 present indices of the real wage and the marginal product of labor in the agricultural sectors of Taiwan and Japan during their well-known successful periods of transition.[22] The indices, normalized to begin at the same point, unambiguously illustrate that in both nations the marginal product of labor in agriculture rose significantly faster than the real wage.

Williamson (1989) presents additional evidence based on historical data from the now developed countries. He shows that during the Industrial Revolution in Britain, the real wage was constant for nearly 40 years, with a commercialized/traditional wage gap of about 2 to 1. The observed phenomenon of rising agricultural productivity and nearly constant real wages after the Enclosure Movement represents additional supportive evidence. Williamson also comments that "[Lewis was] right in viewing the rural sector as an 'industrial labor reserve' such that the urban sector could draw on rural labor supplies during expansion." On a more disaggregated level, Huang (1971) analyzed 1960s data in Malaysia at the province level. He found that in three separate regions the marginal product of family labor rose significantly faster than the real wage and that the wage/marginal product gap was only reduced later with the approach of commercialization. Huang's results are consistent with the initial existence of disguised unemployment and the ultimate equalization of the wage and marginal product when the economy approaches a one-sector neoclassical equilibrium.

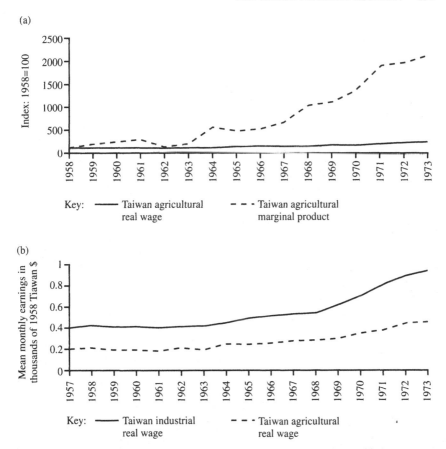

Figure A3.6 Taiwan: real wage and marginal product of labor

Sources: Data for Taiwan was obtained from the UN Food and Agricultural Office (1955–87), the UN Statistical Yearbooks, Ranis (1995a), *Taiwan Statistical Data Books*, *Taiwan Demography*, and *Taiwan Monthly Statistics*.

Along with these trends in labor productivity and wages, other supportive evidence may be cited. One such is concerned with measuring surplus labor in terms of un- or under-employment. Mehra (1966), by estimating the potential number of employment hours available in agriculture and comparing it to actual hours worked and the hours required given prevailing production techniques, found a 17 percent agricultural labor surplus in India. Turnham and Jaeger (1971) found 17.2 percent of rural Thai labor to be surplus in 1971–72 according to the income approach to unemployment based on productivity relative to remuneration.

Another set of empirical evidence rests on analyzing people's willingness to supply additional labor. Sanghui (1969) found that 28 percent of Indian

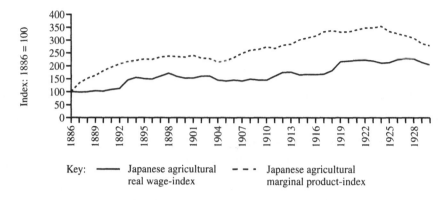

Key: ——— Japanese agricultural   – – – Japanese agricultural
        real wage-index   marginal product-index

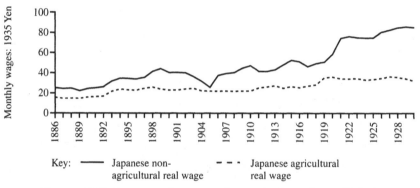

Key: ——— Japanese non-   – – – Japanese agricultural
        agricultural real wage   real wage

Figure A3.7 Japan: real wage and marginal product of labor
Sources: Data for Japan was obtained from Minami (1968)

unskilled male labor in agriculture could be considered "surplus" since male casual workers desired to supply, on average, 28.9 days of labor a month but in reality were able to work only 24.1 days a month. Raj Krishna (1973) and Ahuja (1978) found that at the prevailing wage over 13 percent of the Indian agricultural population was willing to work additional hours. Booth and Sundrum (1985) cite Indonesian government statistics illustrating that in the 1970s the Indonesian agricultural labor force had over 20 percent of its members either unemployed and looking for work or working part time and willing to work more at the present wage.

It will also be useful to relate the results of two studies of Egypt as a labor surplus economy. Hansen (1969) used extensive government survey data from Egypt to conclude that surplus labor was absent, with unemployment near 5 percent and ample work opportunities. He also showed that real wage constancy did not exist, as there was substantial variation in the daily wage in agriculture. However, Hanson (1971) examined the same dataset and argued that Hansen's conclusion of absent surplus labor was erroneous and incorrectly based on Western standards, specifically an eight-hour workday. Adjusting for the seasonality of agricultural production processes, he found that substantial surplus labor was present (especially in the slack season) and that there were few outside work opportunities, thus rendering the labor/leisure trade-off irrelevant and unemployment not voluntary. Hansen's econometric results, which he claimed contradicted the idea of real wage constancy over time, were consistent with a constant hourly wage, where the source of observed wage income variability is the fluctuation in the hours of employment during the peak and slack seasons.

Finally, while most economists are understandably reluctant to venture beyond customary disciplinary boundaries, there is real evidence emanating from anthropological and sociological sources supporting the notion of a bargaining wage at an early stage of the development process. For example, Ishikawa (1975, 1981), a long-time astute observer of Asian economic development, applies the theory of the minimum subsistence level of existence (hereafter MSL) based on an institutional real wage. His theory parallels ours by focusing on the transition process in which "the state of the [traditional] economy's underdevelopment changes in the direction of a more developed market economy." With families in developing nations grouped into distinct economic classes, a large class can be characterized as MSL, which implies income and consumption at the MSL level and some uncertainty about the ability to maintain MSL. The actual concept of MSL includes the minimum means necessary for existence – food, clothing, shelter – along with the means to acquire some minimum standard of "human capabilities" in a socioeconomic sense, including education, basic social abilities, and job skills. Ishikawa documents "a desire of the people in an agricultural society jointly to secure a minimum subsistence level of living" for all individuals (p. 457), a behavior not consistent with the simple version of consumer behavior based on individual utility maximization.

The application of this theory concerns labor supply as a function of wages over a dynamic time path. In a dualistic model with a fixed land quantity, individuals will not supply labor to the commercialized sector at a wage below w, the MSL wage, since prolonged work at a lower wage will not allow the individual to "stay" in the market. Hence real wages in this sector are downwardly rigid at w. This implies a horizontal labor supply curve until all individuals are employed at w. At this point the labor market behaves neoclassically, with a rising wage necessary to induce additional supplies of labor. Upon complete commercialization of both sectors, the MSL wage disappears and the market principle of employment and income distribution replaces the community principle of employment and income distribution.

Ishikawa finds that empirical evidence for Asia as a whole indicates the prevalence of "a community principle of employment and income distribution which promises all MSL families in the community employment, with an income not less than MSL" (p. 474). In pre-war Japan, all working villagers, regardless of social position, were "assured a means of maintaining their livelihood" (p. 465). Pre-Communist Chinese villages "performed important functions in sustaining the economic life of its member families via group management/relief and by providing cooperative public goods" (p. 467). Finally, in India, landowners "were obliged to provide at least a minimum of subsistence to dependent families" (p. 471).

In other studies, Hayami and Kikuchi (1982) found that in Indonesia, "wages do not adjust on the basis of labor's marginal product, but according to subsistence requirements of the time and social conventions" (p. 217). Only over time is there a tendency to adjust towards the neoclassical equilibrium.[23] Scott (1976, p. 41) also documents that most Asian villages have "informal social controls in existence which assure that the minimum needs of all individuals are met."

The transition process *en route* to full commercialization is thus observed to be strongly influenced by something like the MSL concept. As an economy develops, increasingly strong competitive pressures force changes in the prevailing institutions and the ultimate breakdown of the non-commercialized sector. While the notion of an institutional wage may be troubling to some economists, the empirical reality of its existence and validity in the developing world is difficult to deny.

A3.6 Conclusion

We have no inherent conflict with the neoclassical view of LDC agricultural labor markets at the static, microscopic level since our model focuses on dynamic time paths at the macro-level. However, neoclassical economists have taken issue with our results and have rendered the accuracy of the two views of the world mutually exclusive. This appendix is not meant to uphold our position by invalidating the neoclassical model. Rather, it is our intent to demonstrate that we are talking about two different issues. Rosenzweig's empirical findings are inherently reasonable given the normal neoclassical machinery, especially when the individual family's leisure/work trade-off is viewed in its proper LDC perspective. But they are not applicable to our view of an institutional real wage as part of the dynamic transition growth analysis of the dualistic economy.

CHAPTER 3   DEVELOPMENT OF THE CLOSED ECONOMY: A BIRD'S EYE VIEW

NOTES

1   In this chapter we refer to Q_a as the modern input that carries modern science and technology as it flows into the agricultural sector.

2   Given our simplifying assumption that K is deployed only in the non-agricultural sector.

3   Kaldor (1956).

4   Dividing equation 3.1b by L, agricultural labor productivity is $A/L = w_a + TAS/L$, i.e., the sum of IRW and family command over non-agricultural goods per unit of agricultural labor. Thus, the consumption standard of the rural worker is really the sum of IRW and the portion of TAS/L which represents industrial consumer goods acquired in the intersectoral commodities market.

5   In anticipation of our analysis of growth we use η_x to denote the growth rate of any time series $x(t)$ defined as

$$\eta_x = (dx/dt)/x$$

Thus $x(t)$ is the percentage increase of x per unit of time. An elementary well-known theorem applying to growth rates may then be stated as follows.

Let $x(t)$, $y(t)$, and $z(t)$ be three time paths; then

$$
\begin{aligned}
z = x/y \quad &\text{implies } \eta_z = \eta_x - \eta_y \\
z = xy \quad &\text{implies } \eta_z = \eta_x + \eta_y \\
z = x + y \quad &\text{implies } \eta_z = (x/z)\eta_x + (y/z)\eta_y \\
z = x^\alpha \quad &\text{implies } \eta_z = \alpha\eta_x
\end{aligned}
$$

6   Arrow (1988).

7   There may, of course, be other institutional reasons for the maintenance, or even increase, of such a wage gap, e.g., minimum wage legislation, unionization, etc.

8   Thus, S_a constitutes an increase in the household's capital account. Q_a includes current inputs into the farm household, partly as a producing and partly as a consuming unit. This further breakdown of Q_a is rendered more explicit below.

9   Rigorous modeling of the behavior of rural families must obviously be based on utility maximization in the Becker tradition, with these dynamic incentive features added.

10   The division of the total wage bill into Q_i and $S_a + Q_a$ depends on the intersectoral terms of trade d, while the division between the two components of $S_a + Q_a$ depends on farmers' propensities to invest and/or consume. This division is fully investigated in the next chapter.

11   When this percentage is considered in the context of foreign capital inflows to finance growth in the post-war world, reliance on savings in the domestic agricultural sector is far more important than what the system can realistically expect from either the industrial sector or from foreigners.

12 This does not mean that we really believe in the notion of a "zero" marginal product of labor, a statistically highly unlikely event in the real world. The "horizontal" portion of the TPP_L curve should be viewed only as a simplifying assumption.

13 In figure 3.8(b), N^*/d is also represented by the slope of the line $P(0)E$. In diagram 3.8(a) the area $ABCD$ is total agricultural output A and the area $FECD$ is TAS.

14 E.g., Rosenzweig (1988).

15 These concepts are defined rigorously in the next chapter.

16 Other variables, such as additional knowledge about new seeds, etc., may affect the pace of technology change, but we make the simplifying assumption that modern inputs and incentive goods originating in non-agriculture determine the production function in the next period.

17 Suppose the equilibrium d is less than the conjectured d; postulating a slightly lower d leads to a decrease in w_i, and increase in W, a decrease in L as well as A and AAS. This leads to a higher d_e until the postulated d is the equilibrium d.

18 In distinguishing between the traditional and commercialized sectors, it is implicit that the traditional sector correlates highly with agriculture and the commercialized sector correlates highly with industry. However, certain agricultural activities like capitalist plantations can be considered commercialized, while small-scale services and household production of non-agricultural items can be considered non-commercialized.

19 Our model of dualism thus differs explicitly from the original Lewis model which focused only on organizational heterogeneity. For a full discussion of this difference, see Ranis and Fei (1982).

20 For convenience we are assuming a constant population. In the more realistic case, the reallocation rate must exceed the population growth rate if the pool of the underemployed is to decline.

21 For the sake of simplicity we abstract here from the additional Z-goods production within the rural household dealt with in the body of the chapter.

22 Data availability forces us to use an agricultural/non-agricultural instead of a traditional/commercialized sector breakdown.

23 Yet this does not always occur by altering wages to equal the marginal product of labor, which could reduce the wage below the MSL level. Instead, the adjustment occurs institutionally and the MSL wage is not threatened. For example, in Java and the Philippines harvest contracts began to include weeding duties without a complementary rise in the wage rate, thereby not threatening the MSL but making institutional adjustments towards a commercialized economy.

PART III

The Analytics of Growth and Development

4

The Neoclassical Production Function, Growth and Development

4.1 Introduction

It is well known that the heart of economics centers on the analysis of production-related phenomena. For this reason a simple static production function $Q = f(K,L)$ is postulated at the outset, where output Q is specified as a function of the joint inputs of capital K and labor L.[1] Such a production function (equation 4.1a) becomes dynamic when it takes the form of equation 4.1b.

$$Q = f(K,L,\bar{t}) \quad \text{(static production function prevailing at} \qquad (4.1a)$$
$$\text{time } t = \bar{t})$$

$$Q = f(K,L,t) \quad \text{(dynamic production function)} \qquad (4.1b)$$

For any fixed point in time $t = \bar{t}$, equation 4.1a specifies the art of production, while 4.1b specifies the input–output relation prevailing at all points in time. Since change in the static production function between any t and $t+1$ reflects technological change (or innovation), the dynamic production function summarizes all innovation information for any time interval. The dynamic production function thus constitutes a basic conceptual tool to analyze growth-related phenomena after the beginning of the transition to the modern growth epoch (that is, after approximately 1780 in the North) when, for the first time in history, the phenomenon of growth centered on population growth, capital accumulation, and technological change over time.

As a guide to the rest of this chapter, a few general comments are in order on the importance of both the static and dynamic production functions in a growth context. The static production function can be represented by a production contour map formed of output isoquants (figure 4.1(a)). For a typical point $P_0=(K_0,L_0)$ in the input space, nine production-related concepts can be defined as indicated in Column I of table 4.1.

Table 4.1 Growth equations

	Row	Growth performance indices I	Partial elasticity with respect to Labor L II	Partial elasticity with respect to Capital K III	Growth equations Factor quantity effect (A) IVa	Growth equations Innovation effect (Z) IVb
Output-related concepts	1	National income Q	$\phi_L = f_L L/Q$	$\phi_K = f_K K/Q$	T1 $\eta_Q = \phi_L \eta_L + \phi_K \eta_K$	$+J$
	2	Labor productivity $p = Q/L$	$-\phi_K$	ϕ_K	T2 $\eta_p = \phi_K \eta_{K^*}$	$+J$
	3	Capital productivity $d = Q/K$	ϕ_L	$-\phi_L$	T3 $\eta_d = -\phi_L \eta_{K^*}$	$+J$
Factor price-related concepts	4	MPP_L (w)	$-\epsilon_{LL}$	$\epsilon_{LL} = \epsilon_{LK}$	T4 $\eta_w = \epsilon_{LL}\eta_{K^*}$ $= \epsilon_{LL}\eta_{K^*}$	$+H_L$ $+B_L + J$
	5	MPP_K (π)	$\epsilon_{KL} = \epsilon_{KK}$	$-\epsilon_{KK}$	T5 $\eta_\pi = -\epsilon_{KK}\eta_{K^*}$ $= -\epsilon_{KK}\eta_{K^*}$	$+H_K$ $+B_K + J$
	6	$MRS = M$ (w/π)	$M = f_L/f_K$ $-\epsilon$ $(= -\epsilon_{LL} - \epsilon_{KK})$	$+\epsilon$ $(= \epsilon_{LL} + \epsilon_{KK})$	T6 $\eta_M = \epsilon\eta_{K^*}$ $= \epsilon\eta_{K^*}$	$+H_L - H_K$ $+B$
Factor share-related concepts	7	ϕ_L	$\dfrac{f_L L/Q}{= f_L/p}$ $-\epsilon_{LL} + \phi_K$	$\epsilon_{LL} - \phi_K$	T7 $\eta_{\phi_L} = (\epsilon_{LL} - \phi_K)\eta_{K^*}$ $= \phi_K(\epsilon-1)\eta_{K^*}$	$+H_L - J$ $+B_L$
	8	ϕ_K	$\dfrac{f_K K/Q}{= f_K/d}$ $\epsilon_{KK} - \phi_L$	$-\epsilon_{KK} + \phi_L$	T8 $\eta_{\phi_K} = (\phi_L - \epsilon_{KK})\eta_{K^*}$ $= \phi_L(\epsilon-1)\eta_{K^*}$	$+H_K - J$ $+B_K$
	9	r	$\dfrac{\phi_L/\phi_K}{= M/K^*}$ $1 - \epsilon$	$\epsilon - 1$	T9 $\eta_r = (\epsilon - 1)\eta_{K^*}$	$+B$

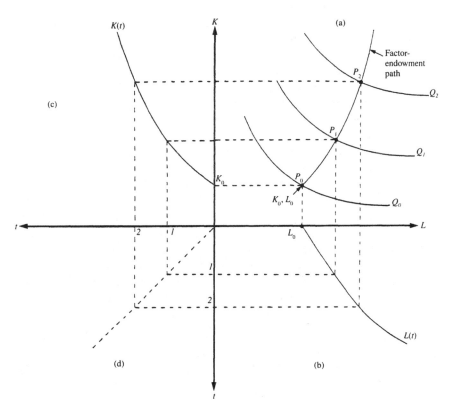

*Figure 4.1 Neoclassical production contours and the factor-endowment
path*

These include three output–related concepts – total output Q, average labor productivity $p = Q/L$, average capital productivity $d = Q/K$ – and three factor price-related concepts – the marginal productivity of labor $MPP_L = f_L$, the marginal productivity of capital $MPP_K = f_K$, and the marginal rate of substitution $MRS = M = f_L/f_K$. Under competitive conditions in labor and capital markets, f_L, f_K, and $M = f_L/f_K$ represent the wage rate w, the rate of return to capital or the profit rate π, and the relative factor price ratio w/π. For this reason these are also referred to as "functional distribution" concepts. Finally, three factor share-related concepts emerge: the labor share $\phi_L = f_L(L/Q)$, the capital share $\phi_K = f_K(K/Q)$, and the relative shares $r = \phi_L/\phi_K$. The above notations for these nine basic concepts are used consistently in this volume. All nine performance indices can be derived from the static production function at any point in time.

These basic production concepts are applied to individual firm analysis in the microeconomics literature. However, we apply it as the aggregate production function for the whole economy (equation 4.1). For this reason, a point in the input space $P_0 = (K_0, L_0)$ is the "factor endowment" or "input point" for the whole economy[2] and Q is national income. Consistently, $p = Q/L$ becomes per capita income and $d = Q/K$ is the productivity of capital (the inverse of which, $1/d = K/Q$, is the capital-output ratio for the whole economy). The MPP_L (or f_L) and the MPP_K (or f_K) are the wage rate w and the profit rate π determined by market forces when the competitive principle of income distribution prevails. When interpreted aggregatively, the nine basic concepts represent the most important growth-relevant performance indices.

Let the time paths of capital $K(t)$ and labor $L(t)$ be exogenous, as shown in figures 4.1(b) and (c), where the time axes are linked by a $45°$ line in figure 4.1(d). A factor endowment path through time can then be determined (figure 4.1(a)). When $K(t)$ and $L(t)$ are substituted in the dynamic production function:

$$Q(t) = f(K(t), L(t), t) \tag{4.2}$$

national income is now a function of time. At every point on the factor endowment path the value of all nine basic production concepts is determined. Thus, when $K(t)$ and $L(t)$ are given exogenously, the time series $p(t)$, $d(t)$, $f_L(t), \ldots$ are all determined. It is obvious that to study the processes of growth at the aggregate level we must be concerned with the dynamic production function determining these time series. Our attention focuses on the rapidity of the growth of these indices as they relate to the (exogenously postulated) growth rates of capital (η_K) and population (η_L), as well as technological change. It can be noted parenthetically that the static pre-World War II version of the neoclassical school – concerned more with general equilibrium theory assuming a multiplicity of commodities – provided a poor response to the challenge of Marx who was concerned with aggregate growth. The dynamic post-war version, however, focusing on capital accumulation and technological change as it affects a single aggregate commodity, does constitute an appropriate, if overdue, response and is of importance to us.

4.1.1 Determination of the growth rates of the performance indices

Instead of studying the nine indices of growth individually, it is helpful to employ an abstract rule which can be applied to all cases. Suppose x is a function of the independent variables y, z, and w. The notation $E(x,y)$ denotes the partial elasticity of x with respect to y, z or w.

$$x = f(y,z,w) \tag{4.3a}$$
$$E(x,y) = (\partial x/\partial y)(y/x)$$
$$E(x,z) = (\partial x/\partial z)(z/x)$$
$$E(x,w) = (\partial x/\partial w)(w/x) \tag{4.3b}$$

Thus, the partial elasticity $E(x,y)$ is the "percentage change in x per unit of percentage change of y." This measures the sensitivity of variation in the dependent variable x when an independent variable varies, all other independent variables being constant. If the independent variables y, z, and w are functions of time, then the dependent variable x also becomes a function of time:

$$x = f(y(t), z(t), w(t)) = x(t) \tag{4.4}$$

η_y, η_z, η_w, and η_x denote the growth rates of y, z, w, and x. We then have the following elementary "chain rule theorem":

$$\eta_x = E(x,y)\eta_y + E(x,z)\eta_z + E(x,w)\eta_w, \text{ where} \tag{4.5a}$$
$$\eta_x \equiv (dx/dt)/x; \ \eta_y \equiv (dy/dt)/y; \ \eta_z \equiv (dz/dt)/z; \tag{4.5b}$$
$$\eta_w \equiv (dw/dt)/w$$

Proof: Differentiating equation 4.4 with respect to t, we have
$$dx/dt = (\partial f/\partial y)(dy/dt) + (\partial f/\partial z)(dz/dt) + (\partial f/\partial w)(dw/dt) \text{ and}$$
$$\eta_x = (dx/dt)/x = (\partial f/\partial y)(y/x)\eta_y + (\partial f/\partial z)(z/x)\eta_z + (\partial f/\partial w)(w/x)\eta_w \quad \text{Q.E.D.}$$

The theorem states that η_x is the additive sum of three terms. Each term is the product of a partial elasticity and the growth rate of that independent variable.

This abstract theorem helps derive all growth equations shown in Column IV of table 4.1, indicating the causation of the rapidity of growth of the nine indices listed. The rapidity of growth of GNP, per capita income, capital productivity, etc. constitute the bread and butter of any quantitative approach to modern economic growth.[3] The abstract chain rule immediately shows that in order to derive the rapidity of any growth indicators, it is essential that the partial elasticities be derived first, with the results summarized in Columns II and III.

The growth equations summarized in table 4.1 amount to a dynamization of the static neoclassical production concepts. The table contains productivity equations (1–3) as well as distribution-related concepts (4–6 and 7–9). The latter are applicable only when the competitive principle of income distribution prevails. The production concepts apply independently of the rule governing income distribution. They represent basic conceptual tools for a rigorous investigation of all the essential growth-related phenomena involving the nine performance indices. In this chapter, the specific properties of the neoclassical production function are introduced in section 4.2 and the partial elasticities in section 4.3. A key dynamic production concept – innovation intensity – is introduced in section 4.4, allowing us to deduce the growth equations for GNP, labor productivity p, and capital productivity d. Another set of dynamic production concepts – those relating to the factor bias of innovations – are presented in section 4.5, permitting us to deduce the growth equations for all other performance indices (f_L, f_K, M, r) of table 4.1.

4.2 Properties of the Neoclassical Production Function

When a static production function is given, we can omit t in equation 4.1b and write:

$$Q = f(K,L) \qquad (4.6)$$

In this section we identify the properties of this production function as postulated by neoclassical economists. For this purpose, the first and second order partial derivatives of equation 1.1 are denoted as follows:

$$(f_L, f_K) = (\partial Q/\partial L, \partial Q/\partial K) \qquad (4.7a)$$

$$\begin{pmatrix} f_{LL} & f_{LK} \\ f_{KL} & f_{KK} \end{pmatrix}_{2\times2} = \begin{pmatrix} \partial^2 Q/\partial L \partial L & \partial \partial Q/\partial K \partial L \\ \partial \partial Q/\partial L \partial K & \partial^2 Q/\partial K \partial K \end{pmatrix}_{2\times2} \qquad (4.7b)$$

Special properties are postulated for the production function (equation 4.6) in terms of the partial derivatives of equations 4.7a and 4.7b. We are interested not only in what properties are postulated, but why they are postulated in the first place. The four conventional axioms are:

Indispensability: $0 = f(0,0)$ (4.8a)
Non-redundancy: $(f_L > 0, f_K > 0)$ (4.8b)
Law of Diminishing Returns: $(f_{LL} < 0, f_{KK} < 0)$ (4.8c)
Law of Complementarity: $f_{KL} = f_{LK} > 0$ (4.8d)

The first axiom states that it takes a positive amount of capital or labor to produce a positive amount of output; "free goods" are not the concern of the economist. The axiom of non-redundancy states that the MPP_L and the MPP_K are positive so that more output can be produced when more labor or capital inputs are added. Chapter 3 showed that labor may not have a scarcity value only when it is redundant $(f_L = 0)$ under the special circumstance of a labor surplus economy. The axiom of the law of diminishing returns states that the MPP_L (MPP_K) declines when more labor (capital) is added. This represents an essential limitation on the art of production since, otherwise, enough food could be grown in the backyard of the typical American family to feed the entire population. Finally, the law of complementarity states that in the joint input process an increase in the quantity of one factor of production benefits the marginal productivity of the other factor(s). If this condition is not satisfied, capital accumulation is useless and unnecessary. Indeed, if any of the above axioms is persistently and significantly violated, economics as a science is at risk.

These four axioms are uncontroversial. In figure 4.2, when the capital stock $K = K_0$ in the production contour map (figure 4.2(a)) is given, the economist routinely draws the TPP_L, $APP_L = p$, and $MPP_L = f_L$ curves (figures 4.2(b), (c), and (d)) with the "correct slopes" ensured by the four axioms. The f_L curve is positive and decreasing by the axiom of non-redundancy and the law of diminishing returns. This implies that the TPP_L curve is increasing and convex because MPP_L is the slope of the TPP_L curve. Since the TPP_L curve cannot start from a negative value, the fact that it is convex implies that the $APP_L = p$ curve is negatively sloped and non-negative – the slope of Oa for the TPP_L curve is p. Finally, the production isoquants in figure 4.2(a) are convex when the following condition is satisfied:

$$d^2K/dL^2 \big|_{Q=\bar{Q}} > 0 \text{ if and only if } 2f_L f_K f_{KL} > f_K^2 f_{LL} + f_L^2 f_{KK} \quad (4.9)$$

The satisfaction of this inequality is ensured by the set of axioms.

In addition to the four axioms, the production function is constant returns to scale (CRTS) when for any factor endowment point (K,L):

$$f(kK,kL) = kf(K, L) \text{ for all non-negative values of } k. \quad (4.10)$$

A geometric interpretation of CRTS is given in figure 4.2(a) where an endowment point $P_0 = (K_0, L_0)$ lies on a radial line OR that represents fixed capital per head $K^* = K/L$. The factor endowment point $P_1 = (kK_0, kL_0)$ lies on the same radial line OR. If the output at P_0 is Q, then the output at P_1

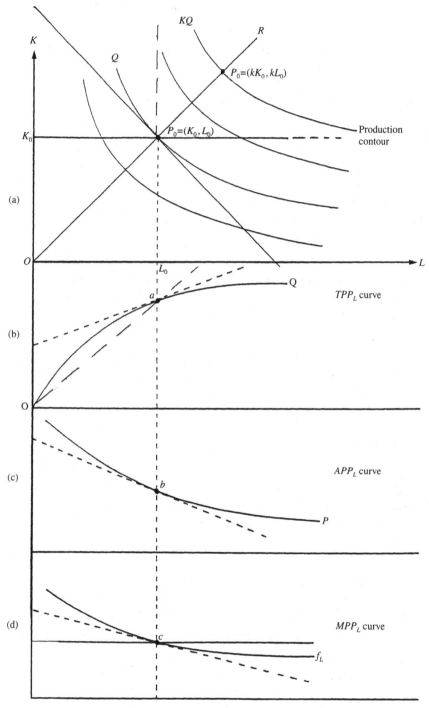

Figure 4.2 Total, average, and marginal productivity of non-agricultural labor curves

must be kQ – the output must change by the same "multiple" when both inputs change by the same multiple (k). A CRTS production function ensures two properties. First, the scale insensitivity property states that all indices of table 4.1 (except Q) take on constant values along any radial line. Formally:

Theorem   Under CRTS, the values of p, d, f_L, f_K, M, ϕ_L, ϕ_K and r are completely determined by the input ratio $K^* = K/L$.

To prove this theorem, first write:

$$M = f_L/f_K \qquad (4.11a)$$
$$\phi_L = Lf_L/Q = f_L/p \qquad (4.11b)$$
$$\phi_K = Kf_K/Q = f_K/d \qquad (4.11c)$$
$$r = \phi_L/\phi_K \qquad (4.11d)$$

Thus, if the theorem is proved for f_L and f_K, then it is also valid for the marginal rate of substitution because M is defined as the ratio f_L/f_K. If, in addition, the theorem is proven for p and d, then the theorem is also valid for ϕ_L (and similarly for ϕ_K) because it is the ratio of f_L to p (and of f_K to d). The theorem is also true for r because it is the ratio of ϕ_L to ϕ_K. Thus, we only need to prove the theorem for f_L and p, since the proofs for f_K and d are symmetrical. To prove the theorem for p:

$$p = Q/L = f(K,L)/L = f(K/L,1) = f(K^*,1) \quad \text{Q.E.D.} \qquad (4.12)$$

To prove the theorem for f_L, we have (by equation 4.12)

$$Q = L f(K^*,1) \qquad (4.13a)$$

Differentiating both sides with respect to L:

$$f_L = f(K^*,1) + L f_K(K^*,1)\mathrm{d}(K^*/\mathrm{d}L) \qquad (4.13b)$$
$$= f(K^*,1) + L f_K(K^*,1) K(-1/L^2)$$
$$= f(K^*,1) - f_K(K^*,1)K^*$$

Thus, the theorem is proved for f_L because only K^* is involved in the expression on the right-hand side.

The importance of the scale insensitivity property cannot be overly emphasized. Most macroeconomic analysis is impossible without it. In growth theory, statements like "per capita income is higher in the US than in India because capital per head is higher," "by increasing capital per head, the wage rate can be increased," or "capital deepening carries a profit depressing effect" – in fact, all our theoretical assertions in Part I – are meaningless without the CRTS hypothesis.

The second major economic significance of CRTS is due to the Euler theorem (ensured by CRTS) which states:

$$Q = f_L L + f_K K, \text{ implying} \qquad (4.14a)$$
$$1 = \phi_K + \phi_L \qquad (4.14b)$$

Equation 4.14a is the "product exhaustion property of the production function with CRTS" which states that if every factor is paid its marginal product, total wage payments $f_L L$ and total profit payments $f_K K$ add up to total output and the two distributive shares add up to 1.

The Euler theorem has historical significance in income distribution theory in that before its discovery by the neoclassical economists, there had been a tendency to regard the pricing of one factor of production as actively determined by its marginal product, with the other factor of production receiving a "surplus value" (for example, rent to the classical economists and profits to Marx). With the discovery of the Euler theorem, the principle of income distribution became symmetrical with respect to both factors of production. In the absence of the Euler theorem:

$$Q > f_L L + f_K K \text{ or} \qquad (4.15a)$$
$$Q < f_L L + f_K K \qquad (4.15b)$$

In either case, the competitive principle of income distribution is impossible. When the factor endowment point $P_0 = (K_0, L_0)$ is given, one cannot be sure whether the wage rate (w) or the interest rate (π) is determined – and, if so, determined by what principle. Simple statements could not be made for the impact of growth on any of the distribution-related indices $(f_L, f_K, M, \phi_L, \phi_K$ or $r)$. Accepting the Euler theorem we have, for later reference:

$$-L f_{LL} = K f_{KL}, \text{ implying } -L f_{LL}/f_L = f_{KL} K/f_L \qquad (4.16a)$$
$$-K f_{KK} = L f_{LK}, \text{ implying } -K f_{KK}/f_K = f_{LK} L/f_K \qquad (4.16b)$$
$$(L f_{LL}/f_L)(f_L L/Q) = (K f_{KK}/f_K)(f_K K/Q) \qquad (4.16c)$$

Proof: partially differentiating $Q = f_L L + f_K K$ with respect to L, we have $f_L = L f_{LL} + f_L + K f_{KL}$, or $-L f_{LL} = K f_{KL}$. This proves 4.16a. The proof for 4.16b is symmetrical.

Together, 4.16a and 4.16b imply 4.16c by taking their ratio and canceling out: $f_{KL} = f_{LK}$.   Q.E.D.

Finally, the four conditions (equation 4.8) are an axiomatic system because they are mutually consistent and collectively independent. That they are mutually consistent can be seen from the Cobb–Douglas production function:

$$Q = K^\alpha L^{1-\alpha}, 0 < \alpha < 1 \qquad (4.17)$$

which satisfies all four axioms. The fact that they are collectively independent is indicated by the fact that one cannot derive any axiom from the other three. When we add the condition of CRTS, the five conditions no longer form an axiomatic system. Equation 4.16a under CRTS means that the law of diminishing returns ($f_{LL} < 0$) and the law of complementarity ($f_{KL} > 0$) mutually imply each other.

4.3 Partial Elasticities of the Static Production Function

When the static production function in equation 4.6 is given, we want to derive and interpret all partial elasticities with respect to labor (column II) or capital (column III) of table 4.1. The first pair are the partial elasticities of GNP with respect to labor and capital:

$$E(Q,L) = (\partial Q/\partial L)(L/Q) = f_L L/Q = \phi_L \qquad (4.18a)$$
$$E(Q,K) = (\partial Q/\partial K)(K/Q) = f_K K/Q = \phi_K \qquad (4.18b)$$

For example, for the factor endowment point P_0 in figure 4.2(a), ϕ_L is the elasticity of the TPP_L curve at point a in figure 4.2(b). The partial elasticities ϕ_L and ϕ_K are recorded in row 1, columns II and III, of table 4.1.

As defined in equation 4.18a, $E(Q,L)$ is a production-related concept – the sensitivity of the variation of output when labor varies. Hence equation 4.18a implies that there is a coincidence between the production interpretation and the distributional interpretation of ϕ_L. Namely, the percentage share of the income of the working class is governed by the labor elasticity of output from the production standpoint.

For industrially advanced countries, the distributive share of labor takes on an order of magnitude of approximately $\phi_L = 0.6$. Thus, a 1 percent increase in the labor force (or population) implies a 0.6 percent increase in national income. The two elasticities ϕ_L and ϕ_K are basic to quantifying the impact of population growth and/or capital accumulation on the growth rate of national income.

Since many of the indices from column I of table 4.1 are ratios, the derivation of their partial elasticities can be simplified with the aid of the following abstract theorem of partial elasticities.

Theorem If $w = x/y$ and if $x = x(z)$ and $y = y(z)$, then

$$E(w,z) = E(x,z) - E(y,z) \qquad (4.19)$$

Proof: Differentiating $w = x/y$ with respect to z,

$$\begin{aligned}
dw/dz &= [(y)(dx/dz) - (x)(dy/dz)]/y^2 \\
&= [(dx/dz)/y] - [(x)(dy/dz)/y^2] \\
E(w,z) &= (dw/dz)(z/w) \\
&= [(dx/dz)/y](z/w) - [(x)(dy/dz)/y^2)(z/w) \\
&= (dx/dz)(z/x) - (dy/dz)(z/y) \\
&= E(x,z) - E(y,z) \qquad \text{Q.E.D.}
\end{aligned}$$

Applying this theorem to the four elasticities involving p and d we have:

$$E(p,L) = E(Q,L) - E(L,L) = \phi_L - 1 = -\phi_K; (E(L,L) = 1)$$
$$E(p,K) = E(Q,K) - E(L,K) = \phi_K; (E(L,K) = 0)$$
$$E(d,L) = \phi_L$$
$$E(d,K) = -\phi_L \tag{4.20}$$

These partial elasticities are recorded in rows 2 and 3 of table 4.1. The economic interpretation of $E(p,L) = -\phi_K$ is that a 1 percent increase in population depresses per capita income by 0.4 percent for $\phi_K = 0.4$. $E(p,K) = \phi_K$ means that a 1 percent increase in capital increases per capita income by the same percentage. Thus, the effects of K and L on per capita income have the same absolute magnitudes but the opposite direction. The same is true for all the pairs in rows 2 to 9, columns II and III, of table 4.1. Thus in figure 4.2(c) the elasticity of the average product curve at point b is $-\phi_K$.

The impact on $p = Q/L$ has important welfare implications because p is per capita income. The impact on the productivity of capital d is no less important, if for an entirely different reason. Letting S be total savings and s the Keynesian average propensity to save, we have the Keynesian saving function:

$$S = sQ \tag{4.21}$$

A large s implies a strong desire for capital accumulation. If S is equated with investment ($S = I$), the growth rate of capital becomes:

$$\eta_K = S/K = sd, 0 < s < 1 \text{ (Harrod–Domar growth rate of}$$
$$\text{capital)} \tag{4.22a}$$
$$\eta_{\eta_K} = \eta_s + \eta_d \text{ (by 4.22a) (capital acceleration)} \tag{4.22b}$$
$$\eta_s = 0 \text{ implies } \eta_{\eta_K} = \eta_d \text{ (constant saving rate)} \tag{4.22c}$$

Thus, when the accumulation of capital is "saving-pushed", its rate of growth is the product of s (the average propensity to save) and d (capital productivity). The interest of the economist in d is due to the fact that when capital accumulation is saving-pushed, the rate of capital acceleration is the sum of η_s and η_d (4.22b). When s is constant, a fall in d ($\eta_d < 0$) implies capital deceleration ($\eta_{\eta_K} < 0$) (4.22c). For example, if $\phi_L = 0.6$, a 1 percent increase in capital implies a 0.6 percent decrease in the growth rate of capital when s is constant. This is the part of the contradiction, sensed by Marx, that the desire for capital accumulation depresses the capital growth rate through its negative effect on capital productivity. For the partial elasticities f_L and f_K:

$$E(f_L,L) = (\partial f_L/\partial L)(L/f_L) = f_{LL}L/f_L < 0 \tag{4.23a}$$
$$E(f_L,K) = (\partial f_L/\partial K)(K/f_L) = f_{LK}K/f_L > 0 \tag{4.23b}$$
$$E(f_K,L) = (\partial f_K/\partial L)(L/f_K) = f_{KL}L/f_K > 0 \tag{4.23c}$$
$$E(f_K,K) = (\partial f_K/\partial K)(K/f_K) = f_{KK}K/f_K < 0 \tag{4.23d}$$

Thus, the law of diminishing returns (4.8c) implies that two elasticities are negative, while the law of complementarity (4.8d) implies that the other two are positive. Equations 4.16a and 4.16b imply, moreover, that the absolute magnitudes of 4.23ab are exactly the same; similarly for 4.23cd. We adopt the notation:

$$\epsilon_{LL} = -f_{LL}L/f_L > 0, \text{ implying } E(f_L,L) = -\epsilon_{LL}; E(f_L,K) = \epsilon_{LL} \quad (4.24a)$$
$$\epsilon_{KK} = -f_{KK}K/f_K > 0, \text{ implying } E(f_K,L) = \epsilon_{KK}; E(f_K,K) = -\epsilon_{KK} \quad (4.24b)$$

where ϵ_{LL} and ϵ_{KK} are defined as positive numbers. These partial elasticities are summarized in rows 4 and 5 of table 4.1. In figure 4.2(d) the elasticity of the demand for labor at point c is $-\epsilon_{LL}$.

The economic interpretation of $-\epsilon_{LL}$ ($-\epsilon_{KK}$) is that it measures the strength of the law of diminishing returns to labor (capital). The larger the absolute magnitude of ϵ_{LL}, the more severe the manifestation of the law of diminishing returns to labor. Symmetrically, ϵ_{LK} and ϵ_{KL} represent the strength of the law of complementarity. The economic significance of $-\epsilon_{LL}$ is that it indicates the adverse impact of population growth on the wage rate when $f_L = w$, with a magnitude proportional to the strength of the law of diminishing returns to labor. The interpretation of $\epsilon_{LL} = \epsilon_{LK}$ is that it measures the beneficial impact on the wage rate due to capital accumulation, with a magnitude proportional to ϵ_{LL} – summarized as the law of complementarity of capital to labor. Thus, both favorable and unfavorable distributional impacts are ultimately traced to the production function and its primary inputs.

While the impact on the wage rate relates to the welfare of labor, the only effective way to raise the economic welfare of a typical fully employed worker is to increase the wage rate. In the long run the wage rate, as determined by competition, reflects the art of production and is independent of the political forces of unionism (in the USA), collectivism (in socialist LDCs), or paternalism (in mixed economy LDCs).

The impact on the profit rate is a different story. While population growth contributes to an increase in the profit rate (ϵ_{KK}), capital accumulation suppresses it ($-\epsilon_{KK}$). Thus, the comparative magnitudes of the capital growth rate and the population growth rate have much to do with the direction of change of the profit rate. A rapid capital growth rate combined with a low population growth rate leads to capital deepening and depresses both the profit rate and the capital growth rate – planting the seeds of the "Marxian contradiction" and long-run stagnation. Applying the elementary theorem (4.19) to MRS = f_L/f_K, we have:

$$E(M,L) = E(f_L,L) - E(f_K,L) = -\epsilon_{LL} - \epsilon_{KK} = -(\epsilon_{LL} + \epsilon_{KK}) = -\epsilon$$
$$(4.25a)$$

$$E(M,K) = E(f_L,K) - E(f_K,K) = \epsilon_{LL} - (-\epsilon_{KK}) = \epsilon_{LL} + \epsilon_{KK} = \epsilon, \text{ where}$$
$$(4.25b)$$

$$\epsilon = \epsilon_{LL} + \epsilon_{KK} > 0 \qquad (4.25c)$$

The positive number ϵ, usually called the elasticity of substitution, should more appropriately be called the "inelasticity of substitution" in accordance with the following definition:

> *Definition*   The inelasticity of substitution ($\epsilon > 0$) is the sum of the degree of the laws of diminishing returns to labor and capital ($\epsilon = \epsilon_{LL} + \epsilon_{KK}$).

Referring to figure 4.2(a), at the input point P_0 a dotted L-shaped (Leontief) production contour implies that K and L are perfect complements (non-substitutable), such that ϵ would have an infinite value.

ϵ and $-\epsilon$ are recorded in columns II and III of row 6, table 4.1. While an increase in labor depresses the relative factor price ratio against the wage rate, the opposite is true for an increase in capital. The quantitative severity of that impact is proportional to the "inelasticity of substitution." The value of ϵ yields the impact of factor scarcities on relative factor prices in the growth process.

Finally, applying equation 4.19 to ϕ_L, ϕ_K and $r = \phi_L/\phi_K$:

$$
\begin{aligned}
E(\phi_L,L) &= E(f_L/p,L) = E(f_L,L) - E(p,L) = -\epsilon_{LL} + \phi_K & (4.26a)\\
E(\phi_L,K) &= E(f_L/p,K) = E(f_L,K) - E(p,K) = \epsilon_{LL} - \phi_K & (4.26b)\\
E(\phi_K,L) &= E(f_K/d,L) = E(f_K,L) - E(d,L) = \epsilon_{KK} - \phi_L & (4.26c)\\
E(\phi_K,K) &= E(f_K/d,K) = E(f_K,K) - E(d,K) = -\epsilon_{KK} + \phi_L & (4.26d)\\
E(r,L) &= E(\phi_L/\phi_K,L) = E(\phi_L,L) - E(\phi_K,L) & (4.26e)\\
&= -\epsilon_{LL} + \phi_K - (\epsilon_{KK} - \phi_L)\\
&= 1 - \epsilon\\
E(r,K) &= E(\phi_L/\phi_K,K) = E(\phi_L,K) - E(\phi_K,K) = \epsilon_{LL} - \phi_K & (4.26f)\\
&\quad - (-\epsilon_{KK} + \phi_L)\\
&= \epsilon - 1
\end{aligned}
$$

These partial elasticities are reproduced in rows 7, 8 and 9 of table 4.1. The following definition is essential to explore the economic interpretation of these partial elasticities:

> *Definition*   The production function is substitution inelastic (substitution elastic) if
>
> $$\epsilon > 1 \ (\epsilon < 1) \qquad (4.27)$$

Substitution inelasticity ($\epsilon > 1$) implies that the combined strength of the laws of diminishing returns ($\epsilon_{LL} + \epsilon_{KK}$) is strong, such that the two factors of production are rigidly combined and are highly complementary and non-substitutable – approaching the Leontief case. Under this condition, an increase in the capital stock raises the share of income of the laboring class (ϕ_L) while depressing the share of income of the property owning class (ϕ_K). The opposite is true when the labor force increases.

In the mature economy, where the production process involves the application of scientific/technological principles of a mechanical or chemical variety, labor is not likely to be readily substitutable for capital. Hence substitution inelasticity is usually thought of as the "normal" case. But this is not inevitable, as we see in our discussion of dualistic development. In that case, when the labor force L increases, labor's share may be raised because the increase in the quantity of labor overwhelms the wage depressing effect of that higher quantity. Equation 4.16c immediately implies:

$$\phi_L \epsilon_{LL} = \phi_K \epsilon_{KK}, \text{ or} \qquad (4.28a)$$
$$r = \phi_L/\phi_K = \epsilon_{KK}/\epsilon_{LL} \qquad (4.28b)$$

The ratio of ϵ_{KK} to ϵ_{LL} is r, the ratio of the relative shares. Although we do not know the absolute magnitude of ϵ_{LL} and ϵ_{KK}, we do know their relative magnitudes, with the law of diminishing returns to capital accounting for the lion's share of the overall inelasticity. Empirically, since ϕ_L is usually around 0.6, r approaches a value of 1.5 – the law of diminishing returns to capital is 1.5 times as strong as the law of diminishing returns to labor. In figure 4.2(a), r is represented by the elasticity of the production contour line at P_0. We readily have:

$$1 + \phi_L/\phi_K = 1 + \epsilon_{KK}/\epsilon_{LL}, \text{ or} \qquad (4.29a)$$
$$1/\phi_K = \epsilon/\epsilon_{LL} \qquad (4.29b)$$

The last equality implies:

$$\epsilon_{LL}/\epsilon = \phi_K \qquad (4.30a)$$
$$\epsilon_{KK}/\epsilon = \phi_L \qquad (4.30b)$$

Since $\epsilon = \epsilon_{LL} + \epsilon_{KK}$, the term ϵ_{LL}/ϵ (ϵ_{KK}/ϵ) is the fraction of the inelasticity of substitution accounted for by ϵ_{LL} (ϵ_{KK}), the law of diminishing returns to labor (capital), empirically approximated by 0.4 (0.6). This may be summarized as a corollary:

The fraction of ϵ accounted for by ϵ_{LL} is the capital share ϕ_K and
the fraction of ϵ accounted for by ϵ_{KK} is the labor share ϕ_L (4.31)

In columns II and III of table 4.1, with the exception of ϕ_L and ϕ_K in the first row, all entries have the opposite signs and the same absolute magnitudes. This may be summarized as follows:

For every index of growth performance in the set (p, d, f_L, f_K, M, ϕ_L, ϕ_K, r), the partial elasticities with respect to labor and capital have the opposite sign and the same absolute magnitude.   (4.32)

This is due to the constant returns to scale (CRTS) property of the neo-classical production function, which lends simplicity to all the growth equations developed in the next section.

4.4 Derivation of Growth Equations

When the capital stock $K(t)$ and the labor force $L(t)$ grow exogenously through time, the growth rate (η) of any performance index x in table 4.1 is composed of a factor quantity effect and an innovation effect. The former refers to the performance in the absence of technological change – when the production function is static. The latter refers to the **additional** performance effect due to changes in the production function as a result of technological change. Using the chain rule of theorem 4.5, the decomposition of η_x into the two effects is:

$$\eta_x = f(K,L,t) = E(x,L)\eta_L + E(x,K)\eta_K + E(x,t)\eta_t, \text{ or} \tag{4.33a}$$
$$\eta_x = A + Z, \text{ where} \tag{4.33b}$$
$$A = E(x,L)\eta_L + E(x,K)\eta_K \text{ (factor quantity effect)} \tag{4.33c}$$
$$Z = E(x,t)\eta_t = (\partial x/\partial t)(t/x)(1/t) = (\partial x/\partial t)/x \text{ (innovation effect)} \tag{4.33d}$$

A, the factor quantity effect, is the additive sum of two terms corresponding to the growth rate of capital (η_K) and of labor (η_L), while Z, the innovation effect, is the percentage change per unit of time when both K and L are constant. The factor quantity effects and the innovation effects are listed separately in columns IVa and IVb of table 4.1. Taking advantage of corollary 4.32 from the last section, we can write the factor quantity effect with reference to the partial elasticities (that is, $E(x,L)$ and $E(x,K)$) of columns II and III. Thus, the factor quantity effect for the growth rate of national income is indicated in 4.34a:

$$A = \phi_L\eta_L + \phi_K\eta_K \tag{4.34a}$$
$$A = E(x,K)\eta_K - E(x,K)\eta_L = E(x,K)[\eta_K - \eta_L] = E(x,K)\eta_{K*} \tag{4.34b}$$

The factor quantity effect for all other indices involves the rate of capital deepening $\eta_{K*} = \eta_K - \eta_L$, as proved in 4.34b. In the absence of technology change, the factor quantity effect represents the total impact of η_K and η_L. We write the factor quantity effect shown in column IVa for all variables in column III by making use of theorem 4.34b. From now on we concentrate on the innovation effect (Z) in 4.33d.

The most important measurement of technological change is the innovation intensity J, defined as follows:

Definition   The innovation intensity J in a dynamic production function is the percentage change of output Q per unit of time when both K and L are held constant:

$$J = (\partial Q/\partial t)/Q = f_t/Q > 0 \quad \text{(by 4.33d)} \tag{4.35}$$

When both inputs are held constant, any output increase through time can occur only through the intensity of innovation. As defined, J is a non-negative number. Substituting Q, p and d for x in equation 4.33d, the various innovation effects are:

innovation effect for Q: $(\partial Q/\partial t)/Q = f_t/Q = J$ (4.36a)
innovation effect for $p = Q/L$: $(\partial p/\partial t)/p = ((\partial Q/\partial t)/L)/(Q/L) = J$ (4.36b)
innovation effect for $d = Q/K$: $(\partial d/\partial t)/d = (\partial Q/\partial t/K)/(Q/K) = J$ (4.36c)

Since the innovation effects for Q, p and d are all equal to J, the relevant growth equations are:

$$\eta_Q = \phi_L \eta_L + \phi_K \eta_K + J \quad \text{(T1)} \tag{4.37a}$$
$$\eta_p = \phi_K \eta_{K*} + J \quad \text{(T2)} \tag{4.37b}$$
$$\eta_d = J - \phi_L \eta_{K*} \quad \text{(T3)} \tag{4.37c}$$

These growth equations are listed in column IV of table 4.1 and indexed by T1, T2 and T3 for ease of reference.

The economic interpretation of T1 is that the growth rate of national income is decomposable into the innovation intensity (J) and a factor quantity effect consisting of a capital contribution term ($\phi_K \eta_K$) and a labor contribution term ($\phi_L \eta_L$). Each term is the product of the factor growth rate and the factor elasticity of output.

The economic interpretation of T2 is that the growth rate of per capita income – the most important index of economic welfare at the aggregate level – is decomposable into the innovation intensity J and the factor quantity effect $\phi_K \eta_{K*}$ – the product of the rate of capital deepening (η_{K*}) and the capital elasticity of output (ϕ_K). The persistent tendency for capital deepening ($\eta_{K*} > 0$) represents a well-known long-run characteristic of the modern growth epoch, even though brief periods of capital shallowing growth may be observed in the commercialized sector of a dualistic developing economy.[4]

The economic interpretation of T3 is that the growth rate of the productivity of capital ($d = Q/K$) is composed of a positive innovation intensity effect (J) and a negative capital deepening effect ($-\phi_L \eta_{K*}$). From the Harrod–Domar growth rate of capital ($\eta_K = sd$) in equation 4.22 we derive

$$\eta_{\eta_K} = \eta_s + \eta_d = \eta_s + J - \phi_L \eta_{K*} \text{ or} \tag{4.38a}$$
$$\eta_{\eta_K} = J - \phi_L \eta_{K*} \text{ (for } \eta_s = 0) \tag{4.38b}$$

Thus, with a constant average propensity to save ($\eta_s = 0$), the growth equation (4.38a) determines the rate of capital acceleration.

Definition A growth process is characterized by capital acceleration (deceleration) if $\eta_{\eta_K} > 0$ ($\eta_{\eta_K} < 0$).

The process of capital acceleration (or deceleration) represents an important growth phenomenon as it relates to both the long-run viability of mature capitalism in avoiding stagnation and the adequacy of balanced growth in the dualistic developing economy. When the economy has a constant average propensity to save (s), the innovation intensity (J) and the rate of capital deepening (η_{K*}) have opposite effects on capital acceleration. A high innovation intensity (J) contributes to capital acceleration, while a high rate of capital deepening (η_{K*}) contributes to capital deceleration. In the absence of technological change ($J=0$), equation 3.6b becomes:

$$\eta_{\eta_k} = -\phi_L \eta_{K*} \tag{4.39}$$

From this we have:

When the average propensity to save is constant ($\eta_s=0$), capital deepening (shallowing) growth implies capital deceleration (acceleration) in the absence of technology change ($J=0$). (4.40)

The preconditions ($J = \eta_s = 0$) of this lemma are satisfied by many "saving-pushed" models in a world with no technological change. The lemma is applicable to all such models, including the Solow model.

A Marxist might interpret a high and constant s as a persistent drive to accumulate capital. The above lemma suggests that, in the absence of technological change ($J=0$), capital deepening growth is always accompanied by a persistent decline of η_K. The capitalists' drive to accumulate can thus only be maintained by a sufficiently strong innovation intensity which compensates for the depressing effects of capital deepening on the capital growth rate.[5]

Returning to the term $E(x,t)\eta_t$ in 4.33d, where x stands for the marginal productivity of labor f_L (similarly for the marginal productivity of capital f_K and $M = f_L/f_K$), H_L, H_K and B are:

$$H_L = E(f_L,t)\eta_t = (f_{Lt}/f_L)(1/t) = f_{Lt}/f_L \tag{4.41a}$$
(innovation effect on MPP_L)

$$H_K = E(f_K,t)\eta_t = f_{Kt}/f_K \tag{4.41b}$$
(innovation effect on MPP_K)

$$B = E(M,t)\eta_t = E(f_L,t)\eta_t - E(f_K,t)\eta_t = H_L - H_K \tag{4.41c}$$
(innovation effect on M)

H_L is the percentage increase of f_L per unit of time (H_K is symmetrical) and B is the percentage change of M per unit of time, all when capital and labor inputs are fixed. These growth equations are listed as T4, T5 and T6 in table 4.1:

$$\eta_w = \epsilon_{LL}\eta_{K*} + H_L \qquad \text{(T4)} \qquad\qquad (4.42a)$$
$$\eta_\pi = -\epsilon_{KK}\eta_{K*} + H_K \qquad \text{(T5)} \qquad\qquad (4.42b)$$
$$\eta_M = \epsilon\eta_{K*} + H_L - H_K \qquad \text{(T6)} \qquad\qquad (4.42c)$$

When x in equation 4.33d stands for ϕ_L, ϕ_K and $r = \phi_L/\phi_K$:

$$E(\phi_L,t)\eta_t = E(f_L,t)\eta_t - E(p,t)\eta_t = H_L - J \qquad (4.43a)$$
$$E(\phi_K,t)\eta_t = E(fK,t)\eta_t - E(d,t)\eta_t = H_K - J \qquad (4.43b)$$
$$E(r,t)\eta_t = E(\phi_L,t)\eta_t - E(\phi_K,t)\eta_t = H_L - H_K = B \qquad (4.43c)$$

These growth equations are listed as T7, T8, T9 in table 4.1:

$$\eta_{\phi_L} = (\epsilon_{LL} - \phi_K)\eta_{K*} + H_L - J \qquad \text{(T7)} \qquad (4.44a)$$
$$\eta_{\phi_K} = (\phi_L - \epsilon_{KK})\eta_{K*} + H_K - J \qquad \text{(T8)} \qquad (4.44b)$$
$$\eta_r = (\epsilon - 1)\eta_{K*} + B \qquad\qquad\qquad \text{(T9)} \qquad (4.44c)$$

We have now derived the growth equations T1–T9; the remainder of this chapter explores the economic significance of these equations. Section 4.5 analyzes the notion of innovation intensity, while section 4.6 explores the factor bias of innovations involving H_K and H_L.

4.5 Innovation Intensity and Growth: Applications

Kuznets pointed out that the major characteristic of the modern growth epoch is the application of science and technology which, together with capital accumulation, contributes to the rapid growth of national income. It fell to Solow to prove, with the help of statistics, that this is indeed the case. The growth equation for national income (T1) leads directly to

$$1 = \alpha^0 + \beta^0 \text{ where} \qquad\qquad (4.45a)$$
$$\alpha^0 = (\phi_L\eta_L + \phi_K\eta_K)/\eta_Q \qquad (4.45b)$$
$$\beta^0 = J/\eta_Q \qquad\qquad\qquad (4.45c)$$

α^0 and β^0 are the fractional contributions to η_Q traced to the "factor quantity effect" and the "innovation intensity effect," respectively. The comparative magnitudes of α^0 and β^0 are indicative of their relative importance as causal factors in the expansion of GNP. To permit an estimation of α^0 and β^0, T1 can also be written as:

$$J = \eta_Q - (\phi_L\eta_L + \phi_K\eta_K) \qquad (4.46)$$

When the time series for $w(t)$ (wage rate), $L(t)$ (labor force), $K(t)$ (capital stock) and $Q(t)$ (GNP) are collected, η_Q, η_L and η_K can all be estimated. The coincidence of the production and distributional interpretations of $\phi_L = w(L/Q)$ allowed Solow to estimate the time series for $\phi_L(t)$ and $\phi_K(t) = 1 - \phi_L(t)$. Thus, all terms on the right-hand side could be estimated and J could be derived as the residual of equation 4.46.

The time series for $\alpha^0(t)$ and $\beta^0(t)$ in 4.45 can then be estimated. One major conclusion of this statistical investigation was that over a long period of time, the average level of $\beta^0(t)$ is far greater (three times as large) than that of $\alpha^0(t)$. This implies that for the expansion of GNP and material well-being, population growth (η_L) and the augmentation of the capital stock by austerity (η_K) are nowhere near as important as the exploration of the frontiers of science and technology requiring human ingenuity, R&D, and the communication of ideas through patents, journals, newspapers and universities, as well as the less spectacular "blue collar" innovations in factory repair shops and on factory floors.

4.6 The Factor Bias of Innovation

4.6.1 Innovation and variations in wage and profit rates

When the dynamic production function $Q = f(K,L,t)$ is postulated, there are two dimensions of technological change through time: innovation intensity J, which we have just analyzed, and the factor bias of innovation, which we discuss in this section. It is in terms of these two dimensions that all innovations can be classified.

From equations T1, T2, and T3 the growth rates of GNP (η_Q), labor productivity (η_p), and capital productivity (η_d) are determined by J when capital K and labor L are constant ($\eta_L = \eta_K = 0$). By the same reasoning, we see from growth equations T4 and T5 that when K and L are constant, the marginal productivities of labor and capital increase by:

$$\eta_w = H_L \text{ when } \eta_K = \eta_L = 0 \qquad (4.46a)$$
$$\eta_\pi = H_K \text{ when } \eta_K = \eta_L = 0 \qquad (4.46b)$$

These results suggest a "verbal" definition of H_L and H_K:

Definition The innovation impact on the wage rate H_L is the percentage increase of the marginal productivity of labor when both capital and labor are constant. (The innovation impact on the profit rate H_K is defined symmetrically.)

The direction of change of the real wage (w) and the profit rate (π) – whether w and π increase or decrease though time – is among the most important growth relevant issues in both LDCs and DCs. In LDCs, whether or not the real wage increases and how fast it rises are key issues related not only to the absolute welfare of the working class, but also to the equity of income distribution.

Moreover, in our analysis of the LDC transition growth process a crucial development characteristic may be the existence of an "unlimited supply of labor" – a state characterized by the near constancy of the agricultural as well as the non-agricultural real wage. In such a situation, industrial sector labor absorption takes place over a considerable stretch of time under the near-constancy of the real wage assumption, and hence the rapidity of capital accumulation and technology change together constitute the principal determinants of the rapidity of labor absorption.

In industrially advanced DCs, to cite just one application, the direction of change of the profit rate π lies at the heart of the thesis of long-run stagnation (which occurs when π declines persistently). In particular, the Marxian thesis of the need for increased labor "exploitation" to maintain the profit rate is related to growth forces determining the direction of the simultaneous change in the wage and profit rates. The concepts H_L and H_K are absolutely crucial for the stability of the relative shares, economic welfare, social harmony, and the long run viability of the capitalist economy in both DCs and LDCs, as is fully demonstrated in later chapters.

4.6.2 Labor or capital-using innovations

To analyze "distributional equity," it is important to know whether technological change caused the wage rate η_w to increase at a rate faster or slower than the profit rate η_π. This leads to the following definitions of the factor bias of innovation:

Definition   The labor-using (capital-using) bias of innovation B_L (B_K) is:

$$B_L = H_L - J \text{ (degree of labor-using bias)} \tag{4.47a}$$
$$B_K = H_K - J \text{ (degree of capital-using bias)} \tag{4.47b}$$

Innovation is labor-using (similarly capital-using) if:

$$B_L > 0, \text{ or } H_L > J \text{ (labor-using bias)} \tag{4.48a}$$
$$B_L < 0, \text{ or } H_L < J \text{ (labor-saving bias)}$$
$$B_K > 0, \text{ or } H_K > J \text{ (capital-using bias)} \tag{4.48b}$$
$$B_K < 0, \text{ or } H_K < J \text{ (capital-saving bias)}$$

Equations 4.48a and b are descriptive of the **direction** of factor-using bias – the innovation is "labor-using" when the marginal product of labor is increased by a percentage greater than J. Equations 4.47a and b are descriptive of the **degree** of factor-using bias – stressing the **amount** of the excess of H_L over J.

The two indices of factor bias (B_L and B_K) are clearly not independent of each other. Under the condition of CRTS:

$$J = \phi_L H_L + \phi_K H_K \qquad (4.49a)$$
$$0 = \phi_L B_L + \phi_K B_K \qquad (4.49b)$$
$$-B_K/B_L = \phi_L/\phi_K = r > 0 \qquad (4.49c)$$
$$B \equiv H_L - H_K = B_L - B_K \qquad (4.49d)$$

Proof: 4.49a follows from the differentiation of $Q = f_L L + f_K K$ with respect to t to obtain

$$\partial Q/\partial t = Lf_{Lt} + Kf K_t = (L/f_L)(f_{Lt}/f_L) + (K/f_K)(f_{Kt}/f_K).$$

4.49b follows from 4.49a and 4.47ab, that is, $J = \phi_L(B_L + J) + \phi_K(B_K + J)$.
4.49c follows from 4.49b.
4.49d follows from 4.47ab   Q.E.D.

Thus, the weighted average of H_L and H_K is J (4.49a) and the weighted average of B_L and B_K is zero (4.49b). Equation 4.49c shows that B_L and B_K always have the opposite sign. Thus, under CRTS a labor-using innovation automatically implies capital saving. The index $B \equiv H_L - H_K$ is also the difference between B_L and B_K. For this reason, B always has the same sign as B_L. All of this may be summarized as:

$$B_L \gtreqqless 0 \leftrightarrow B_K \lesseqqgtr 0 \leftrightarrow B \gtreqqless 0 \leftrightarrow H_L \gtreqqless J \gtreqqless H_K \qquad (4.50)$$

The triplet of inequalities in equation 4.50 identifies three types of innovations according to the following definitions:

Hicksian labor-using or capital-saving: $B > 0$ (or $B_K < 0 < B_L$),
 implying $H_K < J < H_L$ (4.51a)
Hicksian labor-saving or capital-using: $B < 0$ (or $B_L < 0 < B_K$),
 implying $H_L < J < H_K$ (4.51b)
Hicksian neutral: $B = B_L = B_K = 0$, implying $H_L = J = H_K$ (4.51c)

"Labor-using" and "capital-saving" are equivalent (and so are "labor-saving" and "capital-using"), with the pair (H_L, H_K) always straddling J. In the case of a Hicks labor-using innovation, the marginal product of labor is raised by a percentage larger than the percentage increase in the marginal product of capital (with constant K and L). The opposite is true for a capital-using innovation. When $B = 0$ (equivalently, when $B_L = B_K = 0$), the innovation is a Hicks-neutral innovation. In this borderline case, the wage rate and the profit rate are raised by the same percentage corresponding to the innovation intensity J. When K and L are constant, equation T6 implies:

$$\eta_M = B, \text{ if } \eta_L = \eta_K = 0, \text{ implying} \qquad (4.52a)$$
$$\eta_M = 0 \leftrightarrow B = 0 \qquad (4.52b)$$

In the competitive neoclassical case, $w = f_L$ and $\pi = f_K$. Thus, when $\eta_K = \eta_L = 0$, the rate of increase of M is B. The relative factor price ratio M is unaffected if and only if innovations are neutral in the Hicksian sense. M moves in a direction favorable to the wage rate (a higher w/π ratio) if and only if the innovation is labor-using. Thus the labor-using bias of innovations is key for the analysis of the functional as well as the size distribution of income (see chapter 9).

A diagrammatic presentation of factor bias à la Hicks is helpful. Let the production isoquant (the Q curve in figure 4.3(a)), the marginal productivity of labor curve (the f_L curve in figure 4.3(b)) and the marginal productivity of capital curve (the f_K curve in figure 4.3(c)) be given. When the

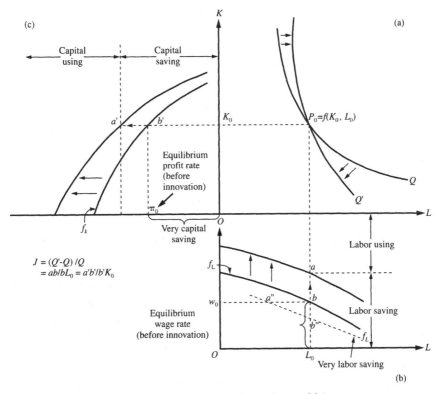

Figure 4.3 Innovation intensity and bias

initial factor endowment point (K_0, L_0) is given at a point P_0 (figure 4.3(a)), the equilibrium wage rate w_0 (the profit rate π_0) is indicated by b (b') in figure 4.3(b) (4.3(c)).

When an innovation takes place, the triplet of curves (Q, f_K, f_L) are all affected as indicated by the double arrows in the diagram. In case of a Hicks-neutral innovation, there is no "swivel" from Q to Q' in figure 4.3(a); only the index is "blown up" by the amount J. At the same time, w_0 and π_0 in figures 4.3(b) and 4.3(c) are raised by the same percentage as the innovation intensity J, as indicated by the points (a, a'). Referring to the points in figures 4.3(b) and (c):

$$J = ab/bL_0 = a'b'/b'K_0 \qquad (4.53)$$

In case of a labor-using innovation, the wage rate is raised to a point higher than a in figure 4.3(b), while the profit rate is raised to a point lower than a' in figure 4.3(c). At the same time, the slope of the Q-isoquant becomes steeper – see figure 4.3(a). The opposite is true when the innovation is capital-using.

4.6.3 Very labor-saving and very capital-saving innovations

If the innovation is very labor-saving, the MPP_L may actually be lowered by the innovation. In other words, an innovation may be very labor-saving or very capital-saving:

$$\text{very labor-saving } (VLS) \text{ when } H_L < 0 \qquad (4.54a)$$
$$\text{very capital-saving } (VKS) \text{ when } H_K < 0 \qquad (4.54b)$$

In figure 4.3b, for VLS the dotted f_L-curve passes through a point b'' lower than b. The concept of "very labor-saving" has an economic significance quite different from that of "labor-saving." When technology change is "labor-saving," we can only be sure that the relative increase in the wage rate is less in comparison with the increase in the profit rate (see equation 4.51b). However, the wage rate decreases absolutely when the innovation is very labor-saving.

The above analysis assumes full employment equilibrium. Hence the factor endowment point (P_0 in figure 4.3(a)) determines equilibrium factor prices (w_0 and π_0). In case unemployment exists, the actual employment of labor may be less than the endowed labor force L_0. For example, if the real wage w_0 is rigid in figure 4.3(b), a very labor-saving innovation reduces the employed labor force (to a'') rather than causing the wage rate to decline (to b'').

This vision of an "underemployment equilibrium" was entertained by Marx for the mature capitalist economy. As capitalists resort to "very labor-saving innovations" to "protect the profit rate" (see equation 4.46b), the working class is "necessarily exploited" by unemployment and/or the suppression of the real wage.

Lewis (1954) and Fei/Ranis (1966) have used the notion of a temporary underemployment equilibrium to study transition growth in a dualistic developing economy. The assumption of an unlimited supply of labor, implying the near-constancy of the real wage in the industrial sector of a dualistic developing economy, means that the factor bias of innovation crucially affects both the rate of industrial sector employment generation and the distribution of income, analyzed in later chapters.

4.6.4 Alternative indices of factor bias

The three Hicksian indices of factor bias (B, B_L, B_K) are intrinsically related (see equation 4.50). To develop these relations further, the symmetry of K and L under constant returns to scale implies:

$$1 = \phi_K + \phi_L \text{ (by CRTS)} \tag{4.55a}$$
$$\epsilon = \epsilon_{LL} + \epsilon_{KK} \text{ (by 4.25c)} \tag{4.55b}$$
$$B = B_L - B_K \text{ (by 4.49d)} \tag{4.55c}$$

Hence:

$$r = \phi_L/\phi_K = \epsilon_{KK}/\epsilon_{LL} = -B_K/B_L \text{ (by 4.49c, 4.28b), implying} \tag{4.56a}$$
$$1/\phi_K = \epsilon/\epsilon_{LL} = B/B_L \tag{4.56b}$$

Proof 4.56b is obtained by adding 1 to 4.56a and applying 4.55. Q.E.D.

From this:

$$\phi_K = \epsilon_{LL}/\epsilon = B_L/B \text{ (by 4.30a)} \tag{4.57a}$$
$$\phi_L = \epsilon_{KK}/\epsilon = -B_K/B \text{ (by 4.30b)} \tag{4.57b}$$

Historically, ϕ_L has fluctuated in the vicinity of 0.6 in developed economies. As stated in equation 4.29, the size of the distributive share is determined by the other factor accounting for a larger percentage of the inelasticity of substitution. But under CRTS, the static concepts ϕ_K and ϕ_L are also factor bias related phenomena via the dynamic concepts B_L, B_K, and B. Moreover, B_L as a fraction of B is ϕ_K, the capital share, while B_K as a (negative) fraction of B is ϕ_L, the labor share. Thus, B, B_L, B_K are related both to the distributive shares and the inelasticity of substitution.

4.7 Factor price and factor share-related growth equations

4.7.1 Factor price-related equations

In an earlier section we derived the growth equations for the triplet $(\eta_w, \eta_\pi, \eta_M)$ involving the terms H_L and H_K (T4, T5 and T6 in equation 4.42). Using the equations that decompose H_L and H_K (4.47ab), these can be rewritten as:

$$\eta_w = \epsilon_{LL}\eta_{K*} + B_L + J \,(= \epsilon_{LL}\eta_{K*} + H_L) \qquad (4.58a)$$
$$\eta_\pi = -\,\epsilon_{KK}\eta_{K*} + B_K + J \,(= -\,\epsilon_{KK}\eta_{K*} + H_K) \qquad (4.58b)$$
$$\eta_M = \epsilon\eta_{K*} + B \qquad (4.58c)$$

These equations are reproduced in table 4.1 (T4, T5, T6). In these equations, the causal factors on the right-hand side are decomposed into a capital deepening effect (involving the term η_{K*}) and an innovation effect (involving B_L, B_K, B and J).

Proceeding again to a preliminary look at the application of these growth equations in the mature economy, the growth phenomenon is increasingly centered on capital accumulation η_K and population growth η_L in the presence of technological change. A long-run characteristic of modern economic growth is a sustained increase in the real wage w that is indicative of the continued exploration of science and technology that benefits workers. The growth equation for w (equation 4.58a) shows that the rapidity of the increase in the wage rate is contributed to by the rapidity of capital deepening ($\eta_{K*} > 0$) and is proportional to the degree of the law of diminishing returns to labor (ϵ_{LL}). Thus, the real wage rises when labor becomes relatively more scarce. A rapid increase in the wage rate can also result from high innovation intensity J and/or high labor-using bias (high positive B_L).

Historically, a sustained increase in w came late in Western Europe's transition process. Throughout the initial period of transition growth (1780–1820 in England, for example), classical economists observed the near-constancy of the real wage w and referred to this phenomenon as the "iron law of wages," believing that the real wage would always remain constant. In modern development economics, the "iron law of wages" became the "unlimited supply of labor" condition, viewed as a temporary transition growth phenomenon in labor surplus LDCs.

The forecasting errors of classical economists can be forgiven because they were unaware that they were living at a time of transition. Since workers had not yet acquired scarcity value, the wage rate was determined by institutional rather than competitive market forces (see chapter 3). They had no idea that the labor surplus condition would soon terminate and that capital accumulation, carrying the full intensity of the technological potential J, would increase the welfare of the working class.

Shortly after the close of the classical period in the nineteenth century, Marx formally analyzed the capitalist growth process and thought he detected a contradiction between the drive for accumulation (high η_K) of the capitalist class and their sensitivity to the level of the rate of profit π under a system of private property ownership. This possible contradiction is shown in the equation for the growth of the profit rate (equation 4.58b). Unless rescued by technological change, the drive for capital accumulation (η_K) easily exceeds the population growth rate η_L and leads to capital deepening ($\eta_{K*} > 0$), which causes the profit rate to decline absolutely ($\eta_\pi < 0$).

The only way that the profit rate (π) can be prevented from falling is for capital-using (or labor-saving) technology change ($H_K = B_K + J$) to occur with sufficient strength to overwhelm the profit depressing effects of capital deepening growth. Capitalists certainly do not hesitate to resort to technological change with high intensity J and/or a high capital-using bias B_K – the two components of H_K.

Equation 4.58c states that the rate of growth of the relative factor price ratio M is proportional to the rate of capital deepening and the "inelasticity of substitution." With increasing capital per head, M increases rapidly (that is, in favor of the working class) if the law of diminishing returns is strong (that is, ϵ is large). A large labor-using bias B works in the same direction.

4.7.2 Distributive shares-related growth equations

The growth equations for the distributive shares (ϕ_L, ϕ_K and $r = \phi_L/\phi_K$) are presented as T7, T8 and T9 in table 4.1. Making use of equations 4.47ab as well as:

$$\epsilon_{LL} - \phi_K = \phi_K\epsilon - \phi_K = \phi_K(\epsilon - 1) \text{ by (4.57a)} \qquad (4.59a)$$
$$\phi_L - \epsilon_{KK} = \phi_L - \phi_L\epsilon = \phi_L(1 - \epsilon) \text{ by (4.57b)}, \qquad (4.59b)$$

these growth equations can be written alternatively as:

$$\eta_{\phi_L} = \phi_K(\epsilon - 1)\eta_{K*} + B_L \qquad (4.60a)$$
$$\eta_{\phi_K} = -\phi_L(\epsilon - 1)\eta_{K*} + B_K \qquad (4.60b)$$
$$\eta_r = (\epsilon - 1)\eta_{K*} + B \qquad (4.60c)$$

The factors on the right-hand side of these equations consist of a capital deepening effect (involving the term η_{K*}) and an innovation bias effect (involving the terms B_L, B_K and B).

In interpreting these equations, the production function is "substitution inelastic" when $\epsilon > 1$. In the modern economic growth epoch, when capital is an "agent" embodying the new ideas of science and technology, it can be assumed that the laws of diminishing returns hold strongly ($\epsilon = (\epsilon_{LL} + \epsilon_{KK}) > 1$) and substitution inelasticity ($\epsilon > 1$) is the empirically "normal" case. The equations in 4.60 imply that a capital deepening growth process ($\eta_{K*} > 0$) causes both the absolute wage share (ϕ_L) and the relative wage share ($r = \phi_L/\phi_K$) to increase. Writing $r = M/K*$ ($= (w/\pi)(L/K)$) implies:

$$\eta_r > 0 \leftrightarrow \eta_M > \eta_{K*} \tag{4.61}$$

Thus, r increases when the factor price ratio (M) increases faster than the factor endowment ratio ($K*$), a condition ensured with $\epsilon > 1$, the normal case as capital deepening occurs.

A labor-using bias ($B_K < 0 < B_L$) contributes to an increase (decrease) in the labor (capital) share. It is evident that a high (or low) intensity of innovation (J) has no impact on the factor shares (ϕ_L or ϕ_K) or the relative factor prices (M) – although it has substantial impact on the growth rate of output (η_Q) and factor productivities (η_p, η_d). Thus, the intensity of innovation (J) has welfare (w, π) and productivity (p, d, Q) effects, while the factor bias of innovations has impact on "equity" and "distributional justice" (M, ϕ_L, ϕ_K, r). Equation 4.56a implies:

$$\eta_r = \eta_{\epsilon_{KK}} - \eta_{\epsilon_{LL}} \tag{4.62a}$$
$$\eta_r > 0 \leftrightarrow \eta_{\epsilon_{KK}} > \eta_{\epsilon_{LL}} \tag{4.62b}$$
$$(\epsilon - 1)\eta_{K*} + B = \eta_{\epsilon_{KK}} - \eta_{\epsilon_{LL}} \tag{4.62c}$$

Equation 4.62b shows that r increases if and only if technological change occurs so that the laws of diminishing returns apply more strongly with respect to capital than labor. This technical interpretation is equivalent to the meaning derived from equation 4.60c tracing the same causal factors stated in equation 4.62c.

4.7.3 Applications of the Growth equations (T1–T9)

In summary, the growth equations (T1–T9) in table 4.1 are derived from the dynamic production function $Q = f(K,L,t)$ that describes production relations at an aggregate level. To the extent that "growth theorizing" is concerned with the rapidity of the growth of the following set of aggregate variables:

$$E = (\eta_Q, \eta_p, \eta_d, \eta_w, \eta_\pi, \eta_M, \eta_{\phi_L}, \eta_{\phi_K}, \eta_r, \eta_{K*}) \tag{4.63}$$

these equations are applicable. Hence, what causally determines growth rates must be at the center of all growth theory – whether concerned with agrarianism, the classical school, Marx, the mature economy, or LDC transition growth. We turn to a fuller analysis of such applications in the chapters that follow.

CHAPTER 4   THE NEOCLASSICAL PRODUCTION FUNCTION, GROWTH AND DEVELOPMENT

NOTES

1   For notational consistency, note that in chapters considering a dualistic economy, such as chapters 3, 7 and 8, we label the industrial labor force "W" and the agricultural labor force "L". However, chapters 4–6 focus on only single-sector economies. In these chapters, we stay with the conventional notation of L representing total labor in the production function.

2   For now we assume that there is full employment so that the endowment and input points coincide.

3   A brief comment on the historical significance of these growth equations may be helpful. Approximately half a century elapsed after the classical writings appeared before Marx took up the cudgel, followed by the neoclassical school which challenged him. However, while Marx was concerned with growth (i.e., long-run stagnation and instability induced by the technology of capitalism), the neoclassical school's analysis was essentially static, focusing on the evolution of a many commodities-oriented Walrasian equilibrium theory with little interest in capital accumulation or technology change. Our analysis here is dynamic but based on the specification of the properties of the so-called static neoclassical production function with constant returns to scale.

4   For example, in Japan between 1880 and 1920; see chapter 7.

5   All arguments are equally applicable to a socialist economy (with public ownership of capital). Socialism and capitalism face the same difficulties in trying to prevent the decline of the capital growth rate. What differentiates capitalism from socialism is a sensitivity to the rate of profit that can only be analyzed with the aid of growth equation T5, involving the profit rate. When the profit rate is not involved, the arguments are institution-neutral.

5
A General Analysis of Growth Systems

5.1 Introduction

Economics is an area of social science concerned with the analysis of human relations. What gives macroeconomics its peculiar characteristic as an academic sub-discipline is the fact that it is concerned with a holistic operational perspective, viewing the totality of all essential economic phenomena – production, consumption, exchange, and income distribution – as forming a related system that can be modeled. Ever since the age of the classical school, economic models have followed this tradition by interpreting "growth" as the movement of a holistic system of related and dated economic variables through time.

Chapter 4 developed a system of growth equations (T1, T2, ... T9) involving the rapidity of the dated variables $(Q, P_1, d \ldots r)$ via production relations. In the construction of economic models it takes a number of these equations to build a growth model incorporating several dynamic variables. This chapter investigates a number of such applications. While the classical economists of the eighteenth century, Marx in the nineteenth, and Schumpeter in the twentieth century were interested in growth in a more "literary" tradition, it was really not until after World War II that the phenomenon was studied rigorously beginning with the "crude" Harrod–Domar model. Moving from that model to the neoclassical growth model of Solow represented an important landmark in the post-war literature that is studied in section 5.2 of this chapter.

In the literary tradition of the nineteenth century, Marx and the classical economists were concerned with a number of "inherent" conflicts – the distributional conflict between wages and profits and the conflict between gains in labor productivity and capital acceleration – of which a rigorous analysis necessitates the use of almost all growth equations simultaneously. In section 5.3 we investigate the relatedness of growth equations by addressing some of these conflicts. The symmetry of capital (K) and labor (L) in the growth equations (T2–T9) suggests a "structural duality" which is explored in section 5.3.

5.2 From Harrod-Domar to Solow

5.2.1 The crude Harrod–Domar model

The first rigorous growth model used by the post-war economists was a crude version of the Harrod–Domar model. In this model the basic assumptions are:

$$\eta_s = 0 \tag{5.1a}$$
$$\eta_d = 0 \tag{5.1b}$$

Thus, in equation 5.1ab, s (average propensity to save) and d (capital productivity) are assumed to be constant. We can then derive the growth rate of capital ($i \equiv \eta_K$):

$$\eta_K = i = (dK/dt)/K \tag{5.2a}$$
$$I = dK/dt = S \tag{5.2b}$$

In this derivation the underlying assumption is the equality of savings (S) and investment (I). Hence the growth rate of capital is determined by savings (or austerity) forces. This savings-pushed characteristic is shared by many growth models.

Since i is constant, the solution of the capital growth path becomes

$$K = K(0)e^{(sd)t} \text{ with} \tag{5.3a}$$
$$i = \eta_K = sd \tag{5.3b}$$

If the population is growing at a constant rate:

$$\eta_L = v \text{ (constant population growth rate), or} \tag{5.4a}$$
$$L = L(0)e^{vt} \tag{5.4b}$$

The rate of growth of capital per head becomes:

$$\eta_{K^*} = sd - v, \text{ implying} \tag{5.5a}$$
$$\eta_{K^*} > 0 \text{ if and only if } sd > v \tag{5.5b}$$

Thus, capital deepening growth occurs if and only if the savings rate (s) is sufficiently large relative to the population growth rate. All early post-war planning efforts were dominated by this model.

5.2.2 The neoclassical growth model of Solow

The Solow–Swan growth model represents the second major model based on the crude Harrod–Domar model. All assumptions of the previous model are kept, with the single exception that a static neoclassical production function ($Q = f(K,L)$) is used, implying non-constant capital productivity (d) when capital and labor are substitutable. Following this seminal contribution of Solow and Swan, a large number of savings-pushed models are produced to investigate growth under the assumption of technological stagnation.

As seen in chapter 4, a CRTS neoclassical production function implies that APP_L (p), MPP_L (f_L), APP_K (d) and MPP_K (f_K) are all functions of K^* – capital per head. These are represented by the four curves in the upper deck (p and f_L) and the lower deck (d and f_K) of figure 5.1, where K^* is measured on the horizontal axis. The APP_L curve is convex and increasing because it represents total output (Q) as a function of K when $L=1$. Thus, the slope of the p curve is f_K, indicated by the MPP_K curve in figure 5.1(b).

At point A of the APP_L curve, the slope of the radial line OA is $p/K^* = d$ as represented by the APP_K curve. The distance AB is $f_K K^*$. Hence the distance BC is equivalent to f_L because $p - AB = p - f_K K^* = Q/L - f_K K/L = (Q - f_K K)/L = f_L$. This implies that the MPP_L curve must

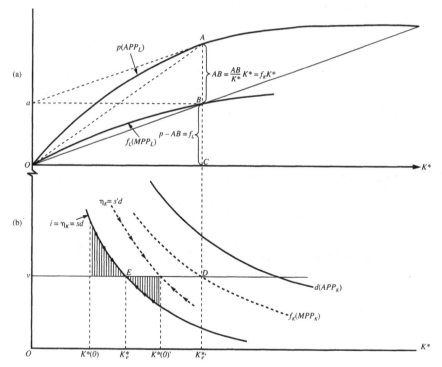

Figure 5.1 Neoclassical growth model with stationary technology

pass through point B. Thus, once labor productivity is given, the other three curves can be derived geometrically. This diagram allows us to investigate movements of the variables p, d, f_K, and f_L as a consistent system when K^* varies.

5.2.3 Determination of capital growth rates

Since the average propensity to save $(0<s<1)$ is a positive fraction, the growth rate of capital $(\eta_K = sd)$ is represented by the curve $i = \eta_K = sd$ in figure 5.1(b). With the constant population growth rate (v) represented by the height (Ov) of the horizontal line, a point of intersection (E) occurs at K_e^*, the long-run stationary value of K^* in the Solow–Swan model.

At a point where $\eta_K > v$ $(\eta_K < v)$, capital deepening (shallowing) growth occurs as K^* increases (decreases). Thus, when the initial value $K^*(0)$ $(K^*(0)')$ is less than (greater than) K_e^*, the value of K^* always increases (decreases) monotonically toward K_e^*. The major conclusion of the Solow-Swan model can be summarized in the following theorem:

Theorem   Given a constant population growth rate (v) and a constant saving rate (s), the growth rate of capital η_K increases (decreases) monotonically to a long-run stationary value K_e^* if the initial value of $K^*(0)$ is less than (greater than) K_e^*, with η_K converging to v.

5.2.4 Classification of solutions and the states of growth

A capital deepening (capital shallowing) growth process is always associated with capital deceleration $[\eta_K < 0]$ (acceleration $[\eta_K > 0]$). The two types of growth are shown in figure 5.2, where η_K approaches the population growth rate and K^* approaches K_e^* from above $(K^*(0)\,)$ or below $(K^*(0)')$.

The theoretical conclusion of Solow and Swan makes it clear that, with stationary technology, two types of growth may be differentiated. On the one hand, there is the notion of a long-run steady state characterized by the constancy of capital per head corresponding to K_e^*. On the other hand, there is the transition growth process toward the long-run stationary state.

The theorem of scale insensitivity implies the following corollary:

Theorem   In the absence of technological change and the constancy of s and v, the economy moves toward a long-run steady state characterized by:

$$\text{constancy of } K^*, p, d, f_L, f_K, M, \phi_L, \phi_K \text{ and } r \qquad (5.6a)$$
$$\eta_Q = \eta_K = \eta_L = v > 0 \text{ (by the constancy of } d) \qquad (5.6b)$$

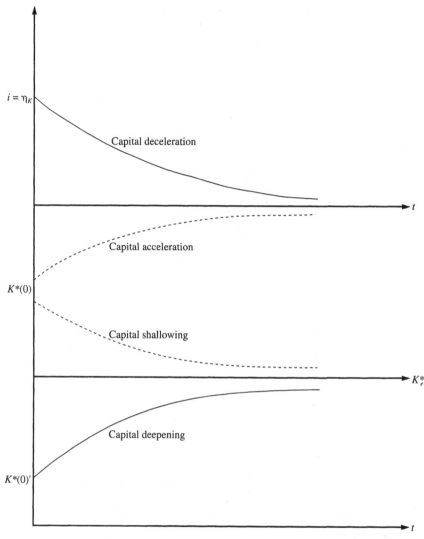

Figure 5.2 Types of growth under technology change

The economy grows at the speed of the population growth rate, but with all essential growth performance indices taking on constant values. This is essentially the von Neumann or Schumpeter state,[1] a long-run vision towards which the mature economy is tending in the absence of technology change.

Equation T2 in table 4.1 of chapter 4 implies a sustained increase in per capita income (η_p) when there is capital deepening ($\eta_{K*} > 0$) and/or high innovation intensity ($J > 0$). In a von Neumann state there is no sustained increase in p because both factors are not operating. Hence, without technological change sustained economic progress is ultimately impossible. This conclusion reinforces the results of a variety of statistical investigations (initially Solow's), that high innovation intensity is the root cause of increases in material well-being in the modern growth epoch.

The most important index of a society's welfare is its per capita consumption standard C^*, where:

$$C^* = C/L \text{ or} \tag{5.7a}$$
$$C^* = (Q - S)/L = p - S/L = p - s(Q/L) = (1 - s)p \tag{5.7b}$$

Hence C^* is the product of labor productivity p (or per capita income) and the propensity to consume $(1 - s)$. The constancy of p and s immediately implies the long-run constancy of the consumption standard in the von Neumann state.

5.2.5 The golden rule and the futility of excessive savings

The von Neumann state raises the question of the significance of possible variations in saving rates. In particular, we are interested in the implied level of the long-run consumption standard when the saving rate is changed.

When the saving rate (s) takes on a higher value, the η_K curve in figure 5.1(b) is raised (for example, to $\eta_K = s'd$; $s<s'$), leading to a higher long-run stationary value $K^*(0)' > K_e^*$. Thus, there are infinitely many von Neumann states – as shown in figure 5.3 – such that a higher saving rate corresponds to a steeper radial line representing capital per head (K_e^*) in a von Neumann state.

An important question is which of these von Neumann states has a perpetually higher level of per capita consumption (C^*). This question is meaningful because saving is only a means to achieve an end (a higher per capita consumption standard). A system which saves very little and has low capital per head is typical of a poor country that cannot afford a high per capita consumption standard. However, a country with high savings (in the extreme, one that saves 100 percent of its income) also cannot maintain a high consumption standard because C^* is zero if all income is saved. Thus, there exists a golden rule of saving where the per capita consumption standard is maximized. To find this golden rule of savings, the per capita consumption standard can be written as:

$$C^* = p - sp, \text{ where} \tag{5.8a}$$
$$sp = vK^* \text{ (per capita investment)} \tag{5.8b}$$
$$C^* = p - vK^* \text{ (by 5.8ab)} \tag{5.8c}$$

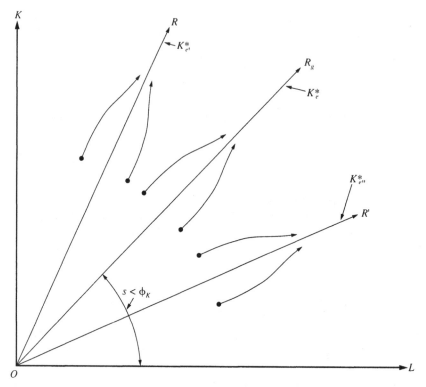

Figure 5.3 Alternative von Neumann states

To prove 5.8ab we have:

Proof $sp = s(Q/L) = I/L = (I/K)/(L/K) = \eta_K K^* = vK^*$ in the von Neumann state.   Q.E.D.

In figure 5.4(a), the p curve of figure 5.1(a) is reproduced. When vK^* of equation 5.8 is represented by a radial line OR, the (shaded) vertical distance between OR and the p-curve is the per capita consumption standard C^* by 5.8c. Since the slope of vK^* is v and the slope of the p curve is f_K, the maximum value of C^* is reached where $v = f_K$, indicated where the tangent line ab is parallel to OR. In other words, C^* is maximized when K_e^* is determined such that v and f_K are equated. This is the Golden Rule:

$$\eta_K = v = f_K \text{ (or } sd = f_K\text{), implying} \tag{5.9a}$$
$$s = S/Q = \phi_K \tag{5.9b}$$
$$C^* = (1 - s)p = \phi_L p = f_L \tag{5.9c}$$

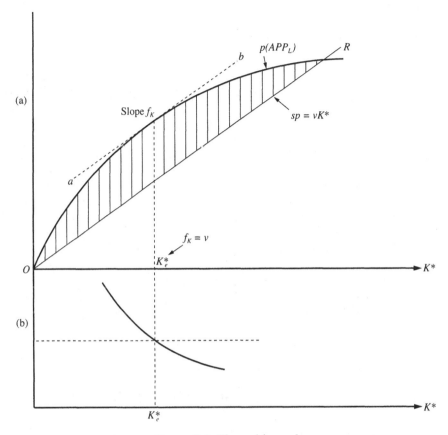

Figure 5.4 The golden rule

Proof: 5.9a implies $I/K = f_K$, or $s = Kf_K$ and $1 - s = Lf_L$. This implies
5.9b.   Q.E.D.

Equation 5.9 implies the classical saving rule (all profit income is saved)[2] and that the profit rate (f_K) is the same as the capital growth rate determined by the population growth rate v (5.9a). All this can be summarized as:

Theorem of the golden rule   The von Neumann state with the maximum per capita consumption is reached when the classical saving rule prevails $(s = \phi_K)$, which implies:

(a) the maximum per capita consumption standard equals the competitive wage rate $(C^* = f_L)$.

(b) the interest rate (f_K) is the same as the growth rate of capital and of population $(\eta_K = v)$. (5.10)

The "golden rule" suggests the futility of excessive savings. Referring to figure 5.3, let OR_g correspond to that von Neumann state which follows the golden rule. Then a higher average propensity to save suppresses the per capita consumption standard to a lower level. Associated with each von Neumann state is a rate of return to capital that is lower for a higher K_e^*. Thus a high saving rate is not practical for an entirely different reason – it depresses the profit rate (f_K) to a level intolerable for the capitalist class. If the profit share ϕ_K is 40 percent, the actual saving rate falls far short of the magnitude consistent with the classical saving rule. A full investigation of the relationship between the profit rate and technological change is postponed to a later section.

The Harrod–Domar model and the Solow neoclassical model thus represent important landmarks in post-war growth theory. Nevertheless, these models are based on an unrealistic assumption: the absence of technological change. The removal of this assumption permits a more realistic analysis of growth in the modern epoch. It is to this issue – consideration of growth when there is technological change – that we turn in the next chapter. Section 5.3 prepares for this effort by analyzing the relatedness of growth systems when technological change is present.

5.3 Growth Conflicts and Technology Change

Since capital (K) and labor (L) are joint and symmetrical inputs, the growth of capital and labor productivity (d, p) and factor rewards (π, w) are determined by a common causal system implicit in the growth process. There is always the possibility of a distributional conflict in that a higher growth of the wage rate (η_w) can only be obtained at the "cost" of a lower growth of the profit rate (η_π). Such a distributional conflict lies at the heart of the class struggle thesis of Marx as well as of the "collective bargaining" school in the second half of the twentieth century – both sides demanding increases in rewards indicated by the two components of a vector $\alpha = (\eta_\pi, \eta_w)$.

In the course of the growth process in the mature economy there is, in addition to the distributional conflict, also a productivity conflict in that at full employment a higher growth rate of labor productivity (η_p) can only be obtained at the cost of a lower growth rate of capital productivity (η_d). To see this, under the assumption of a constant average propensity to save, $\eta_i = \eta_s + \eta_d$ or $\eta_d = \eta_{\eta_K}$. Thus η_d is the same as the rate of capital acceleration. Let β denote the following vector: $(\eta_d, \eta_p) = (\eta_{\eta_K}, \eta_p)$. The productivity conflict is a conflict between high η_p (growth rate of per capita income) and η_{η_K} (capital acceleration). Both conflicts α and β must be resolved if capitalism – or any economic system – is to be viable in the long run.

It is obvious that for the analysis of such "conflicts," the pairs of growth rates $\alpha = (\eta_\pi, \eta_w)$ and $\beta = (\eta_d, \eta_p)$ must be investigated simultaneously. In this section we investigate the distributional conflict (α) and the productivity conflict (β) with the aid of growth equations T1–T9.

5.3.1 The growth versus distribution conflict

As a point of departure, the following theorem follows directly from equations (T4, T5):

Theorem   The innovation intensity (J) is the weighted average of (η_π, η_w), where the weights (ϕ_K, ϕ_L) are the distributive shares:

$$J = \phi_K \eta_\pi + \phi_L \eta_w \tag{5.11}$$

Proof   From T4 and T5, $\phi_L \eta_w = \phi_L \epsilon_{LL} \eta_{K^*} + \phi_L H_L$ and $\phi_K \eta_\pi = -\phi_K \epsilon_{KK} \eta_{K^*} + \phi_K H_K$. The sum leads to 5.11 because η_{K^*} ($\phi_L \epsilon_{LL} - \phi_K \epsilon_{KK}$) = 0 by 4.49a and 4.56a.   Q.E.D.

Let equation 5.11 be represented by the straight line AB in figure 5.5(a), where η_π (η_w) is measured on the horizontal (vertical) axis. The horizontal and vertical intercepts and the slope are defined as:

$$J_K = J/\phi_K \text{ (horizontal intercept)} \tag{5.12a}$$
$$J_L = J/\phi_L \text{ (vertical intercept)} \tag{5.12b}$$
$$J_L/J_K = -1/r = -\phi_K/\phi_L = -\epsilon_{LL}/\epsilon_{KK} \text{ (slope) by 4.56} \tag{5.12c}$$

Since the slope (5.12c) is negative, a higher value of η_w can be obtained only at the cost of a lower value of η_π. Thus there is a distributional conflict for all pairs of points $\alpha = (\eta_\pi, \eta_w)$ on AB. In view of their importance, we adopt the following definitions for J_L and J_K:

Definition J_L (J_K) is the factor augmentation intensity of innovation for labor (capital).

We denote all the points on AB by Ω_J and refer to this as the conflicting choice sets determined by J (with (x, y) referring to the axes in fifure 5.5(a)). Ω_J is partitioned by the vertical intercept (J_L) and the horizontal intercept (J_K) into three segments (subsets), with the following economic interpretations:

$$\Omega_J = ((x,y) / J = \phi_K x + \phi_L y) = \Omega_L \cup \Omega^+ \cup \Omega_K \tag{5.13a}$$
$$\Omega_L = ((x,y) / x < 0, y > J/\phi_L) \text{ (declining profit region)} \tag{5.13b}$$

$$\Omega_K = ((x,y) \mid x > J/\phi_K, y < 0) \text{ (declining wage region)} \qquad (5.13c)$$
$$\Omega^+ = ((x,y) \mid 0 < x < J_K, 0 < y < J_L) \text{ (mutually constrained}$$
$$\text{increasing region)} \qquad (5.13d)$$

We refer to $\alpha = (\eta_\pi, \eta_w)$ belonging to the region Ω_K as the declining wage region to stress the fact that the wage rate declines absolutely (similarly

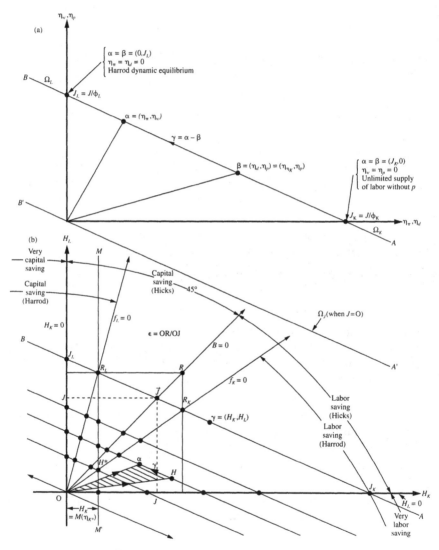

Figure 5.5 Growth and factor rewards

for the declining profit region). The set Ω^+, represented by the line segment $J_L J_K$ in figure 5.5(a), is the mutually constrained increasing region where both factor prices do not decline. This can only happen when the increase in the reward of both factors is constrained. The following corollary follows directly from equation 5.13:

Theorem The reward of a factor of production (η_π or η_w) is diminished (declines absolutely) if and only if the reward of the other factor of production increases at a rate higher than its factor augmentation intensity of innovation:

$$\eta_\pi \gtreqless 0 \leftrightarrow \eta_w \lesseqgtr J_L \qquad (5.14a)$$
$$\eta_w \gtreqless 0 \leftrightarrow \eta_\pi \lesseqgtr J_K \qquad (5.14b)$$

A factor price is constant through time if and only if the other price increases at the factor augmentation rate. In other words, when the interest rate is constant in the long run, the wage rate grows at the rate $J_L = J/\phi_L$. These special cases are represented by the boundary points J_L and J_K on the vertical and horizontal axes in figure 5.5(a). The special point J_L on the vertical axis is important because it corresponds to the long-run constancy of the interest rate.

It is obvious that for the capitalist system to be viable, wages and/or profits cannot decline absolutely and persistently through time. In the long run, an equilibrium value of $\alpha = (\eta_\pi, \eta_w)$ can only be a compromise solution realized somewhere in Ω^+. However, when the innovation intensity J is low, the Ω^+ set degenerates. (In the extreme case when $J=0$, Ω_J is represented by the line passing through the origin ($A'B'$) and Ω^+ contains only a single point – the origin.) It is difficult (and even mathematically impossible) to resolve a distributional conflict if both parties resist reductions of (w, π) and either party insists on some gain.

This distributional conflict is not resolved via the political process of collective bargaining in the twentieth century any more than it was via the "class struggle" of the nineteenth century. Sustained gains in the real wage and returns to capital (w, p) for the economy as a whole are instead determined by growth promotion forces (for example, capital deepening and technology change) which are relatively immune to the influence of the political process. This is not to deny that at a time of high innovation activity in some industries a union can force management to relinquish a part of the "innovation profit."

The fact that it is difficult to expect any class to accept an absolute decline in factor rewards implies that collective bargaining is likely to be more heated when innovation intensity is relatively high (before 1973 in the USA) rather than when it is low (after 1973). This is due to the fact that there is no incentive to bargain hard when there is no room for an increase that both parties know will be resisted by the other party. It is quite evident that the meaningfulness of "collective bargaining" rests firmly on a growth-theoretic foundation.

The two boundary cases – $\alpha = (0, J_L)$ on the vertical axis and $\alpha = (J_K, 0)$ on the horizontal axis – have special economic significance. The boundary case on the horizontal axis $(J_K, 0)$ represents the unlimited supply of labor case $(\eta_w = 0)$ in the transition growth of LDCs (chapter 7). The boundary case on the vertical axis $(0, J_L)$ represents growth in a mature, capital-rich economy under a constant profit rate $(\eta_\pi = 0)$ (section 5.4 of this chapter).

5.3.2 The growth versus rapidity conflict

To consider the growth versus rapidity conflict, the following theorem applies directly from T2 and T3:

Theorem   The innovation intensity J is the weighted average of (η_d, η_p), where the weights are the distributive shares (ϕ_K, ϕ_L).

$$J = \phi_K \eta_d + \phi_L \eta_p \tag{5.15}$$

Proof: From T2 and T3, $\phi_L \eta_p = \phi_L J + \phi_L \phi_K \eta_{K^*}$ and $\phi_K \eta_d = \phi_K J - \phi_L \phi_K \eta_{K^*}$. Their sum leads to 5.15.   Q.E.D.

This theorem states that with the axes of figure 5.5(a) relabeled η_p and η_d, the pair of growth rates $\beta = (\eta_d, \eta_p)$ always fall on the same straight line AB – the same set Ω_J defined in 5.13 – carrying the classification into the same subsets Ω_L, Ω_K and Ω^+ – with a constant average propensity to save $\beta = (\eta_d, \eta_p) = (\eta_{\eta_K}, \eta_p)$. When the intensity of innovation J is given, there is a conflict between a higher η_p (the growth rate of per capita income) and η_{η_K} (the rate of capital acceleration). If the growth rate of per capita income is too high, the growth rate of capital declines absolutely and capital deceleration occurs. The following theorem is symmetrical to equation 5.14:

Theorem   The productivity of a factor (d or p) increases (decreases) if the productivity of the other factor increases at a rate less than (higher than) the factor augmentation intensity.

$$\eta_p \gtreqless 0 \leftrightarrow \eta_d \lesseqgtr J_K \tag{5.16a}$$
$$\eta_d \gtreqless 0 \leftrightarrow \eta_p \lesseqgtr J_L \tag{5.16b}$$

and, under the special assumption of a constant s:

$$\eta_p \gtreqless 0 \leftrightarrow \eta_{\eta_K} \lesseqgtr J_K \tag{5.16c}$$
$$\eta_{\eta_K} \gtreqless 0 \leftrightarrow \eta_p \lesseqgtr J_L \tag{5.16d}$$

In other words, the productivity of one factor is constant if and only if the other factor's productivity increase equals the rate of factor augmentation intensity of innovation. Moreover, under the assumption of a constant saving rate, per capita income increases if and only if the rate of capital acceleration is less than the factor augmentation intensity of capital (5.16c); and capital acceleration occurs if and only if per capita income increases at a rate less than the factor augmentation intensity of labor (5.16d).

5.3.3 Classification of innovations

In this system there are two dimensions of innovation – the intensity (J) and the factor bias H_K or H_L in the Hicksian sense. The two are related by:

$$\phi_L H_L + \phi_K H_K = J \text{ (equation 4.49a)} \qquad (5.17)$$

A particular combination $\vec{\gamma} = (H_K, H_L)$ is represented by an innovation point on line AB in figure 5.5(b). This diagram is reproduced in figure 5.6(a). When the axes are relabeled H_L and H_K, the particular innovation point:

$$\vec{J} = (H_K, H_L) = (J, J) \qquad (5.18)$$

(that is, $H_K = H_L = J$ – Hicks neutral innovation. See equation 4.51c.) is located at the point of intersection $\vec{J}$ of AB with the 45° line OR. The difference between $\vec{\gamma}$ and $\vec{J}$ is:

$$\vec{\gamma} - \vec{J} = (H_K, H_L) - (J, J) = (B_K, B_L) \text{ (by equation 4.47)} \qquad (5.19)$$

as indicated in figure 5.6(a). Thus, a Hicks labor-saving innovation ($B_L > 0$) is represented by a point $\vec{\gamma}$ that lies below $\vec{J}$, while very labor-saving innovations ($H_L < 0$) are represented by any point below J_K. Similarly, a Hicks capital-saving innovation ($B_K < 0$) is represented by a point that lies above $\vec{J}$, while any point above J_L represents very capital-saving innovations. As a point $\vec{\gamma}$ moves upward along AB through four types of Hicksian innovation delineated by three boundary points ($J_K, \vec{J}$ and J_L), innovations become more labor-using.

As innovation intensity J varies, the line AB undergoes a parallel shift (figure 5.6(b)). The two dimensions of innovations are indicated diagrammatically by the length (for J) and the slope (for H_K and H_L) of the innovation points (such as $\vec{\gamma}_1, \vec{\gamma}_2, \vec{\gamma}_3$), now treated as vectors from the origin. This diagram represents an innovation space depicting all possible combinations of innovation intensities and Hicksian factor biases.

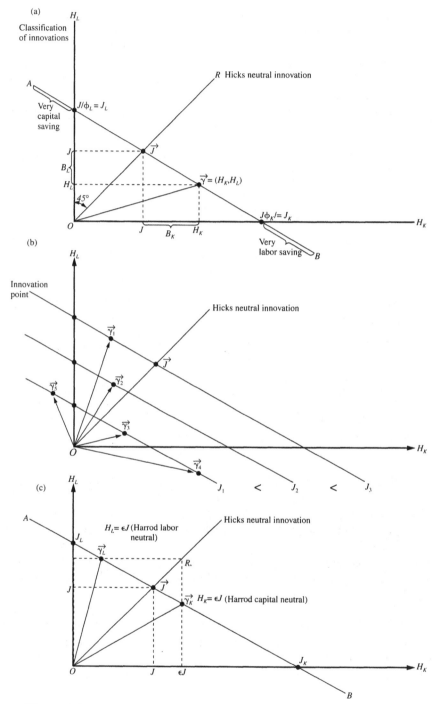

Figure 5.6 Innovation intensity and factor bias à la *Hicks and Harrod*

5.3.4 Harrod factor-using bias

For the study of economic development, Harrod provided another criterion referred to as Harrod-neutral/Harrod-labor capital-using innovations. For simplicity assume that the production function is substitution inelastic ($\epsilon > 1$) – the "normal" case. There are two definitions of Harrod-neutral innovations.

$$\text{Harrod labor-neutral: } H_L = \epsilon J \tag{5.20a}$$
$$\text{Harrod capital-neutral: } H_K = \epsilon J \tag{5.20b}$$

The point of departure for the Harrod classification is the inelasticity of substitution ϵ. Thus, a Harrod labor (or capital) neutral innovation occurs when H_L (H_K) takes on a particular value. To see Harrod-neutral innovations in a diagrammatic form, let ϵJ be marked off on the horizontal and vertical axes of figure 5.6(c). Then point γ_K ($H_K = \epsilon J$) represents a Harrod capital-neutral innovation and the point γ_L ($H_L = \epsilon J$) represents a Harrod labor-neutral innovation. Thus when $\epsilon > 1$, all innovations on AB can be marked off by five boundary points J_K, γ_K, $\vec{J}$, γ_L, and J_L into six subsets with appropriate economic interpretations in terms of Hicks and/or Harrod. As γ moves up along AB, innovations become more labor-using according to both the Hicks and Harrod definitions. Moreover, all points on the half-lines $O\gamma_K$ and $O\gamma_L$ represent Harrod capital-neutral and Harrod labor-neutral innovations, with different innovational intensities J. We make analytical use of the Harrod capital-neutral innovation in a later section.

5.3.5 Causation of factor rewards

The rates of growth of the wage and profit rates are given by the following growth equations:

$$\eta_w = \epsilon_{LL}\eta_{K*} + H_L \tag{5.21a}$$
$$\eta_\pi = -\epsilon_{KK}\eta_{K*} + H_K \tag{5.21b}$$

This attributes gains in factor rewards (η_w, η_π) to capital deepening effects ($\epsilon_{LL}\eta_{K*}$, $-\epsilon_{KK}\eta_{K*}$) and innovation effects (H_L, H_K). These equations can be represented in vector notation as:

$$\vec{\alpha} = \vec{\delta} + \vec{\gamma} \text{ where} \tag{5.22a}$$
$$\vec{\alpha} = (\eta_w, \eta_\pi) \tag{5.22b}$$
$$\vec{\delta} = (\epsilon_{LL}\eta_{K*}, -\epsilon_{KK}\eta_{K*}) = (\epsilon_{LL}, -\epsilon_{KK})\eta_{K*} \text{ (capital deepening} \tag{5.22c}$$
$$\text{effect)}$$
$$\vec{\gamma} = (H_L, H_K) \text{ (innovation effect)} \tag{5.22d}$$

$\vec{\gamma}$ is the innovation point described in the last section. We can refer to $\vec{\alpha}$ (which describes a particular profile of increases of w and π) as the factor compensation point and to $\vec{\delta}$ (which reflects the effects of η_{K*} adjusted by the law of diminishing returns) as the capital deepening effect. Equation 5.22a states that the profile of the factor compensation point ($\vec{\alpha}$) is determined by a capital deepening effect ($\vec{\delta}$) and an innovation effect described by an innovation point ($\vec{\gamma}$). We can investigate the impact of the innovation effect ($\vec{\gamma}$) and capital deepening effect ($\vec{\delta}$) on η_w and η_π simultaneously.

Earlier we developed the following relations:

$$J = \phi_L \eta_w + \phi_K \eta_\pi \text{ (by 5.11)} \tag{5.23a}$$
$$J = \phi_L H_L + \phi_K H_K \text{ (by 5.17)} \tag{5.23b}$$

By re-labeling the horizontal axis of figure 5.6 as η_π or H_K and the vertical axis as η_w or H_L, a factor compensation point ($\vec{\alpha}$) and an innovation point ($\vec{\gamma}$) can be represented on the same straight line AB in figure 5.7. When $\vec{\alpha}$ and $\vec{\gamma}$ are treated as vectors, equation 5.22a implies the capital deepening effect ($\vec{\delta}$) and forms a shaded triangle. The vector $\vec{\delta}$ can be written alternatively as

$$\vec{\delta} = (\epsilon_{LL}, -\epsilon_K)\eta_{K*} = (\phi_K, -\phi_L)\epsilon\eta_{K*} \text{ (by equation 4.30) with a vector}$$
$$\text{slope} \tag{5.24a}$$
$$-\phi_K\epsilon\eta_{K*}/\phi_L\epsilon\eta_{K*} = -\phi_K/\phi_L = -1/r \tag{5.24b}$$

The capital deepening effect has the same slope as AB and a length reflecting the degree of capital deepening (η_{K*}). In the case of capital deepening growth ($\eta_{K*} > 0$) the vector $\vec{\delta}$ points upward (the point $\vec{\alpha}$ lies above $\vec{\gamma}$ on AB). In the case of capital shallowing growth ($\eta_{K*} < 0$), $\vec{\alpha}$ lies below $\vec{\gamma}$ and $\vec{\delta}$ points downward. Some alternative patterns of decomposition (for example, of $\vec{\alpha}^1$, $\vec{\alpha}^2$, $\vec{\alpha}^3$ into the two effects) are provided by the shaded triangles in figure 5.7(b). In each case the innovation effect ($\vec{\gamma}^1$, $\vec{\gamma}^2$, $\vec{\gamma}^3$) takes on different intensities (J) and factor biases (H_K, H_L), and the capital deepening (or shallowing) effects ($\vec{\delta}^1$, $\vec{\delta}^2$, $\vec{\delta}^3$) take on different magnitudes.

Thus, a higher innovation intensity (J) contributes to higher values of η_w and η_π in proportion to the size of J. A higher degree of labor-using bias (a steeper $\vec{\gamma}$) and/or a higher rate of capital deepening (a larger $\vec{\delta}$) leads to higher values of η_w relative to η_π (the ratio η_w/η_π indicated by the slope of $\vec{\alpha}$). In the long run, it is the combined growth promotion forces of innovation intensity, innovation bias, and the extent of capital deepening that determine the rate of growth of each factor's compensation. Political forces such as collective bargaining and government interference in the money market can only affect distributional outcomes in the short run.

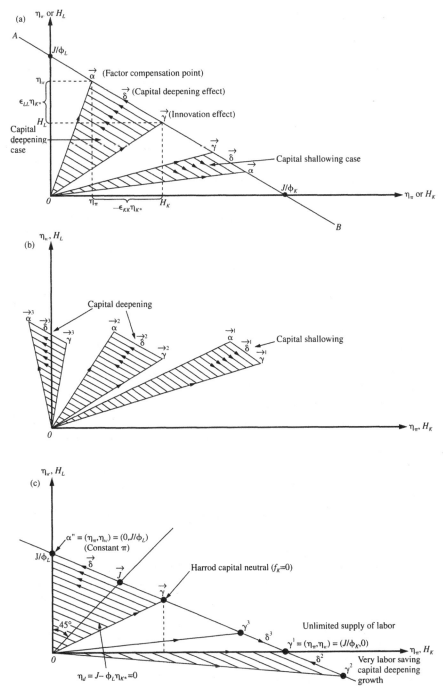

Figure 5.7 Innovation intensity, bias, and capital deepening or shallowing

Figure 5.7(c) provides an application of this framework. In the case of development under unlimited supplies of labor, $\eta_w=0$ and $\vec{\alpha}$ falls on the horizontal axis – implying that the profit rate grows at the same rate as J/ϕ_K (that is, $\gamma^1 = (\eta_\pi, \eta_w) = (J/\phi_K, 0)$). In this case there is capital deepening (shallowing) growth if and only if the innovation is very labor-saving (not very labor-saving) as shown by the innovation point γ^2 (γ^3).

5.3.6 Causation of factor productivity gains

One critical issue is the causation of increases in capital and labor productivity. The growth equations for labor productivity (p) and capital productivity (d) are:

$$\eta_p = J + \phi_K\eta_{K*} \text{ (T2)} \qquad\qquad (5.25a)$$
$$\eta_d = J - \phi_L\eta_{K*} \text{ (T3)} \qquad\qquad (5.25b)$$

In vector notation:

$$\vec{\beta} = \vec{J} + \vec{\delta} \text{ where} \qquad\qquad (5.26a)$$
$$\vec{\beta} = (\eta_p, \eta_d) \qquad\qquad (5.26b)$$
$$\vec{J} = (J, J) \qquad\qquad (5.26c)$$
$$\vec{\delta} = (\phi_K, -\phi_L)\eta_{K*} = (1/\epsilon)(\phi_K, -\phi_L)\epsilon\eta_{K*} = (1/\epsilon)\delta \text{ (by 5.24)} \quad (5.26d)$$

These two decompositions are shown in figure 5.8.

The productivity vector $\vec{\beta}$ describes a profile of gains in labor and capital productivity (η_p, η_d) that is causally determined by an innovation intensity effect (described by the vector $\vec{J}$) and a capital deepening effect (described by the vector $\vec{\delta}$). When the horizontal (vertical) axis is labeled η_d (η_p), the vectors $\vec{\beta}$ and $\vec{J}$ fall on the same line AB of figure 5.8. The vector $\vec{\delta}_1$ (representing the capital deepening effect) leads from the point $\vec{J}_1$ to the point $\vec{\beta}_1$. The two sides ($\vec{J}_1$, $\vec{\delta}_1$) of the shaded triangles represent the decomposition of $\vec{\beta}_1$ diagrammatically. The vector $\vec{\delta}_1$ is merely a (positive) multiple of $\vec{\delta}_1$ in equation 5.26d. Thus, in a capital deepening (shallowing) growth process, the vector $\vec{\delta}_1$ points upward (downward) since $\vec{\delta}_1$ and $\vec{\delta}$ always point in the same direction.

The factor bias of innovation (for example, H_K or H_L) is irrelevant to the decomposition of factor productivity gain $\vec{\beta}$ (from equation 5.25a). In the factor productivity decomposition, the vector $\vec{J}$ always falls on the Hicks neutral line (see figure 5.8(c)). The length of $\vec{J}$ contributes to a proportional gain of the two factor productivities (d, p), while the relative gain is determined by the extent (or degree) of capital deepening or shallowing represented by the length and direction of the $\vec{\delta}$ vector.

When $\vec{J} = 0$, the line $A'B'$ passes through the origin. In this special case (the absence of technology change), with a capital deepening process labor

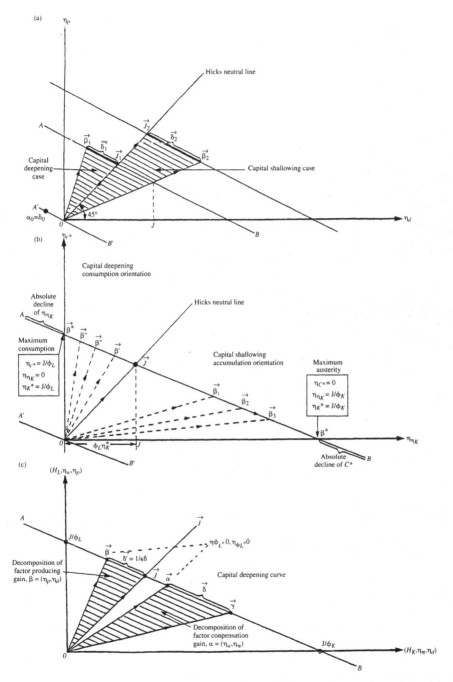

Figure 5.8 Causation of factor productivity gains

productivity increases ($\eta_p > 0$) and capital productivity decreases ($\eta_d < 0$). (The opposite is true for the capital shallowing case.) The decomposition of the productivity gain when J is positive is merely a generalization of the "static case" ($J=0$).

5.3.7   Conflict between consumption and capital acceleration

Under the assumption of the constancy of s:

$$\eta C^* = \eta_p \text{ (by } C^* = (1 - s)p) \tag{5.27a}$$
$$\eta_{m_K} = \eta_d \text{ (by } i = sd) \tag{5.27b}$$
$$\vec{\beta} = (\eta_p, \eta_d) = (\eta C^*, \eta_{m_K}) \text{ (by 5.27ab)} \tag{5.27c}$$

The economist usually believes there exists a conflict between consumption and accumulation. However, the conflict is really between the rate of consumption increase and the rate of capital acceleration. The decomposition $\vec{\beta} = \vec{J} + \vec{\delta}$ illustrates that ηC^* and η_{m_K} are determined by the innovation intensity effect J and the capital deepening effect η_{K^*} – independent of factor bias effects.

$$(\eta C^*, \eta_{m_K}) = \vec{J} + \vec{\gamma} \tag{5.28}$$

Using equation 5.27c and figure 5.8(b) – with the horizontal (vertical) axis relabelled as η_{m_K} (ηC^*) – a movement of the vector $\vec{\beta}$ upward along AB represents enhanced consumption orientation as ηC^* increases and η_{m_K} decreases. Conversely, a downward movement of $\vec{\beta}$ along AB represents increased accumulation orientation and reduced gains in the consumption standard (C^*) while the rate of capital accumulation (η_K) accelerates. In either case there is a "conflict" between a consumption orientation (higher ηC^*) and an accumulation orientation (higher η_{m_K}).

5.3.8   Long-run growth of mature capitalism

The beginnings of the modern growth epoch coincided with the arrival of industrial capitalism. For 200 years development has been characterized by sustained productivity gains and capital deepening. However, one of the amazing aspects of this process is the long-run constancy of the real return to capital. In fact, capitalist society has lived in a world which may be described as exhibiting a tendency towards the long-run constancy of the profit rate.

In this long-run sense, Harrod raised the question of whether a constant η_K can be sustained in a constant profit world. To investigate this issue, given the constancy of the profit rate:

$$H_K = \epsilon_{KK}\eta_{K^*} \quad \text{(by } \eta_\pi = 0 \text{ in T5)} \tag{5.29a}$$

$$\eta_{\eta_K} = \eta_d = 0 \quad \text{(by constancy of } s) \tag{5.29b}$$

$$J = \phi_L\eta_{K^*} \quad \text{(by T3 and 5.29b)} \tag{5.29c}$$

and therefore:

$$J = (\phi_L/\epsilon_{KK})H_K = H_K/\epsilon \quad \text{(by 5.29)} \tag{5.30}$$

It follows that the necessary condition to maintain the constancy of η_K in a constant profit world is that technological change be Harrod-neutral ($H_K = \epsilon J$). The profile of long-run growth in mature economies may therefore be described by the constancy of π, d, f_K, η_K, ϕ_L, and ϕ_K. At the same time, $\eta_c = \eta_p = \eta_w = J_L$ are increasing through time at the rate of J/ϕ_L.

5.4 Structural Duality

The growth equations derived are truisms because they follow from the dynamic production function. Although η_K and η_L are treated as exogenous variables in the derivation of these equations, they can also be treated as endogenous. For example, T4 and T5 imply:

$$\eta_L = \eta_K + H_L/\epsilon_{LL} - \eta_w/\epsilon_{LL} \text{ (}w\text{-exogenous model)} \tag{5.31a}$$

$$\eta_K = \eta_L + H_K/\epsilon_{KK} - \eta_\pi/\epsilon_{KK} \text{ (}\pi\text{-exogenous model)} \tag{5.31b}$$

In this pair of equations, the terms on the right-hand side may be interpreted as causally determining the terms on the left-hand side.

Equation 5.31a is the labor absorption equation applicable to the transition growth process in a labor-surplus LDC. In this application the rapidity of labor absorption (η_L) is causally determined by (η_K, H_L, η_w) – the rate of capital accumulation (η_K), innovation intensity, and labor-using bias ($H_L = J + B_L$) – plus the growth rate of the real wage (η_w). This application is systematically explored in chapter 7 to supplement the earlier analysis of the labor absorption process in a labor surplus dualistic economy.

In this application the rapidity of the change in the real wage rate (η_w) is exogenously determined. Consistent with this interpretation, the labor absorption rate (η_L) is the result of an increase in the demand for labor. An increase in the wage rate only contributes to a slow-down of the labor absorption process.

Equation 5.31b, symmetrical to 5.31a, can be used to analyze the capital accumulation process in the mature capitalist economy. The rapidity of capital accumulation (η_K) is causally determined by η_L (the population growth rate), innovation intensity, and capital-using bias ($H_K = B_K + J$), plus the growth of the profit rate (η_π). An increase in the profit rate contributes to a slow-down of the capital growth rate as investment demand weakens. In this application the interest rate (π) is specified exogenously.

There exist two special cases of 5.31a and b:

$$\eta_L = \eta_K + H_L/\epsilon_{LL} = \eta_K + (B_L + J)/\epsilon_{LL} \text{ (for } \eta_w = 0 \text{ in 5.31a)} \quad (5.32a)$$
$$\eta_K = \eta_L + H_K/\epsilon_{KK} = \eta_L + (B_K + J)/\epsilon_{KK} \text{ (for } \eta_\pi = 0 \text{ in 5.31b)} \quad (5.32b)$$

Equation 5.32b, based on the postulation of constant real wage ($\eta_w = 0$ in 5.31a), is descriptive of the classical model under the assumption of an "iron law of wages". In a modern rendition, this case is descriptive of the "near-constant wage world" of the contemporary LDCs operating under conditions of an unlimited supply of labor (see chapter 7 for more extensive treatment).

Equation 5.32b, based on the postulation of a constant profit rate ($\eta_\pi = 0$ in 5.31b), is descriptive of the mature capitalist economy in long-run historical perspective. Whether or not the profit rate can be sustained at a positive level is not only a crucial issue worried about by classical and Marxist economists, but also lies at the heart of the long-run stagnation thesis (for example, of Hansen) of the 1930s (see chapter 6 for further exploration).

In view of the symmetry between equation 5.32a and b, the analysis of transition growth of an LDC (based on the wage exogeneity of 5.31a) and the analysis of the capital accumulation process in mature capitalism (based on the profit rate exogeneity of 5.31b) can enhance our understanding of both special cases.

CHAPTER 5   A GENERAL ANALYSIS OF GROWTH SYSTEMS

NOTES

1   Von Neumann provided the rigor, but Schumpeter first proposed the idea that in the absence of periodic bursts of technology change, an economy always moves towards a steady state.

2   It should be noted that classical writers of the early nineteenth century believed in the "classical saving rule" as firmly as we deny it at the present time. For before the development of a financial system separated the ownership and management of capital, the working class could not save without assuming the task of management. The class-stratified classical saving rule perpetuated the hereditary class dichotomy of the physiocrats by ruling out interclass social mobility between property-owning and property-less classes.

6

Applications to Modern Economic Growth

6.1 Introduction

As mentioned in Part I, there are three types of growth theories of interest – those applicable to agrarian economies, LDCs in transition, and mature DCs. While we are principally concerned with the transition problem, we first deploy our recently acquired machinery to examine growth in the mature economy.

In chronological order, the growth theoretic ideas examined in sections 6.2 through 6.5 are attributable to the classical school (eighteenth century), Marx (mid-nineteenth century), Schumpeter (the inter-war period), Harrod (mid-twentieth century), and Kaldor and Kuznets (the post-World War II era), respectively. While pre-war contributions were originally made in an ambiguous "literary tradition," we restate these ideas succinctly and rigorously with the aid of the growth equations at our disposal.

In view of the structural duality – the symmetry of K and L in the production relations (equations 5.31ab) – the analysis of capital accumulation (η_K) in a mature economy can also be applied to the analysis of the labor absorption process (η_L) in the commercialized sector of a dualistic economy. We deal with this issue in section 6.6 and with the determination of η_K for industrially advanced countries in section 6.7 of this chapter.

6.2 Classical Growth Theoretic Ideas

The classical school provides the foundation for virtually all growth theoretic ideas. Classical theorists began with a tripartite division of capital (K), land (T), and labor (L) that are joint inputs in a production process described by:

$$Q = f(K,L,T,t) \tag{6.1a}$$
$$w = f_L; \; \pi = f_K; \; n = f_T \quad \text{(factor prices)} \tag{6.1b}$$
$$p = Q/L; \; d = Q/K; \; g = Q/T \quad \text{(factor productivities)} \tag{6.1c}$$
$$\phi_L = w/p; \; \phi_K = \pi/d; \; \phi_T = n/g \quad \text{(factor shares)} \tag{6.1d}$$
$$Q = f_L L + f_\pi K + f_T T \quad \text{(CRTS)} \tag{6.1e}$$
$$\phi_L + \phi_K + \phi_T = 1 \tag{6.1f}$$

We assume a symmetric principle for the determination of the rewards to the three factors of production. Classical economists believed that only the contribution of land was actively determined by its marginal product, while the rest was a surplus out of which labor was paid a subsistence wage. However, we posit the symmetric view (6.1) here.

Factor prices (wage w, profit π, and rent n), factor productivities (of labor p, capital d, and land g) and factor shares (ϕ_L, ϕ_K, and ϕ_T) are defined in 6.1b, c and d, while the assumption of CRTS is maintained even when there are three primary factors of production (6.1e). Define the intensity of innovation (J) and the factor bias of innovation (H_L, H_K and H_T):

$$J = (\partial Q/\partial t)/Q \tag{6.2a}$$
$$H_L = (\partial f_L/\partial t)/f_L; \; H_K = (\partial f_K/\partial t)/f_K; \; H_T = (\partial f_T/\partial t)/f_T \tag{6.2b}$$

The following conclusions can be readily proven and are direct generalizations of the previous "two factor" case given the neoclassical production function:

$$\eta_Q = \phi_L \eta_L + \phi_K \eta_K + \phi_T \eta_T + J \quad \text{(decomposition of } \eta_Q) \tag{6.3a}$$
$$J = \phi_L \eta_w + \phi_K \eta_\pi + \phi_T \eta_n \quad \text{(distributional conflict)} \tag{6.3b}$$
$$J = \phi_L \eta_p + \phi_K \eta_d + \phi_T \eta_g \quad \text{(productivity conflict)} \tag{6.3c}$$
$$J = \phi_L H_L + \phi_K H_K + \phi_T H_T \quad \text{(innovation profiles)} \tag{6.3d}$$

Classical economists argued in terms of:

$$\eta_w = 0 \tag{6.4a}$$
$$\eta_T = 0, \; \eta_K > 0 \rightarrow \eta_{K/T} > 0 \tag{6.4b}$$

Equation 6.4a is the "iron law of wages," that the population always grows to ensure a constant wage rate over time. This is the classical version of the unlimited supply of labor condition. The iron law is really based on a demographic theory in which the population growth rate is controlled by the consumption standard – a theory explored in chapter 3. Equation 6.4b states that land is fixed ($\eta_T=0$) and the capital stock is growing, implying a persistent increase in K/T through time. Equation 6.4a and 6.3b imply:

$$J = \phi_K \eta_\pi + \phi_T \eta_n \tag{6.5a}$$
$$\eta_\pi = -(\phi_T/\phi_K)\eta_n < 0 \text{ if } J = 0 \tag{6.5b}$$

Equation 6.5b states that there is always a distributional conflict between an increase in the rental rate ($\eta_n > 0$) and an increase in the profit rate ($\eta_\pi > 0$). In the absence of any innovation intensity ($J=0$), the profit rate declines absolutely. Because the capital/land ratio increases (equation 6.4b), the value of the rental rate (n) increases and the profit rate must decline over time.

These conclusions led to the stagnation pessimism of the classical economists in terms of the long-run decline of the profit rate ($\eta_\pi < 0$) and the ultimate cessation of capital accumulation. This is due to the classical savings rule which states that of all three distributive shares (ϕ_L, ϕ_K, and ϕ_T) only the profit share is saved, permitting the accumulation of capital. The other shares – ϕ_L and ϕ_T – are consumed.

Classical economists were understandably unaware that they lived at the time of "transition" to the modern growth epoch. The fact that a high innovation intensity (J) can be sustained over several centuries has demonstrated that classical pessimism is unwarranted.

6.3 Marxian Notions of Growth

The appearance of Marxian theory critiquing capitalist growth in the middle of the nineteenth century was certainly a major event. It is appropriate to take a "last look" at this theory just as the socialist real-world experiment is coming to an end.

Marxian theory occupies a special page in the history of growth theory. In speculating pessimistically about capitalist growth, Marx was obviously under the influence of the classical theorists. Like classical economists, his prediction concerning long-run stagnation (the inevitability of the cessation of capital accumulation) was based on distribution arguments – especially the decline in the rate of return to capital. The Marxian notion of a "class struggle" – grounded in the conflict between η_w and η_π – was foreshadowed by the classical conviction that there exists a conflict between rents and profits – η_n and η_π – given an "iron law of wages."

In spite of these cultural linkages, Marxian theory is quite different from classical theory in one major aspect. Classical economists were concerned with the transition of an agrarian economy into the modern growth epoch and were troubled by the law of diminishing returns to capital and labor when land is an essential input to agricultural production. To classical economists, capital was a "wage fund" which had little in common with fixed capital as the carrier of "science and technology" envisioned by Marx. More than 200 years have elapsed since the arrival of the modern growth epoch in the West. In contrast to classical theory characterized by commercial capitalism (1500–1750) when what was being accumulated in the course of the growth process was "liquid capital," the growth theoretic ideas of Marx focused on industrial capitalism and on the accumulation of fixed capital carrying technology.[1]

The core arguments of Marx centered around the following ideas:

1 the contradictions of capital deepening growth;
2 the drive for capital accumulation under the classical saving rule;
3 the resolution of distributional conflicts via technological change;
4 the inevitability of the ultimate atrophying of capitalism.

We can precisely interpret each of these literary arguments with the aid of our growth equations.

6.3.1 The contradictions of capital deepening growth

Ever since the arrival of the modern growth epoch, the mature economy has been characterized by persistent capital deepening growth ($\eta_{K*} > 0$). In the absence of technological change, by $\vec{\gamma}$ in equation 5.22:

$$\alpha_0 = (\eta_w, \eta_\pi) = \delta_0 = (-\epsilon_{KK}, \epsilon_{LL})\eta_{K*} \text{ when } J = H_L = H_K = 0 \qquad (6.6a)$$
$$\eta_\pi < 0, \eta_w > 0 \text{ when } \eta_{K*} > 0 \qquad (6.6b)$$

Thus, in the absence of technological change the point $\alpha_0 = \delta_0$ is shown in figure 5.8(a) of chapter 5 on the line $A'B'$, implying a decline in the profit rate combined with an increase in the wage rate. According to Marx, the working class must be exploited if the capitalist class is to survive. That society is full of "contradictions" is illustrated by the fact that capital deepening growth inevitably ignites the famous "class struggle."

6.3.2 The drive for capital accumulation under the classical saving rule

Capital deepening ($\eta_{K*} > 0$) occurs when the rate of capital accumulation – sustained by the asset accumulation drive of capitalists – exceeds the population growth rate ($\eta_K > \eta_L$). Two different savings rules can be applied:

$$S = sQ \text{ (class-insensitive Keynesian saving rule)} \qquad (6.7a)$$
$$S = \phi_K Q \text{ (class-sensitive classical saving rule)} \qquad (6.7b)$$

The Keynesian saving rule made its appearance more than 100 years after the classical saving rule. Marx utilized the classical saving rule, to arrive at three crucial elements of his "class struggle."

First, there is the uncontrolled drive for capital accumulation as all capitalist income is saved. Second, any inter-class social mobility is effectively forestalled since workers cannot ever join the ranks of the capitalists by saving wage income. Finally, from the classical saving rule (6.7b):

Lemma   Under the classical saving rule ($S = \phi_K Q$ or $S = dK/dt = f_K K$) the capital growth rate is the same as the profit rate ($\eta_K = \pi$) and the rate of increase of the profit rate (η_π) and the capital acceleration rate (η_{η_K}) are also the same.

$$\eta_{\eta_K} = \eta_\pi \text{ (by } \eta_K = \pi) \tag{6.8}$$

Under the classical saving rule, $\alpha_0 = (\eta_\pi, \eta_w) = (\eta_{\eta_K}, \eta_w)$ and the point α_0 in the second quadrant of figure 5.8(a) of chapter 5 implies that $\eta_\pi < 0$ and $\eta_{\eta_K} < 0$ – a persistent decline in the profit rate and capital deceleration. Stagnationists as well as Marxists indeed have been concerned about two presumed features of the mature economy, the tendency towards a persistent decline of the profit rate ($\eta_\pi < 0$), detrimental to the investment incentives of the capitalist class, and a tendency towards a persistent decline in the capital growth rate ($\eta_{\eta_K} < 0$), threatening long-run stagnation. The classical saving rule implies that these two problems always coincide. Furthermore, in the absence of technological change, they always occur in the presence of capital deepening growth.

6.3.3 Resolution of the distributional conflict by technology change

This distributional conflict can be resolved by technology change with sufficiently high innovation intensity (J) and/or capital-using bias (H_K) to compensate for the profit depressing effects of capital deepening growth ($\eta_{K*} > 0$). The growth equation T5 of chapter 4 implies:

$$H_K = \epsilon_{KK}\eta_{K*} + \eta_\pi \tag{6.9a}$$
$$H_K = \epsilon_{KK}\eta_{K*} \text{ when } \eta_\pi = 0 \tag{6.9b}$$

The term H_K in 6.9b is "Marxian compensation" – the level of H_K consistent with profit rate stability when η_{K*} is given. Equivalently, Marxian compensation implies $B_K = \epsilon_{KK}\eta_{K*} - J$. Thus, when the rate of capital deepening ($\epsilon_{KK}\eta_{K*}$) and the rate of innovation intensity (J) are given, capital-using bias must take on a particular value if the profit rate is to be stable. Hence the struggle to maintain profit stability is harder given a

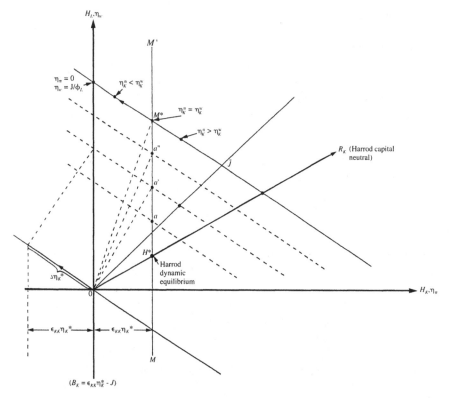

Figure 6.1 The Marxian compensation effect

higher rate of capital deepening and easier with a higher innovation intensity, implying an endogenous theory of innovation. When a certain degree
of capital deepening ($\eta_{K*} > 0$) takes place, innovation activities (H_K) must
satisfy the equality in equation 6.9b to avoid a profit rate decline.

Consider the vertical line MM' in figure 6.1. All points on this line neu-
tralize the effect of a given rate of capital deepening ($\epsilon_{KK}\eta_{K*}$) and forestall
a decline in the profit rate and the capital growth rate – either by a combination of high innovation intensity (J) and low B_K or a low J with a high
B_K. In common sense terms, when innovation intensity is strong the system
need not worry about automation; once innovation activity slackens, however, labor-saving innovation is necessary to avoid a decline in the profit
rate. While the modern entrepreneur worries about this problem at the
microscopic level, Marx was concerned with the holistic view. At the
aggregate level a stable profit rate implies that wages rise at the rate J/ϕ_L.

This historically observed fact, which Marx did not appreciate, is of primary interest to the capitalist class.

For Marx, innovation activity represented another instrument, along with capital accumulation, for the exploitation of labor by monopolists anxious "to save their own necks" (that is, to prevent profits from declining). According to Marx, the class struggle was unavoidable because innovation intensity cannot be sustained indefinitely at a high enough level. For this reason capitalism – which depends crucially on the private ownership of capital and the maintenance of a reasonable profit rate – must eventually give way to socialism.

6.3.4 The inevitable atrophy of capitalism

When the growth theoretic ideas of Marx are presented in an orderly fashion there is nothing logically wrong with the system. Indeed, the very fact that our framework helps identify these "core ideas," given his assumptions, testifies to Marx's keen insight. What is crucially wrong with Marxian theory is his assumption about the necessary inadequacy of innovation intensity (J) to compensate for the profit suppressing effects of capital deepening. Marx had no idea that the western world was about to enter a new growth epoch in which higher innovation intensity implied less need for capital-using bias.

The basic growth promotion force is clearly technology change (J), promising an unlimited potential for the system. In this regard Marx, profoundly pessimistic about the fate of the dominant capitalist industrial sector, committed the same error as the classical economists who predicted the inevitability of long-run stagnation based on the absence of innovative activity in agriculture.

The last 150 years (1850–2000) has been a long enough period to conclude that both the Marxian and classical visions were wrong. The earlier agricultural as well as the more recent second industrial revolution (1950–72) reinforced the conviction that technological potential is virtually unlimited. During this period there has been continuous growth characterized by a constant profit rate and sustained increases in wages accompanied by persistent capital deepening. The statistical refutation of Marx was a major contribution of Kuznets who supplied the empirical long-run growth characteristics of mature capitalist economies.

6.4 Schumpeterian Growth Theory

Theoretical developments after Marxian economics proceeded in two directions until 1950. On one hand, neoclassical "micro" economics (after 1870) was concerned with the efficiency of the utilization and allocation of resources. On the other hand, there was a revival of "macro" economics concerned with the instability of the interwar period (1920–40). Growth was practically forgotten. The exception was Schumpeter, who shared common interests with both micro and macro economists but was concerned with growth.

6.4.1 Technological change and the multiplicity of product growth

As a point of departure, to illuminate the contrasts, the national income accounting framework implicit in Schumpeter's theory is shown (figure 6.2(c)) alongside that relevant to Marx (figure 6.2(b)) and to the classical school (figure 6.2(a)). In all systems, the savings fund (S) finances investment (I), leading to the growth phenomenon of capital accumulation ($\eta_K = I/K$). There is, however, one major difference. Schumpeter was concerned with a multiplicity of products such that the total investment fund (I) had to be allocated to various production sectors ($I_1, I_2, I_3, \ldots, I_n$) to ensure a balanced growth pattern over time. In his concern with resource allocation, the interests of Schumpeter coincide with those of the "microeconomists" and differ in a fundamental sense from the growth theories of both Marx and the classical economists who were concerned primarily with analyzing one aggregate production sector.

Under the assumption of stationary technology, Schumpeter visualized what is now known as a Schumpeter or a von Neumann state in which investment funds are allocated such that the output of all the production sectors grows at a rate determined by population growth. This state, characterized by the stability of proportional sectoral expansion, is disturbed by technological change – when new products are introduced and/or old products can be produced more cheaply. Schumpeter was concerned mainly with the need for such a healthy metabolism – the discovery of new technologies leading to the timely birth of new and death of old products – as a distinguishing characteristic of the modern growth epoch.

6.4.2 Formalization of finance

One essential institutional innovation for flexibility in the allocation of the investment fund ($I_1, I_2, I_3, \ldots, I_n$) in a multiple product world is the development of financial institutions (such as commercial banks, stock markets and saving institutions). These financial intermediaries must channel the saving fund into alternative investment outlets. Schumpeter was very concerned with the special role played by commercial banks when his "steady state" is disturbed by entrepreneurs perceiving a chance for technological change.

A natural victim of the development of financial institutions in the twentieth century is the classical saving rule – shown in figures 6.2(a) and (b) – when only the capitalist class saves. On the other hand, when owners (savers) and managers (entrepreneurs) are separated by financial intermediaries, everyone can save – shown in figure 6.2(c) with a Keynesian saving function. With an increase in inter-class mobility, the nineteenth century concern with distributional conflicts could be put aside and replaced by a concern with allocation.

6.4.3 Allocation orientation and the rate of interest

As long as there is only one return to capital – the interest rate – it can only have distributional significance. For this reason the interest rate was treated by both Marx and the classical economists as a distribution-related concept carrying, in conjunction with the wage rate, equity connotations.

In a world characterized by the multiplicity of products and the necessity of balanced growth, the interest rate (π) takes on allocation-related significance that is independent of the distributional issue. Furthermore, while it was unnecessary to differentiate between "interest" and "profit" in the Marxian case, this no longer holds when the role of the interest rate is centered on the allocation of the investment fund. In a multiple product world the investment fund must be allocated in such a way that investment projects not paying the current market rate of interest are squeezed out. The Schumpeterian state has no innovation profit and investment is allocated by the interest rate alone. In other words, the allocation orientation of the interest rate *à la* Schumpeter is fundamentally different from the distributional orientation of the interest rate *à la* Marx.

In the absence of technology change in the Schumpeterian state, the investment program is determined by mechanisms to equalize the marginal product of investment and the market rate of interest. In fact, the market rate of interest is the only mechanism under competitive capitalism to control the allocation of the saving fund. The profit rate emerges and looms large only when the Schumpeterian state is disturbed by innovations. To Schumpeter, profits are returns to innovation that are gradually annihilated once such innovations have run their course.

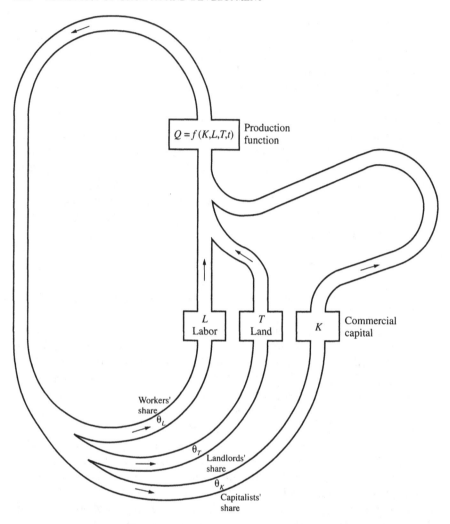

$Q = f(K,L,T,t)$ Production function

L Labor $\quad$ T Land $\quad$ K $\quad$ Commercial capital

Workers' share θ_L

θ_T Landlords' share

θ_K Capitalists' share

Figure 6.2 (a) Classical savings rule

6.4.4 Product metabolism under capitalism

According to Schumpeter, the disturbance of the steady state by technological change is not a smooth process, primarily because of the "bunching
up" or clustering of innovations. In this sense he shares a common interest
with those concerned with "economic instability" – the macroeconomic

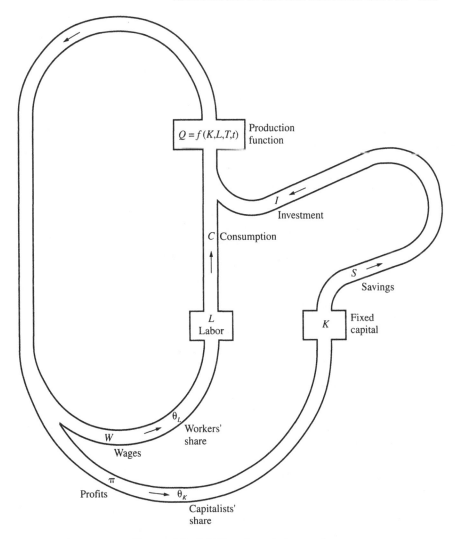

Figure 6.2 (b) Marxian savings rule

theorists of the inter-war, business cycle, and post-war Keynesian periods. To Schumpeter business cycles were a growth-relevant phenomenon when the allocation of the investment fund is disturbed by monetary factors in response to new investment opportunities.

When the entrepreneur perceives the possibility of innovation profits (that is, a premium "on top of" the interest rate), commercial banks are willing to create purchasing power on his behalf. Due to the fact that the supply of bank credit is elastic (the commercial banking system can

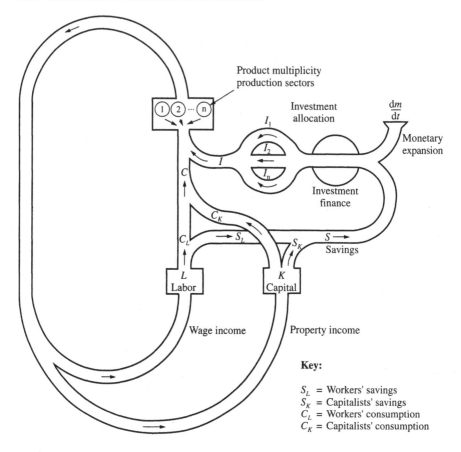

Figure 6.2 (c) Keynesian savings rule

artificially create purchasing power), investment demand can exceed the supply of voluntary saving. What lies behind the "bunching of investment" constitutes temporary "over-investment," representing a conflict of interest between investors and savers, leading to monetary expansion and inflation. This conflict concerning the intertemporal allocation of resources is a far cry from the class-oriented distributional conflict of Marx.

Our above, admittedly sketchy, presentation of Schumpeterian growth theory points out the inadequacy of nineteenth century Marxian analysis for tackling the issues of allocation efficiency and compositional flexibility. A quick glance at a Sears catalogue or the yellow pages of a telephone directory barely 20 years old convinces the reader that structural flexibility is a crucial characteristic of the modern economy, facilitated especially by financial markets regulated by the interest rate.

The fact that there are two interpretations of π – the profit rate interpretation used by nineteenth-century writers and the interest rate interpretation in a multi-product world used by twentieth-century writers – is relevant for the contemporary developing world. In LDCs lacking well-developed financial markets the political penetration of such markets is usually pronounced. As a consequence, LDC governments usually think of π from both a profit rate and an interest rate perspective. The profit rate perspective leads to the covert transfer of profits among classes – favoring the investing class; the interest rate perspective leads to direct investment allocations and bureaucratic interventions substituting for the interest rate as an allocative mechanism. This has been especially pronounced for socialist countries, but is also typical of mixed economy LDCs prior to reform. It is the subject of substantial current policy disputes centering on the role of interest rate interventions in the East Asian success cases.

6.5 The Harrod Theory of "Full Employment Growth"

6.5.1 Historical background

All growth theories for mature capitalist economies (for example, Schumpeter and Marx) must confront the issue of technology change – the *sine qua non* of modern growth. This is also true for the Harrod–Domar model which revived academic interest in growth after War World II. Writing under the influence of the severe unemployment problems of the Great Depression, Harrod was concerned with the difficulties of maintaining growth in mature economies characterized by an "unlimited supply of saving," facing the possibility of massive unemployment.

By the 1930s the modern growth epoch had accumulated a fund of historical experience of some 150 years – long enough to demonstrate the existence of an unlimited technological potential, a truth not perceived by either the pessimistic classical economists or Marx. Benefitted by this historical hindsight, Harrod's central theme was a search for the technological foundations of full employment growth in a high-saving society consistent with the stability of the profit rate ($\eta_\pi = 0$) and of the capital growth rate ($\eta_{\eta_K} = 0$) – the two critical preconditions essential for the long-run viability of capitalism according to Marx (see section 6.3).

While Marx's problem was inherited by Harrod, the latter went several steps further. For one, Marx never recognized technological potential as rendering capitalism viable in the long run; indeed he was not aware of the notion of "Marxian compensation" presented above. For another, Harrod identified a particular type of technological change – capital-neutral innovations – designed to come to the rescue. Harrod's core arguments are based on:

1 Investment incentives, an over-abundance of savings, and the viability of full employment equilibrium.
2 The interaction between the "warranted" and "natural" growth rates of capital.
3 "Harrod capital-neutral innovations" as the foundation for "dynamic equilibrium."

We discuss these ideas in turn.

6.5.2 Saving, investment, and the viability of full employment growth

The appropriate national income accounting framework for the Harrod model differs from the Schumpeter model only in the postulation of a monolithic production sector. However, what is more important is that it also differs from the Marxian (and classical) system by replacing the class-sensitive classical saving function with the class-insensitive Keynesian saving function. But for Marx's use of the classical savings rule and Harrod's choice of the Keynesian savings rule, the two theories are identical.

Harrod accepted the Keynesian saving function ($S=sQ$) along with the Keynesian notion of excess savings proxied by a high average propensity to save (s). The "Harrod–Domar" capital growth rate determined by s is the warranted capital growth rate:

$$\eta_K^w = sd \qquad (6.10)$$

This is a rather "high" growth rate of capital "warranted" by the "push" of full employment savings. If "full employment growth" is sustained, the growth equation T5 (chapter 4) implies:

$$\eta_K = \eta_K^n - \eta_\pi/\epsilon_{KK} \quad \text{or} \qquad (6.11a)$$
$$\eta_\pi/\epsilon_{KK} = \eta_K^n - \eta_K^w \quad \text{where } \eta_K = \eta_K^w \text{ and} \qquad (6.11b)$$
$$\eta_K^n = \eta_L + (B_K + J)/\epsilon_{KK} = \eta_L + H_K/\epsilon_{KK}$$
$$\text{(natural rate of growth of capital)} \qquad (6.11c)$$

Harrod refers to η_K^n in equation 6.11c as the natural growth rate of capital, with its magnitude determined by a quadruplet of exogenous growth promotion forces:

1   a high population growth rate (η_L);
2   a high innovation intensity (J);
3   a strong capital-using bias (B_K); and
4   a weak law of diminishing returns to capital (ϵ_{KK}).

The "natural" growth rate of capital is thus explained by exogenous forces, partly technological and partly demographic in character.

6.5.3 Interaction of the natural and the warranted rates

The juxtaposition of growth rates (η_K^w, η_K^n) – warranted and natural – suggests that capital accumulation through investment is regulated by a "pulling force" and a "pushing force." On one hand, the warranted rate of growth (η_K^w) represents the "pushing force" of the supply of savings. On the other hand, the natural rate of growth (η_K^n) represents the "pulling force" of the demand for investment. Equation 6.11b implies the following results from the interaction between the demand and supply of investment funds:

$$\eta_\pi \gtreqless 0 \leftrightarrow \eta_K^n \gtreqless \eta_K^w \tag{6.12a}$$
$$\eta_\pi = 0 \leftrightarrow \eta_K^n = \eta_K^w = \eta_K \tag{6.12b}$$

The profit rate declines through time $(\eta_\pi < 0)$ if and only if the warranted rate of growth (generated by "high" full employment saving) exceeds the natural rate of growth (determined by "low" demographic and/or technological growth promotion forces) $(\eta_K^n < \eta_K^w)$.

For the first time in the history of growth theory, the "adequacy" of technological progress is directly related to the abundance of the saving capacity and the adequacy of investment incentives. Furthermore, austerity proxied by a high saving capacity that leads to a higher warranted rate of growth of capital may be a curse rather than a blessing – leading to a decline of the profit rate when "investment demand" is deficient.

It is well to recall that under the classical saving rule accepted by Marx $\eta_K = \pi$ and $\eta_\pi = \eta_{\eta_K}$ – the social problems entailed in maintaining the profit rate and the capital growth rate are identical. Harrod replaced this saving rule with the Keynesian rule which represents a realistic theoretical advance. However, the problem is complicated because $\eta_{\eta_K} \neq \eta_\pi$.

From equation 6.12b, the profit rate is constant if and only if the natural and warranted rates of growth of capital are the same. This leads to the following conclusion:

$$\eta_K^n = \eta_K^w \leftrightarrow \eta_\pi = 0 \leftrightarrow H_K = \epsilon_{KK}\eta_{K*} \tag{6.13}$$

Proof   Follows directly from $\eta_K^n = \eta_L + H/\epsilon_{KK}$ and $\eta_K^w = sd$

Thus, technological change relevant to the Marxian compensation effect in equation 6.9b is necessary for the constancy of the profit rate.

For long-run viability of capitalism, in addition to the constancy of the profit rate, the growth rate of capital must not decline persistently through time. In the Marxian system the classical saving rule implies the coincidence of the constancy of the profit rate and the constancy of η_K. When the classical saving rule is dropped, this coincidence disappears. In other words, by the twentieth century when all classes are permitted to save (as the Keynesian saving function prevails), Harrod is forced to search for specific innovation characteristics consistent with $\eta_\pi = \eta_{\eta_K} = 0$. The acceptance of the classical saving rule by Marx and of the Keynesian saving rule by Harrod, brought about by the development of financial institutions and the broadening of the basis of savings, is the only major difference between the two theories.

6.5.4 Harrod capital neutrality and dynamic equilibrium

The following definition of a "dynamic equilibrium" is attributable to Harrod:

> *Definition*   A dynamic equilibrium (in the Harrod sense) is a state of growth characterized by the constancy of the profit rate (π) and the growth rate of capital (η_K) through time ($\eta_\pi = \eta_{\eta_K} = 0$) when full employment savings are persistently invested.

The following theorem identifies the technological foundations of dynamic equilibrium and is the central contribution of Harrod:

> *Theorem*   When the average propensity to save (s) is constant, innovations with capital neutrality in the Harrod sense are a necessary condition for dynamic equilibrium:

$$\eta_\pi = \eta_{\eta_K} = 0 \rightarrow H_K = \epsilon J \text{ (see equation 5.20)} \qquad (6.14)$$

To see the essence of the proof, the Harrod dynamic equilibrium implies:

$$\eta_\pi = 0 \text{ implies } H_K = \epsilon_{KK}\eta_{K*} \text{ (from T5)} \qquad (6.15a)$$
$$\eta_{\eta_K} = \eta_d = 0 \text{ implies } \eta_{K*} = J/\phi_L \text{ (from T3)} \qquad (6.15b)$$
$$H_K = \epsilon_{KK}J/\phi_L = \epsilon J \text{ (by equations 6.15ab and 4.30)} \qquad (6.15c)$$

However, Harrod capital neutrality is a necessary but not a sufficient condition for Harrod dynamic equilibrium. Another necessary condition is the

Marxian compensation effect. The set of necessary conditions for Harrod dynamic equilibrium are:

$$H_K = \epsilon J \qquad \qquad (6.16a)$$
$$H_K = \epsilon_{KK}\eta_{K*} \text{ or } B_K = \epsilon_{KK}\eta_{K*} - J \text{ (by equation 6.9)} \qquad (6.16b)$$

It follows that as a high saving rate "pushes" the system along a capital-deepening growth path, technological change must be of a special kind to achieve Harrod dynamic equilibrium.

Although the notion of a dynamic equilibrium was invented by Harrod in order to establish the technological foundation for "full employment growth" in a high-saving society in the short run, the notion has profound long-run historical implications. Ever since the arrival of the modern growth epoch more than 200 years ago, mature capitalist economies have developed with certain long-run stylized characteristics. Prominent among these are sustained gains in labor productivity, per capita consumption, capital per head, and the real wage, while the capital-output ratio (K/Q), profit rate (π), labor share (ϕ_L) and capital growth rate (η_K) all exhibit long-run stability in the sense that they all move within a narrow band around a constant trend. The notion of a Harrod neutral innovation as a precondition for dynamic equilibrium – defined as the constancy of the profit rate and of the growth rate of capital – is historically important because it is the technological precondition for the observed long-run stylized facts of mature capitalism.

6.5.5 Growth theories for mature economies after World War II

The revival of growth theory after World War II proceeded along two fronts: a revival of the "transition theory" of the classical school, and work on the theory of growth in the mature economies following in the footsteps of Marx, Schumpeter and Harrod.

Analysis of growth in recent decades has advanced along empirical as well as theoretical lines. On the empirical front, Kuznets and Denison have tried to statistically identify the long-run stylized facts. On the theoretical front, Kaldor, Solow, and others have constructed growth models to explain them. The econometric work of Solow deserves special mention because his efforts represent the first attempt at a formal statistical proof of what was known intuitively (for example, by Kuznets). In fact, a key comment in Solow's Nobel lecture was that "the main result of that 1957 exercise was startling. Growth of output per hour of work in the US economy doubled between 1909 and 1949; and some seven-eighths of that increase could be attributed to technological change in the broadest sense."[2]

Table 6.1 Profile of transition growth of LDC industrial sector (exogenous *w*)

Analysis of rapidity of	Decomposition into coefficients of					Decomposition Under Unlimited supply of labor ($\eta_w = 0$)				Decomposition when $\eta_w = F_L = 0$		
	Growth rate	J	B_L	η_K	η_w	Growth rate	$J_K = J/\phi_K$	F_L^a	η_K	Growth rate	J_K	η_K
	(I)	(II)	(III)	(IV)	(V)	(VI)	(VII)	(VIII)	(IX)	(X)	(XI)	(XII)
a) Labor absorption	η_L =	$1/\epsilon_{LL}$	$1/\epsilon_{LL}$	1	$-1/\epsilon_{LL}$	η_L =	1	$1/\phi_K$	1	η_L =	1	1
b) Output expansion	η_Q =	$1 + r/\epsilon$	r/ϵ	1	$-r/\epsilon$	η_Q =	1	r	1	η_Q =	1	1
c) Capital deepening	η_{K^*} =	$-1/\epsilon_{LL}$	$-1/\epsilon_{LL}$	—	$1/\epsilon_{LL}$	η_{K^*} =	-1	$-1/\phi_K$	—	η_{K^*} =	-1	—
d) Labor productivity growth	η_p =	$(\epsilon-1)/\epsilon$	$-1/\epsilon$	—	$1/\epsilon$	η_p =	—	-1	—	η_p =	—	—
e) Capital productivity growth	η_{ld} =	$1 + (r/\epsilon)$	r/ϵ	—	$-r/\epsilon$	η_{ld} =	1	r	—	η_{ld} =	1	—
f) Profit rate variation	η_π =	$1/\phi_K$	—	—	$-r$	η_π =	1	—	—	η_π =	1	—
g) Variation of distributive shares	η_r =	$-(\epsilon-1)/\epsilon_{LL}$	$1/\epsilon_{LL}$	$-(\epsilon-1)/\epsilon_{LL}$	$-(\epsilon-1)/\epsilon_{LL}$	η_r =	—	$1/\phi_L$	—	η_r =	—	—

$^a F_L = B_L/\epsilon - (\epsilon-1)J/\epsilon = H_L/\epsilon - J$

Recent "new growth theory" efforts have concentrated on endogenizing technology change by focusing on externalities related to investments in education and research and development (Lucas, Romer, Barro) as a way to preserve the viability of capitalist economies. The basic notion remains that the primary growth promotion force during the modern epoch is the persistent exploration of the technological frontier followed by the institutionalized application of that knowledge. While this volume is focused on the transition growth of developing countries *en route* to economic maturity, the reader should not lose sight of the fact that the very notion of "maturity" can only be defined in terms of a society's technological competence.

6.6 Structural Duality

6.6.1 Symmetry of K and L

There is a basic symmetry between capital and labor in the growth equations of table 4.1 of chapter 4. Furthermore, by changing the causal order of determination we have identified two types of real world problems:

$$\eta_L = \eta_K + (B_L+J)/\epsilon_{LL} - \eta_w/\epsilon_{LL} \quad \text{(Labor absorption in the LDC)} \quad (6.17a)$$
$$\eta_K = \eta_L + (B_K+J)/\epsilon_{KK} - \eta_\pi/\epsilon_{KK} \quad \text{(Capital accumulation in the mature DC)} \quad (6.17b)$$

While equation 6.17a envisions labor absorption analysis to determine η_L (the rapidity of labor absorption) in the context of a contemporary dualistic LDC, equation 6.17b is concerned with the economic forces that determine the growth rate of capital (η_K) in a mature capitalist economy. The symmetry between K and L allows us to transfer knowledge from one growth system to the other.

In equation 6.17a we see that η_L is affected by η_w (the behavior of real wages) while in equation 6.17b η_K is affected by η_π (the behavior of the profit rate). To carry the notion of duality one step further, we have the following special case:

$$\eta_L = \eta_K + (B_L+J)/\epsilon_{LL} \text{ (by } \eta_w = 0) \text{ (unlimited supply of labor)} \quad (6.18a)$$
$$\eta_K = \eta_L + (B_K+J)/\epsilon_{KK} \text{ (by } \eta_\pi = 0) \text{ (unlimited supply of capital)} \quad (6.18b)$$

Equation 6.18a is the labor absorption equation under the condition of an "unlimited" supply of labor, while equation 6.18b is the capital accumulation equation under the condition of an "unlimited" supply of capital.

Table 6.1 (based on equation 6.17a) and table 6.2 (based on equation 6.17b)

Table 6.2 Profile of mature economy growth

	Decomposition into coefficients of					Decomposition with rate ($\eta_\pi = 0$)				Decomposition when $\eta_w = F_K = 0$		
Analysis of rapidity of	Growth rate	J	B_K	η_L	η_π	Growth rate	$J_L = J/\phi_L$	$F_K^{\,a}$	η_L	Growth rate	Coefficients of J_K	η_L
	(I)	(II)	(III)	(IV)	(V)	(VI)	(VII)	(VIII)	(IX)	(X)	(XI)	(XII)
a) Capital accumulation	$\eta_K =$	$1/\epsilon_{KK}$	$1/\epsilon_{KK}$	1	$-1/\epsilon_{KK}$	$\eta_K =$	1	$1/\phi_L$	1	$\eta_K =$	1	1
b) Output expansion	$\eta_Q =$	$1 + (1/r\epsilon)$	$1r/\epsilon$	1	$-r/\epsilon$	$\eta_Q =$	1	$1/r$	1	$\eta_Q =$	1	1
c) Capital deepening	$\eta_{K^*} =$	$1/\epsilon_{KK}$	$1/\epsilon_{KK}$	—	$-1/\epsilon_{KK}$	$\eta_{K^*} =$	1	$1/\phi_L$	—	$\eta_{K^*} =$	1	—
d) Capital productivity growth	$\eta_d =$	$(\epsilon - 1)/\epsilon$	$-1/\epsilon$	—	$1/\epsilon$	$\eta_d =$	—	-1	—	$\eta_d =$	1	—
e) Labor productivity growth	$\eta_p =$	$1 + (1/r\epsilon)$	$1/r\epsilon$	—	$-1/r\epsilon$	$\eta_p =$	1	$1/r$	—	$\eta_p =$	1	—
f) Wage rate variation	$\eta_{lw} =$	$1/\phi_L$	—	—	$-1/r$	$\eta_{lw} =$	1	—	—	$\eta_{lw} =$	1	—
g) Variation of distributive shares	$\eta_r =$	$(\epsilon - 1)/\epsilon_{KK}$	$-1/\epsilon_{KK}$	—	$-(\epsilon - 1)/\epsilon_{KK}$	$\eta_r =$	—	$-1/\phi_K$	—	$\eta_r =$	—	—

$^a F_K = B_K/\epsilon - (\epsilon - 1)J/\epsilon = H_{K'}/\epsilon = H_K/\epsilon - J$

each contains a number of growth equations. Since these two tables are completely symmetrical with respect to the roles of capital and labor, we can concentrate on the derivation of the growth equations in one (for example table 6.1) with the understanding that the equations in the other table can be derived by applying the rule of symmetry. We begin with the analysis of the labor absorption problem in a dualistic economy (equation 6.17a) in the course of transition.

6.6.2 Development of the commercialized sector in the dualistic economy

In analyzing transition growth in the labor surplus economy, there is recognition of the dualistic nature of the system – the coexistence of "non-commercialized" and "commercialized" sectors. The interaction of these two differently behaved sectors constitutes a fundamental difference between our approach and that of the classical school's "iron law of wages" or even that of Arthur Lewis.

Our general growth equations can be applied to the commercialized sector of a labor surplus economy as well as to an aggregate one-sector neoclassical system. Consistent with this interpretation, equation 6.17a is the labor absorption equation identifying the causal factors determining its rapidity when the growth of the real wage rate is exogenously determined.

We envision a situation in which an unlimited supply of labor ($\eta_w = 0$) prevails in its extreme form as specified in the special case of equation 6.18a. Alternatively, we can envision the more general case when $\eta_w > 0$, which may be interpreted as the labor absorption equation if there is some upward creep of the industrial real wage as the labor surplus condition gradually terminates. A more sustained increase in the non-agricultural real wage is likely to take place only after the commercialization point has been reached. For analytical reasons, these two cases must be distinguished conceptually. In applying growth equations T1–T9 (table 4.1, chapter 4), all indicators refer to the commercialized or non-agricultural sector of a dual economy. For example, η_Q is the rate of growth of output of that sector while ϕ_L is its labor share.

6.6.3 Derivations of growth equations in the labor absorption process

From equations T1–T9 we can see that all the growth rates, η_Q, η_p, η_d, $\eta_w, \ldots$ are determined by exogenous η_K and η_L. In particular, with the exception of η_Q in T1, all other growth rates (T2–T9) involve the term η_{K*}. With equation 6.17a as a labor absorption equation when η_K is treated exogenously:

$$\eta_L = \eta_K + H_L/\epsilon_{LL} - \eta_w/\epsilon_{LL} \qquad (6.19a)$$
$$\eta_{K*} = \eta_w/\epsilon_{LL} - H_L/\epsilon_{LL} \qquad (6.19b)$$
$$H_L = B_L + J \qquad (6.19c)$$

When the terms on the right-hand side are treated as exogenous, endogenous η_L and $\dot\eta_{K*}$ (when substituted into T1–T9) determine the growth equations in table 6.1. In each row the growth rate of a variable is decomposed into an additive sum with coefficients attached to η_w, η_K, B_L, and J. This set of growth equations is useful to analyze the growth rates of all the endogenous variables relevant to the labor absorption process, as indicated in column I of table 6.1.

6.6.4 Rapidity of labor absorption (η_L) and output expansion (η_Q)

The rapidity of labor absorption (η_L) and industrial output expansion (η_Q) are:

$$\eta_L = (1/\epsilon_{LL})J + (1/\epsilon_{LL})B_L + \eta_K - (1/\epsilon_{LL})\eta_w \text{ (by 6.19)} \qquad (6.20a)$$
$$\eta_Q = (1 + r/\epsilon)J + (r/\epsilon)B_L + \eta_K - (r/\epsilon)\eta_w \qquad (6.20b)$$

Proof $\eta_Q = J + \phi_K\eta_K + \phi_L(\eta_K + J/\epsilon_{LL} + B_L/\epsilon_{LL} - \eta_w/\epsilon_{LL})$
$\qquad = J + \eta_K + (r/\epsilon)(J + B_L - \eta_w) \text{ (by } \phi_L/\epsilon_{LL} = r/\epsilon)$
$\qquad = \eta_K + J(1+r/\epsilon) - (r/\epsilon)\eta_w + (r/\epsilon)B_L.$ \qquad Q.E.D.

The proofs of equation 6.20ab require only routine substitutions of 6.19 into the relevant growth equations of table 4.1 of chapter 4. Equations 6.20a and b are listed in rows a and b of table 6.1, with η_L and η_Q in column I decomposed into four effects corresponding to the coefficients of (J, B_L, η_K and η_w) as listed in columns II–V.

Columns II and III describe the technological effects, while column IV indicates the capital accumulation effect. The impact of an increasing wage rate (assuming $\eta_w > 0$) is given in column V. If a strict unlimited supply of labor condition exists, all effects indicated in column V vanish because $\eta_w = 0$. Before the commercialization point $\eta_w > 0$ is likely to be small due to the "upward creep" in the institutional real wage in agriculture, while it is likely to be large thereafter.

From equation 6.20ab, given the unlimited supply of labor condition ($\eta_w = 0$), a faster rate of labor absorption (η_L) and output expansion (η_Q) are driven by high innovation intensity (J), high labor-using bias (B_L), and a high capital growth rate (η_K). It is hardly a surprise that in a labor surplus economy, severe austerity (high η_K) and strongly labor-using inno-vations (B_L) contribute to both industrial output expansion (η_Q) and the solution of the "underemployment problem" (η_L). Hence there is unlikely to exist a conflict between output and unemployment effects. However, to the extent there is an upward "creep" in real wages before the turning point and an upward "gallop" thereafter, the rate of industrial employ-ment expansion and output are slowed down.

6.6.5 The rate of capital deepening (η_{K*})

The rate of capital deepening given by equation 6.19b is reproduced in row c of table 6.1. When an unlimited supply of labor exists, the equation reduces to the special case:

$$\eta_K^* = -H_L/\epsilon_{LL} \qquad (\eta_w = 0) \qquad (6.21a)$$
$$\eta_K^* = -J/\epsilon_{LL} - B_L/\epsilon_{LL} \qquad (\eta_w = 0) \qquad (6.21b)$$

Whether or not capital per head (K^*) should be expected to increase or decrease through time is a debatable issue. While persistent overall increases in K^* are a well-known stylized fact in the typical mature eco-nomy, an increase in K^* in the commercialized sector of the dual economy while the unlimited supply of labor condition prevails may be an indica-tion of a flawed development strategy as suggested by the following restatement of equation 6.21a:

$$\eta_K^* \gtreqless 0 \leftrightarrow H_L \lesseqgtr 0 \text{ (from equation 6.21a)} \qquad (6.22)$$

In other words, when the real wage is constant a capital deepening process results $(\eta_K^* > 0)$ if and only if technological change is very labor saving $(H_L < 0)$. An upward creep of w contributes to the same result. In post-war LDC experience, a development strategy aimed at increasing K^* is often associated with a "big push" for modernization via the importation of "turn-key" projects, embodying very labor-saving innovations while ignoring both the existence of alternative technological import choices and the possibility of exploring labor-using adaptations of that technology. The fallacy of such a "big push" strategy is clearly demonstrated as it con-tributes to a slowing down of both output expansion and labor absorption, with a negative H_L implying a negative B_L in equation 6.21ab. A fuller analysis of capital deepening or shallowing in the context of Japanese his-torical and Indian post-war development experience is undertaken in chapter 7.

As seen in column IV of table 6.1, the growth rate of capital (η_K) exer-cises a positive and proportional impact on η_L and η_Q but has no effect whatsoever on $\eta_K{}^*$, η_p, η_d, η_π, η_r. Hence the savings rate also does not affect these indicators.

6.6.6 Growth of labor productivity (η_p) and capital productivity (η_d)

In a labor surplus economy, the rates of increase of labor and capital productivity in the commercialized sector are reproduced in rows d and e of table 6.1. A large J and/or B_L contribute unambiguously to an increase in capital productivity (large η_d). In contrast, a large J and/or B_L affect labor productivity (η_p) differently. A labor-using bias $(B_L > 0)$ lowers labor productivity (η_p). Even a large J can lower labor productivity if the law of diminishing returns does not operate strongly (that is, $\epsilon < 1$). Thus, if the LDC makes an effort to engage in labor-using innovations or to ameliorate the law of diminishing returns to labor (that is, make fuller use of its surplus labor force), the average productivity of labor is expected to decline as more workers are absorbed by the industrial sector.

Before the commercialization point is reached there arise such debatable issues as the possible conflict between employment generation (η_L) and output or productivity generation $(\eta_Q$ or $\eta_p)$ associated with technological choice. The question is whether the employment objective must be sacrificed when a high productivity objective is pursued. The possibility of such a conflict is analyzed further in chapter 7.

6.6.7 Variations in the profit rate

The growth rate of profit in the course of the transition growth process is listed in table 6.1, row f. Given $\eta_w = 0$:

Definition   The growth rate of profits (η_π) is insensitive to the factor bias and/or the growth rate of capital.

Thus, the coefficients for B_L and η_K are zero. The economic significance of this result is that when individual entrepreneurs face a strictly unlimited supply of labor – a constant real wage rate – they are interested in the highest possible innovation intensity effect but do not care whether the innovations are labor-saving or labor-using. This situation does not change when an upward creeping or galloping real wage adversely affects the profit rate. The direction of change in the profit rate remains insensitive to the factor bias of innovation. This is a now familiar finding in the microeconomics of innovation literature.

6.6.8 Variations in the distributive shares $(r = \phi_L/\phi_K)$

Variations in the distributive shares $(r = \phi_L/\phi_K)$ are shown in table 6.1, row g. A labor-using bias $(B_L > 0)$ contributes to an increase in the wage share (ϕ_L) and thus in r. Under "normal" conditions $(\epsilon > 1)$ the wage share increases when the real wage rises $(\eta_w > 0)$, while a higher innovation intensity (J) lowers the wage share. When the laws of diminishing returns operate less strongly $(\epsilon < 1)$, both $B_L > 0$ and a larger J increase the wage share. We return to this issue when analyzing income distribution in chapter 9.

6.6.9 Innovation characteristics under unlimited supply of labor conditions

When the unlimited supply of labor condition applies strictly, the terms in column V of table 6.1 drop out and the growth equations for (p, d, π, r) can be written in simplified form. We use the following definitions:

$$J_K = J/\phi_K > 0 \quad \text{(capital augmentation innovation intensity) (6.23a)}$$
$$F_L = 1/\epsilon(H_L - \epsilon J) \quad \text{(Harrod labor-using bias)} \qquad \text{(6.23b)}$$

Equation 6.23 leads to the following theorem:

Theorem Under the condition of an unlimited supply of labor $(\eta_w=0)$, the growth equations of $(\eta_p, \eta_d, \eta_\pi, \eta_r)$ take on the following form:

$$\eta_p = -F_L \qquad \text{(6.24a)}$$
$$\eta_d = J_K + rF_L \qquad \text{(6.24b)}$$
$$\eta_\pi = J_K \qquad \text{(6.24c)}$$
$$\eta_r = F_L/\phi_L \qquad \text{(6.24d)}$$

The proof of this theorem follows directly from the equations indicated in columns I to IV plus:

$$F_L = B_L/\epsilon - (\epsilon - 1)J/\epsilon \text{ (from equation 6.23b and } B_L \equiv H_L - J) \text{ (6.25)}$$

The equations in 6.24 are recorded in columns VI to IX of table 6.1. The performance of the industrial sector under the condition of an unlimited supply of labor can be analyzed most conveniently in terms of these equations.

J_K and F_L appear naturally among the derivations of the growth equations of table 4.1 in chapter 4. The economic significance of these equations is facilitated when their intuitive meaning is first explored.

6.6.10   Factor intensity of innovations and factor bias à la Harrod

The economic interpretation of the following pair has been previously established:

$$J_K = J/\phi_K \quad \text{(capital augmentation innovation intensity)} \quad \text{(6.26a)}$$
$$J_L = J/\phi_L \quad \text{(labor augmentation innovation intensity)} \quad \text{(6.26b)}$$

For the other dualistic pair:

$$F_L = 1/\epsilon(H_L - \epsilon J) \quad \text{(Harrod labor-using bias)} \quad \text{(6.27a)}$$
$$F_K = 1/\epsilon(H_K - \epsilon J) \quad \text{(Harrod capital-using bias)}^3 \quad \text{(6.27b)}$$

In section 5.3.4 of chapter 5 we defined the direction of factor bias (F_L and F_K) of innovation in the Harrod sense. In the case where we have Harrod-neutral factor bias, $F_L = F_K = 0$. A positive F_L (F_K) implies a Harrod labor-using (capital-using) or capital-saving (labor-saving) bias. The relatedness of Harrod neutrality and Hicksian neutrality for the "normal" case of $\epsilon > 1$ was analyzed in the context of figure 5.6(c) in chapter 5.

6.6.11   Transition growth under unlimited supplies of labor

Making use of J_K and F_L, the equations in table 6.1 provide a complete profile of transition growth of the commercialized sector as described by the titles indicated in the various rows of that table (for example, "labor absorption", "output expansion," "capital deepening," ... "variations in the distributive shares.") In all cases the rapidity of growth is causally determined by (J, B_L, η_K, η_w). However, under the condition of an unlimited supply of labor, the causal factors can also be stated in terms of the triplet (J_K, F_L, η_K) as indicated in columns VI to IX. Furthermore, when technological change is Harrod labor neutral ($F_L=0$), the growth equations reduce to the special case indicated in columns X, XI and XII.

For the triplet (p, π, r):

Theorem   Under the condition of an unlimited supply of labor:

$$\eta_\pi = J_K \quad \text{implying } \eta_\pi \geq 0 \quad \text{(6.28a)}$$
$$\eta_\pi = -F_L \quad \text{implying } \eta_\pi \gtreqless 0 \leftrightarrow F_L \lesseqgtr 0 \quad \text{(6.28b)}$$
$$\eta_r = F_L/\phi_L \quad \text{implying } \eta_r \gtreqless 0 \leftrightarrow F_L \gtreqless 0 \quad \text{(6.28c)}$$

Equation 6.28a states that under conditions of an unlimited supply of labor the industrial entrepreneur is assured of a rising profit rate determined by the always positive capital intensity of innovation. Equation 6.28b states that industrial labor productivity rises or falls in relation to whether or not innovations are Harrod labor-saving or labor-using. Equation 6.28c states that the trend of the relative shares also depends on the direction of bias *à la* Harrod.

For the pair (η_{K^*}, η_d) under an unlimited supply of labor:

$$\eta_{K^*} = -J_K - F_L/\phi_K = -H_L/\epsilon_{LL} \qquad \text{implying } \eta_{K^*} \gtreqless 0 \leftrightarrow H_L \lesseqgtr 0 \tag{6.29a}$$

$$\eta_d = J_K + rF_L \qquad\qquad\qquad \text{implying } \eta_d \gtreqless 0 \leftrightarrow F_L \gtreqless -J_K/r \tag{6.29b}$$

Equation 6.29a implies that capital deepening occurs if and only if innovations are very labor-saving *à la* Hicks. Equation 6.29b illustrates that capital productivity is constant if and only if innovations are sufficiently labor-saving *à la* Harrod.

Finally, when $\eta_w = F_L = 0$:

$$\eta_L = \eta_Q = J_K + \eta_K \tag{6.30a}$$
$$\eta_d = \eta_\pi = -\eta_{K^*} = J_K \tag{6.30b}$$
$$\eta_r = \eta_p = 0 \tag{6.30c}$$

Thus, when the economy approximates a labor surplus condition and Harrod labor-saving neutrality, industrial labor productivity is constant (6.30c); both capital productivity and the profit rate rise in the presence of capital shallowing (6.30b); and output and employment growth are equal at the positive $J_K + \eta_K$ rate (6.30a). This summarizes the growth profile in the extreme labor surplus economy case. Given the symmetry between labor and capital, the contents of table 6.2 can now be utilized to analyze growth in the mature economy.

6.7 Growth in the Mature Economy

6.7.1 Growth rate of capital in the long and short run

Table 6.2 contains growth equations that can be used to analyze the growth profile of mature economies. Our point of departure is the interpretation of equation 4.58b – the capital accumulation equation reproduced in row a. The causation of the rapidity of capital accumulation η_K is decomposable into four terms, with coefficients attached to J, B_K (representing the (positive) technology effect), η_L (representing the (positive) population growth effect), and η_π (representing the (negative) real interest rate effect). It is obvious that higher exogenous values of J, B_K, and η_L contribute to more rapid capital accumulation.

There is a short-run and a long-run interpretation of the exogenous interest rate (η_π). In contemporary (Keynesian) macroeconomics, in the short run, it is traditional to treat the interest rate (π) as exogenously determined by monetary considerations subject to the control of monetary authorities. In this tradition, variations in the interest rate determine the short-run value of investment ($I=dK/dt$) based on assumptions concerning the marginal productivity of capital. The growth rate of capital is determined by the interest rate when the "initial capital stock" is given.

The exogenous treatment of the return to capital in the short run is ultimately traced to the fact that there exist two diametrically opposed notions of the interest rate – one which is liquidity-sensitive and one which is savings rate-sensitive. Keynesian economists (for example, Tobin), given their interest in the short run, believe that savings is irrelevant for the determination of the interest rate – a fact that provides the basis for the short-run exogenous treatment of π. In the long-run, in sharp contrast, "liquidity" is irrelevant and the interest rate at any moment in time is determined by "austerity" approximated by the savings capacity – for example, a high saving rate depresses the long-run interest rate. Thus, in the long-run we accept the classical savings-sensitive theory of interest.

Whether we accept the long-run or the short-run interpretation, the direction of impact of an increase in the interest rate on capital accumulation is negative, with a coefficient (of absolute magnitude $1/\epsilon_{KK}$) inversely related to the severity of the law of diminishing returns to capital (ϵ_{KK}). When the law of diminishing returns is strong, the marginal product of capital curve is steep and variations in the interest rate do not affect investment and capital accumulation. The same savings coefficient ($1/\epsilon_{KK}$) applies to the positive effect of J and B_K – explained similarly in terms of the strength of the law of diminishing returns. These are the growth-theoretic contributions to short-run macroeconomic analysis.

6.7.2 Growth profile

The growth profile of a mature economy in the long and short run is provided through the equations for η_Q, $\eta_K{}^*$, η_p, η_d, η_w, and η_r (in rows b to g of table 6.2), derived from η_K according to the principle of duality. In theory, the use of an (exogenous) interest rate policy has an impact on all the variables indicated. The population growth rate η_L only affects η_K and η_Q and does not affect the value of any other variable. A higher innovation intensity (J in column II) exercises a positive impact on all variables given the "normal" case of substitution inelasticity ($\epsilon > 1$). A higher rate of profit increase (η_π) depresses labor productivity (row e) and the wage rate (row f). Thus, an expansionary monetary policy calculated to lower η_π (especially when rendering it negative) is always popular with the working class – since the wage rate rises – as well as with the entrepreneurial class – since the rate of capital accumulation increases. However, it violates our sense of equity to see beneficial effects achieved by Keynesian money printing. In the long run, such benefits disappear, as the next section shows.

6.7.3 Long-run growth profile of mature capitalism

The long-run growth profile of mature capitalism is indicated in columns VI-XII of table 6.2 when the rate of interest is constant ($\eta_\pi = 0$) – the economy remains in the constant real interest rate world (for example between 3 percent and 5 percent) that has persisted for the nearly 200 years since the industrial revolution. Exogenous factors are represented by the triplet of terms J_L (the effect of labor augmentation intensity), F_K (the effect of Harrod capital-using bias), and η_L (the effect of population growth).

A positive capital-using innovation in the Harrod sense ($F_K > 0$) hurts capital productivity ($\eta_d < 0$ in row d) and the labor share (row g) as expected. Otherwise, the impact of a positive F_K and J_L is non-negative for all variables. In the constant profit world, the wage rate always increases at the positive rate J_L – the labor augmentation innovation intensity.

6.7.4 The dynamic equilibrium of Harrod

In long-run perspective the development of mature capitalist economies is characterized by the constancy of the growth rate of capital (η_K) as well as the constancy of the interest rate. Empirically, the growth rate of capital ($\eta_K = sd = s/(K/Q)$) has been approximately 2.5 percent over time, with s varying from 10 percent to 20 percent and K/Q between 4 and 5, yielding a narrow band of 2 percent to 5 percent for η_K. The so-called "dynamic equilibrium" of Harrod ($\eta_\pi = \eta_{\eta_K} = 0$ in equation 6.13) is a special case of the constant profit world when the additional condition of constant capital growth rate ($\eta_{\eta_K} = 0$) is imposed. Theorem 6.14 and equation 6.16 established that the necessary conditions for a Harrod dynamic equilibrium are that innovations be capital neutral in the Harrod sense ($F_K=0$) and that the Marxian compensation effect ($H_K = \epsilon_{KK}\eta_{K*}$) occurs. When these conditions are imposed, the growth equations reduce to those shown in columns X-XII of table 6.2:

$\eta_K = \eta_Q = J/\phi_L + r$ (long-run growth rapidity)   (6.31a)

$\eta_p = \eta_w = \eta_{K^*} = J/\phi_L > 0$ (constancy of the growth rate of p, w, and K^*)   (6.31b)

$\eta_\pi = \eta_d = \eta_{\phi_L} = \eta_{\eta_K} = 0$ (constancy of the level of d, π, ϕ_L, and η_K)   (6.31c)

The sufficient condition for Harrod dynamic equilibrium is thus the constancy of J, ϕ_L, and r.

The Harrod dynamic equilibrium describes the long-run growth profile of mature industrial capitalism when capital and GNP grow at a constant rate ($J/\phi_L + r$) – a demographic and technological phenomenon (6.31a). The necessary conditions for Harrod dynamic equilibrium exist, as $\eta_{\eta_K} = \eta_\pi = 0$, but sufficiency is lacking since J is not constant in the most general case. In the long run p, w, and K^* all grow at the constant rate J/ϕ_L (6.31b), completely driven by technology. There is a persistent gain in labor welfare, labor productivity, and capital deepening. There also exists a domination of welfare by technology as savings and demographic forces are irrelevant. Finally, given the background of a continuous expansion in size (6.31) and gains in consumer welfare (6.32b), mature capitalism is characterized by the long-run constancy of the triplet (π, d, and ϕ_L) – the well-known Kaldor constancies. This equilibrium represents a long-run generalization of the result achieved by Solow. Assuming $J=0$,

$\eta_Q = \eta_K = r$ (by 6.31a)   (6.32a)

$\eta_w = \eta_p = \eta_{K^*} = \eta_\pi = \eta_d = \eta_{\phi_L} = \eta_{\eta_K} = 0$ (by 6.31b)   (6.32b)

Our general model, including $J > 0$, is more realistic and allows us to apply the notion of structural duality to tables 6.1 and 6.2.

CHAPTER 6   APPLICATIONS TO MODERN ECONOMIC GROWTH

NOTES

1   Marx did not exclude liquid capital, but it was not at the core of his theory.
2   Solow (1988, p. 313).
3   As the name "Harrod" suggests, the F_K concept (i.e., capital using innovation in the Harrod sense) was first proposed by Roy Harrod for the study of growth in the mature economy. The F_L concept is symmetrical to F_K, first proposed by Fei and Ranis (1965).

PART IV

Applications to Growth and Development Under Dualism

7

Transition Growth in the Closed Dualistic Economy

7.1 Introduction

The previous three chapters developed conceptual tools to analyze growth and development in various general settings, while this chapter focuses specifically on transition growth in the closed dualistic economy. The overall analysis of transition growth of chapter 3 serves as the theoretical parent of this chapter, while the tools fashioned in chapter 4 are applied to the analysis of the labor reallocation process. Focusing on labor absorption is important in this context because it represents the main indicator of successful balanced growth in the underlying labor and commodity markets. We have seen that such labor absorption is driven by two causal agents: capital accumulation η_K and technological change (J and B_L). The impact of these two factors – both heavily emphasized in chapter 4 – is considered when each is viewed as independent as well as when there is a degree of interdependence between them.

Section 7.2 explores the logical necessity for continuous labor reallocation as **the** indicator of successful balanced growth in the intersectoral labor, commodity, and financial markets. Section 7.3 advances the critical minimum effort criterion for developmental success and explores the impact of technology change and capital accumulation on the rate of labor reallocation in greater detail. Section 7.4 illustrates the real world relevance of our analysis by drawing on empirical evidence from two developing countries and section 7.5 addresses the potential conflict between maximizing output and employment objectives during the labor reallocation process.

7.2 Balanced Growth and the Necessity for Labor Reallocation

The typical labor surplus dualistic economy, thoroughly portrayed in chapter 3, is initially faced with an unfavorable resource endowment, that is, a high labor/land ratio and increasing population pressure at the margin. In this situation the "balanced" reallocation of underemployed labor from the agricultural to the non-agricultural sector represents a basic policy goal. Such a process of labor reallocation must be sufficiently rapid to shift the economy's center of gravity if commercialization is to occur and occur quickly enough. The process must, by necessity, entail agricultural productivity increases which are sufficiently large to allow the release of labor, as fewer workers must be capable of feeding the total population. At the same time, the industrial sector must expand its capital stock and/or its technological progress rapidly enough to provide employment for the released labor. If either side of this process fails, successful transition will not occur.

To illustrate the notion of balanced growth in the labor market, let $P(t)$ be the time path of the total population or labor force, with $W(t)$ and $L(t)$ the industrial and agricultural labor forces, respectively: $\theta = W/P$ is the fraction of the population allocated to the industrial sector, while $(1 - \theta) = L/P$ is the fraction remaining in the agricultural sector. θ is a rough proxy for the degree of labor reallocation, with $W/L = \theta/(1 - \theta)$ representing the number of industrial workers "supported" by one agricultural laborer. The goal is for labor reallocation θ to increase at a rate exceeding the population or labor force growth rate.

In this simple framework there are thus three possible real world cases:

$$\eta_P > \eta_W \quad \text{(failure)} \qquad (7.1a)$$
$$\eta_P = \eta_W \quad \text{(stagnation)} \qquad (7.1b)$$
$$\eta_P < \eta_W \quad \text{(success)} \qquad (7.1c)$$

In the failure case, the proportion of the total labor force absorbed by the non-agricultural sector is falling, as the rate of population growth overwhelms labor reallocation efforts. This result can be driven by either insufficient demand by non-agriculture or an explosion in population (and labor force) growth. The stagnation case features a stand-off, represented by a constant θ. In the success case of equation 7.1c, θ is increasing, signifying an increase in the fraction of the labor force engaged in commercialized activities. The three cases can be depicted graphically in figure 7.1(a).

Figure 7.1(b) emphasizes the time dimension of this reallocation process. *RIC*, related to the population or labor force growth curve, denotes the "required industrial labor curve," that is, it describes the labor

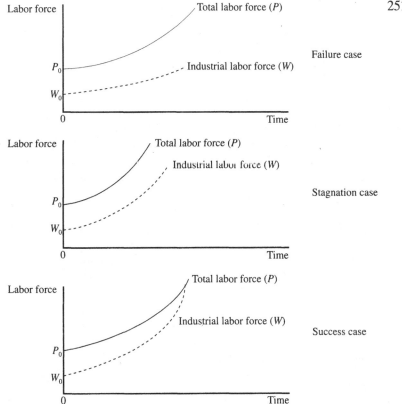

Figure 7.1 (a) Alternative reallocation scenarios

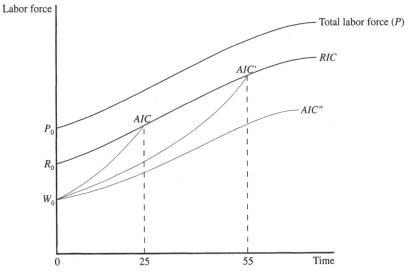

Figure 7.1 (b) Reallocation and the time dimension

reallocation which must have already taken place **if** commercialization were to occur at each possible point in time, while *AIC* denotes the "actual industrial labor curve," that is, the reallocation path that has actually been followed. Both the failure and stagnation cases of figure 7.1(a) are represented by an *AIC* curve which never "catches up" with the *RIC* curve, as the end of labor surplus is never reached. *AIC″* illustrates such a possibility. On the other hand, *AIC* and *AIC′* each illustrate a possible success case. However, commercialization occurs much earlier in the *AIC* case compared to *AIC′*, rendering the former clearly superior. In fact, if the time required is too long even *AIC′* may be viewed as politically unsustainable.

While these dynamic effects provide a coherent overview of the development possibilities in the most general and simplified framework, to analyze the specific process of labor reallocation we must look deeper into these conditions. Using equations 3.4a and 3.18a from chapter 3, the growth rate of the total labor force can be decomposed as follows:

$$\eta_P = \theta \, \eta_W + (1 - \theta) \, \eta_L \quad \text{where} \tag{7.2a}$$
$$\eta_W \to \eta_P \text{ as } \theta \to 1 \tag{7.2b}$$

The population growth rate is the weighted average of η_W and η_L (7.2a), where η_W approaches η_P as θ approaches 1 (7.2b). In this successful case, the historical population pressure on land in the agricultural sector is reversed as η_L may even turn negative as L declines absolutely after some point.

In any dualistic economy under population pressure, only equation 7.1c can be termed successful. The stagnant case entails no mopping up of the "reserve army" of the underemployed, and the failure case denotes an increase in that pool. While the change in the percentage of the total labor force reallocated to the industrial sector is not the sole measure of success or failure in development, it is one of the most important performance indicators summarizing the extent to which balanced inter-sectoral growth has managed to extricate the economy from its initial labor surplus condition. It is important to realize that θ represents only a proxy for these underlying forces of balanced growth, that is, agricultural productivity increase and non-agricultural labor absorption. The commercialization process can only be understood by considering the full interaction of both sectors in the intersectoral commodity, labor, and financial markets.

Equating development success with a sufficiently rapid reallocation of agricultural labor in a balanced growth context is corroborated by the evidence of some of today's developed economies like Japan, as well as today's successful NICs like Korea and Taiwan. Empirically, approaching the modern growth epoch can be linked to success in reaching the end of labor surplus, for example, around 1920 in Japan and around 1970 in East Asia, as signalled by the first sustained rise in unskilled real wages.

The argument for shifting the center of gravity of an economy to its non-agricultural sector is also supported by Engel's law. As long as agricultural labor productivity expands, industrialization is an inevitable and natural consequence. Given higher incomes, individuals prefer to consume proportionally more non-agricultural products, forcing a reallocation of labor to the industrial sector as fewer agricultural workers are necessary to support the food consumption of the entire population. We should recall that as long as the unlimited supply of labor condition lasts, real wages are unlikely to rise markedly in either sector. Engel's law comes into play, nevertheless, as a consequence of higher employment raising family wage incomes, even as wage rates rise only very modestly before the commercialization point. While much of the economy's surplus will be saved and invested, we can expect the wage bill to increase modestly for two additional reasons. First, there may be an upward creep in wage rates driven by agricultural productivity increase, and, second, there are possible changes in the inter-sectoral wage gap due to minimum wage legislation, unionization, etc.

Our emphasis on agricultural productivity increase and labor reallocation does not depend on the premise of a closed economy. Opening the dualistic economy to trade provides an additional production function enabling the system to obtain goods, possibly including food, more cheaply. But, as we show in chapter 8, this does not invalidate the necessity of balanced growth in all three inter-sectoral markets.

Figure 7.2 provides an operational perspective of a closed dualistic economy showing the various inter-relationships between the agricultural and non-agricultural sectors. Each sector is divided into a production sector and a household sector. The linkages are classified into three types, shown by the three circles at the center of the diagram: (1) the dualistic commodity market; (2) the dualistic financial market; and (3) the dualistic labor market. The arrows indicate the direction of the flow of real goods and services, while movements in the opposite direction imply the flow of money payments.

With respect to the intersectoral commodity market, a portion of the total output of the agricultural sector A goes to agricultural households for self consumption, C_A, and a portion flows to the non-agricultural sector, a flow we have labeled TAS – total agricultural surplus. This is a commodity surplus – the agricultural output in excess of the consumption of those working in agriculture. Part of it is consumed by non-agricultural households, C_{NA}, and part of it is an intermediate input into the industrial sector, C_M.

Total industrial sector output Q is partly consumed by industrial

Non-agricultural sector   Agricultural sector

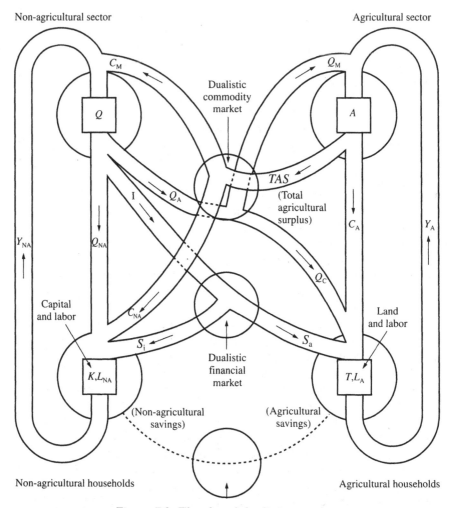

Figure 7.2 The closed dualistic economy

households, Q_{NA}, while the rest is divided into investment goods, I, and goods purchased by the agricultural sector, Q_A. The latter is used either for consumption by agricultural households, Q_C, or as inputs into agricultural production, Q_M.

The agricultural production sector receives land and labor services, Y_A, as well as intermediate inputs, Q_M. The incomes received by agricultural households are either spent on consumption, $(C_A + Q_C)$, or saved, S. Similarly, in the non-agricultural sector household factor payments Y_{NA} are either consumed, $(Q_{NA} + C_{NA})$, or saved, S_i. Together $S + S_i$, the savings out of the agricultural surplus plus the profits or savings of the industrial sector, constitute the savings fund of the closed dualistic economy financing non-agricultural investments via the dualistic financial market, as indicated in figure 7.2. If we accept the simplifying assumptions that land and labor are the only factors of production in agriculture, and capital and labor the only factors of production in non-agriculture, all capital goods produced are destined for investment in the latter sector. S_a thus represents the amount of financial credit extended by the agricultural sector to the industrial sector. Given an initially large agricultural sector, savings out of the agricultural surplus serve as the main fuel initially for the continued growth of the dualistic economy, dwarfing the savings of non-agriculture in the early stages.

In the intersectoral commodity market the participants are, on one side, the owners of the agricultural surplus who sell surplus food and, on the other side, the newly allocated industrial workers who possess wage income in the form of industrial goods and are anxious to exchange these goods for the food "left behind." Once these transactions are completed, the newly allocated industrial workers find themselves in possession of the agricultural goods which they want to consume. In this way, the intersectoral commodity market is indispensable for creating a wages fund for newly allocated industrial workers. At the same time the owners of the agricultural surplus must be compensated by becoming owners of a portion of the newly formed industrial output. Depending on the depth and diversity of the financial network, such claims will be in the form of savings or bank deposits, postal savings deposits, stocks and bonds, and, of course, direct ownership. The financial network must provide the financial assets acceptable to various owners of the agricultural surplus, enabling the dualistic economy to convert its rural savings into productive industrial investments. The satisfactory performance of these two markets is clearly an inter-related package.

The third intersectoral market is the labor market, through which low marginal productivity agricultural workers must be reallocated to more productive employment in the industrial sector. As we have seen earlier, the empirical reality is that up to 80 percent of the labor force may initially find itself in non-commercialized agriculture. In the course of a successful development effort this number may drop drastically over a few decades. The intersectoral labor market is based on the initial condition of an agricultural sector facing high man/land ratios, traditional technology, and production units frequently coincident with households. In the industrial sector commercialized activities predominate, especially urban large-scale activities operating on the basis of modern technology and specialization. This concept has been thoroughly analyzed in our chapter 3 discussion of the dualistic labor market.

Working through these three intersectoral markets and their implications for balanced growth, we see the need, on the one hand, for the agricultural sector to yield sufficiently large agricultural surpluses and to preserve a sufficiently large part of such surpluses for productive investment in industry; simultaneously, the industrial sector, financed by this agricultural surplus, plus the reinvestment of industrial profits, must grow fast enough to absorb the labor being reallocated. Over time there must clearly be a balance between capital accumulation, allocated mainly to industry, and technology efforts in both sectors to approach balanced growth. As we have just seen, such balanced growth must, moreover, proceed at a pace which not only exceeds the rate at which population growth yields additions to the labor force but which also satisfies a society's impatience for emerging from its dualistic condition.

In summary, balanced growth is defined by three criteria. One is that the volume of agricultural workers freed up through agricultural productivity increase is not too far out of line with the volume of new employment opportunities created in non-agriculture. A second is that the intersectoral commodity markets for agricultural and industrial goods clear without a major change in the intersectoral terms of trade. A third is that intersectoral financial markets clear, that is, *ex ante* agricultural and non-agricultural savings are converted into non-agricultural investment.

In the context of a market economy, where relative prices provide the main signals for investment opportunities and technological efforts in the two sectors, the dynamics of the dual economy's balanced-growth path can be illustrated by adding consumer preference and the terms of trade between agricultural and non-agricultural goods to the dual economy setting we have previously outlined.

Figure 7.3, while ignoring the flows of intermediate inputs, can be used to show balanced growth in our three intersectoral markets. To accurately illustrate this point, the "balance" criterion must hold for each of the three intersectoral markets. Given a fixed supply of land we can represent per capita agricultural output for the economy as a whole by the Q_A^* curve in quadrant II, with the total population or labor force shown on the horizontal axis. In other words, given agricultural technology, every point on Q_A^* describes the food supply per capita for different possible levels of allocation of the total labor force OP_0. At one such possible point of allocation, P_0L_0 workers have been reallocated with OL_0 remaining in agriculture.

Assume that the average agricultural worker receives an institutional wage equal to $c = Ow_a$ in terms of agricultural goods and wants to consume some agricultural goods (A on the vertical axis) and some non-agricultural goods (NA on the horizontal axis). The actual consumption mix chosen by the typical worker will depend on his preference map and its points of tangency with the terms of trade or budget line, w_aw_{na}, shown in quadrant I.

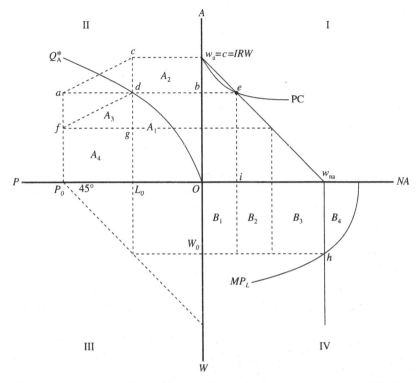

*Figure 7.3   Balanced growth in a closed dualistic economy: equilibrium
position*

At these terms of trade the non-agricultural real wage in terms of non-agricultural goods (and assuming no intersectoral unskilled wage gap) is equal to Ow_{na}. Assuming the same indifference map for both agricultural and allocated workers, we can trace out the price–consumption (PC) curve describing the locus of all possible equilibria, given different terms of trade.

Point e on the PC curve indicates one such possible equilibrium in the commodity market for the typical unskilled worker, regardless of whether he is engaged in agricultural or non-agricultural production. Consistent with his per capita demand for food Ob, at these terms of trade, is a per capita supply of food of L_0d describing one possible equilibrium position along the balanced growth path. This equilibrium assumes that P_0L_0 workers have already been allocated out of agriculture, with OL_0 workers remaining. Allocated workers P_0L_0 can also, with the help of the 45° line in quadrant III, be translated into OW_0 workers in quadrant IV. In this quadrant we can observe equilibrium at h where the demand for non-agricultural labor, represented by the MP_L curve, intersects the supply at the fixed institutional wage Ow_{na}. This MP_L curve is generated for a given technology and capital stock K_0, not shown here. Thus, we have equilibrium in the labor market, with the number of workers supplied by agriculture equal to those demanded by non-agriculture.

Turning to equilibrium in the commodity market, we can see that total agricultural output in the economy is the area $ObaP_0=A_1+A_3+A_4$, which is sufficient to meet the food consumption requirements of every individual in the economy at level Ob. This total agricultural supply of food can be divided into agricultural labor's share and the landlords' share. At the Ow_a wage level the total agricultural labor share is $Ow_acL_0=A_1+A_2$. To determine the residual or landlords' share we can draw a line from c to a in quadrant II and a line parallel to ca from d, locating point f. By the law of similar triangles, the ratio gd/db equals the ratio cd/ad, and hence $dbcd = gdad$. Thus, area A_2 is equal to area A_3 and agricultural labor's share can also be written as A_1+A_3. Consequently the residual of total agricultural output that accrues to the landlord class is $(A_1+A_3+A_4)-(A_1+A_3) = A_4$.

Turning to non-agriculture, the total quantity of non-agricultural output in this economy equals $B_1+B_2+B_3+B_4$. The industrial labor share is $B_1+B_2+B_3$, with OW_0 workers employed at the wage w_{na}. The residual profit share accruing to capitalists is B_4.

We can now indicate the required balance in the intersectoral commodity and financial markets. In order for everyone to arrive at the same equilibrium consumption point e each industrial worker will want to exchange $w_{na}i$ units of industrial goods for ei units of food at these terms of trade. Each agricultural worker will similarly wish to exchange bO units of food for be units of industrial goods. Industrial workers as a whole will want to exchange B_2+B_3 industrial goods for $A_1+A_3+A_4$ or $A_1+A_2+A_4$ agricultural goods. Industrial workers can be thought of as exchanging B_2 for A_3 ($=A_2$) with agricultural workers and B_3 for A_4 (the agricultural surplus) with landlords. This clearly establishes balance in the intersectoral commodity market, with all workers (assumed not to save) consuming at point e and landlords (who, like the capitalists, are assumed not to consume) owning an inventory of B_3 ($=A_4$) of industrial goods. Returning to the financial market, the investment fund for the next period is equivalent to the agricultural savings (equivalent to agricultural surplus here) of A_4, plus non-agricultural saving, equivalent to capitalist profits, that is, $I=A_4+B_4=B_3+B_4$.

Figure 7.3 can be reproduced (see figure 7.4(a)) to illustrate the process of balanced growth in the closed dualistic economy. As we have noted, a condition for the maintenance of "balance" is that the increase in agricultural labor productivity and that in non-agricultural labor productivity allows about the same number of workers to be released and absorbed, while the commodity markets continue to clear at the initial terms of trade. Consider an increase in agricultural productivity that allows agricultural labor to be "released" to industry (an increase in θ), represented by an upward shift of Q_A^* to $Q_A^{*'}$ in figure 7.4(a). At this higher level of productivity, a smaller agricultural population (OL_1) is needed to support the average food consumption of everyone at level e. The allocated non-agricultural labor force rises to P_0L_1 (equal to OW_1 in quadrant IV). The same real wage in terms of non-agricultural goods is now equal to the MP_L at h'. At this new point along a balanced growth path we also have a larger agricultural surplus (A_4) and non-agricultural profits (B_4) – see figure 7.3 – leading to a larger investment fund.

Notice that Dhh' in quadrant IV describes the "horizontal" unlimited supply of labor curve of Arthur Lewis and Fei/Ranis. In the real world, given the likelihood of some upward adjustment in the agricultural real wage at its source and the possibility of the existence, and enlargement, of an intersectoral unskilled wage gap, we do not expect Dhh' to be "flat" over time. We do, however, expect it to be only gently rising before the commercialization point. This is in sharp contrast to what can be expected to happen in the case of "unbalanced growth." This case resulted from the idea, quite popular in the 1950s and 1960s, that industrialization is tantamount to successful development and can drag the agricultural sector along with it. In the absence of adequate agricultural productivity increases to accompany the "push" for industrialization, we get the phenomenon of food shortage-induced inflation and a premature rise in the non-agricultural real wage. Consider figure 7.4(b), which reproduces the initial equilibrium in all three intersectoral markets as presented in figures 7.3 and 7.4(a). However, consider now an effort to reallocate workers by the same numbers as before, that is L_0L_1, but now in the absence of any increase in agricultural productivity. The per capita demand for food can be brought down to the now lower level of per capita supply only by re-establishing equilibrium at e' via a change in the terms of trade, from $w_a - w_{na}$ to $w_a - w_{na'}$. The new non-agricultural real wage $Ow_{na'}$ now intersects the non-agricultural labor demand curve MP_L at h'' instead of at h'. Consequently, the non-agricultural labor supply curve $w_{na}hh''$ is no longer horizontal (or gently upward sloping) but rises sharply, endangering the entire transition growth process long before the commercialization or Lewis turning point is reached. Food shortage-driven inflation often leads to further inflationary consequences, validated *ex post* by monetary expansion. Not until the 1970s did most policy makers realize the importance of agricultural mobilization as an essential ingredient of successful balanced growth.

Finally, we need to illustrate the termination of a balanced growth

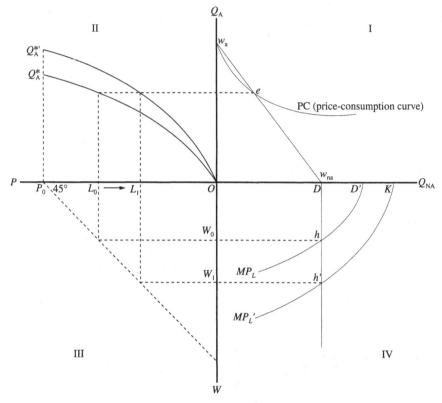

Figure 7.4 (a) Balanced growth: comparative static equilibrium

process, that is the achievement of commercialization. The reader will recall that this point is marked by the advent of neoclassical equality between the marginal product of labor and the real wage. We can illustrate such termination of the dualistic condition with the help of figure 7.4(c), an extension of figure 7.4(a). With the institutional real wage fixed at w_a, quadrants II and IV illustrate successive balanced increases in agricultural and non-agricultural labor productivity, each allowing labor to be released to the industrial sector as the agricultural labor force declines. We can draw a marginal product of agricultural labor curve in quadrant II (MP_L, MP_L', MP_L'') for each level of per capita food supply (Q_A^*, $Q_A^{*'}$, $Q_A^{*''}$). As the marginal product rises, the gap between it and the IRW at each point of allocation declines. Finally, when technology change in agriculture has yielded a marginal product (along MP_L'') equal to the (constant) agricultural wage, the economy has achieved commercialization, ending the dualistic character of the economy as all labor, agricultural as well as non-agricultural, will now be paid its marginal product.

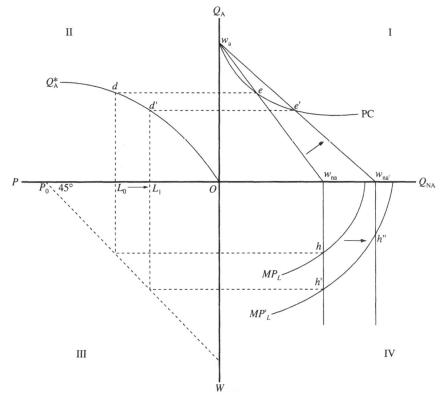

Figure 7.4 (b) Unbalanced growth: comparative statics

Note that in this case we have explicitly held the agricultural real wage constant; if, as we have pointed out earlier, it rises gently, but lags behind average agricultural labor productivity increases, the level of w_a in figure 7.4(c) would have to be raised. In such a case the balanced growth process would play itself out as before, except that the *IRW* would now present a moving target and it would therefore take longer for the balanced growth process to yield commercialization with a higher MP_L required to achieve equality at the point of allocation.

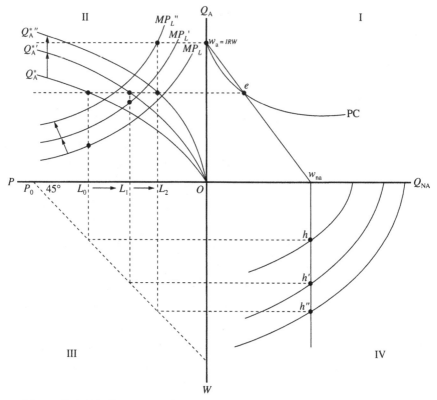

Figure 7.4 (c) Commercialization at the end of a balanced growth path

7.3 Underlying Conditions for Success

We defined the necessary condition for developmental success as the growth rate of the industrial labor force exceeding the growth rate of the total population or labor force (equation 7.1c). Assuming that the extreme labor surplus condition of a constant institutional real wage ($\eta_{w_{na}} = 0$) holds, we can combine the success criterion with our growth equations. Using the labor absorption equation 5.31a of chapter 5, the minimum labor reallocation condition for successful development (see equation 7.1c) becomes:

$$\eta_P < \eta_W = \eta_K + (B_L + J)/\epsilon_{LL} - \eta_{w_{na}} / \epsilon_{LL} \qquad (7.3a)$$

This equation states that the development effort can be related to five causal factors, the combined magnitude of which must exceed the rate of overall labor force or population growth for success to occur. In other words, the rate of industrial capital accumulation η_K must be large enough, the intensity of innovation J high enough, the labor-using bias of innovation B_L strong enough, the growth in wages $\eta_{w_{na}}$ small enough, and the law of diminishing returns to labor ϵ_{LL} weak enough so that their combined effect on the industrial sector demand for labor exceeds the population growth rate.

The extent to which the real wage rises ($\eta_{w_{na}} > 0$), the forces of demand, η_K, J and B_L, are weakened, that is, they fall on price rather than quantity. In actuality w_{na} is likely to increase slightly over time, even in the presence of an unlimited supply of labor condition, due to an upward creep in the agricultural wage as agricultural labor productivity rises, plus possible increases in institutional interventions in non-agriculture, including minimum wage legislation and union pressure. In the extreme case of an unlimited supply of labor condition ($\eta_{w_{na}} = 0$) equation 7.3a is modified to yield:

$$\eta_P < \eta_W = \eta_K + (J + B_L)/\epsilon_{LL} \qquad (7.3b)$$

which represents the simplified condition for successful development.

While the above critical minimum effort criterion may not be met every year, it cannot be consistently violated if successful development is to occur. Such a violation implies that the underemployed population in agriculture is being augmented faster by demographic pressures than it is being diminished by the reallocation of workers. The center of gravity of the economy can only be shifted if equation 7.3b is satisfied over the long run.

Thus, given exogenous demographic pressures, success is determined largely by capital accumulation (η_K) and technological change ($B_L + J$), the two most important growth concepts. In fact, equation 7.3b can be decomposed further. Using the production function described in chapter 4, the corresponding equation (4.22a) allows us to explain more precisely the rate of capital accumulation and its impact on the minimum labor reallocation condition for successful development:

$$\eta_P < \eta_W = \eta_K + (B_L + J)/\epsilon_{LL} = sd + (B_L + J)/\epsilon_{LL} \qquad (7.3c)$$

where s is the measure of national austerity (average propensity to save) and d is the level of capital productivity. This decomposition is important because $\eta_{\eta_K} = \eta_s + \eta_d$, so that capital deceleration or acceleration in the growth process can be determined from the interaction of these two variables. Technology takes on an even more important role in this framework, as capital productivity is directly dependent on technological progress.

The causal factors behind η_P, η_K, J, B_L, plus how close the system is to sustaining the unlimited supply of labor condition $\eta_{w_{na}} = 0$, clearly determine the success or failure of a particular economy's development effort. Some of these factors are more easy to influence via policy than others. For example, the rate of capital accumulation can be enhanced via domestic austerity programs by reinvesting a larger volume of industrial profits and/or channeling more agricultural savings into industrial investment. However, other factors are harder for policy makers to influence precisely. Current knowledge about the intensity of innovation and the degree of labor-using bias of innovation is not very precise, especially since the two factors are not necessarily independent of each other. The quality of innovations is linked to the incentives faced by industrial entrepreneurs and to the activities of government – activities which may bias the direction of innovations. Indeed, the burgeoning field of the so-called "new growth theory" is focused on trying to render this black box less opaque and more transparent.

Similarly, endogenous explanations of the population growth rate remain less than satisfactory. While mortality determinants are reasonably well understood, there does not yet exist a fully reliable theory to explain the movement of fertility over time – in spite of substantial efforts at the micro or household level in recent decades. We have learned a good deal about the importance of women's education and wages as well as concerning the impact of infant mortality on fertility. Yet we are still not in a position to determine exactly what determines a household's demand for children. Consequently, policies aimed at reducing population growth have had a mixed record of success – performing quite well in some nations but poorly in others.

Finally, an approximation to the constant institutional real wage hypothesis ($\eta_{w_{na}} = 0$) implies the persistence of an agricultural reserve army. The near constancy of the real wage, with only a modest upward drift to be reasonably expected until the turning point has been reached, means that most of the impact of the forces of demand, that is, capital accumulation and technological change, falls on the quantity of labor absorption rather than on its price, that is, the non-agricultural real wage.

The critical minimum effort criterion of equation 7.3a thus represents a convenient framework for summarizing the forces which determine the success or failure of development in the dualistic economy. Even if our understanding of the determinants of each of the elements of equation 7.3a is less than perfect, the framework permits quantitative inductive analysis through which the absolute and relative importance of

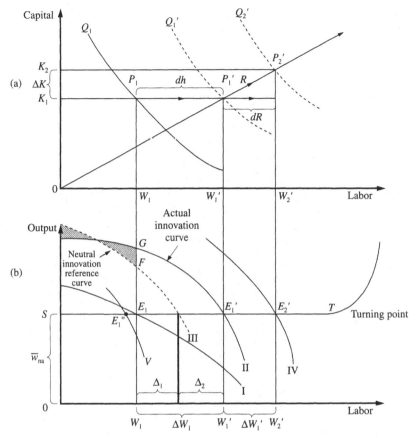

Figure 7.5 Production contour map, industrial sector

capital accumulation and innovative activities, as well as of "premature" wage increases, on industrial sector labor absorption can be assessed.

It might be useful to explore industrial sector labor absorption a bit more fully with the help of figure 7.5. Figure 7.5(a) illustrates the production contour map of the industrial sector (Q_i) for varying combinations of capital and labor. Figure 7.5(b) shows the unlimited supply of labor curve (ST) at a constant industrial real wage $\bar{w}_{na}$. For any initial capital stock, for example K_1, we can show the relevant labor demand or MP_L curve, that is, curve I in figure 7.5(b), yielding the equilibrium points E_1 and P_1, with K_1 and W_1 units of inputs yielding Q_1 units of output.

Let us now assume that an innovation occurs at this initial point in time. In this case the MP_L curve shifts, say, from position I to II, which implies new equilibrium points E_1' and P_1', respectively. With the capital stock still fixed at K_1, ΔW_1 units of additional labor are absorbed by the industrial sector at the new equilibrium shown on the labor axis of figure 7.5(b), due exclusively to innovative activity. To determine the relative contributions of innovational intensity and bias we can draw a reference curve (curve III) which traces a neutral innovation, with the intensity or strength of innovation J equivalent to that of the actual real world innovation, that is, the areas of the two shaded triangles are equal. Since point G lies above point F, that is, the MP_L at the pre-innovation input point has risen more than it would have if the innovation were neutral, the actual innovation is labor-using (or capital-saving). Had the innovation been neutral, Δ_1 additional labor would have been absorbed due to the innovation. However, since the innovation is labor-using, the actual amount of labor absorbed is $\Delta_1 + \Delta_2$, the innovation intensity effect, Δ_1, plus the labor-using bias effect, Δ_2. In general, we can use figure 7.5(a) to show the total magnitude of labor absorbed due to innovations, for a given capital stock, as a function of:

1   The "height" of point F relative to the pre-innovation point E_1, representing the intensity of the innovation, that is, how much the initial production contour has been "blown up."
2   The "height" of point G relative to point F, representing the degree of labor-using bias of the actual innovation.
3   The "steepness" or "flatness" of the II curve, representing the relative strength or weakness of the law of diminishing returns to labor. (The "flatter" the curve the further to the right is equilibrium point E_1'.)

Given this and equation 7.3, more labor will be absorbed if innovation intensity (J) is high, innovation bias is labor using (high B_L), and if the law of diminishing returns to labor is weak (low ϵ_{LL}). J/ϵ_{LL} is the innovation intensity effect that determines the magnitude of Δ_1, while B_L/ϵ_{LL} is the labor-using bias effect that determines Δ_2.

Let us now assume a change in the capital stock (ΔK) from K_1 to K_2 in figure 7.5(a). This means that the marginal product in the new, post-innovation family shifts from position II to IV in figure 7.5(b) leading to a demand for labor at E_2' and a new equilibrium input position at P_2' in figure 7.5(a). Notice that the same capital-labor ratio is maintained, as P_1' and P_2' lie on the same radial line as capital accumulation occurs. This is due to our CRTS assumption which implies a constant MP_L along any radial line as long as we have real wage constancy. Notice also that an additional $\Delta W_1''$ units of labor are now being absorbed by the industrial sector due to capital accumulation. Our diagrammatic representation of equation 7.3 shows the simultaneous impact of technology change, in both its intensity and bias dimensions, and that of capital accumulation.

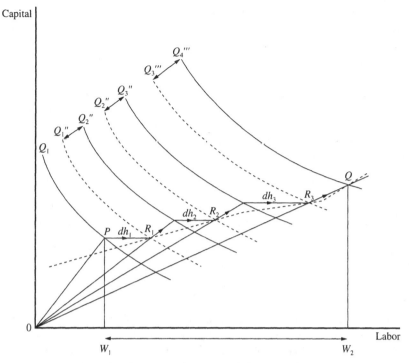

Figure 7.6 Decomposition of the growth path

Labor absorption due only to technological change is represented by a horizontal movement to the right (*dh*), while the labor absorption due only to capital accumulation is represented by a radial movement (*dR*). Considering the two concurrently – and they are, of course, likely to be behaviorally related – allows us to explore the effects of continuous innovation and capital accumulation activity on labor absorption over time.

Figure 7.6 illustrates what may happen to the capital/labor ratio over time as long as innovations are not very labor saving – in which case the horizontal movement would be to the left. The horizontal effects are represented by dh_i, while the radial effects are projected as R_i. The output (Q) contour map reflects changes in the production function due to technological change, for example from Q_1 to Q_1' as well as increased output along the same production function due to capital accumulation, for example from Q_1' to Q_2'.

As long as we maintain the simplifying assumption of a constant real wage, capital shallowing growth – a declining capital-labor ratio – will result as long as innovations are not very labor saving, that is while every radial movement R_i leaves the capital-labor ratio unaffected, each horizontal movement dh reduces it.

However, innovations that are very labor saving would result in capital deepening growth. For example, returning to figure 7.5(b), a very labor saving innovation would imply that the post-innovation MP_L curve (V) intersects the supply curve at a point E_1'' to the left of E_1; since the marginal product at the initial input point K_1W_1 is now below the pre-innovation level, less workers will be demanded. The result can also be seen by rewriting equation 7.3 as:

$$\eta_{K/W} = -(B_L+J)/\epsilon_{LL} \tag{7.4}$$

Given that ϵ_{LL} is always greater than zero, capital deepening will occur only if (B_L+J) is negative – our definition of a very labor-saving innovation.

If the constant real wage case does not quite hold, equation 7.3a becomes:

$$\eta_W = \eta_K + (B_L+J/\epsilon_{LL}) - (\eta_{w_{na}}/\epsilon_{LL}) \tag{7.5}$$

where, in the absence of an unlimited supply of labor ($\eta_{w_{na}} > 0$) the effect of increases in capital accumulation, innovation intensity, or labor-using bias on the rate of labor absorption is weakened if they simultaneously cause movements in the real wage – that is, we have both quantity and price adjustment.

This section has traced the effects of the underlying demand for labor as part of the balanced growth process in a closed labor surplus economy. The remaining sections of the chapter demonstrate what actually occurred in some real world economies historically, as well as to indicate the result when assumptions like the constancy of the real wage, or that of a closed economy, are relaxed.

7.4 Historical Analysis of the Labor Reallocation Process

Section 7.2 illustrated the importance of the labor reallocation process as an index of developmental success in the dualistic economy. Two possible archetypes of success or failure can be illustrated by comparing the relevant period of development experience in historical Japan (1880–1930) and that of post-independence India (1950–80). We chose these two periods and economies because they represent equivalent sub-phases of the development process in two situations which experienced very different outcomes. Japan will be shown to have consistently satisfied its critical minimum effort criterion, by marshalling a sufficient demand for labor reallocation in the dual economy context, while avoiding substantial increases in the industrial real wage.

Post-independence India also represents a dualistic economy, pursuing many of the same development objectives as Japan in the latter half of the twentieth century. However, India did not meet its critical minimum effort criterion in a balanced growth context. With the rate of labor reallocation serving as the index of success, India may, at least until very recently, be viewed as a stagnation or failure case which has not yet reached commercialization.

These general propositions can be illustrated empirically. The first step in an inductive analysis of the labor reallocation process is to decompose industrial labor absorption into a horizontal effect (labor absorption caused by innovation) and a radial effect (labor absorption due to capital accumulation). Using equation 7.3, since the rate of increase in industrial employment η_W and the rate of increase of the industrial capital stock η_K can be independently measured, the rate of labor absorption due to capital accumulation η_K is the radial effect (R) and the difference between η_W and η_K is the horizontal effect (h), a good proxy for the rate of labor absorption due to innovation activity:

$$\eta_R = \eta_K \qquad \text{(radial effect)} \qquad (7.6a)$$
$$\eta_h = \eta_W - \eta_R = (B_L + J)/\epsilon_{LL} \qquad \text{(horizontal effect)} \qquad (7.6b)$$

As we have seen, success requires η_W to be consistently larger than η_P. Given a population growth rate, success is clearly dependent on the rate of capital accumulation, the quality of technical progress, and the extent to which increases in unskilled real wages are contained as long as the labor surplus condition persists.

7.4.1 The case of Japan

Figure 7.7(a) shows that Japan consistently met its critical minimum effort criterion, with η_W exceeding η_P during its unlimited supply of labor phase in the late nineteenth and early twentieth centuries. Japan's escape from the Malthusian trap is more impressive since the agricultural labor force (η_L) not only decreased relatively, but declined absolutely after 1897.

Decomposing the total amount of labor absorbed (η_W) into its radial (η_R) and horizontal (η_h) components yields figure 7.7(b). Here we can clearly see that, early on, innovations (horizontal movements) played an important role relative to capital accumulation (radial movements) in the

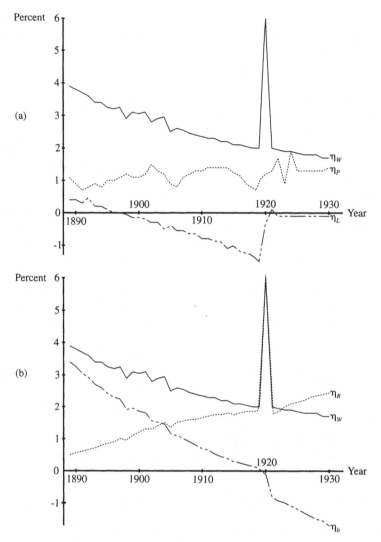

Figure 7.7 Japanese labor absorption – decomposition analysis

labor absorption process accounting for the lion's share (80 percent) of total labor force reallocation. Over time the relative contributions of these two factors reversed themselves. Clearly the Japanese case illustrates the case of successful balanced growth. It is interesting that even at the aggregate industrial sector level, we can observe capital shallowing taking place (see figure 7.8) up to about 1920; this means that in spite of shifts in the

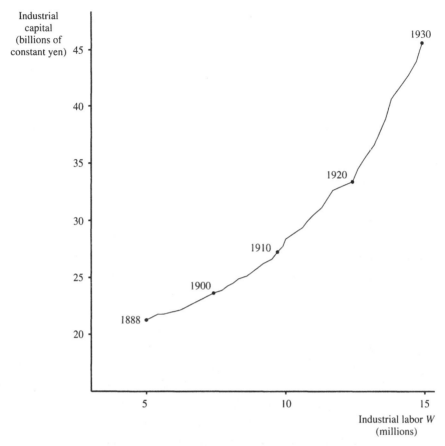

Figure 7.8 Japanese aggregate industrial capital-labor ratio growth path

output mix, which can be assumed to be in a more capital-intensive direction, innovations were sufficiently labor-using (or at least not very labor-saving) to yield declines in the overall capital-labor ratio.

If we are able to disaggregate, that is, concentrate on only one industry, such as cotton spinning, thus eliminating the output mix change problem (see figure 7.9), we can observe a similar trend. Japanese cotton spinning exhibited, initially, pronounced capital shallowing, with the advent of capital deepening only after 1915. Fortunately, we can also check this performance against available unskilled real wage data in the cotton spinning industry. This yields figure 7.10, indicating that a strict labor surplus condition seems to have obtained, at least up to 1895. Unskilled real wage data

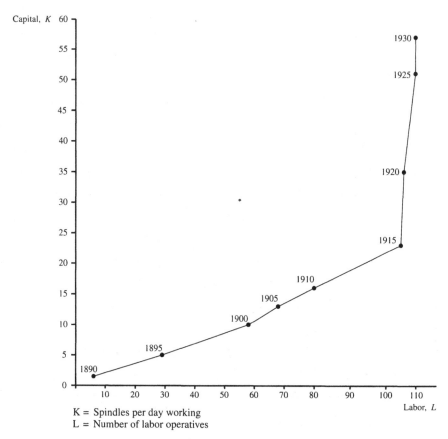

Figure 7.9 K/L *ratio in Japanese cotton spinning*

Source: Japan Cabinet Statistical Bureau. *The Japan Annual Statistical Report #10–40.* Tokyo.

for the industrial sector as a whole, presented in the appendix to chapter 3, lend additional support to our story.

7.4.2 The case of India

Applying the same approach to India during the 1950 to 1985 period illustrates a less favorable outcome. Figure 7.11(a) indicates that the critical minimum effort criterion is frequently not met. Except for one year in the 1950s and short periods in the early 1960s and late 1970s, population growth (η_P) substantially exceeded the rate of labor absorption by the industrial sector (η_W). The main cause of this failure – in addition to a higher population growth rate – is clearly demonstrated in figure 7.11(b),

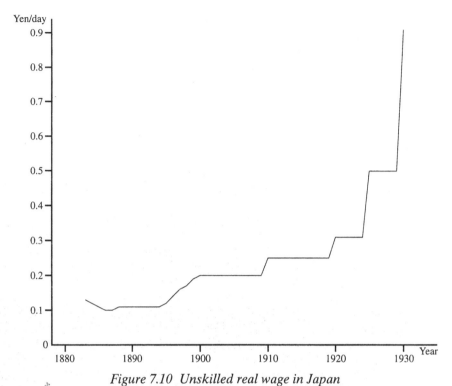

Figure 7.10 Unskilled real wage in Japan
Source: Otsuka, K., G. Ranis, and G. Saxonhouse. *Comparative Technology Choice in Development. London: Macmillan, 1988.*

that is, while the rate of growth of capital (radial movements) was respectable, and the unskilled industrial real wage was not permitted to rise (see figure 7.13), innovation activity was almost always very labor-saving (horizontal movements to the left), yielding a low η_W. It should not surprise us, therefore, that, almost from the outset, India experienced capital deepening in its industrial sector (see figure 7.12). This is in spite of the fact that the non-agricultural real wage during this period remained broadly constant (see figure 7.13).

   Disaggregating once again, and concentrating on the cotton spinning industry, yields similar results. Figure 7.14 presents the capital-labor ratio in this industry over time, and while capital deepening is less severe than in the aggregate case, the technology response to the labor surplus condition (see figure 7.15 for industry-specific unskilled real wage data) is again shown to be unsatisfactory. Instead, from 1950 onwards growth in this industry is basically capital deepening. Such capital deepening at both the aggregate and industry levels during a time of labor surplus, is the antithesis of the successful balanced growth archetype we have been analyzing.

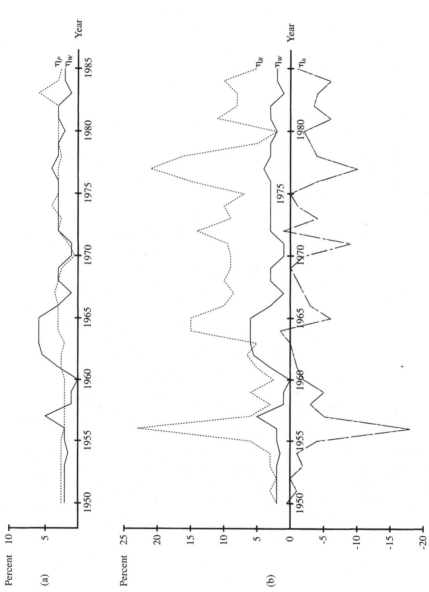

Figure 7.11 Indian labor absorption – decomposition analysis

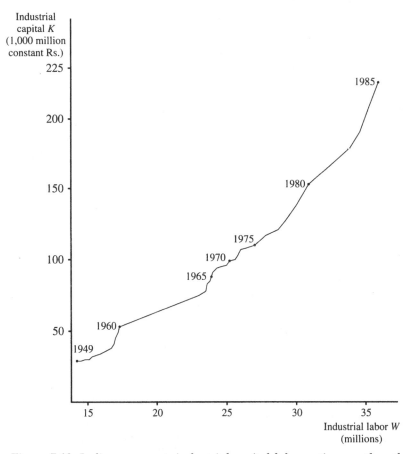

Figure 7.12 Indian aggregate industrial capital-labor ratio growth path

The contrast between these two country cases at both aggregate and industry levels is thus quite clear. Continuous capital shallowing growth in Japan between 1888 and the end of World War I provides strong evidence that Japan made maximum use of its abundant unskilled labor force by adopting labor-using innovations. The continuously positive rate of labor absorption due to innovations (η_h) and the initial capital shallowing growth followed by capital deepening only when the surplus labor condition had ended and real wages began to rise markedly corroborates this finding. India, on the other hand, resorted to very labor-saving innovations from the beginning of the development effort at both the aggregate and industry levels, yielding to the temptation of an increasingly

Figure 7.13 Unskilled real wage in India

Source: United Nations. *International Yearbook of Labor Statistics.* Geneva, various years.

capital-intensive industrial structure and neglecting the use of its abundant unskilled labor force while the surplus labor condition was still very much in evidence. Overall, these two cases illustrate the extremes of a successful versus an unsuccessful balanced growth process within a closed dual economy. Differences in the quantity and quality of technology change were clearly crucial to this outcome.

7.5 Employment/Output Trade-offs

Our analysis and policy conclusions have been based on the rate of labor reallocation to the industrial sector as **the** summary index of a "successful"

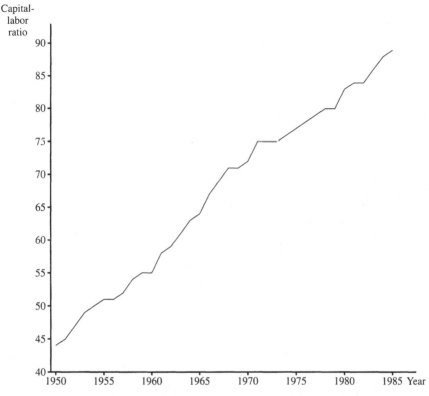

Figure 7.14 India cotton spinning K–L ratio

Sources: *Statistical Abstract of British India.* New Dehli, various years. Pearse, A. *The Indian Cotton Industry.* Manchester, England, 1929. De Costa, E. 'The Cotton Textile Industry,' in M. Ghandi, ed., *The Indian Cotton Textile Industry.* Calcutta: G. N. Mitra Publishing, 1930.

development effort. Most governments include a "maximum industrial employment growth" objective among their priority goals, but the overriding objective customarily is the achievement of maximum output growth. If there is a conflict between maximum employment and maximum output, real or imagined, it is customarily resolved in favor of the seemingly more urgent maximum output objective, with the absorption of surplus manpower often viewed as the "supplementary" strategy. In the context of a labor surplus economy it is, however, extremely unlikely that there exists a conflict between the reallocation of labor and industrial growth objectives.

To analyze this issue, let us recall, from the growth equations of chapter 4, that under the condition of an unlimited supply of labor, capital accumulation (η_K) and innovation activities (J, B_L) determine not only the rate of labor absorption and industrial employment, but also the rate of expansion of industrial output. The relevant growth equations for output and

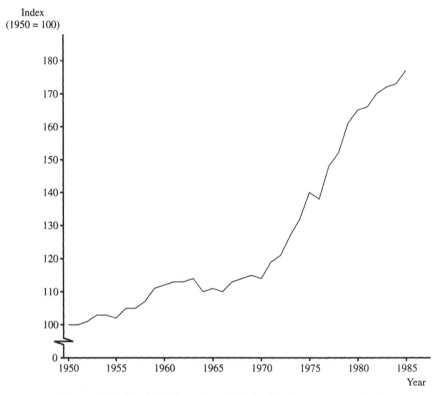

Figure 7.15 Unskilled real wage in India (cotton spinning)

Source: Mukerji, K. 'Trends in Real Wages in Cotton Textile Industry,' in *Artha Vijnana*, Vol. 1, No. 1 (1959).

industrial labor in table 4.1 of chapter 4 can be rewritten, given that $H_L=J + B_L$, as:

$$\eta_Q = \eta_K + J(1+\phi_L/\epsilon_{LL}) + B_L(\phi_L/\epsilon_{LL}) \qquad (7.7a)$$
$$\eta_W = \eta_K + J/\epsilon_{LL} + B_L/\epsilon_{LL} \qquad (7.7b)$$

Holding η_K constant, the two equations in 7.7 can be represented by two systems of parallel lines in the (J, B_L) space of figure 7.16. Equation 7.7a is represented by a dotted system of "equal rates of growth of industrial output" contour lines, while equation 7.7b is represented by a solid system of "equal rates of growth of industrial employment" contour lines. A country should clearly direct its resources and policies in the direction of securing values of J and B_L as far to the "northeast" as possible since higher values of J and B_L contribute to both greater employment and output.

Given a level of η_K at any point in time, it is, however, impossible to

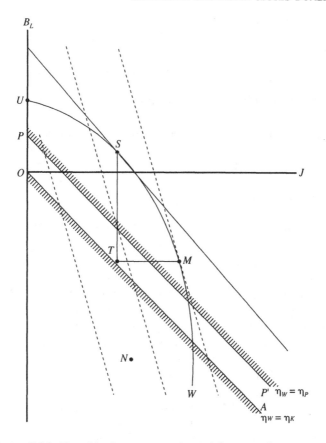

Figure 7.16 Graphical representation of the growth equations

increase both J and B_L without limit. Otherwise, all economic problems would be instantaneously solved. Indeed, a given year's investment fund and innovative energies may be directed either towards the use of the latest imported "modern" processes and products or their adaptation, plus the generation of domestically generated counterparts. The former are likely to be characterized by high innovation intensity (J) and only modest or negative labor using bias (B_L), the latter by a relatively low J and high B_L. Such a choice among a limited volume of innovation activity can be represented by the negatively sloped innovation frontier in figure 7.16, indicating that J and B_L are both limited in volume and substitutable. Such an innovation frontier is drawn for a given rate of capital accumulation; that is, a higher η_K would move the entire frontier outward. Given such an innovation frontier, the maximum employment criterion can be indicated at S (at tangency with one member of the solid system of equal employment growth contours of equation 7.7b) and the maximum output criterion at M (at tangency with one member of the dotted system of equal output growth contours of equation 7.7a). Since the slope of the dotted system ($=1+\epsilon_{LL}/\phi_L$ from equation 7.7a) is steeper than that of the solid system ($=1$ from equation 7.7b), S must lie above M on the innovation frontier. This indicates that in order to maximize output, the maximum employment criteria may have to be sacrificed along the frontier by choosing innovations with relatively higher intensity (J) and a lower labor-using bias (B_L). Thus, a conflict between growth of output and employment objectives would seem to exist. However, a particular developing society is not likely to be on the frontier nor even in the arc under the SM segment where such a conflict seems likely.

A comparison of the afore-mentioned performances of Japan and India in reference to figure 7.16 may help clarify the issue. The contour line OA in the solid system of equal employment growth contour represents the boundary ($B_L + J = 0$ or $J = -B_L$) between very labor-saving and not very labor-saving innovations. Another contour line in the same system PP' can be located when $\eta_W = \eta_P$, the exogenously given population growth rate. Since this solid line represents a rate of industrial labor absorption equal to the rate of population growth (the stagnation case), the entire region above it meets the criterion for successful development $\eta_W > \eta_P$. Unlike OA, whose position is fixed, PP' may lie above or below OA, depending on the relationship between η_K and η_P for any given country case. Assume that PP' lies above OA; then the (J, B_L) space can be partitioned into three regions with different economic interpretations. In the region above PP', equation 7.3, the criterion for successful development, is satisfied with the help of capital shallowing ($\eta_W > \eta_K$) growth. In the entire region below PP', equation 7.3 is not satisfied. This is because for most of the region – below OA – there is capital deepening ($\eta_K > \eta_W$). However, in some cases – the region between PP' and OA – equation 7.3 may not be satisfied even in the presence of capital shallowing. In this area population growth η_P is so high relative to capital accumulation η_K that capital shallowing, while helpful, is not strong enough to make it possible for the economy to meet its critical minimum effort criterion.

As our empirical analysis in the previous section indicates, pre-World War I Japan may be represented in almost any year by a point in the success area above PP'. It is, moreover, the case that PP' lies below OA historically. Assuming that Japan was already operating on or near its innovation frontier, we may locate it somewhere between the maximum employment criterion S and the maximum output criterion M. On the other hand, if we construct a similar diagram for India, our empirical results indicate that its performance is located somewhere below OA in figure 7.16, as equation 7.3 is not satisfied in the presence of capital deepening. India's position can be represented by a point such as N. Location substantially within the frontier could result from entrepreneurial and/or administrative incapacity to perceive or act on the fact that both J and B_L can be increased simultaneously without the need to sacrifice one for the other. In either case, India's performance is suboptimal since it could, with improved policies, obtain more of both the employment and output objectives by moving upward towards M. It is in this context that we conclude in this heuristic fashion that the maximum employment and maximum output objectives are not likely to be in conflict in the typical developing economy before commercialization has occurred.

The LDC that desires to escape its labor surplus trap should not disregard its labor-using innovation possibilities. The experience of Japan in the nineteenth century indicates that in the early stages of a country's development there are many opportunities to adopt such innovations requiring only modest amounts of capital, and thus incur minimal sacrifice in terms of innovation intensity. In Japan such innovations included the survival of modernizing Z-goods, the adoption of multiple shifts and other core process-related innovations, as well as the widespread substitution of surplus labor in all sorts of activities peripheral to the machine process.[1] Most innovations of this type represent unspectacular readjustments or rearrangements of the production process and require only entrepreneurial attention or official policy reorientation rather than large amounts of capital. What is involved is the adaptation of imported technology as well as the acceptance of an entirely indigenous production function. It is essential to resort to this reservoir of innovative ideas if the economy's abundant factor – surplus agricultural labor – is to be utilized effectively. Failure to do so, owing to the premature emphasis on modern industries, state of the art technology, capital-intensive production, and neglect of domestically generated innovation possibilities, may well condemn an economy to continued failure.

CHAPTER 7   TRANSITION GROWTH IN THE CLOSED DUALISTIC ECONOMY

NOTES

1   For more on this, see Ranis (1973). For a comparison of technology choice and technology change in India and Japan historically, also see Otsuka, Ranis and Saxonhouse (1988).

8
Transition Growth Under Open Dualism

8.1 Introduction

Chapter 7 illustrated successful balanced transition growth in a closed dualistic labor surplus economy. Based on the production functions derived in chapter 4, labor absorption and growth are driven by capital accumulation (η_K) and technological change (J and B_L), with the relevant commodity prices determined by the terms of trade between the agricultural and non-agricultural sectors. While this closed economy case represents a natural construct in which to initially consider the growth problem, as the typical LDC moves into an increasingly integrated "world" economy considering the international aspects of transition growth becomes a logical necessity.

Trade constitutes a powerful new production function available to the economy through which both traditional and non-traditional goods can be converted into imported capital goods and raw materials. The availability of this additional production function permits the developing country to harvest the conventional static and dynamic gains from trade. Even more to the point, LDCs operating well inside their production possibilities curve, as a consequence, following the "vent for surplus" approach convert previously under-utilized resources in the form of raw materials and/or unskilled labor into importability.

The openness of the economy also permits foreign capital, public and private, to support the balanced growth process. While such flows exist during the colonial period, they tend to be limited in terms of both purpose and impact. An important corollary advantage, of course, is the range of additional technological alternatives opened up both via embodiment in imported machinery and via the sheer impact of additional foreign contact. The most successful choice of technology is ultimately likely to result from suitable domestic modification and adaptation, but ideas carried by trade often represent the primary stimulant. Picking and choosing from the international technology shelf and innovating on that basis means that the less developed dualistic economy is in a position to get the most labor absorption with output growth, in terms of J and B_L, from a given rate of capital accumulation.

As we have seen, the successful transition of the open dualistic economy depends on the success of synchronized efforts to mobilize the agricultural sector in balanced interaction with domestic non-agriculture. Domestic balanced growth remains the centerpiece of success in the open economy, even in relatively small country cases. But the open economy can be of considerable help loosening the strait-jacket of resource constraints and inherited autarky, aiding the domestically-driven growth of the dualistic LDC.

To illustrate the potential benefits from an open economy in this context, consider the typical dualistic labor-surplus economy at an early stage of development, characterized by a scarcity of capital goods. If trade occurs, then this nation can export labor-intensive industrial goods and import the capital goods necessary to accelerate balanced growth and the transition to the status of an industrial economy. Factor mobility increases the availability of capital, and it also facilitates the absorption of labor by the industrial sector since foreign capital can increase domestic capital accumulation and advance technological change. Thus, all four components to the internationalization of a closed economy – trade, capital and labor mobility, and technology – facilitate successful balanced growth and development in a labor surplus economy.

The optimistic scenario illustrated above is not, however, meant to suggest that the international sector is either necessary or sufficient for successful transition growth to occur in a labor surplus LDC, especially given the existing – and often dismal – international evidence. While chapter 7 illustrated the emphasis on domestic success driving the process of balanced growth, there exist substantial risks to an international focus (for example Dutch Disease and the collapse of the import-substitution oriented economies). The importance of analyzing the international sector even with the necessity of success in the domestic market is important for two reasons. Considering the international aspect of growth and development more accurately describes the real world and leads to a better understanding of the complex interactions a developing country faces. More importantly, the central conflicts faced by LDCs are domestic in origin and effort, especially the reallocation of surplus agricultural labor to the industrial sector. The resolution of these conflicts, however, can be assisted – but not solved – by the international economy, a fact which renders the analysis of transition growth in an open economy of major importance.

The importance of integrating international trade and factor movements with our theory of growth is increased by the pre-eminence of international issues in the development strategy of most current LDCs. Given the multiplicity of policy options available in today's international environment – ranging from institutional aid, import substitution, export promotion, favorable trade status, etc. – any discussion of growth in an open economy immediately takes on a normative aspect with policy implications. This heterogeneity of international policy possibilities is further complicated by the lack of homogeneity among the LDCs themselves – especially variations in comparative advantage that change over time. However, even with these formidable difficulties in analyzing the open economy aspect of a theory of growth, we remain firm in our conviction that the domestic side of the economy presented in chapters 1–7 constitutes a valid approximation of the real world problems of the contemporary labor surplus LDC, and that the addition of an international production function is only a modification of our basic approach.

Section 8.2 of this chapter focuses on the importance of international trade, analyzing the benefits in both a static and dynamic context before exploring transition growth in the open labor surplus dualistic economy. After exploring this model fully, we contrast it with the alternative theories of export pessimism and agricultural neglect. We then emphasize domestic linkages and international trade, as well as explore new theories of trade. Section 8.3 concentrates on the increased factor mobility brought about by the open economy. This dimension of development has two components. First, increased capital inflow quantitatively enhances output growth and labor absorption. The success of this factor's use also depends on the qualitative dimension and time phasing within which it is applied. Second, international factor mobility brings labor issues to the forefront, where both migration of unskilled labor and movements in skilled labor must be addressed. Finally, section 8.4 emphasizes the importance of foreign technology to dualistic LDCs in an open economy, especially its adaptation to specific needs as well as its importation. The analysis in this chapter is based on the system of growth equations derived in chapters 4 and 5, where balanced growth in the open economy is the primary concern. While empirical support for specific points is included in this chapter, empiricism related to total performance of growth in an open economy is reserved for the policy discussion in chapter 10.

8.2 International Trade and Growth in the Labor-surplus Economy

8.2.1 Gains from Trade

That positive benefits from free trade accrue to an economy is an economic truism with roots in the writings of the classicists (see, for example,

Ricardo, 1897). In simplest form, gains from trade occur via greater consumption possibilities for a country with a given labor input. More formally, trade facilitates an increase in national income attained by an optimal allocation of resources on a worldwide basis – Pareto international efficiency. The size of the gains from trade depend on a nation's comparative advantage and terms of trade – both in terms of commodities and in terms of income, the latter adjusting the former for changes in export/import volume. Unfortunately, changes in the international terms of trade alone cannot explain observed changes in the gains from trade – we must determine the underlying forces affecting both the terms of trade and the export volume.

While this classical and neoclassical view of trade is essentially static, there also exist dynamic gains from trade that are of equal importance. While the static benefits from trade are basically demand-side phenomena, dynamic gains occur via supply-side effects. Specifically, free trade promotes increased productivity, or "X-efficiency," (Liebenstein, 1966) in a dynamic sense as international trade augments the production function to increase efficiency. Dynamic gains from trade can be summarized as a movement along the production function without changing the cost conditions. This, according to Haberler (1959, p. 14), is analogous to an outward and upward shift of the production function over time due to the dynamic gains from international trade, above and beyond the static gains.

8.2.2 The open dualistic economy and balanced growth

This section broadens the closed dualistic analysis used in chapters 1–7 to include the reallocation of surplus labor over time in the presence of international trade. The purpose of the analysis is to identify the structural changes which occur between the initial and terminal years in the open dualistic labor surplus economy. This structure can be described by the indices derived in our theoretical growth model of chapter 4, including production, consumption, labor allocation, savings, investment and international trade/factor movements – the latter the addition to our growth system addressed by this chapter.

While chapter 7 analyzed closed dualism, the system can be expanded to illustrate the open economy case. Once exports are allowed, a triangular relationship is established among the cash crop export sector, the foreign sector, and the food-producing domestic agricultural sector. Cash crops are sent abroad in exchange for producers' capital goods, intended to further the expansion of export activities, plus industrial consumer goods to induce agricultural workers to move out of food-producing agriculture and into export-oriented cash crop activities. The export-oriented cash crop agricultural subsector generates foreign exchange earnings used to import capital goods necessary for the construction of a new industrial sector producing the previously imported consumer goods for the domestic market. These exports, converted into industrial capital goods imports, also provide a second source of agricultural surplus – supplemented by the inflow of foreign savings – to help finance non-agricultural growth in a balanced growth context. This triangular relationship between two kinds of commercialized activities, one agricultural and one non-agricultural, and the food-producing agricultural hinterland replaces the colonial triangle of chapter 7.

As with the closed economy case, for an open economy balanced growth requires that the intersectoral commodity, labor, and financial markets must clear, though now international trade changes the dynamics of this process. Figure 8.1, while ignoring the flow of intermediate inputs, illustrates balanced growth in the open economy. The individual worker consumes two kinds of commodities – agricultural (A) and

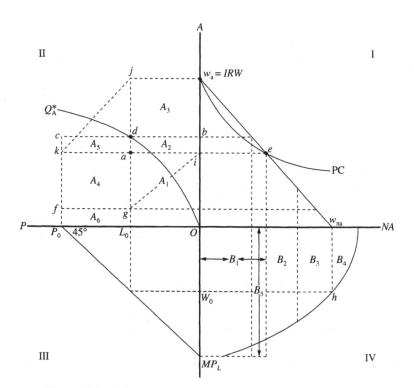

Figure 8.1 Balanced growth in an open dualistic economy

non-agricultural (NA) goods measured on the vertical and horizontal axis of quadrant I of figure 8.1. In this context with no intersectoral unskilled wage gap, Ow_a (Ow_{na}) is the real wage in terms of agricultural (non-agricultural) goods, with the slope of the budget line $w_a w_{na}$ the initial terms of trade between the agricultural and the industrial sectors. In the context of a labor surplus dualistic economy, the real wage in terms of agricultural goods Ow_a is an institutional real wage (IRW) determined by the institutional forces prevailing in the agricultural sector. Adding the identical preference map for agricultural and non-agricultural workers to quadrant I, we get the actual consumption mix between the two types of goods for the typical worker. Changing the terms of trade allows us to trace out the price–consumption (PC) curve denoting the set of possible equilibria in this market.

With a fixed land supply we can use figure 8.1 to represent the per capita agricultural supply for the economy as a whole via the Q_A^* curve in quadrant II, with varying labor input shown on the horizontal axis. Thus for a given technology each point on Q_A^* describes the food supply per capita for different levels of allocation of the total labor force. In this case with P_0 workers in the economy, OL_0 of them remain in agriculture, providing per capita food supply of Ob ($=L_0 d$). The intersection of the worker's budget line $w_a w_{na}$ with the price–consumption curve – point e in quadrant I – is the initial consumption equilibrium point. At point e the corresponding per capita food demand is Oi, which is less than the per capita supply Ob at this terms of trade. Given this, a substantial agricultural export surplus per head equal to ib (or ad) exists when the equilibrium point e occurs below the Q_A^* curve for the given agricultural labor force OL_0.

Two factors differentiate the industrial and agricultural sectors: (1) the primary factors of industrial production are – as our growth system in chapter 4 describes – labor (W) and capital (K); and (2) the industrial sector is commercialized – the real wage equals the marginal product of labor. To show the industrial sector equilibrium position with an initial agricultural labor force OL_0, we can project the labor force $P_0 L_0$ already allocated to industry to the downward vertical axis. Using the 45° line in quadrant III, $P_0 L_0$ workers in industry can be translated into OW_0 workers in quadrant IV. With the initial non-agricultural real wage Ow_{na}, this labor supply intersects the MP_L curve in quadrant IV at equilibrium point h. Here $P_0 L_0$ units of non-agricultural labor are demanded via the MP_L curve and equated to the labor supply determined by the fixed industrial real wage Ow_{na}. This yields labor market equilibrium as the workers supplied by agriculture equal those demanded by non-agriculture.

In this export case where the consumption equilibrium point e is below per person agricultural supply Ob there is a pattern of triangularism. The agricultural sector produces an exportable surplus (*ib* per person) which provides the import capacity used for two types of industrial imports – consumer goods and producer capital goods. The same agricultural exports generate income and demand for a larger volume of industrial consumer goods now produced at home. In this manner the agricultural sector can fuel import-substitution (IS) growth as producer capital goods imports permit the continued build-up of the domestic import substitution capacity that gradually replaces consumer goods imports.

In terms of commodity market equilibrium, we can examine the role of savings in this process. In figure 8.1 we have the initial equilibrium position in an open economy with an agricultural labor force OL_0. This agricultural labor force produces a per capita agricultural supply Ob, allowing total agricultural output to be represented by the area $OP_0cb=A_1+A_2+A_4+A_5+A_6$. With respect to the allocation of this output, we see that, since the real wage in terms of agricultural goods is Ow_a, agricultural labor's share is $Ow_aJL_0=A_1+A_2+A_3$. Staying with our assumption that wage earners do not save, then the consumption by farmers of food is A_1 (at the consumption standard for agricultural goods Oi determined by point e), while the income exchanged by farmers for industrial consumer goods is its remaining share, A_2+A_3. To see the magnitude of the landlord or rent share, draw the auxiliary straight line jk; then from point i let a straight line parallel to jk be constructed to the agricultural labor supply L_0, thus obtaining point g. The area A_4 ($=gfka$) then equals A_2+A_3 by construction. Since the wage share is $A_1+A_4=(A_1+A_2+A_3)$, the remaining total output or rent share is $A_2+A_5+A_6$. Under the assumption that all rental incomes are saved and there are no other leakages, this constitutes agricultural saving (S_a).

The total output of agriculture is thus allocated in the following way: A_1 is consumed by agricultural workers, A_2+A_5 is exported (ad or ib being exports per capita), and the remaining output A_4+A_6 is destined for consumption by workers in the industrial sector. The latter two types of shipments summarize the contribution that agriculture makes to non-agricultural development: first providing import capacity (A_2+A_5) and second providing food for industrial workers (A_4+A_6).

We can similarly consider the allocation of industrial output, where the equilibrium is established at point h where the MP_L curve intersects the real wage level in terms of industrial goods Ow_{na}. With a given industrial labor force (P_0L_0), the total industrial output is divided into the wage share ($B_1+B_2+B_3$) and the profit share (B_4), the latter constituting industrial saving (S_i). Out of the total wage share based on consumption equilibrium point e, B_1 is consumed by industrial workers, while B_2+B_3 is exchanged for agricultural goods for purposes of consumption. At the given terms of trade, the exchange value of B_2+B_3 is A_4+A_6. B_2 comprises industrial consumer goods exchanged for A_4 units of agricultural goods delivered by the farmers; B_3, on the other hand, represents investment goods exchanged for the landlord's agricultural saving A_6. Total agricultural export proceeds (A_2+A_5), which also accrue to the owners of the agricultural surplus, enable the system to import B_5 units of investment goods. Thus the total domestic investment fund is $B_3+B_4+B_5$ and is financed in the following way: $I = S_a+S_i$, where $S_a=(B_5+B_3)$ and $S_i=(B_4)$.

What we have just presented is the agricultural exporting case, which could easily be modified to capture the importing case. In the latter case the consumption equilibrium point e occurs above the per capita agricultural goods supply (Ob), necessitating food imports. In such a case the agricultural sector is not a dynamic element of the growth process, but is a hindrance to growth. Not only is importing food a disincentive to increases in agricultural productivity, but it slows the industrialization process by requiring industry to not only produce an exportable surplus to finance capital goods imports, but also to finance the import of foods. Finally, the analysis of productivity increases in agriculture, unbalanced growth, and reaching the commercialization point in this open economy can be done parallel to the closed economy analysis in chapter 7 using figure 8.1.

In terms of income distribution, labor's share in any sector s, as discussed in chapter 3, is $\phi_s = (L_sW_s)/Z_s$, where Z_s is the total output in that sector. Consequently, the rate of increase of ϕ_s is:

$$\eta_{\phi_s} = \eta_{W_s} - \eta_{Z_s/L_s} \tag{8.1}$$

where equation 8.1 is the difference in the rate of increase of the real wage and the rate of increase of labor productivity in that sector. Thus, in each sector – including the international one – the distribution of income moves against labor when increases in the real wage lag behind productivity increases – the behavior implied by our model in chapters 4 and 5 in a dualistic LDC during the unlimited supply of labor phase.

Examining the non-agricultural sector in the same comparative static setting, a dramatic increase in either the percentage of the population in industry or an increase in agricultural productivity leads to a large increase in the per capita output of industrial goods. Although there is increase in the domestic use of industrial output, the most conspicuous result is the increase in industrial exports. An increase in the external orientation of the industrial sector brings a corresponding change in the structure of foreign trade. First of all, in terms of the overall involvement in trade – measured by the export ratio – the export ratio rises substantially. Furthermore, the initial export dominance of the agricultural sector is completely reversed so that, as development proceeds, most exports become explicitly non-agricultural.

The previous framework illustrated the initial and terminal conditions of transition growth in the dualistic economy with an international perspective. However, it is inadequate in the sense that we do not have a comprehensive picture of the process of continuous development over time. We can, however, highlight this process in terms of turning-points by which the phases of transition growth measuring the behavior just discussed can be marked off. In what follows we explore the economic significance in the open dualistic LDC of four turning points: commercialization, reversal, export substitution, and switching.

Using the transition growth analysis of chapter 7, in a **closed** labor surplus dualistic economy the commercialization point indicates the end of the surplus labor condition. From this point on, the real wage in agriculture equals the marginal product of labor, which signifies that labor is now a scarce factor and the wage increases rapidly. This concept is also applicable to the open dualistic economy.

In the open economy case, the arrival of the commercialization point is found in combination with the "push" effects of technological change in agriculture and the "pull" of industrial labor demand, both augmented by access to the international economy. In figure 8.2 – an enhanced version of quadrant II in figure 8.1 – M_i represent the changing marginal product of labor curves in agriculture as technological change takes place. The dynamic process of labor reallocation is depicted by a sequence of points e, which show an absolute increase in agricultural population (e_1 to e_4) followed by an absolute decrease (from e_4 onward). Thus the open economy commercialization point at which the MP_L exceeds the IRW at W_a arrives earlier the faster the upward shift of the MP_L, the slower the rate of population growth, the slower the upward creep in the institutional real wage, and the faster the demand for labor increases in the industrial sector.

An increase in the real wage while the economy moves toward the commercialization point has a profound impact on income distribution, savings capacity, and the economy's consumption pattern. As income distribution shifts in favor of labor, any decline in the propensity to save is accompanied by sustained expansion of the domestic market for consumer goods. In other words, the open economy commercialization point is the end of the natural austerity typical of the unlimited supply of labor condition. After the commercialization point the savings rate and GDP growth rate level off. Furthermore, in an open dualistic labor surplus economy the commercialization point is also likely to change the structure of international trade. The external orientation of the industrial sector – previously based on entrepreneurs taking advantage of cheap labor – gives way to the incorporation of skills and capital goods as the basis for exports. Simultaneously the orientation of the industrial sector shifts to satisfy the growing domestic market for industrial consumer goods. The phases of

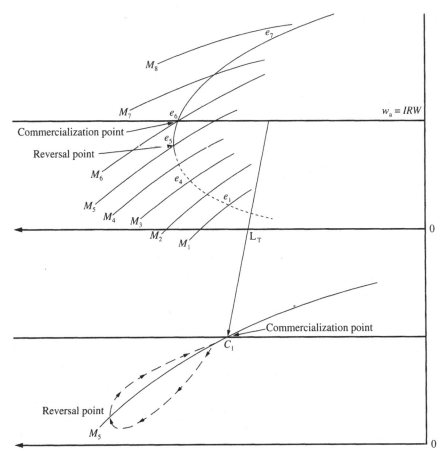

Figure 8.2 Technological change in agriculture and commercialization

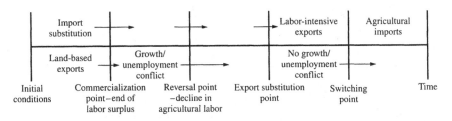

Figure 8.3 Phases of growth and resource flows

growth and resource flows for each of the turning points are illustrated in figure 8.3, with the specific flows leading up to the commercialization point depicted in figure 8.4.

The second turning point is the reversal point signifying an absolute decline in the agricultural labor force. The analysis of chapters 3 and 7, using equations 7.3a and 7.5, shows that when the growth of the industrial

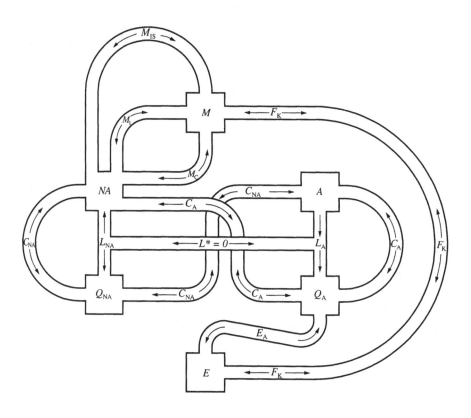

A	Agricultural sector	M	Imports
L_A	Agricultural labor force	M_C	Imported consumer goods
Q_A	Agricultural output	M_I	Industrial imports
C_A	Consumer goods for agricultural workers	M_{IS}	Import substitution goods
F_K	Foreign capital flows to balance imports	M_A	Agricultural imports
	and exports	NA	Non-agricultural sector
L^*	Movement of surplus labor from	L_{NA}	Non-agricultural labor force
	agriculture to non-agriculture	Q_{NA}	Non-agricultural output
E	Exports	C_{NA}	Consumer goods for non-agricultural workers
E_A	Agricultural exports	E_{NA}	Non-agricultural exports

Figure 8.4 The end of labor reallocation: commercialization point

labor force (η_W) is sustained long enough at a level above the growth rate of the total labor force (η_P), not only does $\theta = W/P$ increase continuously, but a reversal point is reached when the absolute increase of the agricultural labor force gives way to an absolute decline. In figure 8.2, the initial labor allocation point e_1 changes and the open economy movement of the labor allocation point through time is driven by productivity increases allowing labor to be reallocated to industry until the reversal point. This behavior can also be represented by the sequence of resource flows in figure 8.5 as the agricultural labor force declines absolutely while reallocating to the industrial sector.

When the supply of land is fixed, the arrival of the reversal point signifies that the law of diminishing returns is beginning to work in the reverse direction, as the marginal and average productivities of labor in both sectors increase even when technological change is stagnant. This implies that pressure exists to adopt labor-saving technology in agriculture since there

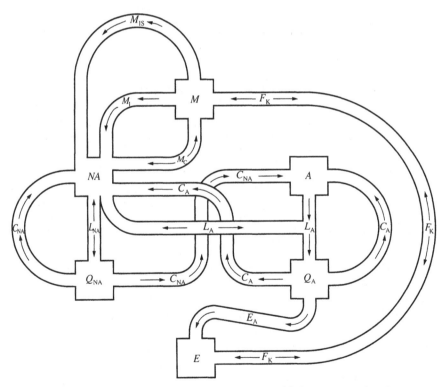

Figure 8.5 Absolute decline in agricultural labor: reversal point

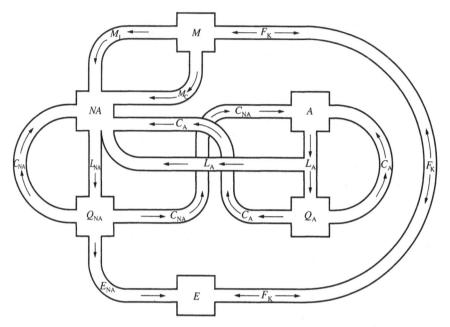

Figure 8.6 Non-agricultural instead of agricultural exports: export substitution point

is a "shortage" of manpower under the original technology.

The third turning point in an international context is the export substitution point, where resource flows are depicted in figure 8.6. During the long period of growth prior to transition growth, the economy is land-based and fueled by primary product exports. During the import substitution phase which characterizes the initial period of transition growth, the open economy relies on agricultural land-based exports to build up and sustain its import substitution industries. The import substitution strategy usually adopted by the government (high tariff protection for domestic import substituting industries, overvalued domestic currency in the world market by the official exchange rate, artificially low domestic interest rates, etc.) encourages the use of foreign exchange earned by traditional exports to develop and subsidize import substitution industries. Export substitution occurs when labor intensive manufacturing replaces traditional exports as the dominant export items of the economy.

When the domestic markets for industrial consumer goods are supplied almost exclusively by import substituting industries, the import substitution phase comes to an end. In the case of a small labor surplus economy, the natural development is the emergence of an export substitution phase – selling labor-intensive manufacturing exports in the world market. This transition is facilitated by changes in government policy to promote exports (for example realistic exchange rates) based on labor efficiency.

The emergence of the export substitution phase replacing the import substitution phase is a highly important phenomenon for the labor surplus economy analyzed here. While the import substitution phase was not conducive to full employment – leading to the "necessary" conflict between employment and growth – there is no such conflict when the export substitution phase arrives since labor is embodied in exports, which is conducive to both rapid growth and full employment. As this process advances, it leads to the "commercialization" and "switching" points, signifying the termination of the labor surplus condition in the economy as a whole, as well as in the agricultural sector in particular.

The final turning point in the transition of the open dualistic economy is the switching point. It is based on the notion that countries at some time become net importers of agricultural goods, as pictured in figure 8.7. In general, the phenomenon of land-based exports at the beginning of the transition to the modern industrial economy is a temporary phenomenon. A "switch" from an agricultural exporting to an agricultural importing economy is bound to occur at some stage of the successful development process. But when it occurs, and on the basis of what kind of agricultural

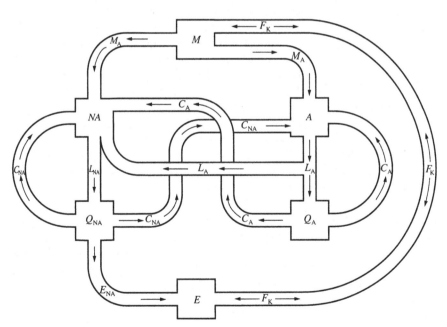

Figure 8.7 Imported agricultural instead of industrial goods: switching point

performance, remains an all-important issue. It matters greatly whether or not existing reserves of agricultural productivity have been harnessed *en route* to successful balanced transition growth in the LDC. The alternative is a failure of the total development effort – true for many contemporary LDCs – or an unacceptable reliance on foreign capital.

The array of government policy measures (for example, tariffs, exchange controls, etc.) adopted to facilitate the import substitution process via the exclusion of foreign competition and the augmentation of profits of the domestic industrialists are subject to change. Stabilization plus dismantling direct controls trade and exchange rates creates a more market-oriented economy conducive to the utilization of the economy's abundant resource – surplus labor – via embodiment in labor-intensive industrial exports. Concurrent to this, the open dualistic labor surplus economy is likely to move from the successful exploitation of its agricultural potential to a long-term position as an agricultural importer as the industrial sector becomes successful. The arrival of such a switching point signifies that the LDC ultimately accelerates its industrial exports to acquire needed food and raw materials. Finally, an absolute decline in the agricultural population shifts the policy focus towards labor-saving techniques in agriculture to prolong the labor-using phase in industry as the economy gets ready for the skill- and capital-intensive phase.

This section has focused on expanding our growth model to incorporate international trade as an additional input to the production function in an open dualistic LDC. The characteristics of the transition growth process in the presence of international trade are determined by the location of the initial consumption equilibrium point and are functions of technological change, capital accumulation, and population growth. In this framework open transition growth is successful given the postulated factor behaviors. However, there are other theories with alternative transition growth outcomes based on the inclusion of international trade in the production function. Two of these are agricultural neglect and export pessimism, and we briefly explore each of these ideas to complete our analysis of international trade in the open dualistic economy.

During the interwar period (1920–40) foreign trade originating in developing countries performed dismally. This dismal performance led many LDCs to adopt an "inward-oriented" development strategy, even though models such as the one presented in this chapter and almost all traditional "outward-oriented" trade theories illustrate substantial gains from trade as a strong complement to domestic activities. This early empirical performance by developing nations gave rise to export elasticity pessimism in these countries, in which both the earnings from trade and foreign demand for LDC exports were considered highly inelastic. This idea, coupled with perceived insufficient demand, placed a barrier on industrial development in developing nations due to a perceived lack of ability to generate foreign exchange, making development of industrial sector exports an unlikely contributor to growth over time.

The key characterization of export pessimism is that this perceived shortage of foreign exchange can be a major constraint on successful economic growth and development. One expression of this view is:

> The majority of underdeveloped countries are ... dependent for their earnings of foreign exchange on a single commodity. These earnings are highly inelastic. ... At the same time, nearly all the plant and machinery they require has to be imported, so that industrial development is limited by the foreign exchange available to pay for it. (Cairncross, 1960)

While this perspective occupied many early international trade models of growth, its inapplicability became clear in the post-war era as the failure of inward-oriented development (for example, import substitution) was quite pronounced by the late 1960s.

The idea of export elasticity pessimism is quite unrelated to our model of development, where the successful utilization of domestic surplus labor, not foreign exchange, is the constraint on industrial development. Our model corresponds more closely to the real-world case by not assuming a highly inelastic foreign demand for exports – in either the agricultural or the industrial sector. Instead, our model of successful transition growth passed through a series of phases, each illustrated in figure 8.3. All phases feature varying export and import compositions. The composition varies over time as the economy's resource needs and availabilities evolve, and as long as the foreign exchange criteria can be met. For example, for successful transition growth to occur the foreign exchange from primary product exports must be sufficient to allow the importation of industrial capital goods. In our model the "phases" do not occur out of order – specific export and import compositions during each phase depend on the foreign exchange generated in the last phase. This is not to imply that foreign exchange shortages do not occur. It does imply, however, that their occurrence is due not to export elasticity pessimism, but to deviations from the proper transition growth phases (for example, trying to move too quickly to an export substitution phase with unallocated surplus labor in the agricultural sector). This point is the major difference between our model's implications and the results from the theory of export elasticity pessimism.

Another alternative theory of growth and development in an open economy is based on the concept of agricultural neglect.[1] Our model emphasizes capital accumulation, technological change, and labor reallocation. This combination leads to successful balanced growth and development in both the non-agricultural and the agricultural sectors in dualistic LDCs with surplus agricultural labor, where successful development is characterized by balanced growth in output, consumption per capita, and increases in the standard of living in both the agricultural and non-agricultural sectors. The theory of agricultural neglect, however, rejects this conclusion. Instead, it argues that most poor people in LDCs located in the agricultural sector will be kept poor even with overall growth by the emphasis on industrial/urban activities and the neglect of the agricultural sector.

Agricultural neglect is built on two forms of bias in favor of the urban sector – efficiency and equity. Efficiency bias in favor of non-agriculture – based on the maximization of output – is supposedly demonstrated if output would rise over time if resources were shifted **to** the agricultural sector. This concept is in direct conflict with our model, since in dualistic LDCs the prevalent resource is surplus labor initially located in the agricultural sector, and any allocation of such resources should be from agriculture **to** industry where productivity is undoubtedly higher. In our analysis this reallocation of labor from agriculture to industry increases the long-run output of the economy (and is the driving force behind balanced growth). In terms of efficiency, our model is diametrically opposed to the concept of agricultural neglect.

The other measure of agricultural neglect is by equity – demonstrated if "rural workers are being enriched more slowly than urban workers" (Lipton, 1976, p. 56). This is a very normative measure of neglect, one which does not occur in our model when balanced growth exists since both sectors experience rising wages until the commercialization point is reached and the agricultural/industrial distinction no longer applies.

In an open economy, the conclusions from the theory of agricultural neglect become even more extreme. In this context international trade enriches the urban center at the expense/exploitation of rural agriculture, contributing to increased agricultural neglect. In contrast, trade is a positive complement to balanced growth in our model. In general it is methodologically difficult to compare our model with the theory of agricultural neglect because we are really addressing development issues from a different premise. We recognize the dualistic nature of most LDCs, but view the agricultural/industrial distinction as a strength, as the interaction and subsequent labor reallocation between the two sectors drives balanced growth which benefits both sectors of the economy. The theory of agricultural neglect, however, interprets the two sectors of the economy as necessarily in conflict for a limited amount of resources. In this scenario the two sectors do not positively interact – industry is favored at the expense of the agricultural sector, hurting the agricultural sector in both equity and efficiency measures.

This section has presented our model of balanced growth under open dualism, explored many of its intricacies, and compared it to two alternative development concepts. The important point to emphasize is that we view international trade not as the source of growth, but as a complement to the domestic linkages which are the primary source of balanced growth, an idea we turn to again in the next section.

8.2.3 Domestic linkages in the open economy

While international trade is an important component of growth and development in the open dualistic labor surplus economy – allowing an additional production function with easier access to capital goods, the availability of new technology, and a new source of private capital and savings – in our model it is the domestic arena in which the necessary conditions for successful transition growth must be met. Growth cannot be driven by international trade alone if domestic linkages are neglected. Instead, international trade facilitates growth in dualistic LDCs in conjunction with successful domestic policies. To illustrate the importance of domestic linkages, we return to the Z-goods model presented in chapter 2 and expand it to include international trade in an open economy. This section also illustrates that there is a substantial policy component attached to international trade which cannot be divorced from the success or failure of a growth and development effort.

Section 2.3 of chapter 2 illustrated the growth dynamics of a colonial economy with pre-existing Z-goods activity. While Hymer and Resnick (1969) explained the decline of rural non-agricultural activities (RNA) in the colonial era and Resnick (1970) provided empirical collaboration, they did not extend their model to the post-colonial era. This extension is critical since international rural development experiences in the post-colonial period are by no means homogenous, with some countries experiencing rapid rural industrialization and others having only a modest amount of RNA activity in evidence.[2]

This section illustrates the importance of not neglecting domestic linkages in the face of international trade by expanding the Z-goods model to encompass the post-colonial era in an open dualism context, while simultaneously analyzing the major determinants of dynamism in rural development. The extent of such dynamism is crucial for determining the success of the development process as a whole, where success is defined in terms of equity across families and regions as well as economic growth. Since the basic Z-goods model has been formulated in chapter 2, we do not repeat that analysis here. Instead, we extend the model to accommodate necessary changes in its assumptions. We use the model to analyze the post-colonial era, addressing both the favorable and unfavorable development scenarios. In our policy chapter – chapter 10 – we present empirical evidence from Taiwan and the Philippines corresponding to the favorable and unfavorable archetypes discussed here.

Assumptions The Hymer–Resnick (H–R) model for the colonial era is based on assumptions not applicable with respect both to likely movements in the international terms of trade and to the inferior character of Z-goods once international trade opportunities arise in the post-colonial era. To analyze growth dynamism and RNA with an international perspective, we make three departures from the basic model.

First, a major development of the post-colonial era is the emergence of a modern industrial sector in urban areas. This sector (the U-sector) is devoted to replacing imports during the import-substitution phase. In the presence of a U-sector, H–R displacement of Z-goods by imports is no longer a dominant feature of an economy's development. Instead, goods from the U-sector replace Z-goods domestically without the help of external economies. This displacement, labeled U-displacement, forces the assumption that labor is the only factor of production in non-agriculture to be dropped as the U-sector can import capital goods in exchange for cash crop exports (A_E).

Second, LDC agriculture (A) is not the homogenous sector assumed by H–R. Instead, it is composed of two sub-sectors – a cash crop export sector (A_E) and a domestic food producing sector (A_D). In the post-colonial era domestic agriculture has the potential for dynamic growth since it is subject to productivity-raising technological change. This domestic feature of the A sector – ignored by the H–R model – has two important consequences. First, this sector releases land and labor for use in the production of both Z-goods and cash crop agriculture (A_E) as fewer resources are required to feed the total population, permitting an outward shift of the production possibilities frontier. Second, a dynamic A sector strengthens the linkages between domestic agriculture and rural non-agriculture compared to those from export agriculture. These stronger linkages run both from A to RNA and from RNA back to A, including improved consumption and production linkages, rising internal terms of trade, and additional technological knowledge.

Finally, H–R assume improving external terms of trade for the A_E sector. In the post-colonial era this does not correspond to the facts: most LDCs' terms of trade have remained constant or deteriorated over time.[3] In fact, if deteriorating international terms of trade occur in the H–R model, Z-goods production tends to increase. We assume constant terms of trade in the following analysis, which explores the implications for rural development and the economy extending the Z-goods model to the post-colonial era with the aforementioned departures from the basic assumptions. Since the achievement of rural balanced growth is by no means a certain occurrence, we contrast the unfavorable and favorable archetypes of the Z-goods model.

The Unfavorable Post-Colonial Archetype The major development of the post-colonial era is the emergence of a U-sector as developing nations engage in import substitution. In the unfavorable case urban industry is encouraged at the expense of both Z-goods production and domestic agricultural activities by government policies that affect the internal terms of trade, the exchange rate, the interest rate, and the allocation of foreign exchange while neglecting domestic linkages. In this case, the U-sector is composed of large-scale domestic enterprises and MNCs financed by foreign institutions interested in promoting the urban-oriented import substitution process. Within agriculture, export crops whose earnings fuel the import substitution process are favored relative to food crops. Land and income remain unequally distributed, especially in A_E activities, with increases in purchasing power directed towards U-goods. Consequently, domestic and rural linkages are weak as a result of the neglect of the food producing agricultural sector and the U-displacement process – the displacement of Z-goods by the newly developing urban consumer goods industries. While some Z-goods production continues – due to the persistence of rural poverty and the natural protection afforded by shipping costs – the potential development of the Z-sector is severely limited.

Figure 8.8 illustrates the unfavorable post-colonial case. The horizontal axis to the right of the origin indicates a combination of U-goods and imported consumer goods (M_C), where the proportion of imports in the supply of total consumer goods declines as import substitution proceeds. Productivity in the A_E sector is represented by the $A_{E0}Z^0$ curve in quadrant II. Earnings from agricultural exports are spent increasingly on capital good imports (M_K) and less on imports of consumer goods (both shown on the vertical axis below the origin). The capital goods are used to produce domestic urban factors – consumer or U-goods shown on the horizontal axis of quadrant I. The slope of the $M_{K0}U^0$ line in quadrant IV is likely to be less than 45 degrees depending on the capital-output ratio. The consumption possibilities curve in quadrant I represents possible combinations of Z-goods and U-goods. As illustrated in the diagram, once imported consumer goods have been fully replaced by capital goods imports, the proceeds from agricultural exports are translated into large amounts of capital goods imports and then through domestic production into larger volumes of U-goods.

In the unfavorable case, even when the productivity and output of A_E in figure 8.8 increases from A_{E0} to $A_{E'}$, the productivity of the Z-sector is unchanged and the production possibilities curve shifts outward to $Z^0A_{E'}$. The consumption possibilities curve then shifts correspondingly to Z^0U'

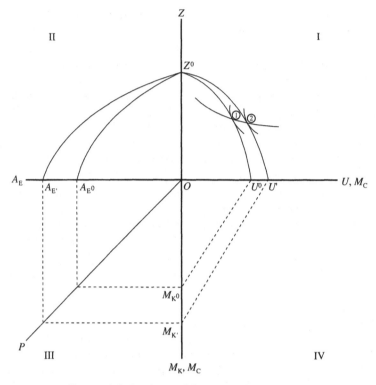

Figure 8.8 Unfavorable post-colonial case

from Z^0U^0. The substitution effect reduces the consumption of Z-goods and increases the consumption of U-goods. Since the Z-sector is overwhelmingly focused on traditional goods, the income effect is also negative since Z-goods are inferior, which also reduces Z-goods consumption. Consequently, the equilibrium position moves from (1) to (2), with reduced production and consumption of Z-goods and worsening welfare for the economy even with international trade.

The Favorable Post-Colonial Archetype   In more favorable post-colonial circumstances, the Z-goods sector represents a dynamic element of interaction with a growing food producing agricultural sector as domestic linkages are encouraged. This results from a more favorable environment in a number of dimensions. First, in this case the government does not discriminate against domestic agriculture relative to traditional primary export activities. Consequently, productivity expands in the A_D sector as land and labor resources are released, allowing additional production in other sectors of the economy. Second, income generated within A_D is more equally distributed than within A_E, especially when land-saving or labor-saving technologies are adopted. Given this, the A_D sector's expansion generates demand for the output of RNAs. Third, government domestic policy with respect to the allocation of infrastructure and the macroeconomic environment is more evenhanded between rural and urban industry as well as between agriculture and industry.

This positive environment allows the rural industrial sector more favorable conditions from the perspective both of demand via linkages with agriculture and of supply via the dynamics of investment and the adoption of new technology. The resulting modernization transforms Z from a sector composed of small, low productivity household and village enterprises producing traditional goods to one increasingly represented by modern activities – small factories using modern (often imported and adapted) technologies and producing products of a more uniform (and often higher) quality than the traditional Z-goods. These goods sell at favorable prices relative to the output of the U-sector and imports. The modernized Z-sector eventually exports, either directly or through subcontracting relations with the U-sector. Modern goods displace traditional ones, and the Z-goods sector retains substantial importance until the labor surplus condition has been eliminated.

U-displacement is less evident in this case since the U-sector is forced to compete with, or induced to establish complementary relations with, the Z-goods sector. At some point the U-sector begins to supply domestically manufactured capital goods, while the Z-sector supplies the U-sector with partly processed agricultural goods and/or serves as a subcontractor for the production of U-goods. Far from exhibiting H–R stagnation, with strong domestic linkages the Z-sector becomes a dynamic element in industrial development with a high rate of capital accumulation, technological change, and employment expansion. This stimulates agricultural growth through RNA to A linkages. This pattern of development is associated with a high overall rate of growth, an egalitarian income distribution, and better regional balance – all in contrast to the unfavorable archetype.

Figure 8.9 represents the favorable post-colonial case. Productivity increases in the A_D sector release land and labor that is used to enhance the production of both A_E and Z goods as the production possibilities curve shifts out in quadrant II. Moreover, the increase in productivity enhances the potential production of Z-goods. The outward shift of A_E is, however, smaller than in the unfavorable case since less attention is paid to that sector and more to domestic agriculture A_D. In this case the income as well as the substitution effects on Z-goods consumption are positive because of the modern characteristic of Z-goods, leading to a new equilibrium at (2) in quadrant I. Both Z-goods production and consumption

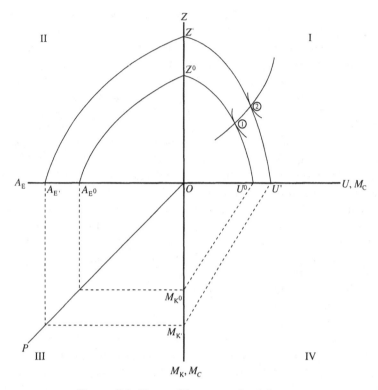

Figure 8.9 Favorable post-colonial case

expand, supported by strong domestic linkages with agriculture and expanding complementary relations with the U-sector over time, all of which combine in the open economy to increase the economic welfare of the LDC as successful balanced growth and development occur.

8.2.4 New trade theory

The previous sections illustrated the importance of international trade in our model of transition growth in a dualistic labor surplus economy. This importance stems both from the additional inputs which trade brings to the neoclassical production function via the facilitation of capital and technological imports and from the complementarity of international trade with favorable policies emphasizing domestic linkages as illustrated in the Z-goods model. Throughout this analysis trade is viewed explicitly as a complementary factor in the growth process – one which only facilitates domestically driven growth by the utilization of surplus labor, and does not drive growth alone. However, recent theoretical work in international trade, based on the tenets of industrial organization theory and the new growth theory discussed in chapter 1, emphasizes trade as a source of growth independent of domestic linkages. While we do not embrace this approach or agree with its conclusions, we mention it here to provide a more holistic perspective on trade and growth.

The new trade theory is based on the work of Krugman (1979, 1980) in which the LDC industrial production processes are explicitly assumed to be increasing returns to scale (IRTS) and to operate in a monopolistically competitive environment. The new models of international trade were formulated to explain some departures from traditional trade theory – the existence of intra-industry trade, economies of scale in production, and the intense concentration of industry in many developing countries. The models use monopolistic competition with IRTS in production to explain these facts quite easily. Also, in contrast to traditional trade theory, the new models allow gainful exchange to occur even between two identical countries. The resulting monopolistic competitive equilibrium generates a role for active strategic trade, compared with the "passive" trade embraced by traditional theories and our model.

This model differs from ours not only in its assumptions and results, but also in its policy implications. With IRTS in the LDC production processes, the new trade models imply that an active import-substitution strategy is not only feasible, but can be the key to successful LDC growth. In such models, as an LDC imports industrial goods and expands its production process, production becomes more efficient due to the IRTS economies, allowing it to capture a larger share of the market. In this model, when the import-substitution process supplies the domestic markets, import-substitution does not "falter" and give way to an export-substitution phase as in our growth model, but remains a dynamic element of the economy's production function, keeping IRTS production of certain goods at a comparative advantage with respect to developed countries. This provides a mechanism by which LDCs can have an active import substitution policy and use exports to DCs as the driving force yielding positive and increasing growth rates.

We reject this analysis for reasons both methodological and empirical. First, we rely on a CRTS production function and consider the existence of IRTS as technological change composed of changes in the intensity of innovation and factor bias – without which the growth equations we believe to be useful and realistic cannot be applied. Second, our analysis focuses on dynamic transition growth for a dual sector LDC, while the new trade theory is concerned with the analysis of steady state trade results for a homogeneous static economy. Third, while we have presented some simple active policy implications from the Krugman model, in reality the policy implications from the model are far from obvious. The case for strategic intervention is very sensitive to the model's assumptions and specification. Also, the arguments for trade intervention from this theory (for example, the import-substitution argument presented above) cannot be taken as analytic support for particular interventions used by LDCs in a different context.

8.3 Factor Mobility

While trade is the most prominent and visible international aspect of the open LDC economy, in a sense successful trade augmenting growth and development is an indicator of balanced growth in the underlying labor and capital markets. The model of growth with international trade presented in section 8.2 was based on, and constrained by, the underlying availability of capital and labor. The open economy allows access to capital and labor markets which facilitates economic growth by providing an additional source of supply of each resource, leading to a more rapid growth path. In this section we first look at the quantitative effect of the increased availability of foreign capital, and then explore the qualitative dimension of foreign capital availability. Finally, we explore international movements of labor, emphasizing time phasing, skilled labor, and migration pressure.

The potentially large benefits of openness for a dualistic economy with surplus labor are easy to see within our growth model. On the broadest level, successful balanced growth over time is driven by, on one side, surplus labor and/or agricultural productivity increases releasing labor to the industrial sector, and by, on the other side, the expansion of the capital stock in the industrial sector providing employment for the released labor. The failure of either side renders successful industrialization impossible. However, access to foreign capital and capital goods ensures that capital accumulation on the industrial side will be unconstrained, such that not only can balanced growth occur, but it can occur at a faster rate than in the closed economy case, especially during the surplus labor phase when the capital capacity of the industrial sector to provide employment for the underemployed labor in agriculture is the limiting condition for growth. In this framework, allowing international factor mobility in the open dualistic economy provides an additional production function enabling the economy to obtain capital goods more efficiently, especially capital goods that usually require a long gestation period if produced domestically.

Moving deeper into the growth process, we can illustrate the positive quantitative effect of foreign capital mobility on both output growth and labor absorption using our growth equations from chapters 4 and 5. We have defined the condition for successful economic development in a labor surplus LDC as:

$$\eta_p < \eta_W = \eta_K + (J+B_L)/\epsilon_{LL} \tag{8.2}$$

from equation 5.31a of chapter 5. This equation illustrates that the labor absorption process is driven by four causal factors – the rate of industrial capital accumulation, the intensity of innovation, the labor-using bias of innovation, and the law of diminishing returns to labor. Once foreign capital is available to the LDC industrial sector, the rate of industrial capital accumulation is positively augmented, leading to a more rapid rate of labor absorption and a faster successful growth and development process.

While the last paragraph utilized the labor absorption growth equation, we can use the output expansion growth equation from table 4.1 of chapter 4 to further this analysis:

$$\eta_Q = \eta_K + J(1+\phi_L/\epsilon_{LL}) + B_L(\phi_L/\epsilon_{LL}) \tag{8.3}$$

This equation immediately illustrates how foreign capital can quantitatively enhance output growth. The availability of foreign capital increases industrial capital accumulation, which directly augments and enhances output growth – the main indicator of development success.

While the importance of foreign capital to enhance both output growth and labor absorption is readily apparent, the availability of foreign capital has other, more qualitative, effects on development in a dualistic labor surplus economy. For example, chapter 7 illustrated that a dualistic economy attempting to move forward with an unlimited supply of labor is faced with a conflict. On the one hand, natural austerity forces the expansion of the industrial sector toward the production of investment goods. On the other hand, the production of investment goods must be as labor-using as possible to utilize the economy's abundant resource – redundant labor. The conflict arises because the basic capital goods industries are capital-using rather than labor-using, even though the prescription for successful development is to transfer as much labor as possible from the agricultural sector to the industrial sector where labor-using technology exists. However, once it is possible for the dualistic economy to access foreign capital goods, domestically produced industrial goods that are labor-intensive can be exported in exchange for foreign capital goods with less labor absorptive capacity. In this fashion the open economy permits the domestic production of any good that can take advantage of the economy's surplus labor endowment which can be exchanged for the needed capital goods from abroad. Thus, under open dualism the advantages of natural austerity in terms of an increased savings capacity in the economy are preserved while the maximum amount of redundant labor can be used in domestic production processes with the necessary capital imported from abroad.

There is also an important qualitative aspect of international capital mobility for dualistic developing countries to consider if the full effect of factor mobility in an open economy is to be measured. The qualitative side of capital inflows – in terms of the way the foreign capital is utilized – can either sink a country's development effort or alleviate some of the usual tensions a developing country can experience on the balanced growth path. The possible adverse effect of foreign capital – in a qualitative sense – on growth and development in an open labor surplus dualistic economy has already been analyzed empirically within the closed economy framework for India in chapter 7.

Post-war India followed a development strategy relying heavily on natural austerity driving the rate of capital accumulation, where the growth rate of capital (η_K) is equal to the product of the national savings rate (austerity) and the level of capital productivity. The Indian development strategy was to use extremely capital-intensive investment goods in production – many of them imported from abroad – and to neglect the economy's abundant resource – surplus labor. This qualitative misuse of a higher capital stock, some of which was available due to foreign capital mobility, kept India from experiencing successful transition growth. Labor actually moved from industry to agriculture as the empirical analysis of chapter 7 illustrated, and the industrial sector became even more labor-saving over time – the exact opposite of the prescription for successful development from our model. While the increased level of capital in India would have a positive impact on its growth and development in a quantitative sense if correctly utilized, the qualitative abuse of the foreign capital in terms of the type of industrial processes chosen created a road block on India's path to balanced growth.

While the evidence from India illustrates the qualitative abuses of foreign capital that can occur in an open labor surplus dualistic economy, the opening of an economy to international capital mobility can have a positive growth effect through qualitative factors. The positive growth effect occurs if capital inflows are appropriately utilized through an enhancing effect on domestic variables. While this topic could be the basis for a book of its own, here we only analyze one application of the positive qualitative dimension to capital inflows – the one that is due to a discovery of large amounts of natural resources.

One of the best illustrations of a positive qualitative effect from capital inflows in an open labor surplus dualistic economy is consistent with a successful development response to the discovery of a large amount of a tradeable natural resource. This latter phenomenon, commonly known as "Dutch disease," has two specific effects in developing countries. First, in a domestic sense the increased income from natural resource exports generates an income effect that increases consumption and shifts the orientation of the economy away from the manufacturing sector. This "crowding out" of manufacturing occurs as the comparative advantage of the economy shifts dramatically towards the natural resource sector. Second, in an international sense, the discovery of a tradable resource causes a real appreciation of the exchange rate, which also crowds out the domestic manufacturing sector and contributes to the shift in the economy's focus away from industry. These two effects generate the dilemma that once the natural resource is exhausted, the economy is left with an undeveloped industrial base incapable of sustaining balanced growth over time.

However, an economy with access to foreign capital flows can avoid the problems generated by Dutch disease. In the closed economy case with Dutch disease there is a strong link between high natural resource revenues and total expenditures leading to the crowding out of the industrial sector, while with an open economy this link can be broken using foreign capital. If the increased revenues from exports of the tradable natural resource are used to accumulate foreign assets (in the form of capital goods to be used in the industrial sector, for example), the current account can effectively smooth expenditures and subsidize the industrial sector over time. If this occurs, once the natural resource is exhausted the economy is not in dire straits. Both income from foreign capital assets and output produced by the imported foreign capital goods in a vibrant industrial sector can sustain the economy along a path of balanced growth, especially if the industrial sector chooses labor-using technology to absorb the surplus labor from the non-agricultural sector. Thus, an intelligent use of capital inflows can positively impact domestic variables and have a strong qualitative effect on successful balanced growth over time as the use of foreign capital mobility to alleviate the pressures of Dutch disease has illustrated.

While the expansion of our model to allow for capital movements from abroad represents a significant step forward from the closed economy framework, up to this point we have explicitly ignored the possibility of movement in the other factor in the production function 4.6 of chapter 4 – that is, labor. In fact, since we consider the domestically driven closed economy case an accurate first approximation of the true development process, considering international labor mobility is a few steps away from our basic model, with both international trade and capital mobility occupying a higher causal order of importance. However, in the real world, migration cannot be dismissed and in fact has been quite important for some nations in the post-war era, as movements of labor from Asia to the USA illustrate. In theoretical fact, one of the basic tenets of economic theory is an underlying tendency towards international factor price equalization. While most of this equalization occurs through international trade of goods which incorporate both capital and labor inputs, some of it is accomplished directly by the movement of capital from rich to poor nations, the latter having a higher marginal productivity of capital. The final component of this price equalization is the migration of labor from poor to rich countries.[4]

Labor movement ranks last in importance because it has substantial restrictions when compared to the relatively free flow of both goods and capital. These restrictions usually occur from both sides – on the one hand there are limits to the number of immigrants a rich nation will allow and on the other hand there are psychological (desire) and physical (ability) restrictions faced by individuals in developing countries as barriers to migration.

Given the place of international migration within our model, we do not explore every aspect of the international labor reallocation process. Instead, we focus on the effective demand for migration and its determinants from the developing world (labor-abundant) to the modern industrial nation (capital-abundant), keeping in mind the discouragement factor and the pressure for illegal migration when effective demand for migration exceeds legally permitted levels.

The effective demand for migration can be decomposed into individuals' desire to migrate and their ability to migrate. The desire to migrate from one nation to another is a function of three factors. First, the absolute size of the current differences in "average" income, public amenities, and the status level between the two countries.[5] Second, the extent of individual agents' information, specifically the knowledge or lack of knowledge about these differences. Third, the individual agents' probability assessments of the chance of achieving a given income and status level in the potential destination nation relative to the country of origin. All three factors are dynamic, in that any desire to migrate takes future information into account and the decision is re-evaluated at each point in time.

The ability to migrate places the greatest barriers on individual agents since many of them are set by the destination country's government. There are five determinants of the ability to migrate. First, the precise level and quality of barriers to immigration in the destination country. This barrier can affect migrant groups differently, as, for example, US immigration policy treats Western European immigrants far more liberally than those from Africa or Latin America. Second, the distance, transportation, and initial fixed costs to move to the destination country. Third, the extended family's financial resources – in both the country of origin as well as in the destination country – and its willingness to support the individual agent's decision to migrate. Fourth, the extent of and access to official capital markets to finance the agent's migration decision. The fifth and final determinant of the ability to migrate is the home country government policies encouraging or discouraging emigration.

To illustrate the myriad of influences of these factors, we can consider the "successful" and "unsuccessful" growth path examples of international migration.[6] The unsuccessful case is illustrated by the Philippines. The Philippine economy experienced a premature shift to capital-intensive output, with little balanced growth since the Philippines did not encourage dynamic labor reallocation from the agricultural sector to the urban industrial sector. There was almost no small-scale industrial activity, and rural non-agricultural activities were wholly neglected. This unbalanced growth led to sluggish demand for labor and the existence of massive under and un-employment in the urban sector. The Philippines never structured its economy to take advantage of its abundant resource – labor – and the system's continuation of this inefficient growth path for decades drove one of the highest national rates of migration to the USA. This narrow, compartmentalized nature of the growth path leading to a falling living standard for the average Filipino drove the rise in the demand for migration over time.

The migration implications of this case for unskilled workers is illustrated in figure 8.10(a). The unsuccessful growth path leads to a rising desire to migrate as their frustration at home continues to rise. The ability of individual agents to migrate also rises slowly as income growth occurs, even if the income growth is unequally distributed. These trends, plus an only slowly rising legal limit in industrial nations, constitute an increasing gap between the desire to migrate and the binding quality constraint, leading to a growing volume of excess migration demand which is inherently volatile and causes both tension and efforts at illegal migration.

In contrast, the East Asian nations represent the case of a successful growth path, with balanced growth, successful reallocation of labor from agriculture to industry, the emphasis on rural non-agricultural activities, and a more equal distribution of income.[7] Given these conditions, international unskilled labor migration follows the pattern of figure 8.10(b). The desire to migrate rises for a time, but ultimately declines once the labor surplus condition ends, NIC status is achieved, and the income differential with the modern industrial nation becomes smaller than the costs of migrating. In fact, it is likely that there is ultimately a reversal point as net migrants return – an experience currently occurring in Taiwan. The ability to migrate also rises over time as the growth of equally-distributed income occurs and more agents have access to liberalized credit markets. What is of critical importance is that the gap between the desire to migrate and the

(a)

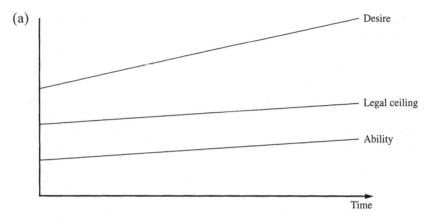

(b)

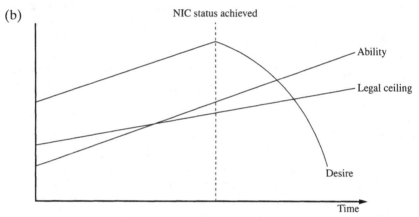

Figure 8.10 (a) Unskilled labor migration with an unsuccessful growth path; (b) Unskilled labor migration with a successful growth path

binding supply side constraint – excess demand for migration – declines and is ultimately eliminated.

While up to this point our discussion of labor and international migration has focused on unskilled labor from the urban sector, there is also the issue of movements in skilled labor. While "brain drain" from developing countries is well understood since opportunities to utilize human capital investments are greater in the modern developed country than in the dualistic developing economy, a few former LDCs have begun to experience factor mobility via a return of skilled labor (especially Taiwan).

Since 1951 Taiwanese graduate students have been allowed to study abroad (most notably in the USA), with the number increasing rapidly from 558 in 1951–52 to 7182 in 1988.[8] Of these students, in 1952 (1988) only 48 (2296) returned to Taiwan. This loss of highly educated manpower reduced the supply of professional people available within Taiwan. However, since this "brain drain" originated from the lack of opportunities for university people in the Taiwanese job market, this labor movement alleviated the pressure on the labor market to find jobs for highly educated workers within Taiwan. Also, family and social connections from Taiwan to the USA enhanced technological communications. Now that ample opportunities and needs for skilled labor exist in Taiwan, the first priority in developing its resources is to give incentives to the foreign educated students to return to and stay in Taiwan.

8.4 Technology

Our system of growth equations has illustrated that changes in technology – represented by innovation intensity and factor bias – are, along with capital accumulation, the most important source of growth in the post-war era. This importance of technological change is a fact that transcends the usual economic disagreements regarding methodology and is accepted by nearly all modern economic theories – from the neoclassical growth theory of Solow and its "new" extensions by Romer, to real business cycle theory à la Kyland and Prescott, and to our own form of nonstochastic modeling with its intellectual origins in Kaldor and Kuznets. There is, however, one differentiating factor concerning technology with respect to transition growth under open dualism in our model. While most economists embrace technological change in the form of new discoveries/innovations driving growth in developed countries, the issue with respect to developing countries is quite different.

Most LDCs have no "new discoveries" of the type that would be considered technological change by developed country standards. Instead, in the dualistic labor surplus economy technological change is represented by the adaptation, implementation, and innovation of technology imported from the developed world. This distinction can be broken down in a manner consistent with our growth model of chapter 4. Using equation 4.35 of chapter 4, the most important measurement of technological change is the innovation intensity J. This corresponds to the adaptation of foreign technology to domestic production processes, which allows output to increase without necessitating a rise in the domestic capital or labor stock. For example, Otsuka *et al.* (1988) comment that in most successful dualistic LDCs these domestic inventions modified advanced foreign technology.

The other side of technological change, using equation 4.47, is the factor bias of production B_L. This is determined by the **choice** of imported technology, whether it is labor or capital saving, etc. With the increase in concern about the link between transition growth and technology as a choice variable, analyzing transition growth under open dualism must include a focus on the role of technology importation and adaptation in the open labor surplus dualistic economy. Overall, we must recognize the importance of improving the quality of LDC technology since it has direct positive consequences for productivity and balanced growth as well as the achievement of a more employment-intensive growth path.

The most important point to be kept in mind when analyzing the choice of technology in a developing country is that it is driven by what is occurring in the rest of the world, regardless of that nation's attitude toward the rest of the world. Thus, the choice of technology embraced in more advanced countries powerfully affects what technology gets implemented in developing countries. This occurs via what technology is chosen by a LDC without modification or what is carefully searched for and then adapted. These later modifications constitute the real changes in technology as far as developing countries are concerned. While differentiating between alternative choices of technology and changes that result from domestic adaptations of imported technology is important in theory, these alternatives are hard to differentiate empirically. While we are not concerned with empirical distinctions here, it should be clear that we are discussing both choice among different available technologies/processes and the ability to make modifications in one direction or another – labor-using or labor-saving, for example – to make the final process most suitable for local conditions.

"Appropriate" technology choice is the joint selection of processes and product qualities to "maximize" a society's growth and equity objectives subject to the binding physical production constraints. This definition illustrates the dynamic nature of technological choice (change) in developing countries. "Appropriate" is not necessarily small-scale or large-scale, labor-intensive or capital-intensive, but that which fits the existing resource endowment at a particular point in time, both with respect to technique choice and product quality. Under this – now that the idea of fixed factor proportions and fixed attribute bundles has been discarded by the majority of both economists and engineers – there is more opportunity to focus on the political economy governing the search for technological alternatives in developing countries appropriate to the particular situation as well as the appropriate innovation inducement mechanisms at the individual firm level.

In the open dualistic developing country perspective, we can distinguish between the demand and supply sides governing the choice of technology and direction of innovative activity. By demand side we mean that attention must be paid to the macroeconomic environment that determines the extent to which individual economic agents are concerned with the issue of alternative technology choice – as part of their profit maximizing calculus. In other words, if the macroeconomic environment provides individual actors with large unearned rents, regardless of the choice of technology, then there clearly exists a greater tendency for satisfying behavior, as people will maximize with respect to other arguments in their utility function.

The most important dimension of the effective demand for more, rather than less, appropriate technological choices in the above sense is based on the competitive pressure on entrepreneurs – public or private – to seek out the most appropriate techniques and product attributes. This ability to create and maintain an environment placing competitive pressure on the decision makers is crucial to both the technology choice and the direction of technological change. The second important dimension of effective demand deals with the distortion of relative factor and product prices which drives a wedge between private and social choice. In this sense, the key to the exploitation of technology is the adoption of strategies and policies by the government and firms that reduce price distortions and barriers to competition, achieving a better functioning market which facilitates the continuous absorption of new technologies. In terms of the latter dimension, the East Asian nations and Japan have been the most successful during their development in removing price and output distortions, while most developing countries have kept large relative factor price distortion because of government intervention and repressed financial markets. The price distortions commonly observed in developing countries are likely to result both in inappropriate technology choice and in inappropriate directions of technological change. An important point to keep in mind is that the absence of deliberate market intervention policies helps both to ensure an efficient choice of imported technology and to adapt during and after the labor surplus phase has come to an end.

The Japanese development experience also demonstrates the importance of the quality dimension of technological choice and change – a subject often ignored by economists but at the heart of business' entrepreneurial options. When one can change attribute mixes and weights within reasonably well-defined products – quality variations – in the specification of final goods or in the quality of intermediate inputs deployed, this can represent an intentional effort to procure more labor-intensive combinations and supply differentiated markets. During their development phase the Japanese were successful, in part, by carefully exploring technological complementarity and substitution possibilities throughout the economy, making it possible to produce goods of a given quality using fewer or lower-quality inputs and a larger volume of unskilled labor. This utilization of surplus labor has already been cited as the key to successful development in a dualistic labor surplus economy. Thus, with a low capital-labor ratio, the labor-intensive technology choice allowed Japan to "stretch" its scarce capital while utilizing its abundant resource. The national increase in total factor productivity at the same time indicates that the new technological packages chosen – using a combination of substitution and innovation – represented a clear demonstration of the power of technological adaptation and diffusion within a competitive environment with few factor price distortions.

Similarly, the East Asian NICs also maintained an environment conducive to appropriate technological choice during their post-war development. Interest rates were high even while most LDC rates were low or negative. The NICs also refrained from artificially raising the cost of labor – via government intervention, minimum wage legislation, etc. In other words, relative factor prices were less distorted in the NICs compared to the rest of the developing world. Similarly, relative output prices – even during the primary import-substitution subphase – were not distorted, as the internal terms of trade against agriculture were positive enough to lead to no food rationing and no wage/price controls. In summary, the demand for the most appropriate technological processes and choices in East Asia and Japan is in consonance with shadow prices of both goods and factors, and thus is more "appropriate" in the sense the term is used here. In our model this translates into a milder use of import-substitution policies and an earlier transition from such policies into the export-oriented subphase of transition growth.

Even more important on the demand side of appropriate technology choice is the effect of different macro-policies in the institutional dimension rather than the simple question of relative factor prices that have been discussed in the literature and in this chapter. The basic point is that import substitution policies – especially in countries that persevere in that regime longer and in an inflexible fashion – provide levels of protection to domestic industrial producers that become entrenched. This translates into the expected continuous dispensation of many non-competitive favors, not just to insure protection, but also to provide monopolistic advantages in the domestic market – for example, the government denying free entry to other firms, overvalued exchange rates, artificially low interest rates to favored borrowers, etc. All these advantages represent measures aimed at ensuring continued profits and safety for the no longer infant industrial entrepreneurs.

This perseverance of import substitution policies means that an entrepreneur in a protected industry is guaranteed profits. His impetus to seek out the most appropriate technology is severely blunted as a consequence. The usual profit-maximizing assumptions are likely to be invalid since the choice of a non-optimal technology leads to only a small loss in profits, especially given the monopoly windfalls guaranteed by government action. Such "satisficing" behavior was mostly absent in Japan and the NICs since their periods of import-substitution were mild and short. The prevalence of satisficing behavior in industry – with firm energy directed toward seeking government favors and ensuring the maintenance of their monopoly position rather than towards a search for more appropriate technological processes – cannot be overestimated. Economists usually do not give this dimension its proper weight because the profession is reluctant to abandon the profit maximizing behavior assumption. An alternative to the satisficing explanation is to think in terms of utility maximization that includes a preference for specific attributes and/or prestige among competitors. In a basic sense, if the typical entrepreneur is not "up against it" in a competitive sense and is instead guaranteed good profits via government policy, he is much less likely to search out better technological choices.

In summary, the macro policy setting and relative factor prices combine to determine the assiduousness with which the demand-side search for technological improvements occurs, ultimately leading to development success. Our concern here is the reasons why – with respect to the role of technological choice – these successes become possible. It is important to remember that macroeconomic policies not promoting sustained import-substitution ensure that the demand for the selection of appropriate technologies and the search for new ones remain strong. But development success also requires complementary policies to ensure that there exists an ample supply of technological alternatives. It is to the availability and capacity to utilize these alternatives that we now turn.

In terms of the supply side of technology choice, there is an array of organizational dimensions that permit those who are actively searching for technological alternatives to have access to real world choices. The expansion of existing technological choices via technological change is subject to policy actions – government ones both internal and external to the economy – in part determined by the international economic environment.

While there is a usual perception of a "technology shelf" through which technological processes can be chosen once search costs are incorporated, in reality, there is a lack of illumination about technological choices as well as a limited capacity to obtain information, even about processes that may have been in use years ago or are currently used in other countries. In other words, the technology shelf is a mistaken concept from the point of view of the development of information about viable alternatives. Instead, there is a remarkable lack of information in the hands of most individual decision-makers, even if they are motivated to search out these alternatives. Consequently, there are high search costs involved in finding a range of technological processes or quality levels.

While we have so far illustrated the search for and supply of technological advances as a private venture, there is also a public aspect to it. In agriculture especially, the search for new technologies represents a public sector activity, as does the diffusion of new technology via extension services. Since we must also be concerned with the non-agricultural sector to have balanced growth, the private appropriability of innovation profits is an important consideration, and government devices such as patents are important as a method of diffusing new information.

The most important supply-side conclusion with respect to technological change is that, in developing countries, the most relevant technological improvements and adaptations in both the process and qualitative dimensions take place within repair shops and on the floors of small-scale firms. This is facilitated by the growth of such firms in successful dualistic LDCs – for example the NICs – and a rise in the number of patents. It is interesting to note that total factor productivity moves closely with domestic patents – indicating the importance of indigenous technological change. Thus, inflow of new ideas from advanced nations is the initial stimulus to technological change "supply" in LDCs, but most of the credit thereafter belongs to domestic adaptations. One illustration of this is that in successful dualistic LDCs – such as Japan – there was an early existence of a domestic machinery industry facilitating the modification and adaptation of initially imported foreign technology. This industry served as a temporal link between the initial importation of foreign capital goods and the production of modified capital goods required for the technological flexibility of other industries.

The importance of this type of technological change is linked to the organizational structure of industrial activities. Technological change potential is normally discovered in the context of repairing imported machinery – even when the technology is transported "as is" from abroad, most companies are willing to alter factor proportions and/or product specifications in response to suggestions from "below." This sequence of importing new foreign technology – either embodied in capital goods or disembodied as technical knowledge – followed by domestic innovation and the large-scale domestic production of new capital goods supports a supply-side technology-push hypothesis asserting that new technological knowledge provides a stimulus to further technological developments. In this perspective, there is little doubt that domestic innovative activity in successful transition growth LDCs (for example Japan and the NICs) was heavily influenced by the inflow of new technological ideas from advanced countries.

Another technological supply-side characteristic important in the success of some developing dualistic economies is the deployment of foreign technicians and engineers. The successful case features selective use of foreign advisors – including local engineering consultants – with most used for only a few years and then sent home. The crucial part is that once the foreign advisors are gone, subsequent adaptations can be made by locals on the advice of the shop floor. Many LDCs that have not successfully utilized foreign technology kept long-term engineering personnel from abroad, stifling the opportunity for the adaptation of the technology to local process needs.

The institutional capacities we analyze thus not only entail the ability to make the "right" choice in search of technologies which exist in the rest of the world, but also the ability to diffuse the imported or adapted technology. Fundamental to this supply-side issue is the human capital capacity required to ensure better choices in terms of the initial imported technology as well as the capacity to make important innovations and adaptations. This requires a minimum of technological capacity based on technical literacy not present in all societies.

CHAPTER 8   TRANSITION GROWTH UNDER OPEN DUALISM

NOTES

1   See Lipton (1976) for a complete survey.
2   Evidence of both expanding and declining RNA can be found in the following publications: Ho (1979); Anderson and Leiserson (1980); Shand (1986); Haggblade, Liedholm, and Mead (1986); and Bagachwa and Stewart (1991).
3   Spraos (1980); Grilli and Yang (1988).
4   Once the Heckscher–Ohlin assumption of equal technological knowledge is abandoned, the transfer of technology also contributes to international factor price equalization.
5   "Average" income does not necessarily refer to an arithmetic mean, but to a general comparison of the standard of living likely to be realized by an individual in the two nations.
6   For a more detailed analysis, see Ranis (1992a).
7   For a complete description and empirical analysis of the successful case for East Asia, see, for example, Ranis (1978, 1992b); Ranis and Fei (1975); and Ranis and Stewart (1993).
8   All statistics from Liu (1992).

9
Growth, Equity and Human Development

9.1 Introduction

Throughout much of this volume "success" in economic development has focused on employment and output growth. However, as we have stressed both in the generation and interpretation of our growth equations and in our applied chapters, transition growth also has important implications for income distribution outcomes relevant to both theorists and practitioners. Indeed, the "bottom line" of successful development must ultimately be judged in terms of its contribution to poverty reduction and, moving beyond incomes, to changes in the quality of the lives of human beings over time. It is these dimensions that distinguish the concept of "development" from that of simple "economic growth" in much of the literature.

The close links between growth and development are simultaneously a matter of importance as well as a frequent source of confusion. There is no doubt that, all things equal, an increase in per capita income is also likely to make a positive contribution to the quality of life of most of the people; but it is by no means certain. It was quite natural that the early writings in development economics concentrated on ways of first achieving economic growth, increases in per capita GNP and employment, leaving distributional and quality of life issues which might possibly interfere with that objective for "later." Implicit in this stance was also the notion that, since the rich have higher saving propensities than the poor, if saving and investment rates are to rise a society must first allow income distributions to worsen before it is in a position to redistribute. Earlier cross-sectional evidence, indicating a worse distribution of income in middle-income countries, seemed to support this view (Kuznets, 1955). The basic argument was that as growth proceeds, the property (rent plus profits) share rises at the expense of the wage share, which is kept low by the abundance of cheap labor. Consequently, as development is associated with a shift of families from a more egalitarian agricultural sector to a less egalitarian urban industrial sector, the society can be expected to accumulate more as income distribution worsens. Only later, when surplus labor has disappeared and modern economic growth has been reached, can the economy "afford" higher wage rates and greater equity. Kuznets thus, at least implicitly, accepted Arthur Lewis's dualistic economy framework, and both Nobel prize winners accepted the notion that "things had to get worse before they could get better" in the equity dimension.

In recent decades it has, however, become increasingly clear that the consideration of how income, and especially the command over the basic necessities of life is shared not only matters now, and therefore cannot be put off to some uncertain future, but also that the assumption of a necessary conflict among growth and equity objectives over time may be quite false. It is, of course, possible for a country to experience an expansion of GNP per capita while the distribution of GNP becomes more unequal, with the poorest groups possibly becoming even absolutely poorer. But it is not inevitable and few analysts or politicians today would accept a view of economic progress based on GNP growth without raising the relevance of distributional and other equity-related dimensions of change.

In the early post-war national plans and programs, straightforward growth was generally the principal stated objective. While there were some notable exceptions – India's early five-year plans included extensive references to poverty alleviation and Sri Lanka's six-year plans emphasized employment creation – the overall performance of a given society was almost always assessed relative to the UN target of a 2.5 percent annual growth of per capita income. While this target was usually more than met – at least on average – equivalent success was by no means achieved in the realm of income distribution, which was generally bad initially and probably worsened over time in much of the developing world. But such concerns were not at center stage.

During the late sixties and early seventies this view began to erode, partly because of an enhanced concern with the overall quality of life, absolutely and relatively, partly because poor people's and poor regions' faith in the political will and technical capacity to effect redistribution "later" began to waver, but mostly because the assumption that savings rates associated with more equally distributed incomes are necessarily lower was shown to be empirically false. Moreover, there appeared on the scene a few real world counter-examples, especially in East Asia, in which savings rates were seen to rise with increased equity and faster growth.

Thus, supposed iron law conflicts between equity and savings and between equity and growth were shown not to be inevitable (see Ranis, 1978). At the same time the empirical reality in most third world contexts remained that income distribution persisted at unfavorable levels over four decades of unprecedentedly high growth. The typical experience consisted of substantial increases in income per capita associated with relatively smaller increases in the incomes of the poor, rendering the latter absolutely better but relatively worse off.

Whether or not absolute poverty, in terms of the percentage of LDC populations falling below some arbitrary poverty line, actually fell or increased is a more controversial subject and undoubtedly differs markedly by country. It has been conjectured that in some countries increases in per capita GNP have actually been accompanied by rising levels of absolute poverty among the lowest income groups. Fields (1980), for example, presents evidence that absolute poverty grew in India in the presence of little overall growth, in Argentina with moderate overall growth, and in the Philippines with substantial overall growth. The Indian case is the least surprising, but the possibility that absolute immiserization can indeed occur in the midst of reasonable growth, as in the Philippines, is clearly disturbing and needs to be better understood. It is generally agreed that renewed interest in income distribution was shown in the 1960s and 1970s, and once again in the 1990s; moreover, such concerns are now increasingly accompanied by the search for underlying measures of the state of the human condition, such as life expectancy, literacy and other elements of well-being. The UNDP's *Human Development Reports*, initiated in 1990, reflect this trend. And even the traditionally growth-oriented World Bank's President Preston called poverty alleviation **the** basic objective of all international support efforts.

Such concern with "bottom line" human development is, of course, not new in the history of economic doctrine. In fact, it could well be argued that growthmanship has played the role of temporary intervenor in history of economic thought terms (see Smith, 1776; Marx, 1975; Pigou, 1912, 1920, and 1955, for example). During the 1980s, distribution and poverty-related issues were temporarily pushed off the international research and policy agenda by the pervasive debt and adjustment crisis. Disenchantment with income transfer programs at home and an ideological turn to the right in most OECD countries seemed to legitimize a shift away from direct concerns with poverty and income distribution objectives or constraints in formulating economic policy (Adelman and Robinson, 1989). However, the more recent return to basic longer term development concerns, coupled with the increased sensitivity to the issue of "safety nets" in the wake of the debt crisis, shifted attention back to the need for the resumption of growth to be accompanied by a concern for the quality of life of those at the lower end of the distribution.[1]

A growing focus on the limits of social and political tolerance for absolute income declines among the poor, plus progress in adjustment and debt reduction efforts, coupled with a decline in global inflation and interest rates, seems to have refocused attention on the underlying LDC development problem. Consequently, the public policy agenda is now more sensitized to the issue of the impact which past and current structural adjustment programs have had on disadvantaged groups in society, compared to what would have happened in their absence. Also as a consequence, the distributional, poverty, and human development implications of alternative macro-economic growth and structural adjustment patterns are being carefully examined, and even the IMF now lists them as important items for study and policy attention.

The analytical support for some of these concerns has initially been focused on the question of what happens to the distribution of income over time as growth occurs, that is, relative poverty, as well as what happens to the proportion of families who are poor, that is, experiencing absolute poverty. Such poverty can, of course, be measured in income terms, in terms of the absence of the satisfaction of certain basic needs provided by a combination of private and public goods, or in terms of the achievement of certain "capabilities," using Sen's language. Ultimately, it is the improved quality of life of individuals or families, not their incomes or even their consumption bundles, which really matters.

This chapter supplements our prior analysis of transition growth by linking it to various dimensions of equity and human development. We begin (in section 9.2) at the more rigorous end of the spectrum, that is, income distribution, which can be more readily related analytically to the body of growth theory explored earlier in the course of this volume. We subsequently turn (section 9.3) to relevant dimensions of poverty, the satisfaction of basic human needs, and the quality of life dimensions that are critical but also represent analytically more difficult terrain.

9.2 Income Distribution and Growth

It is well understood that GNP per capita by itself gives no indication as to who benefits from economic growth. The use of the real growth rate as an index of social welfare over time and/or as a method of comparing the performance of different LDCs assumes that the same welfare weight is attached to the income growth of each family or each income group. In reality, these welfare weights are likely to be very different. At one extreme, one could define social objectives largely in terms of the income growth of the lowest quintile, placing little or no value on growth in the upper income groups. Alternatively, we might have an ascending set of weights as we move down the distribution.

Atkinson (1970) has made it clear that every measure of inequality implicitly assumes an underlying social welfare function. Any income distribution index is a multi-dimensional object, with potentially as many variables as there are people and categories into which to place them. These variables can only be ranked by being reduced to a scalar, and this is what a social welfare function does. It is a comparatively recent undertaking to take the traditional inequality measures – such as the Gini coefficient, the Theil index, the Kuznets index, the coefficient of variation – and investigate what welfare judgments are really implied (see Fei and Fields, 1978). The choice of index relates to the analytical purpose. One summary scalar measure which is both commonly used and has the required linear additionality feature is the Gini coefficient, the (implicit) welfare properties of which have been analyzed by Fei and Fields (1978). It is the most widely used measure and also employed in this volume.

Although the third world has experienced faster rates of growth in the post-war era compared to the industrial countries – doubling GNP every 25 years[2] – there is a widespread perception that in most LDCs this average has been distributed in increasingly unequal ways. Indeed, based on Kuznets's (1955) pioneering essay, a general view has evolved that there exists a natural and unavoidable conflict between growth and equity during transition growth. The seemingly incontrovertible nature of Kuznets's cross-sectional evidence, accompanied by some plausible, if loose, hypotheses as to its causes, seemed sufficient – especially in the absence of rigorous efforts to link growth theory of whatever vintage to measured distribution.

The main schools of thought relevant here can be classified as essentially classical or neoclassical. The classical models of Malthus, Ricardo, and Mill focused on the functional distribution of income and posited that the distribution of both power and income among classes was defined by their respective ownership of the factors of production in both rural and urban locations: the landlord elites, the rising groups of industrial entrepreneurs, and the peasants and workers whose "surplus" supply was holding wages near subsistence levels. These classical models were rooted in the characteristics of the production process and its evolution over time. In the Ricardian case, for example, diminishing returns to capital and labor applied to the fixed land drive the profit rate to zero, while Malthusian assumptions inhibit increases in the real wage. Landlords benefit at the expense of both capitalists and workers and in the course of time their unwillingness to save, plus the absence of technology change, brings the upturn to a halt!

In Marxian theory, industrial capitalists keep the wages of workers down through labor-saving innovations and the maintenance of an industrial "reserve army of the unemployed." Increasing inequality is the explicit cause of capitalism's demise as a result of labor's immiserization and the consequent limitations on the expansion of demand and society's development potential as reflected in a declining profit rate.

Kaldor (1956) proposed an alternative distribution theory based on Keynesian analysis, in which differences in the propensity to save between wage earners and capitalists and variations in the rate of investment interact to determine the functional distribution of income. Given the assumption that capitalists and workers have different propensities to save, and that the ratio of investment to national income is exogenous, the required *ex post* equality of savings and investment means that there exists only one division of income between workers and capitalists which sets the resulting weighted average savings rate equal to the investment rate.

The work of Kaldor (1956) and Kalecki (1971) along similar, if more subtle, lines has been used by Taylor *et al.* (1980) and Taylor (1991) to construct models that link the macroeconomic behavior of the economy to inevitably worsening distributional outcomes. The most recent incarnation of this approach is the Latin American structuralist school, which focuses on the "necessarily" regressive impact of stabilization and adjustment packages on LDC equity.

In neoclassical theory, based on the Walrasian model of competitive equilibrium, all factors are paid the value of their marginal products, all markets clear, and the resulting equilibrium is Pareto efficient. In this theory relative shares change as the combined consequence of the quantities of factors employed plus technical change (see Clark, 1899). Neoclassical theory indicates that when in a one-sector commercialized world, secularly increasing levels of capital per worker can be assured, as our growth equations in chapter 4 tell us, if the elasticity of substitution (ϵ) is less than unity such capital deepening raises the share of labor, but also reduces labor-saving innovations, explaining the observed stability in the relative shares.

Kuznets's empirical observation can be differentiated from the prevailing wisdom in at least two important respects. For one, he focused on the family or size distribution of income and not exclusively on the class or functional distribution of income. For another, he saw the developing world in terms of non-homogeneous two-sector systems. Accordingly, his own explanation of the empirically observed inverse U-shaped phenomenon – with Gini coefficients on the vertical and per capita increases on the horizontal axis – leaned on divergent inter- as well as intra-sectoral phenomena. Supplementing his cross-sectional LDC data with the long-term analysis of now developed countries, Kuznets found that, while early economic growth produced increasing inequality, the size distribution of income in these nations ultimately improved. The more recent work of Jeffrey Williamson on England and Wales (table 9.1), as well as the explosion of

Table 9.1 Growth and income distribution in England and Wales

Year	Average income[a]	Gini coefficient[b]	Annual income growth (%)
1823	15.7	0.400	—
1830	16.1	0.451	0.4
1871	24.3	0.627	1.2
1891	34.9	0.550	2.2
1901	40.4	0.443	1.6
1911	41.7	0.328	0.3
1915	42.3	0.333	0.4

[a]per capita income in 1890£.
[b]for households.
Source: Williamson (1985, p. 226).

cross-sectional empirical studies in the 1970s, if some admittedly based on non-comparable data, also fit the Kuznets hypothesis.[3]

For a time the World Bank as well as many academics charted scenarios for worsening inequality in the developing world in the decades ahead.[4] Kuznets himself, more cautious than many of his followers, remained skeptical about the necessary universality of his findings,[5] and by the late 1970s enough time series data had accumulated to permit another look. This "second look" at the inverse *U*-shaped hypothesis had three discernable dimensions:

1   questions concerning the necessary relevance of the pattern for any individual country over time;
2   questions concerning **data** and **econometric specifications**; and
3   questions concerning the **causes** of changes in equality observed in the course of growth.

On the question of determinism, the most serious cross-sectional empirical study of the relationship – by Ahluwalia, Nicholas, Carter, and Chenery. (1979) – did not consider the Kuznets generalization to be an "iron law." Like any other "economic law," it only laid a claim for stochastic regularity as a generalization of "typical" experience. Many observations of individual countries were found to lie well off their estimate for inequality regressed against a quadratic function of per capita income change.

Most individual countries did show an initial worsening of income equality in the early stages of their transition growth effort. But the presence of countries like Taiwan in which inequality declined to "world record" low levels in the context of rapid growth clearly demonstrates that there is no "law of nature" to which all countries must conform. The Taiwan case is thus important, from both a practical policy and an economic theory perspective, for understanding the relationship between growth and equity. The careful examination of a successful counter-example to any "historical necessity" is bound to provide relevant policy conclusions concerning the precise conditions under which "things do not have to get worse before they can get better." As Srinivasan (1979) put it, "the deviation of an individual country observation from the estimated [Kuznets] curve should be viewed as the effect of policies being followed as well as other specific features of that country."

The obvious next question – given the presence of successful deviant cases – is whether the Kuznets curve represents enough of a statistical regularity to merit our styling it as a fact. Some historical records of currently developed countries (for example, table 9.1) exhibit a pattern supporting the hypothesis; others are ambiguous. Continuing to use cross-sectional data to analyze evolutionary phenomena in the post-war LDCs is, however, increasingly problematic. The early cross-sectional data set collected by Jain (1975) and initially used extensively by students of income distribution has been widely criticized for a number of reasons: inconsistencies in the grouping of income recipients (by deciles, quintiles etc. which affects the level of the Gini); heterogeneity in the units of recipients being compared (for example, households, families, individuals, income earners); and data based on heavily urban-biased household surveys, mixed in with others.

By the end of the 1970s, enough time series data for selective individual countries had been accumulated to subject the Kuznets hypothesis to intertemporal tests much more likely to avoid these problems. For example, Fields (1980) analyzes comparable data on changes in inequality for 13 developing countries and found surprisingly little association between rapid economic growth and inequality change. Some countries such as Brazil and the Philippines grew rapidly while inequality increased; however, income inequality declined in Costa Rica, Pakistan, Singapore, Sri Lanka, and Taiwan. A decade later, Fields[6] advanced a set of hypotheses and findings on poverty, inequality, and growth, using new data and found no systematic tendency for inequality to increase or decrease with economic growth.

Several other critics have noted similar problems. Papanek (1978), for example, points out that while the two tails of the Kuznets curve seem to exist – both really poor countries and very rich countries are reasonably egalitarian – some countries are much more egalitarian than others at all levels of per capita income. In other words, using cross-sections for time-series predictions is not warranted.

Saith (1983), moreover, shows that the statistical results obtained from the data by Ahluwalia (1976b) are not robust to several reasonable redefinitions of the sample. For example, once the six socialist countries are excluded, the fit for the log-quadratic U-curve drops precipitously. Papanek and Kyn (1987) test a number of related hypotheses using different econometric specifications and data samples. They find that the inclusion of Taiwan reverses the signs of the purely intertemporal Kuznets curve, but in the case of the combined cross-country intertemporal curve it only weakens the Kuznets effect; while Taiwan clearly is an outlier in the cross-section analysis, there is no reason to exclude it. Finally, Fields and Jakubson (1990) estimated the inequality-development relationship using alternative econometric methods. While the basic cross-section estimates of most authors use only the most recent observation per country, they deploy pooled data and an innovative "fixed effects" model which allows individual countries to be on higher or lower Kuznets curves by assigning each its own intercept in the regression. They find that use of this model reverses the shape of the Kuznets curve in every statistical specification.

Although most countries can be captured by a Lorenz curve of the *OWZH* type (see figure 9.1), what is clearly needed is an effort to move beyond essentially descriptive statements to relate robustly estimated income distribution time series rigorously to the nature of the growth process. One such effort, initiated by the present authors and described here, proposes the use of a Gini decomposition into additive factor Ginis approach to forge that analytical link. As the empirical case, the Kuznets curve counter-example of Taiwan is deployed, with a dramatically improving income distribution especially during the period (1953–70), which was also characterized by sustained and rapid growth (see table 9.2), that is, prior to the rise of real wages at the end of labor surplus.

In building on the fact that total household income is composed of various factor income components, we can be sensitive to some of the central features of successful growth as analyzed earlier in this volume, that is, the reallocation of labor from agricultural to non-agricultural activities and the impact of technology change and capital accumulation on employment and output. Using this Gini decomposition method we are then able to trace the causes of a change in the level of overall inequality, both before and after the commercialization or turning point. Only if we are able to analyze the behavior of an economy during the transition growth process and relate such behavior to distributional outcomes can we proceed to analyze the "inequality histories" of individual developing countries and come up with policy-relevant conclusions. We believe that this effort is a necessary condition for the construction of a theory of causal interaction between the nature of the growth path and equity.

We proceed with the analysis in three steps.[7] First, we demonstrate the decomposition of the overall Gini coefficient into its factor components.

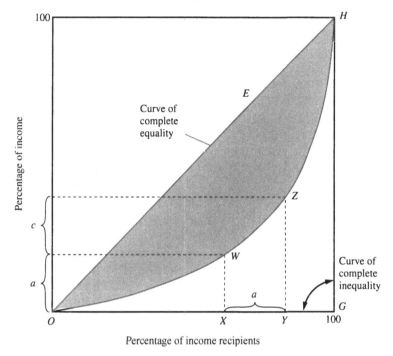

Figure 9.1 The Lorenz curve

We then derive the basic equations analyzing changes in the distribution of income in the course of growth. Finally, we relate these changes in the Gini to growth theoretic constructs, some macroeconomic in character and some relating to particular sectors or markets.

The sources of income inequality are as many-dimensional as the factors of production from which households derive income. Overall inequality obviously derives from differences across households in terms of the quantity of various assets (human or physical) held as well as in the rate at which they are compensated.

Because we can measure the Gini coefficient of each factor component of income as well as the Gini of overall income, it might appear that one way to decompose the overall Gini $[G_y]$ would be as the sum of the n factor Ginis $[G_i]$, for example, labor, property income, etc., weighted by each factor share $[\phi_i]$. This basic decomposition equation would be of the following form:

$$G_y = \phi_1 G_1 + \phi_2 G_2 + \ldots + \phi_n G_n. \quad (i = 1, \ldots, n) \qquad (9.1)$$

Such an exact decomposition would be in error, however, because it ignores the fact that the rank ordering of households by total income is not

Table 9.2 Taiwan: growth with improving equity

Year	Real per capita income growth rate (%)[a] in 1981 NT$	Gini coefficient[b]
1953	8.3	0.558
1959–60	3.1	0.440
1961	3.3	0.461
1964	10.1	0.323
1968	6.7	0.326
1970	8.7	0.294
1973	10.1	0.287
1976	12.8	0.280
1978	9.8	0.287
1980	2.8	0.277
1982	2.7	0.283
1984	10.4	0.287
1987	12.2	0.299
1988	6.1	0.303
1990	6.2	0.312
1991	3.8	0.308

[a]Source: *Taiwan Statistical Databook*
[b]DGBAS

necessarily the same as the rank ordering by each component factor income. Only in the case where the orderings are identical in all factors, that is, the richer family always gets more wage and property income, is this weighted average an exact equation. In all other cases we must correct for imperfect rank order correlations between each factor's rank ordering and the ordering of income as a whole. We do this via a linear estimation for each factor Gini, adjusted to take account of the rank order correlation of each component increase to total income. The exact decomposition equation, presented in Fei, Ranis, and Kuo (1978, 1979), yields $G_y = \phi_1 R_1 G_1 + \phi_2 R_2 G_2 + \ldots + \phi_n R_n G_n$, where the R_i's represent the respective rank order correlations. Notice that when the non-linearity errors are small (that is $R_i \rightarrow 1$), the approximation $G_y \approx \phi_1 G_1 + \phi_2 G_2 + \ldots + \phi_n G_n$ can be used.

We define the factor incomes distributed among families as either of Type One, Type Two, or Type Three. The specific characteristic of Type One income is that richer families on average have both absolutely and proportionately more such income than poorer families; property income, rents and profits, is a good example. The characteristic of Type Two income is that richer families have, on average, absolutely more but proportionately less such income than poorer families; wage income, wages and salaries, is a good example. Type Three income, on average, declines absolutely as families' total income rises, that is, it is an income distribution equalizer; examples are transfer payments or unskilled labor income.

To carry out a precise test of the degree to which each factor income's distribution differs from that of overall income, we can estimate a vector of all income from factor j going to household i, $\{\vec{W^j} = W^j_i\}$, based on the linear model:

$$\vec{W^j} = b^j + a^j Y \tag{9.2}$$

subject to the restrictions $\Sigma_j b^j = 0$, $\Sigma_j a^j = 1$. Let $Y = \{Y_i\}$, $j = \{1,2, \ldots, r\}$, $i = \{1,2, \ldots, N\}$, and the N households be ranked in their order of overall income so that $Y_i < Y_{i*} \Leftrightarrow i < i*$.

Using this framework we can distinguish the three income types by restrictions on the signs of their coefficients:

Type One income: $a^j > 0, b^j < 0$
Type Two income: $a^j > 0, b^j > 0$
Type Three income: $a^j < 0, b^j > 0.$

Figure 9.9 depicts the three income types as linear functions of total income Y, with b_1, b_2, and b_3 as intercepts and a_1, a_2, and a_3 as slopes. In the linear model a useful linking equation is $G_i = e_i G_y$, where $e_i = a^i Y/W^i > 0$ is the elasticity of Type I income at the mean point. Whether G_i is greater or less than G_y depends on whether e_i is greater or less than unity, which depends, in turn, on b^i and a^i. Making use of the information about the signs of the coefficients for each income type:

Type One income: $G_1 = [a^1 Y/(b^1 + a^1 Y)]G_y$ implies $G_1 > G_y$ as $a^1 > 0$, $b^1 < 0$
Type Two income: $G_2 = [a^2 Y/(b^2 + a^2 Y)]G_y$ implies $G_2 < G_y$ as $a^2 > 0$, $b^2 > 0$

We can therefore conclude that Type One income is distributed more unequally than total income, while Type Two income is distributed less unequally. Furthermore, the share of income due to the ith factor is:

$$W^i/Y = b^i/Y + a^i \tag{9.3}$$

Hence, for Type One (Two) income, since $b^i < 0$ ($b^i > 0$) the share of factor income increases (decreases) with total income.

We are now in a position to explore the linkage between the overall income distribution measured by G_y and the basic growth-related forces at work in the economy. To illustrate this, assume initially a one-sector economy with two factor components ($n = 2$) – capital (K) and labor (L) –

with ϕ_w and ϕ_π the distributive shares and negligible non-linearity errors. We then have:

$$G_y = \phi_w G_w + \phi_\pi G_\pi \qquad (9.4)$$

Differentiating equation 9.4 with respect to time:

$$\begin{aligned}
dG_y/dt &= D + B, \text{ where} &(9.5a)\\
D &= (G_w - G_\pi)d\phi_w/dt &\text{(functional distribution effect)} (9.5b)\\
B &= \phi_w(dG_w/dt) + \phi_\pi(dG_\pi/dt) &\text{(factor Gini effect)} (9.5c)
\end{aligned}$$

This equation attributes changes in G_y over time to two growth-relevant effects. The first – the functional distribution effect – describes the change of G_y due to changes in the relative shares of capital and labor. The second – the factor Gini effect – captures the change of G_y due to the effect of favorable or unfavorable changes in the two factor Ginis. Thus, the change in the overall G_y can be traced precisely to changes in the functional distribution of income as well as to changes in the family ownership of physical and human assets.

Equation 9.5b tells us that since wage income is always distributed more equally than property income ($G_w < G_\pi$), a change in the functional distribution in favor of labor (that is, increasing ϕ_w) always improves the overall distribution of income. In fact, this establishes support for the accepted popular notion that an improvement in the functional distribution of income (in favor of labor) also implies an improvement in the size distribution of income. However, contrary to the popular view, there is also the factor Gini effect to consider.

The analysis of the impact of the functional distribution effect, that is, the direction of change in the functional distribution of income or the relative shares, is central to the effort to link growth theory to distributional outcomes. This is true for any growth theory – neoclassical, classical, Kaldorian, Marxist, Schumpeterian or hybrid. In the context of this volume we apply the analysis of the functional distribution effect to the labor surplus developing economy undergoing two distinct historical phases – before the turning point, when labor is in excess supply, and after the turning point, when surplus labor has been fully absorbed by commercialized activities. Before the turning point, wages are approximately constant, or only gently rising, and after the turning point they rise rapidly since labor is a scarce factor of production. Using the growth equations developed in chapter 4, we can show the following propositions to hold:

Proposition 1   Before the turning point – as long as the real wage approaches constancy – ϕ_w increases when the degree of the labor-using bias of innovation overwhelms the innovation-intensity effect.

Proposition 2 After the turning point, when the real wage is rising, ϕ_w increases only when there is capital deepening or when innovations are biased in a labor-using direction.

The equation relevant to the analysis of the direction of change of ϕ_w after the turning point, from table 4.1 is:

$$\eta_{\phi_w} = (1 - \phi_w)\eta_{K/L}[(1/\epsilon)-1] + B_L \qquad (9.6)$$

where ϵ is the elasticity of substitution and B_L is the degree of the Hicksian labor-using bias of innovation.

Substituting equation 9.6 into 9.5b, the functional distribution effect becomes:

$$D = \phi_w(G_w - G_\pi)\eta_{\phi_w} \qquad (9.7a)$$
$$D = \phi_w(G_w - G_\pi)[(1 - \phi_w)\eta_{K/L}[(1/\epsilon)-1] + B_L] \qquad (9.7b)$$

Equation 9.7b shows that, after the turning point, when wages are upwardly flexible, household income distribution improves when technological change is biased in a labor-using direction ($B_L > 0$) or there is overall capital deepening ($\eta_{K/L} > 0$) because only then is the impact of the functional distribution effect definitely favorable ($D < 0$).[8]

On the other hand, as long as there exists an unlimited supply of labor and therefore near constancy in the real wage as assumed in chapters 7 and 8, equation 9.6 reduces to the following special form:

$$\eta_{\phi_w} = B_L\epsilon - J(1 - \epsilon) \qquad (9.8)$$

which implies that $\eta_{\phi_w} > 0$ if and only if $B_L > J(1/\epsilon - 1)$, with $1/\epsilon > 1$.

Using equations 9.8 and 9.4, we have

$$D = \phi_w(G_w - G_\pi)[B_L\epsilon - J(1 - \epsilon)] \qquad (9.9)$$

Consequently, as long as the unlimited supply of labor condition lasts, the functional distribution effect helps income distribution when technology is sufficiently biased in a labor-using direction to overcome the innovation intensity effect, a form of growth wholly consistent with the conditions for balanced growth put forth in chapters 7 and 8. In the "normal" case ($\epsilon < 1$) high innovation intensity leads to more labor absorption and a lower K/L ratio, decreasing labor's share. Thus, a high B_L contributes to both employment (and hence growth via equation 7.5 of chapter 7) and egalitarian income distribution objectives, while a high J contributes to the first but not to the second objective. In the "less normal" case when the technology is substitutable ($\epsilon > 1$) a high J also contributes to a better income distribution, that is in that case both a high J and a high B_L contribute to the elimination of unemployment and the improvement in the distribution of income. Independent estimates of ϵ are hard to come by, but it is likely that under LDC conditions of borrowed technology and massive adaptation the case of $\epsilon > 1$ may well not be so abnormal.

As we saw earlier, a high innovation-intensity effect (J) and a high degree of Hicksian labor-using bias of innovation (B_L) contribute to the economy's meeting the "critical minimum effort criterion" and thus the elimination of surplus labor and the arrival of the commercialization point. However, the distribution of income may become more unequal if $\epsilon < 1$ and the intensity effect $J(1 - \epsilon)$ overwhelms B_L. After the turning point a higher value of B_L, combined with capital deepening, contributes to the improvement of the family distribution of income.

As far as the factor Gini effect (equation 9.5c) is concerned, it demonstrates that changes in the overall distribution of income are also affected by changes in the distribution of individual factor incomes. This is where various micro theories focusing directly on capital and/or labor markets can be linked up with distributional outcomes. Such theories include analyses of changes in physical or human asset distribution and in their rate of remuneration, whether based on neoclassical or bargaining-determined rules of the game. For example, $dG_\pi/dt < 0$ could result from land or capital reform, a change in inheritance laws, or a reduction of discrimination in financial markets. Similarly, labor incomes can be more equally distributed, that is, $dG_w/dt < 0$, when lower income families acquire better access to educational opportunities or there is a reduction in discrimination in labor markets.

Before applying the above model empirically to the Taiwan case, the explicit dual characteristic of the economy before commercialization needs to be accommodated. While urban families receive incomes primarily from non-agricultural production (that is, wage and property income from urban industry and services), rural families usually receive income from both agricultural production (that is, merged wage and property income from agriculture) and from non-agricultural production (wage and property income from rural industry and services). This real world complexity motivates the treatment of all LDC households by segmentation into three subgroups – urban families, rural families, and all families. If we were interested in only the urban families, the decomposition equation 9.4 could be applied directly. But if we want to know about all families, including rural families, our analysis linking growth and distribution must be modified and enriched.

With respect to non-agricultural production, the two distributive shares (wage and property income) are treated explicitly, while in the farm family type of agriculture income cannot practically be divided into that

emanating from labor and that from land except by highly artificial impu-
tation procedures. In order to reflect the dualistic character of our economy, we therefore modify equation 9.4 as follows, where ϕ_A is the share
of agricultural income and ϕ_X the share of non-agricultural income; ϕ_X is
decomposed into labor and capital shares, with ϕ_w' and ϕ_π' representing
their relative weights within total non-agricultural income. Thus

$$G_y = \phi_A G_A + \phi_X G_X \qquad \text{where} \qquad (9.10)$$
$$\phi_X = \phi_w + \phi_\pi, \phi_X + \phi_A = 1; \quad \text{and}$$
$$G_X = \phi_w' G_w + \phi_\pi' G_\pi \qquad \text{where}$$
$$\phi_w' = \phi_w/\phi_X, \phi_\pi' = \phi_\pi/\phi_X, \phi_w' + \phi_\pi' = 1$$

Differentiating G_y in equation 9.10 with respect to time, we obtain

$$dG_y/dt = R + D + B, \text{ where} \qquad (9.11a)$$
$$R = (G_A - G_X)d\phi_A/dt \text{ (reallocation effect)} \qquad (9.11b)$$
$$D = (G_w - G_\pi)(d\phi_w'/dt)\phi_X \text{ (functional distribution effect)} \quad (9.11c)$$
$$B = \phi_A(dG_A/dt) + \phi_w(dG_w/dt) + \phi_\pi(dG_\pi/dt)$$
$$\text{(factor Gini effect)} \qquad (9.11d)$$

Equation 9.11 now can help us attribute overall changes in G_y over time
to three distinct growth-relevant effects. Two are already familiar to the
reader. The functional distribution effect reflects the impact of capital
intensity, the elasticity of substitution and the character of technological
change on the distributive shares, as previously analyzed, and can be summarized in terms of ϕ_w' and ϕ_π', which move in the same direction as ϕ_w
and ϕ_π, respectively; hence our previous discussion relevant to the one-
sector case continues to hold, that is, income distribution is improved as
long as $d\phi_w'/dt > 0$. With respect to the factor Gini effect, which now has
three components, the same considerations hold as before, except that we
need to separately consider what happened to the distribution of agricultural income dG_A/dt, as a consequence, say, of land reform or changes in
the agricultural output mix. In other worlds, whatever facts or theories are
found relevant to explain the distribution of each of the explicitly identified distributive shares can, in this fashion, be explicitly and quantitatively
linked to changes in the distribution of income.

The new expression in equation 9.11, compared to 9.5, is the reallocation effect R, reflecting the relevance of the shift of the economy's center
of gravity from its agricultural to its non-agricultural sector. This, presumably inevitable, shift in any successful LDC case can be proxied by a
decline in ϕ_A, the share of agricultural income in total income, when such
reallocation takes place over time, that is, $d\phi_A/dt < 0$. Thus, the impact of
the reallocation effect on overall income distribution equity G_y in equation
9.11b depends on the sign of the term $(G_A - G_X)$. When agricultural
income is of Type Two $(G_A < G_y)$, G_X must be of Type One $(G_X > G_y)$.

Hence $G_A - G_X$ must be negative, which means that the reallocation effect reduces the overall equality of income distribution. Conversely, when agricultural income is of Type One, $G_A - G_X$ is positive and the reallocation effect improves the overall family distribution of income. In other words, if Kuznets' prediction – that agricultural incomes are more equally distributed than non-agricultural incomes – is correct, the reallocation effect makes a negative contribution to the overall distribution of income. If his intuition is wrong, reallocation improves overall income equity.

In summary, changes in the overall inequality of income G_y can thus be traced to three growth-related forces. The first is changes in the functional distribution of income based on factors such as the production function, capital intensity and technological change. The second is changes in the distribution of factor incomes due to changes in asset structure, patterns of private and public saving, and the extent of earnings discrimination in various markets. The third is the reallocation of labor from agricultural to non-agricultural activities. The first and third effects provide a direct link between macro-economic theories of growth and the measured distribution of income. The second is more traceable to specific microeconomic events in the labor, land and capital markets affecting the distribution of human and property assets and the competitiveness of their compensation across income groups.

Our decomposition equation 9.11, focusing on these three dimensions, thus provides an analytical framework for examining growth and the distribution of income in a developing economy context. It enables us to make qualitative statements about the direction of the impact of a given pattern of growth on equity. More than that, it permits us to make precise quantitative statements about the importance of various individual effects as they contribute to overall changes in income equality or inequality over time.

The easiest way to demonstrate the analytical and policy usefulness of our decomposition technique is to examine the case of Taiwan which clearly constitutes a major counter-example to Kuznets's thesis. As table 9.2 and figure 9.2 show, the critical 1953 to 1970 period, encompassing both the import substituting 1950s and the export substituting 1960s, decades of rapid growth, also witnessed a continuous substantial improvement in income distribution equity. The improvement after the turning point is consistent with Kuznets and not surprising; the slight deterioration in the late 1980s is not really relevant to our story and undoubtedly due to policy changes in the virtually mature economy.

We can deploy our Gini decomposition technique to help us understand the underlying causes of this extraordinary pattern, between 1964, when detailed household survey data first became available, and 1968, and

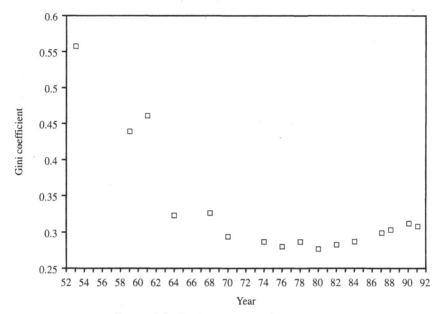

Figure 9.2 Taiwan income distribution

Sources: *Taiwan Statistical Databook*; Directorate-General of Budget, Accounting and Statistics

between 1968 and 1972, that is, for four years before and four years after the commercialization point. Table 9.3 demonstrates the quantitative contribution of the various aforementioned "effects" to the overall improvement in the distribution of income while figures 9.3 and 9.4 illustrate Gini coefficients and income shares over time by component parts. Table 9.3

Table 9.3 Distribution of change in overall Gini allocatable to various effects (%)

	1964–68	1968–72
Total Gini reduction	−100	−100
Reallocation effect	−20	23
Functional distribution effect	−2	−18
Factor Gini effect	−78	−105
of which agricultural Gini	−183	−30
non-agricultural Gini	105	−75
of which property Gini	10	−28
wage Gini	95	−47

Source: Table 3.5 in Fei, Ranis, Kuo (1979)

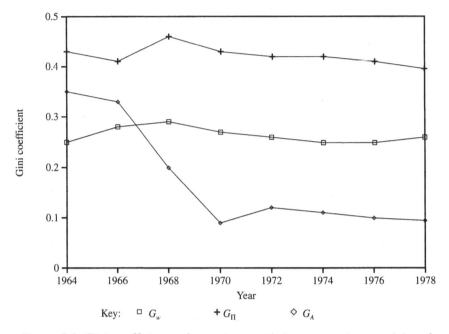

Figure 9.3 Gini coefficients of wage income (w), property income (π) and agricultural income (A) – Taiwan

shows that the functional distribution effect, summarized by changes in the relative share of labor, is helpful (that is $dw/dt > 0$, which also means $d\phi_w'/dt > 0$) throughout the period, if more pronouncedly after the turning point. As we pointed out earlier, the relative share of labor, a proxy for the labor intensity of non-agricultural production, depends heavily on the choice of technology, both in its process and product dimensions.

The range of process choice has three dimensions: exploring labor intensive choices and making labor-using adaptations within the core production process; exploring similar possibilities in activities ancillary to the core process, for example, raw materials receiving, storing, intermediate goods conveying and final goods packaging; and plant-saving innovations via sub-contracting, trading company utilization, etc.. The range of choice in the realm of product specifications is at least equally large, focusing on the search for more "appropriate goods," that is, goods with attributes meeting specific niche demand patterns, while enhancing the possibilities for efficient labor utilization. Thus, the final technology chosen in terms of our aggregative J and B_L-focused growth equations is a composite of a large number of product and process innovations, combining what is on

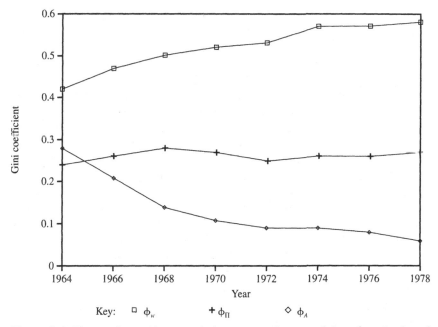

Key: □ ϕ_w + ϕ_Π ◇ ϕ_A

Figure 9.4 Share of wage income (w), property income (π) and agricultural income (A) – Taiwan

offer from abroad with the equally important domestic adaptations to local conditions. It should also be noted that the ratio of the relative shares ϕ_w/ϕ_π was consistently higher – and rising – for rural than for urban non-agricultural activities (see Fei, Ranis, and Kuo, 1978, 1979). This means that the decidedly rural orientation of non-agricultural activities in Taiwan during the critical 1960s – the only known case where rural non-agricultural employment grew faster than urban – kept overall income distribution from being adversely affected by the inevitable shift in the output mix in a more capital intensive direction.

Turning to the factor Gini effect, the largest contribution to improved equity was made by the decline in the agricultural income Gini.[9] On the other hand, the non-agricultural income Gini effect, especially for wages, was not helpful before the turning point, probably due to the impact of increasing labor force heterogeneity – a neoclassical human capital phenomenon in a growing economy – plus the increased segmentation of the labor market due to sex, family affiliation and other kinds of discriminatory behavior.[10] This situation seems to have reversed after the turning point when the economy presumably became more competitive.

This leaves us the task of analyzing the impact of the reallocation effect of equation 9.11b. Given that agriculture's distributive share declines persistently throughout the period, that is, $d\phi_A/dt < 0$, this effect, as we have noted, hurts or helps the overall distribution of income depending on whether or not agricultural income is of Type One or Type Two. In other words, if agricultural income is more equally distributed than non-agricultural income, as Kuznets predicted, and people are therefore being reallocated from a "more equal" to a "less equal" sector, the reallocation effect hurts the distribution of income. On the other hand, if this does not hold, Kuznets's intuition is wrong. As it turns out, during most of the 1960s agricultural income on Taiwan was of Type One, which means that, counter to Kuznets, reallocation entailed a shift from a less egalitarian (if improving) agricultural sector to a more egalitarian non-agricultural sector. As a consequence, the reallocation effect contributed 20 percent to the overall Gini decline during the 1964–68 period (see table 9.3). This unexpected result derived from the pronouncedly rural and increasingly labor-intensive nature of non-agricultural activities on Taiwan. Surveys by the Joint Commission for Rural Reconstruction show that the poorest rural families, proxied by those with the least land, earned almost two thirds of their incomes from non-agriculture even in the 1950s, as they participated more than proportionately in these initially domestic and increasingly export-oriented activities. Not only did the non-agricultural labor force grow by a remarkable 80 percent during the 1960s, compared to only 35 percent in the 1950s, but employment in dispersed rural industries and services grew faster than its urban counterpart and thus rapidly emerged as the major source of additional employment and income for rural families. By 1968 rural non-farm activities had become the dominant source of rural family incomes and the main destination of agricultural labor reallocation. In 1980, 67 percent of rural families' employment and 60 percent of rural families' income was drawn from such rural non-agricultural pursuits. The unusually decentralized and labor-intensive character of the industrialization process on Taiwan – concentrated initially in constant returns to scale food processing and textile activities – thus helped improve the overall distribution of income via both the functional distribution and reallocation effects.

This example of balanced growth between agricultural and non-agricultural activities has major advantages, not only in terms of stimulating a virtuous cycle of rapid inter-sectoral productivity growth but also in ensuring increased distributional equity before the turning point.[11] In mathematics, only one exception is required to render a "law" inoperative. In economics, the case of Taiwan clearly indicates that Kuznets and Lewis, endorsed in this instance by neo-Marxist and dependency theorists (for example, Cline, 1975), were wrong. There clearly exists no "law of nature" dictating an initial worsening of distribution as the necessary price of growth (Ahluwalia, 1976b). The fault, as Shakespeare put it, "is in ourselves; not our stars," that is, appropriate policies can eliminate, or at least soften, any conflict between these two key social objectives. Taiwan's experience should not, therefore, be viewed as unique or virtually unobtainable for the "ordinary" LDC (see Ranis, 1978). Moreover, we have evidence that a similar pattern in other developing nations undergoing transition growth is possible, at least over more limited periods of historical time.

In Colombia, for example, most of the evidence indicates an initial worsening of income distribution during the post-World War II import substitution era, through the middle of the 1950s.[12] The Lleras Government subsequently introduced liberalization policies, permitting a shift into export substitution, accompanied by enhanced growth and an improvement in its (highly inequitable) distribution of income in the 1960s and a slight worsening once again in the 1970s which continued into the late 1980s. Figure 9.5(a) illustrates the trend in the Colombian Gini coefficient over time. Ranis (1980) found, not surprisingly, that Colombia's wage income was consistently more equitably distributed than its property income in the 1960s and 1970s, but that overall equity levels continued to be unfavorable even as factor Ginis were falling $(G_w, G_\pi) = (0.64, 0.74)_{1968}$, $(0.57, 0.63)_{1971}$, and $(0.43, 0.47)_{1974}$ (Ranis, 1980, table 2). This is because the non-agricultural labor share (ϕ_w), a key ingredient in assessing the contribution of the functional distribution effect, rose consistently, from 0.53 to 0.59 in the 1960s, before declining to 0.52 by 1972 and further during the decade.[13] Unlike Taiwan, Colombia clearly used increasingly capital-intensive technologies and output mixes which, when linked with the high effective levels of industrial sector protection, contributed to an overall worsening of the distribution of income.

In Pakistan, the 1960s showed a similar steady growth in per capita income as a consequence of liberalization and a shift from import to export substitution policies under President Ayub. Between 1964 and 1971, the Gini coefficient depicted in figure 9.5(b) declined from 0.361 to 0.322 (and further declined to 0.29 by 1991), while per capita income growth averaged more than 3 percent per year.[14] The main contributor to this case of trade-off avoidance between growth and equity was the factor Gini effect. The wage Gini (G_w) declined from 0.438 in 1964 to 0.380 in 1971 and the self-employed income Gini (largely property), which carried a large weight in the total, fell from 0.325 in 1964 to 0.277 in 1971.

With additional household data becoming generally available, it should be possible to carry out additional Gini decomposition exercises, especially for countries experiencing improved distributional outcomes accompanied by accelerated growth, such as Chile and India, which have managed to shift from an import to an export substitution orientation. But

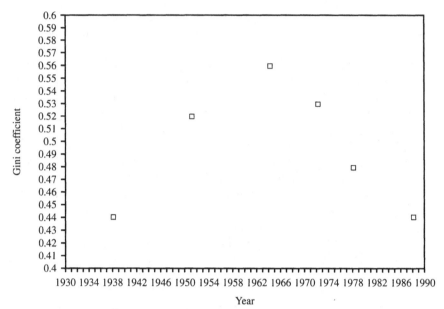

Figure 9.5 (a) Overall Ginis for Colombia
Sources: World Bank (1993b) and London (1990)

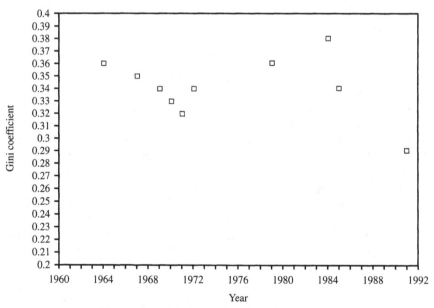

Figure 9.5 (b) Overall Ginis for Pakistan
Sources: World Bank (1993b), London (1990) and Fields (1989b)

the central point has, hopefully, been made – that is, that there is sufficient evidence to indicate that policy change can render growth and equity not only compatible but mutually reinforcing; moreover, that precise causal relationships can be established linking our favorite macroeconomic growth stories and our favorite understanding of micro factor markets to distributional outcomes.

In our effort to understand the determinants of the distribution of income in a developing country, we have emphasized results which emerge from the way income is generated via the production process itself and de-emphasized what could be achieved "later" as the consequence of redistribution through tax and transfer policies. This is because we believe that, at least in the mixed economy developing country context, the "primary" income distribution mechanism largely determines the final distributional outcome, since fiscal incapacity and political obstacles render "secondary" redistribution mechanisms highly doubtful. India's past experience with "post-office socialism" indicates that when governments intervene directly on behalf of the poor, the poor often find themselves worse off. What all too frequently results is hijacking by the middle classes, sometimes intentional, sometimes the result of inadequate administrative, planning, and implementation capacity. While governments can admittedly help (see below) by increasing and reallocating expenditures on health, education, and other public goods from the urban rich to the rural poor, there is growing agreement among analysts that in mixed economies it is the way primary output is generated and the way families are compensated for their contributions that has to bear most of the explanatory burden. Redistribution efforts or poverty programs directed at the tail of the distribution exist almost everywhere, but usually have small impact, while public works programs intended to mop up large-scale residual unemployment, while temporarily helpful, are difficult to blueprint, finance, and sustain.

Along with asset redistribution and institutional change, the choice of development strategy affecting the way output is generated remains the principal means of raising the relative incomes of the poor and relieving income inequality. Although well-designed asset redistribution policies can clearly be helpful to effect desirable distributional outcomes, much of the difference in the level and trend of income distribution rests on alternative policy paths to achieve transition growth. The selection of such a path is, moreover, not made once and for all; instead, the choice is likely to be evolutionary and reversible, continuously influenced by changing economic conditions, internal as well as external, as a society passes through the various sub-phases of transition growth.

9.3 Poverty Reduction, Basic Needs, and Human Development

We have seen that the post-war era has witnessed substantial success – substantially in excess of early post-war expectations – in terms of per capita income growth, but only modest success in combining growth with improvements in income distribution equity. The consequences for absolute poverty reduction have been even more ambiguous. It had been erroneously assumed that growth would automatically bring with it a reduction in the proportion of a population below the poverty line. But, partly due to the arbitrariness of that poverty line and partly due to our analytical shortcomings in addressing the poverty problem, we have encountered considerable confusion on both empirical and analytical grounds.

It is clearly necessary to link poverty outcomes rigorously to what else we know in development theory, that is, how growth is generated and how growth and income distribution interact. If we accept purely national definitions of poverty lines there is no reason to assume any relationship between restored growth and poverty reduction – witness the adage that "the poor are always with us."

Indeed poverty lines are usually drawn on the basis of minimal caloric and other requirements which are then translated into poverty income levels by the inverted use of Engel's curve calculations. Although a number of poverty indices have been put forward, the most common is the head-count ratio, reflecting the number of families below such a poverty line. These calculations of course differ across countries for physiological, climatic, as well as for cultural and economic reasons. Clearly daring, in the light of this, has been the attempt by the World Bank and others to establish an international poverty line and estimate the purchasing power equivalent in each country's currency *en route* to global poverty estimations. While such a ratio and changes in it over time are easy to calculate and understand, it clearly has many shortcomings, chief of which is that they do not capture the "degree" of people's poverty – individuals' distance from the poverty line – and are insensitive to shifts between the relatively poorer and relatively richer households among the poor.

Such considerations have led to the development of alternative measures of poverty. Some have calculated a "poverty gap" measuring the total income necessary to raise every poor family to the poverty line; this can be combined with a "redistribution potential" tied to the amount of total non-poor incomes and the effective (that is, politically and administratively feasible) marginal tax rate. Others have focused on the income-gap ratio – the mean shortfall of the poor from the poverty line. While the head-count ratio is insensitive to the extent of poverty shortfall per family, the income-gap ratio is insensitive to the numbers involved. Sen has endeavored to combine the two, (1973, 1979, and 1992) while Foster, Greer, and Thorbecke (1984) have prepared a poverty measure which reflects the non-discrete or continuous nature of poverty while it is also sensitive to the income distribution among the poor.

The choice of a poverty index should also be dictated by the conceptual context and its use can therefore be expected to lead to a number of different policy conclusions. Use of the simple head-count ratio, for example, would seem to imply that income changes be allocated to those just below the poverty line, while the Foster–Greer–Thorbecke index, which assigns weights to poor households varying inversely with their level of income, would favor income changes among the poorest of the poor.

As an illustration, table 9.4 presents one such estimate of the extent of absolute poverty (the proportion of a country's population with real income below the international poverty line) and its numerical magnitude (the actual number of people who can be classified as "absolutely poor") at a particular point in time. The data are from 35 developing countries in Latin America, Asia, and Africa. Using relatively conservative estimates, 38 percent of their populations were living at absolute poverty levels. The proportions were much higher in a number of heavily populated individual low-income countries like Bangladesh (64 percent), India (46 percent), and Indonesia (59 percent). High per capita income does not necessarily preclude substantial absolute poverty, but, for countries at similar levels of per capita income, poverty is likely to be more serious where there is high income inequality. For example, Colombia (19 percent) and Peru (18 percent) have much higher percentages of population in poverty than Taiwan (5 percent) or Korea (8 percent), although in 1975 they belonged to approximately the same per capita income cohort.

One serious defect with an exclusively incomes-based approach to defining poverty is that it fails to allow for command over minimal levels of public goods, such as health, education, access to potable water and sanitation. An effort to incorporate these dimensions of the quality of life led, in the late 1970s and early 1980s, to the so-called "basic needs" approach to assessing levels of development.[15] This approach specified that basic needs include not only certain minimum requirements of a family for private consumption, such as adequate food, shelter, and clothing, but also minimal levels of essential services provided by the government. This approach to poverty alleviation emphasizes the delivery of a basket of "basic needs" to the target groups, presumably via a combination of the market and its primary income generation plus some sort of national or international public sector "supply management" or "delivery system." In a system in which production and consumption decisions are mediated

Table 9.4 Extent and magnitude of absolute poverty in developing countries

Country	1975 GNP[a] per capita (US dollar)	Population 1975 (millions)	Percentage of population in poverty	Number of population in poverty (millions)
Group A (<$350)				
1. Bangladesh	200	80.7	64	52
2. Ethiopia	213	27.3	68	19
3. Burma	237	30.9	65	20
4. Indonesia	280	130.0	59	76
5. Uganda	280	11.5	55	6
6. Zaire	281	20.6	53	11
7. Sudan	281	18.1	54	10
8. Tanzania	297	14.8	51	8
9. Pakistan	299	73.0	43	32
10. India	300	599.4	46	277
Group B ($350–$750)				
11. Kenya	413	13.4	55	7
12. Nigeria	433	75.3	35	27
13. Philippines	469	42.5	33	14
14. Sri Lanka	471	14.1	14	2
15. Senegal	550	4.3	35	1
16. Egypt	561	37.2	20	7
17. Thailand	584	41.6	32	13
18. Ghana	628	9.8	25	2
19. Morocco	643	17.3	26	4
20. Ivory Coast	695	5.9	25	1
Group C (>$750)				
21. Korea	797	34.1	8	3
22. Chile	798	10.6	11	1
23. Zambia	798	4.9	10	0
24. Colombia	851	24.8	19	5
25. Turkey	914	39.7	14	6
26. Tunisia	992	5.7	10	1
27. Malaysia	1006	12.2	12	1
28. Taiwan	1075	16.1	5	1
29. Guatemala	1128	5.5	10	1
30. Brazil	1136	106.8	15	16
31. Peru	1183	15.3	18	3
32. Iran	1257	33.9	13	5
33. Mexico	1429	59.6	14	8
34. Argentina	2094	24.9	5	1
35. Venezuela	2286	12.2	9	1
Total	577	1695.3	38	644

[a]Using Kravis adjustment factors.

Source: Tables 1 and 2, Ahluwalia, Carter, and Chenery (1979).

largely through the market, the failure of the poor to obtain their basic needs requirements could thus reflect not only the unequal distribution of private purchasing power, but also the inegalitarian allocation decisions with respect to public goods on the part of governments. In such a context, income redistribution alone may be insufficient to ensure that the poor receive their basic needs.

If direct delivery to the poor of both the private and public goods components of basic needs can be accomplished, this approach may lead to the alleviation of poverty at much lower levels of aggregate income per capita – that is, earlier in the course of the transition growth process. It could even be argued that, in the absence of information and knowledge relevant to the choice of basic needs goods, poor families may not make the optimal consumption decisions. For instance, if targeted poor people are ignorant of nutritional principles or if they prefer less nutritious foods as their incomes rise, it is possible that tackling nutritional deficiencies using the income route may be inefficient. These propositions are not likely to be very convincing. On the other hand, to the extent basic needs are public goods in mixed economy systems, the direct targeting of the poor may be an essential ingredient in alleviating the problem.

The basic needs concept was at one time quite popular among international and national aid agencies, but received with considerable skepticism by recipients and some analysts. Its proponents saw an opportunity to short-circuit the need to raise per capita incomes over time in order to reach specific target groups as efficiently and quickly as possible. Its opponents saw it as a device to justify lower levels of international assistance and objected to the paternalistic assumption that local, national, and international agencies would be in a position to determine the differentiated basic needs of individual LDC localities and, even if they could, to solve the implied delivery and sustainability problems. In any case, for this approach to the poverty problem to have any chance of survival, it was felt it needs to be tied analytically to the rest of what we know about development.

Figure 9.6 considers basic needs (BN) in the context of the economy as a whole. The economy's total productive resource endowment is indicated at level I. Various production sectors are postulated, as shown at level III, including BN and non-BN sectors. During any given year productive resources are allocated as inputs to sectors such as education (R_e), health (R_h), food/nutrition (R_f), and others (R_o). This sectoral representation points out that the BN approach is concerned with the specific output mix, indicating the inescapable allocation choice of inputs between BN and non-BN activities. The output (Q_o) of the non-BN sector is divided into "luxury" consumption goods C and investment goods I. The products of the BN sector are education services Q_e, health services Q_h, food Q_f, etc.

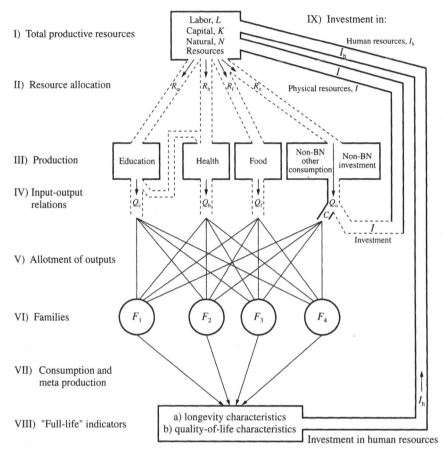

Figure 9.6 Framework of basic needs in a general economic system

A society's *n* families – represented by $F_1, \ldots, F_4$ at level VI in figure 9.6 – represent the basic units of social organization. The composition of these families, including their labor endowment and dependent populations, is taken as given. Beyond the output mix encountered at level III, the BN approach is concerned with the determination of the allotment, either by way of family incomes and the market or by government provision, of Q_o, Q_e, Q_h, Q_f, etc. to the individual families.

Families derive benefit from consuming both BN and non-BN goods. These benefits are conventionally treated in "utility" analyses and can be viewed in terms of some basic "full-life" indicators indicating the level of human development. One type of full-life indicator emphasizes longevity characteristics – life expectancy at birth or infant mortality rates; another stresses such quality-of-life characteristics as literacy rates and morbidity. The not very well understood functional relationships between the pattern of consumption of various BN goods, public and private, and these full-life indicators may be called the meta production function. More formally, letting $q_i = q_{ie}, q_{ih}, q_{if}, q_{io}$ represent the consumption pattern of BN and non-BN goods for family i, and, letting $J = (J_1, J_2, \ldots, J_k)$ be a set of k full-life indicators, the meta production function represents a mapping $J = F(q_1, q_2, \ldots, q_n)$. Conceptually there, of course, exist both a variety of substitution and complementarity possibilities along such a meta production function, such that various alternative combinations of private and public goods can achieve any defined level of the "full-life," but presumably only one can do so at minimum cost.

An implicit assumption of the BN approach is that the meta production function is a relatively stable relation that can be approximated empirically. While hard evidence exists with respect to some of these relations, most are only hypothesized about and on many there are only rough approximations. With the exception of economic demographers studying nutrition and education specialists studying literacy, economists have paid relatively little attention to the meta production function. Yet we cannot approach meeting BN requirements efficiently without a better notion of just how full-life indicators flow from the allocation of primary resources and the allotment of various combinations of BN outputs. Even if we accept the (usual) assumption that individuals know what is best for them as they participate in the private commodities market, to the (considerable) extent that BN goods are public goods and interact with private goods, this remains a serious problem. In any case, a sensible BN approach should not be subject to the accusation of commodity fetish.

Improvements in the full-life indicators at level VIII of figure 9.6 do not, of course, only represent ends in themselves, but they also constitute an investment in human capital in both the quantitative (for example, labor productivity) and qualitative (for example, literacy) senses and thus help augment the system's productive capacity next year. Such feedback relations are traditional and better understood than the aforementioned meta production function.

Adherents of the "new household economics" have pointed out that the value of output in the market sector seriously understates the full income of a household and thus of the economy. While an effort is usually made to estimate non-market food production, by omitting parts of the non-monetized sector, such as the child-rearing activities of family members, national income may still be underestimated by as much as 40 percent. "Full income" is a concept especially relevant here because of the overwhelming importance of families in BN production, especially in the realm of providing education and health services; it is difficult to name a significant household production activity whose output does not critically enter the meta production function, affecting the full-life indicators of the family.

The resource flow framework of figure 9.6 is institution neutral in the sense that the same set of functions (allocation, production, allotment, consumption, meta production, investment in physical and human resources) must be performed regardless of the broad institutional arrangement (for example, government or market) or the specific organizational device (such as local government or NGOs). This differentiation is considered in figure 9.7. All productive resources in the economy are transformed into services via four alternative modes of economic organization: the private market P, within the family F, by government G, or by community groups U such as farmers' associations or neighborhood associations. Each organizational/institutional mode can, of course, produce BN and non-BN goods, as indicated at level IV. In the health sector, for example, the total output of health services (Q_h) is the sum of the outputs P^h (representing private hospitals and clinics), F^h (family health care), U^h (communal fly-eradication groups), and G^h (public health and sanitation activities).

The critical question is how families, poor and non-poor, gain command over these allotments of BN and non-BN goods under whatever institutional auspices. Figure 9.8 presents a framework analogous to figures 9.6 and 9.7 in which to consider this question. A family's full income (F_i) is seen to consist of wages (W_i), property income (π_i), household and extended community income (d_i), plus provisions from government made up of monetary transfers (T_i) and goods and services (g_i). The distribution of full incomes is described by the pattern of wages, property income, transfers, publicly provided goods and household incomes. The allotment of primary incomes (Y), composed of W, π and d, has received most of the attention in the literature, but the provision of public goods must also be included for BN analysis.

Families thus receive the right to claims or actual allotments and must decide how to allocate W_i, π_i, and T_i among BN consumption goods C_b, non-BN consumption goods C_n, and savings S. For income from g_i and d_i, however, the allotment and consumption choices are usually identical and made simultaneously. Thus each family's full income is expended in seven ways – (C_b, C_n, d_b, d_n, g_b, g_n, and S).

The crucial element in our analysis of basic needs and its relation to income distribution and growth is this allotment of income. It is useful to consider the factors determining each of the seven allotment patterns separately for market sector goods (C_b, C_n, S), government sector goods

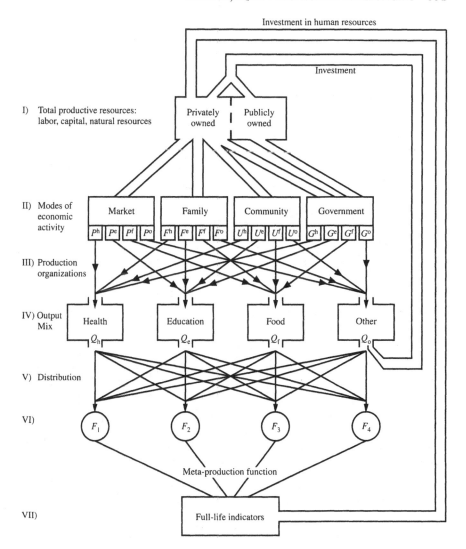

Figure 9.7 Organizational choices

(g_b, g_n), and household sector goods (d_b, d_n). We first examine how income is distributed among families and then how it is disposed of with respect to BN and non-BN goods, noting again that these two stages are independent only with respect to market sector goods. Earlier in this volume we analyzed the causes of income growth, as well as the distribution of income, and its relation to growth. We now analyze the relationship between per

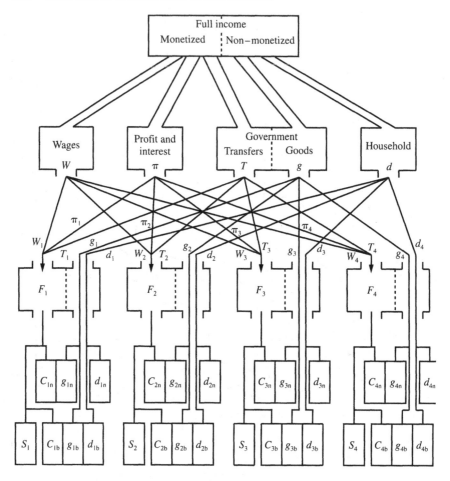

Figure 9.8 Income distribution and basic needs

capita income $(\bar{Y})$, the Gini coefficient G_y, and the satisfaction of BN via the market.

Figure 9.9 depicts the allocation of total income by all the families (F_i) to the patterns C_b, C_n, and S, observing the identity $Y = C_b + C_n + S$. Family incomes, going from poorest to richest, are arranged on the horizontal axis and the expenditure of income by these same families on BN and non-BN consumption goods and savings are shown on each of the vertical axes. To simplify the exposition, we assume that the consumption and savings functions are linear, with b_1, b_2, and b_3 as intercepts and a_1, a_2, and a_3 as slopes, such that $b_1 + b_2 + b_3 = 0$ and $a_1 + a_2 + a_3 = 1$.

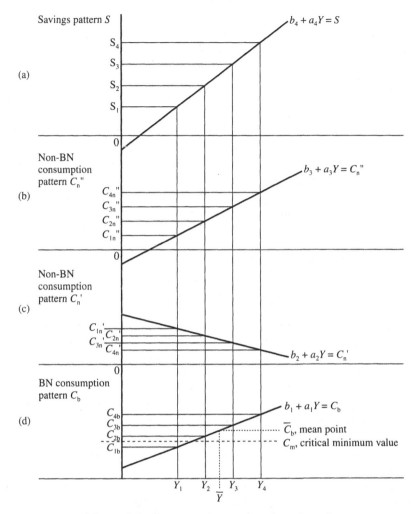

Figure 9.9 Consumption and savings functions

The mean value of BN consumption is $\bar{C}_b$. The inequality of Y is measured by G_y and the inequality of BN consumption is measured by G_b. The critical minimum level of BN consumption C_m, corresponds, for example, to minimum caloric food requirements.

In the linear model, a useful linking equation is:

$$G_b = e_b G_y, \text{ where } e_b = |a_i| Y/C_b > 0 \tag{9.12}$$

This is the elasticity of the BN consumption function at its mean point. In the case of BN goods this elasticity is likely to be less than 1, that is, BN goods are likely to be of Type Two in the earlier language of this chapter, as richer families consume absolutely more than poorer families, but less than proportionally so. In other words, we can assume that $b_1 > 0$ and $a_1 > 0$ because families at all income levels must consume positive amounts of BN goods and, as income rises, families will increase their consumption of BN goods less than proportionally. In that case $G_b < G_y$, that is, BN consumption is distributed more equally than family income. Non-BN goods are likely to be of Type One, described in figure 9.9(b), with rich families consuming proportionally more than poor families and $G_n > G_y$. The Type Three case illustrated in figure 9.9(c) is possible but highly unlikely to occur.

Our earlier linking equation can now be used to analyze the impact of an increase in income per family on the satisfaction of basic needs, our main objective being to link basic needs, growth and distribution. Substituting $\bar{C}_b = b_1 + a_1\bar{Y}$ into the expression for e_b, the elasticity of expenditures on basic needs relative to income change, yields

$$G_b = e_b G_y = \frac{a_1\bar{Y}}{b_1 + a_1\bar{Y}} G_y \qquad (9.13)$$

Changes in G_b over time are thus determined by both $\bar{Y}$ and G_y. If an increase in per capita income occurs without any change in G_y, given $a_1 > 0$, $b_1 > 0$, e_b rises and therefore G_b increases, approaching G_y in the limit.

In other words, the inequality of BN consumption increases as income per family increases. At the same time, the number of families falling below a minimum level of BN consumption C_m is likely to decrease. While BN advocates regard the process of increasing BN consumption through growth as too slow, it may well be the most feasible and sustainable solution. Of course, if, simultaneously with the growth of income $(\bar{Y})$, income distribution (G_y) can be improved, G_b can fall. This supports the argument that, as the experience of East Asia indicates, rapid and increasingly equitable growth is likely to simultaneously solve the BN poverty problem. But even if there is a conflict between growth and equity, the number of families below critical minimum levels of BN consumption may decline, even if at a slower pace.

We now turn to the provision of BN goods via the government, that is, public goods. In this area analysis is more difficult. Some of the literature assumes a positive association between the distribution of money income and the distribution of publicly provided goods such as national security. In countries with a more egalitarian distribution of income, there is a tendency for a more egalitarian distribution of public goods and a higher proportion of public goods to be BN goods. Greater income equality may mean a more equitable distribution of political and economic power leading to greater equality in G_b and G_n. There is, however, no guarantee that this is the case. It may be that the consumption of public goods imposes complementary costs that can be better met by consumers with higher incomes. Examples in education would be the opportunity cost of attending school and the complementary costs of clothing and transportation. Most public goods are likely to be allocated in Type Two fashion, though we cannot exclude the possibility of Type One if elitist interest groups are really powerful. Transfers, for example welfare payments, can be expected to be of Type Three but, given the hijacking ability of the middle class, often turn out empirically to be of Type Two. Admittedly, both the overall magnitude of public goods and their distribution, in relation to $\bar{Y}$ and G_y, are difficult to determine and we are less confident about the stability of these relations. Consequently, the task of changing the quantity, BN content, and distribution of public goods in a desired direction is not an easy one.

Finally, we explore the relationship between $\bar{Y}$, G_y and BN goods produced by the household and other private co-operative institutions. Recent research into the distribution of household income has produced the expected result that d_n and d_b are more equally distributed than Y. A related dimension of BN satisfaction is the provision of goods by NGOs, rural co-operatives, and other elements of a system's civil society. It is now sometimes being claimed that such institutions represent the most efficient and dependable avenue for getting the appropriate BN goods to target groups. Some OECD countries have even announced that they intend to channel most of their future foreign assistance through NGOs.

Whether or not such institutions are really seven feet tall and are able to overcome problems of bureaucratic or paternalistic character remains to be seen. But certainly the methods of the planning school represented by Chenery, Tinbergen and others could be adapted to examine such alternative channels for achieving BN satisfaction in a given country at minimum cost over a specified period of time. Meeting BN goals requires productive resources, and the usual dynamic conflict between BN satisfaction today and investment, permitting more BN satisfaction tomorrow, also cannot be ignored. Such conflict can, however, be reduced when we recognize the feedback effects of BN satisfaction today on labor productivity tomorrow – quite aside from the direct impact of today's BN satisfaction on today's quality of life indicators.

Though simple enough in theory, only a BN-focused dynamic planning effort would, however, be difficult to implement, largely because of the problem in estimating the meta production function. As we have pointed out, a substantial number of complementary and substitute relations exist among BN inputs for inducing changes in the quality of life indicators. Without education, for instance, health services may be much less effective in yielding a longer life. Food may be a partial substitute for health services. Moreover, producing increments in "literacy" or "long life" indices may entail the effects of BN consumption over a considerable stretch of time.

A whole set of equally challenging but more manageable problems arise when we focus on quality of life indicators as also constituting human resource investments that augment the system's total productive capacity. Leading examples are the "feed-back" effects of literacy and improved health status on worker productivity. Here we have much more to go on since there exists a substantial literature in the microeconomic labor market and human capital literature.

We clearly have a variety of policy instruments and organizational choices available to the majority of "mixed economy" LDCs interested in improving BN performance. In the simplest case relative BN/non-BN commodity prices are assumed not to be affected, even if extreme redistributional policy were able to transfer incomes until all are equalized; complete income equality would be tantamount to the complete equality of private BN consumption. If the critical minimum BN consumption level of figure 9.9(d) were to lie below the mean consumption level, one solution would be to transfer incomes until the income of the poorest person were sufficient to reach the critical minimum BN level. Of course, if the mean consumption level were to lie below the critical minimum level, such internal transfers would not solve the BN problem, but would only result in an equal sharing of poverty. In this case income growth clearly becomes necessary. Governments may also change families' consumption patterns at given levels of income in order to increase the proportion of income spent on BN goods by controlling their relative price or by education policies aimed at shifting the slope of the BN consumption function. Although everyone would consume more BN goods, low income families would increase their consumption more than high income families, reducing G_b so that BN goods would be more equally allotted and a_1 is reduced. Fewer families would then remain below the deprivation line, even if overall and per capita income levels were not affected.

There are two arguments against such income transfer policies providing a sufficient level of BN consumption via the market. One is that such *ex post* income equalization efforts may hurt economic growth due to disincentive and harmful savings effects; current literature, including our own work, indicates that such harmful effects of a more equal distribution of income on growth have been much exaggerated. More critical is the absence of the necessary administrative and political capacity to effect the fiscal transfers and ensure they indeed reach the intended target groups. The empirical evidence here suggests that governments rarely succeed in greatly reducing income inequality through transfers, particularly when primary income inequality is substantial.

Increasing the volume of publicly provided BN goods, possibly includ-ing not only health, water, education, etc., but also food, represents a more direct method of ensuring minimal BN availability. However, the identifi-cation of needs, the management of the transfers, the avoidance of hijack-ing, and the sustainability of such programs all represent difficulties which, as we have pointed out above, need to be taken into consideration.

The desirable mix of public and market activity in ensuring that BN goods reach target groups of course involves a choice concerning the orga-nizational forms best suited to the task. We clearly need to move beyond simple-minded prescriptions which would tend to leave all such activity in private market hands. Much depends on a country-specific assessment of the relative past performance of various organizational forms and/or the special circumstances that have favored one form over another – for exam-ple, centralized or decentralized governments, NGOs or family-based community organizations, and the structure of civil society generally. Identifying and filling in the relevant knowledge gaps remains an impor-tant ingredient for closing the analytic circle and being able to address the policy issue.

To complicate matters even further, the efficiency of a given set of orga-nizational choices may, of course, not be the only criterion. Participation and the chance to "take control of one's own life" may itself also be signifi-cant, not only as a "full-life" indicator but also as a crucial instrument in ensuring the long-run sustainability of the system, especially when recur-ring costs must be met locally. Undoubtedly, more emphasis should be given to the comparative efficiency of BN production within families and other communal arrangements like farmers' co-operatives, as well as to the comparative ability of local governments to raise additional resources and deploy them effectively. Such BN production/distribution patterns are likely to make a much smaller claim on a system's total capacity, including on what is required for the growth of the non-BN portions of income over time.

The validity and survival value of any approach which focuses on improvements in the basic quality of life and views income as an interme-diate product depends very much on the extent to which it can be inte-grated within the analytical framework of contemporary development theory and policy. A better understanding of the meta production function and of the various organizational choices available is required if such an integration is indeed to be accomplished over time.

Although the literature is far from "convergent" on this topic, a fuller integration indeed necessitates a departure from the excessively inductive and commodity-focused basic needs approach. An early indication of the direction in which we are heading was given by Sen (1984) who focused attention on the human welfare implications and practical economic effects of defining a bundle of basic "entitlements" for a population. The connection between what is "just" and what is "efficient" is the fact that the essence of deprivation includes constraints on income, mobility, health, education and, ultimately, choice itself. Sen suggested that, rather than trying to specify the complete social welfare function over all possible social states, the proper approach may be to identify the most "binding" of these constraints and work on them first.

The profession is indeed gradually returning to one of the old verities – that the ultimate end of economic activity is the enlargement of people's choices, the most critical being a long and healthy life, an adequate level of education, and access to enough resources so that an individual's basic needs can be met. Income growth, its distribution, as well as the provision of public goods out of that income are essential to the advancement of the human condition but they are the means to an end, not an end in themselves.

At the same time, human development, in the form of enhanced health, literacy, etc., feeds back on economic development in the next period via its enhancement of labor productivity, the enhancement of entrepreneurial funding, the efficiency of R&D, etc., combining with investment and other traditional inputs. What we thus encounter is a closed circle, or general equilibrium system, linking human development and economic development. Whether this circle is virtuous (that is, describing an upward spiral) or vicious, depends on the strength of the various links between them – including income distribution and poverty levels affecting household expenditures on food and other basic needs, plus the quantity and quality of government social expenditures per capita affecting educational enrollment ratios, health service coverage and the like. Figure 9.10 indicates the various main elements or links in the human development–economic development cycle.

The gradual rediscovery of this basic truth, that people reside at the center of development, not only as a contribution to it, but also as an end in itself, has been increasingly reflected in the recent literature as well as in the changing emphasis by international organizations such as the United Nations Development Programme (UNDP). The first UNDP Human Development Report (HDR), in 1990, appeared at the same time as a World Bank Development Report focused on income poverty. This coincidence helped demonstrate the switch in analytical as well as policy emphasis. The HDR defined human development as a combination of literacy, life expectancy and command over enough resources to obtain one's basic needs. The approach sought to demonstrate that various combinations of income growth, income distribution, and the public provision of BN goods can achieve an improved level of human development, and moreover

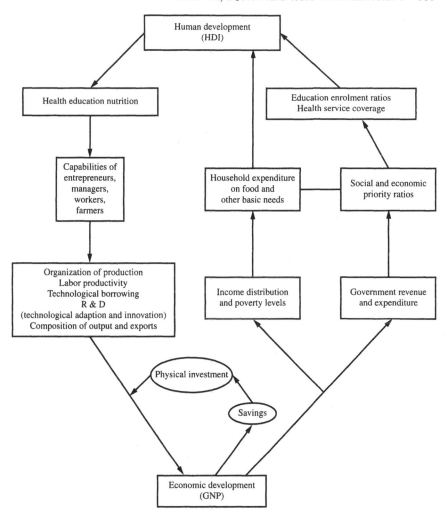

Figure 9.10 The human development–economic development cycle

sustain such improvements over time. The proposed use of a, necessarily rather arbitrary, human development index combining income and quality of life objectives – which has perhaps received undue attention – is less critical than the substantive shift of the analytical and policy focus from mere means to ultimate ends. The central message of this new focus is that while growth in national income is absolutely necessary to provide both the resources and the choices which promote human development in a dynamic context, it is not sufficient. In this respect, human development is a more comprehensive concept, simultaneously concerned with the generation of economic growth as well as with its distribution and the enhancement of basic quality of life indicators via the provision of BN goods.

In this connection it is instructive to note that there exist alternative real world scenarios for achieving improvements in the human condition, depending on differing points of departure, endowments, etc.[16] For the 1960–86 period, for example, it was found useful to disaggregate the overall developing country experience into cases of sustained human development, disrupted human development, and missed opportunities for human development; and, more importantly, to note that success can be achieved via alternative combinations of initial conditions and policies over time.

As we have already noted, the "human condition" has a number of dimensions, such as life expectancy at birth, infant and child mortality, female and male literacy, and nutritional status. There is, however, widespread consensus as well as statistical evidence that such quality of life indicators generally move together. Therefore, for purposes of illustration, a single index such as under five mortality can be used as a proxy to measure relative success in human development.[17]

A tentative study of the trends in human development in different developing countries serves to illustrate a variety of possible patterns for achieving success and sustaining it. Growth remains essential for sustainability, and an improving distribution of income as growth proceeds is clearly of great help; the ability to reach particularly disadvantaged segments of the population with BN-type goods is, moreover, essential to assure the distributional equity of HDI and its components.[18]

Substantial improvements in these basic quality of life indicators can clearly be achieved relatively quickly and indeed the gap between rich and poor country average levels has narrowed dramatically over the past few decades. Table 9.5 summarizes the trends in some of the basic indicators of the human condition, such as infant mortality, life expectancy at birth, and female literacy for a number of countries. The important questions that remain are: what conditions, including government policies, were responsible for effecting such dramatic changes and, more importantly, what conditions need to be satisfied to ensure that these improvements are sustained.

For this purpose we clearly need to focus on the association between the observed patterns of human development performance, countries' initial conditions, the macroeconomic policies pursued, as well as the patterns of government tax and expenditure policies in the human development domain. The most important macroeconomic determinants turn out to be, not surprisingly, the initial levels and rates of growth of income per capita plus income distribution levels and trends. Together these macro concepts determine the level and changes in income at the household level. The other main instrument of human development-oriented policies is the

Table 9.5 Trends in basic indicators of human development

	Infant mortality rate			Life expectancy			Adult literacy			
							Female		Male	
	1960	1975	1987	1960	1975	1988	1970	1985	1970	1985
	(per 1000 births)			(Years)			(%)			
Country										
1. Taiwan	32	14	7	62	68	78	68	85	89	96
2. Singapore	36	16	9	64	70	73	55	79	92	93
3. Cuba	62	NA	15	63	72	74	87	96	86	96
4. South Korea	85	40	26	54	64	69	81	88	94	96
5. Sri Lanka	70	52	34	62	66	70	69	83	85	91
6. Malaysia	73	37	24	54	64	70	48	66	71	81
7. Botswana	119	92	68	46	52	59	44	69	37	73
8. Jamaica	62	23	18	63	68	74	97	NA	96	NA
9. Kenya	124	99	73	45	52	59	19	49	44	70
10. Costa Rica	84	40	18	62	69	75	87	93	88	94
11. Chile	114	58	20	57	65	72	88	96	90	97
12. Zimbabwe	110	84	73	45	53	59	47	67	63	81
13. China	209[a]	49	50[b]	35[a]	64	64[b]	NA	56	NA	82
14. Colombia	103	63	46	55	61	65	76	87	79	89
15. Brazil	116	89	64	55	61	65	NA	56	69	79
16. Nigeria	183	146	106	40	46	51	14	31	35	54
17. Pakistan	162	136	110	43	50	57	11	19	30	40

[a] average of 1959–61.
[b] 1984.
Source: China's data on life expectancy and infant mortality rates are from Judith Bannister's unpublished work. All other data are from UNDP sources, except the following: Taiwan – *Statistical Yearbook of the Republic of China*; Female and male literacy – UNICEF, *State of the World's Children*, 1989.

provision of public goods via a tax and expenditure system which emphasizes "priority" activities in the social sector as well as in the realm of economic infra-structure. Within each sector of activity one can usually distinguish between the relative impact of different types of expenditures, such as primary versus tertiary education, preventive versus curative health care, recurrent versus capital expenditures, etc.. Here the literature does provide some help, indicating the relative priority which should be given to primary education and preventive health care in terms of human development, both as an end in itself and, via rates of return calculations, as a means of generating additional resources next year.[19] Moreover, care must be taken that even priority expenditures are provided in a way that does not discriminate unduly among different social groups or regions – for example, universal food subsidy systems, primary education programs, or immunization programs. Such across-the-board policies need to be

Table 9.6 Strategies towards human development

Country category	Current 'initial' conditions	Illustrative current country examples	Priority policies	Examples of successful historical cases (startig with these conditions and following these policies)
I	Poor human development, low income, bad income distribution	Nepal Sierra Leone Sudan	Improving growth and distribution; meso: reallocate to and restructure social sectors; use targeting	Botswana Kenya[a] Zimbabwe[a]
II	Poor human development, middle income, bad income distribution	Brazil Gabon Nigeria	Improve distribution and sustain growth; meso: reallocate to and restructure social sectors; use targeting	Malaysia
III	Moderate human development, low income, moderate income distribution	Egypt India Indonesia	Improve growth and maintain distribution; meso: reallocate to and restructure social sectors; use targeting	China South Korea Sri Lanka Taiwan
IV	Moderate human development, middle income, moderate income distribution	Thailand Tunisia	Sustain growth and maintain distribution; meso: reallocate to and restructure social sectors; use targeting	Chile Colombia Costa Rica Cuba Jamaica[a] Singapore

[a] The historical record on income distribution for these countries is somewhat ambiguous.

compared with the targeted provision of such goods in the attempt to cover only the needy members of a particular, say ethnic or geographic, group — for example, a food stamp program for the very poor or supplementary feeding programs for malnourished children.

While we have emphasized that human development-focused provisions by government are usually concentrated in the so-called "social sectors" – such as health, education, and potable water – this is not exclusively so; for instance, they sometimes extend to food when the "primary" incomes of the population are insufficient or insufficiently well distributed. Where per capita primary incomes are too low, across-the-board provisions may be required; where distribution is bad, targeting the poorer segments of society may be the preferred strategy even if it is not always easy to achieve.

The overall evidence indicates that even poor countries can make substantial progress in improving the human condition, but that it is difficult to maintain good performance in the absence of sustained economic growth. When growth is accompanied by a fairly equal distribution of income, improvements in the human condition are feasible with only moderate provision of public goods beyond ensuring universal access to primary education and health care. Especially during periods of required socio-economic adjustment, it is as important to monitor the quantity and quality of public sector human development oriented expenditure as it is to watch the macro-economic fiscal and monetary indicators which are currently still getting most of the attention.

In order to ensure sustained progress in human development, both a system's initial conditions and the actions pursued over time in generating primary income and the public provision of BN goods are relevant. For purposes of illustration only, in table 9.6 we differentiate four categories (and examples) of countries according to their initial conditions and the combinations of subsequent actions taken to ensure success.[20] The most difficult situation is represented by category I countries which have low income, poor human development performance, and poor income distribution as initial conditions. Nonetheless, some low-income countries of this type – Zimbabwe and Kenya – have managed to improve their human development performance significantly. On the other hand, poor human development performance by the category II countries is difficult to justify since their initially higher income levels put appropriate policies within easier reach. Such countries need to improve their primary income distribution, but could partially compensate for inadequate primary income distribution by strong and well-structured government BN allocations. Malaysia is a middle income country which succeeded in raising human development levels in this way.

The prospects of category III countries are significantly better than for category I, although they also start with low levels of per capita income. These countries have already registered good levels of human development because of their relatively equitable distribution of income. However, they need continued growth and expansion of appropriate across-the-board BN provision to accelerate progress. Historically, Taiwan, China and Sri Lanka have followed this strategy successfully – with Taiwan relying relatively more on primary income growth and its equitable distribution than the others. Lastly, category IV countries – for example, Costa Rica and Chile – should be able to attain and surpass DC levels of human development within a few years if they continue to combine appropriate public sector BN strategies with generally good growth and equity-oriented macro policies.

It should be emphasized that while well-designed public sector BN allocations can partially compensate for poor primary income distribution, they cannot make up for the absence of adequate economic growth over time. Consequently, policies to sustain or restore economic growth are necessary, if not sufficient, for every type of developing country.

CHAPTER 9   GROWTH, EQUITY AND HUMAN DEVELOPMENT

NOTES

1 A substantial literature dealing with this topic has followed the pioneering effort by Cornia, Jolly and Stewart (1987).
2 Ahluwalia, Nicholas, Carter, and Chenery (1979, p. 294).
3 See also Paukert (1973); Chenery, Ahluwalia, Bell, Duloy, and Jolly (1974); Ahluwalia (1976a, 1976b); Ahluwalia, Carter and Chenery (1979); Bacha (1978). In spite of the serious data shortcomings in many of these compilations, the basic Kuznets hypothesis seems to have been supported.
4 Ahluwalia, Carter, and Chenery (1979).
5 See also Fields (1988).
6 Fields (1989); Fields and Jakubsen (1990).
7 For a fuller exposition of our methodology and its application, see Fei, Ranis and Kuo (1979).
8 This statement is true for the "normal" case of production complementarity — that is, when $\epsilon < 1$. For the case of production substitutability — that is, when $\epsilon > 1$ — it is true when there is capital shallowing ($\eta_{K/L} < 0$) instead of capital deepening.
9 This was even more true during the fifties for which the absence of comprehensive family survey data rendered careful decomposition analysis impossible. Rural income data provided by the Joint Commission for Rural Reconstruction indicate that the marked fall in G_A during the 1950s can be

traced to Taiwan's well-known three-step land reform (1949–51) and its aftermath, plus enhanced multiple cropping and the shift in the composition of agricultural output from land-intensive sugar to labor-intensive vegetables which followed.

10 See chapter 6 of Fei, Ranis, and Kuo (1979) for a fuller analysis.

11 For a fuller assessment of the benefits of rural non-agricultural development in the dual economy setting, see Ranis and Stewart (1993).

12 Berry and Urrutia (1976).

13 See Berry and Soligo (1980); and Ranis (1980, table 4).

14 The discussion here follows Ayub (1977).

15 First introduced by the International Labour Office (1977).

16 The discussion of country scenarios which follows draws heavily on Chapter II of the *1990 Human Development Report*, in whose preparation one of the authors served as a consultant.

17 Improvements in other dimensions of the human condition — nutritional status, particularly that of pregnant mothers, infants and children, as well as educational achievement — are usually reflected in reductions in infant and child mortality rates. Estimates of life expectancy are strongly influenced by infant and child mortality rates. Of these two mortality rates, child death rates are likely to be less subject to erratic annual fluctuations. An examination of long-run trends in child mortality rates is, therefore, likely to provide a good summary index of the pattern of changes in the human conditions over long periods of time across different developing countries.

18 One of the serious problems facing us is that data on life expectancy, infant mortality, etc., are often interpolated and otherwise deficient. Moreover, except for rural/urban break-downs, such basic quality-of-life indicators usually do not carry distributional information, only average for the population as a whole.

19 In a recent series of studies Behrman and Schneider (1992, 1993) used World Bank data from 1965 to 1988 to examine the human capital and quality of life investments of the developing world and found support for this proposition.

20 Table 9.6, as well as the discussion relating to it, is largely based on the UNDP's *1990 Human Development Report*.

PART V

Conclusions for Policy

10

Policy and Political Economy in the Transition to Modern Economic Growth

10.1 Introduction

Earlier in this volume, we examined the theory of transition growth in the closed and subsequently the open dualistic economy. It is our purpose now to extend the framework of our analysis to the more realistic level of "open dualism," in which interactions with foreign countries, in terms of trade, capital movements, and technology constitute the additional critical dimensions of the analysis of modernization of the contemporary less developed economy.

The analysis of growth in the "open" dualistic economy represents a significant theoretical extension because the typical contemporary LDC initiated its post-war transition process based on a colonial heritage characterized by "openness" in both the economic and political senses. Such agrarian dualism or colonialism is pictured in figure 10.1. In the economic sense, colonialism implied long-run capital inflows aimed at the expansion of primary product exports from the enclave to the world market when the price trend of the primary product was favorable. Otherwise (that is, when the price trend was unfavorable) outward capital migration (long-run capital export) would occur to promote expansion at home or of primary products in other countries. In the political sense, colonialism implied domination by "imperialist" foreigners, much resented in the age of decolonization after World War II.[1] In long-run historical perspective, the demand for political and economic modernization by the ex-colonies was primarily a drive to emulate the economic system as well as the polity of the DCs.

With respect to economic modernization, the achievement of success in the context of "dualism" now, as before, requires the dynamic interaction between modernizing agricultural and non-agricultural sectors. We have already shown, in the closed economy context, that the agricultural sector can indeed only be effectively modernized via such interaction, so that

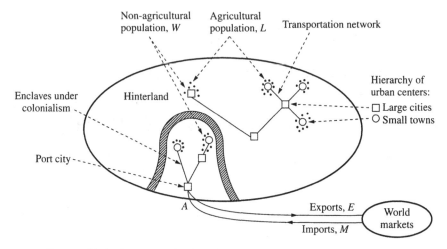

Figure 10.1 Agrarian dualism/colonialism in spatial perspective

agricultural productivity can be raised both by the infusion of modern inputs produced in the non-agricultural sector and the additional incentives provided by the appearance of new investment and consumption opportunities for successful farm families. On the other hand, the key to the continued growth of the non-agricultural sector is really centered in the acquisition of innovative capacities to produce an increasingly wide variety of new products, giving that sector a dynamic structural flexibility (that is, reflecting Akamatsu's "flying geese" or Vernon's product cycle) that reminds us of the development path of Japan over the past century.

Both of these basic economic tasks must be performed as well in the open economy setting, that is, the two sectors must learn not only to interact with each other but also with the rest of the world. Openness provides additional opportunities as well as challenges. New types and qualities of output, new processes, and additional capital now become potentially available. Not all foreign technologies are "appropriate" and there may be "neo-colonial" trade or capital export restrictions to contend with. However, if the developing economy makes itself master of its own house and chooses wisely, the advantages of openness hugely outweigh its risks. Imported technologies can be carefully selected and adapted to differing LDC conditions and restrictive foreign capital inflow conditions rejected. The tell-tale bottom line of success in mastering the open economy is that domestic producers gradually acquire the capacity to persistently sell a wide variety of continuously changing new products into world markets.

With respect to political modernization, the transition process implies a rearrangement of the relationship between government and society at large. Given the post-war climate of anti-colonialism, the new sovereign states find it essential to adopt growth promotion policies with certain distinguishing characteristics defining a particular mode of government-society relations. On the one hand, such policies are typically addressed to repair market failure and to exclude foreign influence, partly as an expression of a new-found sense of nationalism. Many contemporary LDCs thus initiated their transition process within a highly politicized economic framework and a distinct orientation toward autarky. The more heterogeneous the society, the more the government often found it necessary to supplement organic with synthetic measures to generate such nationalist impulses.

A central theme of this chapter is that, seen in long-run historical perspective, LDCs which start out with such a highly politicized economic system, associated with the so-called "import substitution syndrome", will ultimately experience a process of liberalization defined as the gradual reduction of such political interventions in the economy. We therefore suggest that to the six stylized facts of modern economic growth advanced by Kuznets[2] must be added this institutional aspect of gradual depoliticization of economic transactions. This process results from both a maturing of the political culture of "nationalism" and the increasing complexity of the production structure. Together, they gradually force the replacement of bureaucratic discretion by market mechanisms which, themselves deficient, are gradually repaired by government action in the course of the transition process.

In analyzing the growth experience of a contemporary LDC, one can choose to emphasize the quantifiable aspects of performance of the economy by describing "growth rapidity" indicators (for example, population, GNP or per capita GNP growth rates) and/or "structural changes" (such as the allocation of labor between the agricultural and non-agricultural sectors or the value of exports as a fraction of GNP) by the use of statistical data. These ways of tracing success have been the subject of extensive treatment in the profession[3] and will also be dealt with by us, if in a somewhat different, that is, evolutionary context. However, a central theme of this chapter will be to emphasize to the analytical economist what will appear to be an elusive and nebulous topic – that is, that of the institutional changes that must be accomplished if a traditional agrarian society is to be effectively modernized. Statistical data can play a useful, but nevertheless only a limited role, since institutional change involves changes in the mode of organization (for example, features relating to the relative roles of government policy and markets) as well as to so-called cultural values, including ideas and ideology.

Our analysis of the politico-economic institutional changes suggests that transition growth must indeed be viewed as a long-run evolutionary process requiring a "framework of thinking" as well as a "methodology" that will be sketched out in this chapter. While we intend to formally illustrate successful transition with the help of the experience of one particular case, Taiwan, our basic purpose is to propose a generally applicable methodology for the analysis of institutional change in an evolutionary context.

We shall, in section 10.2, briefly describe the key features of our proposed methodology for the study of transition growth in later sections.

10.2 Design for an Evolution-oriented Methodology

To the modern analytical economist, the methodology of evolutionary analysis is something of a lost art. In the early post-war period most attention was focused on cross-sectional approaches *à la* Chenery. More recently, micro-focused deterministic models have gained ascendancy.[4] Evolutionary analysis or analytical economic history is only very recently coming back into favor, witness the World Bank's recent multi-country comparative studies, including its "East Asian Miracle" effort.

At the heart of our evolutionary approach to transition growth as pursued in this chapter are five central ideas: (1) a holistic operational perspective; (2) a metamorphic sensitivity; (3) the notion of the conformity of policy evolution; (4) gradual depoliticization; and (5) typological specificity. These methodological features will be illustrated with the help of the specific Taiwan case to guide our discussion in later sections. It is useful to spell out these five dimensions in somewhat greater detail.

10.2.1 Holistic operational perspective

Ever since the French physiocrats, professional economists have used a holistic operational framework to provide an integrated treatment of production, consumption, exchange and income distribution, in a multi-sectoral context, covering the whole economy. (See chapter 1.) In fact the *tableau economique*, with its duality of production and household structures as between the agricultural and non-agricultural sectors, needs to be modified only slightly via the addition of a "foreign sector" to yield a holistic framework suitable for the analysis of the open dualistic economy. Figures 10.2–10.6, to be taken up in detail in section 10.3 below, provide a concrete view of the holistic perspective applied to our specific problem.

10.2.2 Metamorphic sensitivity

Post-war transition growth may be interpreted as a metamorphic process as both the "forms" (morphology) and "rules of operation" (physiology) went through evolutionary phases. For example, Taiwan, emerging from its pre-war 1895–1950 colonial state, passed through three clearly demarcatable sub-phases of transition growth: Phase I, the import substitution (IS) sub-phase (approximately 1950–62); Phase II, the external orientation (EO) sub-phase (approximately 1962–80); and Phase III, the science and technology orientation (TO) sub-phase (1980–).

The transition process over these three phases is shown in the sequence of circular flow diagrams (figures 10.2–10.6) depicting a metamorphic process beginning with the heritage of "agrarian colonialism" (premodern phase) and moving into the epoch of modern economic growth that follows sub-phase III. In the open dualistic economy, the modernization of the agricultural and industrial sectors must occur via the interaction among three sectors, agriculture, non-agriculture and the foreign sector. The focal point of our analysis is laying stress on the logical necessity of the evolution from one sub-phase to the next if there is to be success, a process that implies the modernization of both the agricultural and non-agricultural sectors.

10.2.3 Conformity of policy evolution

A central component of the evolutionary approach to transition growth is to regard changes in policy as accommodating or conforming to changes in the underlying conditions of the economy as it passes through various sub-phases. In this regard, what differentiates the contemporary LDC from the typical DC (at its starting point) is, as we have already pointed out, the large array of direct growth promotion policies typically in place early on. We shall find it useful to differentiate between two types of such policies, that is, those that are pervasive or across-the-board (in the sense of affecting all sectors) and those which are non-pervasive or sector-specific. Typical pervasive growth promotion policies, sometimes called macro-economic policies, include:

1 domestically oriented fiscal policies;
2 external trade related fiscal policies;
3 monetary policies related to the interest rate;
4 monetary policies related to the foreign exchange rate;
5 policies on international capital movements.

Typical sector-specific growth promotion policies, sometimes called structural policies, include:

6   management of public sector enterprises and the construction of economic and social infrastructure;
7   specific agriculture- or industry-oriented policies;
8   manpower, labor and education-focused policies;
9   development of science and technology-oriented policies;
10   development policy and planning.

The conformity of policy evolution with the notion of transition through sub-phases represents the key methodological innovation of this chapter. It is demonstrated by application to the particular case of Taiwan and depicted in the policy matrix of table 10.1. While the ten categories of policies (I–X) are indicated in the rows, the three main sub-phases are indicated along the horizontal time axis. The policies enacted at any point in time are indicated in the boxes of this evolutionary chart. Given our approach to the problem of understanding the transition process, the more than 100 major policy events summarized in this policy matrix constitute the equivalent of primary statistical data.

In comparative economic theorizing, the adoption and implementation of policy is usually regarded as an "exogenous event" (the occurrence of which really need not be explained) such that the analytical focus falls entirely on the prediction of the behavior of the so-called "endogenous" variables, for example, growth and/or equity performance in terms of our model. While inquiries into the precise impact of various policies still have a major role to play, the notion of the conformity (or lack of conformity) of policy with basic evolutionary forces suggests that tracing such impacts is by no means our exclusive or even main purpose. Indeed what we are searching for is an improved understanding of the causation of policy formation itself, that is, rendering it akin to an endogenous phenomenon as part of our evolutionary approach to the transition process.

10.2.4 Depoliticization

In our view, the timely appearance and disappearance of particular policies carries its own logical necessity as part of a causation system that can be identified only when examined in the context of the metamorphosis of the operations of the entire system over time. In this regard, growth promotion policies should be viewed as but a part of changes in the politico-economic institutions in the long term direction of depoliticization or liberalization, a trend that can be revealed by the policy content. In other words, a policy evolution matrix is useful because it is focused on the specific issue of depoliticization which is the central theme of this chapter.

The enactment and implementation of a growth promotion policy always involves a political process. For this reason, the policy content of any measure is always the product of the political culture or the current societal consensus concerning the appropriate role of government and of markets. As an economy moves towards economic maturity, entailing increased complexity in technology, output mixes, and trade patterns, changes in the ideal role of public and private sector activities represent an important component of the meaning of modern economic growth.

Institutional change involves both the materialism associated with economic efficiency and ideology associated with the power of ideas. Depoliticization or liberalization must ultimately occur because the modernizing economy becomes increasingly too complicated to be directly planned and commanded by bureaucrats; since government interventions to address various types of market failure may be quite pervasive early on, its role is bound to change gradually once people believe that the time has come. When we examine in a concrete successful case, such as Taiwan's, the evolution of policies within a holistic operational perspective we can obtain a clear and concrete view of the necessity of a changing role for government from one directly guiding the economy via specific "horizontal" actions, to one creating the institutions which will permit its more general "vertical" actions to work themselves out via the improved functioning of various markets.

10.2.5 Typological sensitivity

In order to illustrate our methodology, we really have no alternative but to choose some country, preferably one which has been successful, such as Taiwan. Clearly, as we shall see below, there is no inevitability attached to the accommodative nature of policy change. Moreover, we acknowledge that to a certain extent the experience of each and every country is unique. But that does not mean that we cannot deduce general lessons from such an analysis. Certainly there exist strong family resemblances among groups of countries which encourage the use of a typological approach to individual country experience. Thus, an analysis of the evolution of Taiwan over a period of some 40 years has transferable value even if it cannot capture all the details relevant to other members of the family, not to speak of countries belonging to different families of LDCs.

The basic "uniqueness" of types rather than simply individual countries is traceable to differences definable in terms of certain initial endowments of the economic-geographic variety (for example, a relative abundance of

Table 10.1 Policy matrix for the Taiwan economy

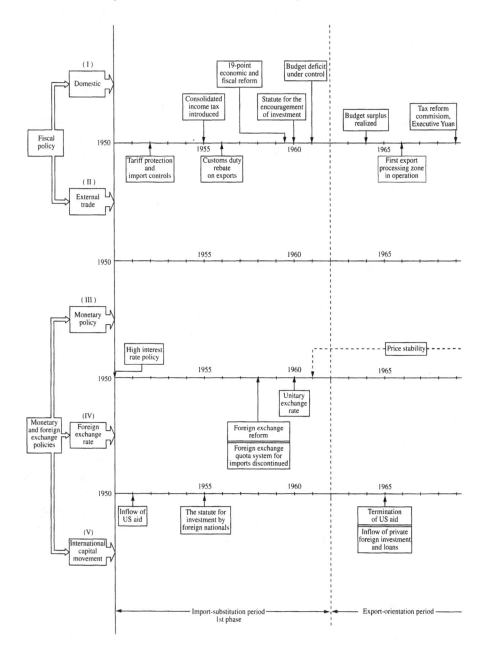

Table 10.1 cont'd

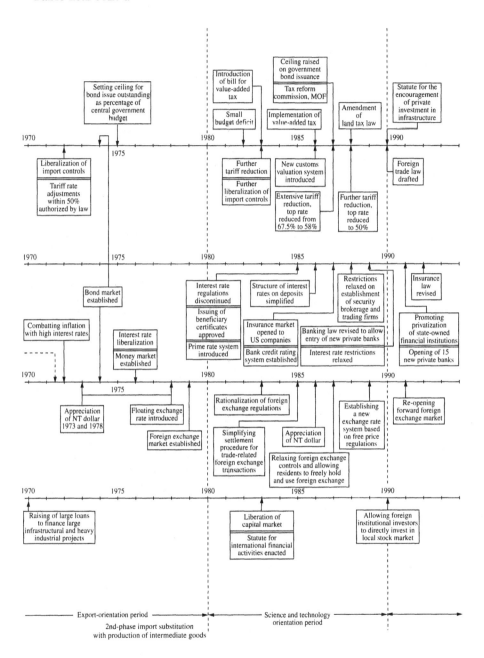

Table 10.1 cont'd

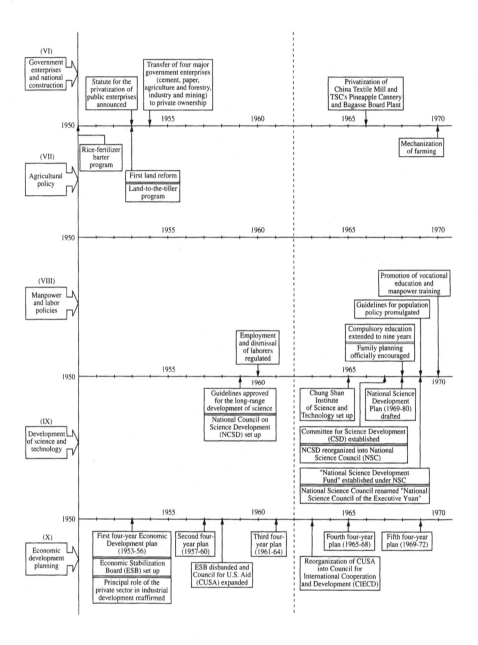

Table 10.1 cont'd

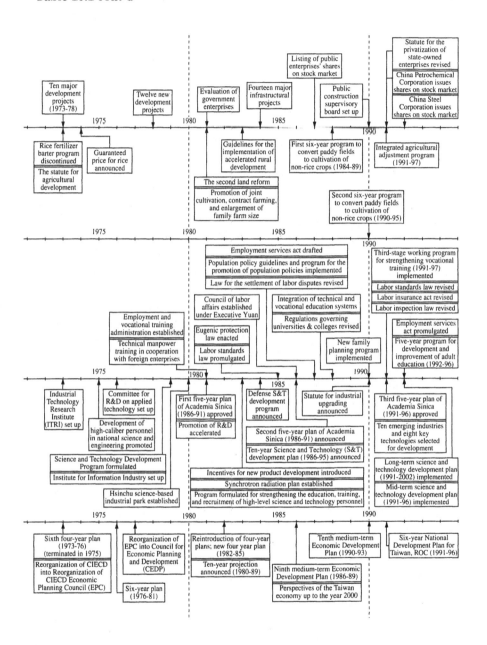

labor, land or natural resources) and/or of the historical-cultural variety (for example, colonial experience and the tradition of education or commercial entrepreneurship that broadly defines the attribute of "human resources"). The transition growth of Taiwan is relevant to the type of LDC characterized by the deficiency of natural resources and the abundance of low cost but relatively high quality human resources.

Typologically speaking, the transition growth experience of Taiwan thus represents that of a labor surplus open dualistic economy, relatively small and characterized by heavy population pressure on the land, a shortage of natural resources and a favorable human resource base. It also represents a case of outstanding developmental success. Along with South Korea, Hong Kong and Singapore, these four NICs have demonstrated the importance of a shift from a land-based to an unskilled labor-based and ultimately a human resources-based development pattern. Korea and Taiwan, undoubtedly less "special" and therefore more generalizable than the two city-states, are clearly about to terminate their transition journey and join the ranks of the industrially advanced countries. Others in the region, including Thailand, Indonesia and Malaysia, are currently in the process of pursuing a somewhat similar path.

The rest of this chapter follows the "methodological design" outlined above. We shall first analyze the evolutionary process through its various sub-phases (section 10.3). This is followed by an examination of the policy sequence traced by means of the policy evolution matrix, with a view to analyzing policies within our holistic operational perspective (section 10.4). Finally, in section 10.5, we briefly discuss the political economy dimensions of policy and policy change from this evolutionary perspective.

10.3 Evolution through Sub-phases

10.3.1 Agrarian dualism or colonialism as the initial condition

We shall begin with an analysis of the metamorphic evolution of the economic system from its initial colonial or open agrarian status. In the economic sense such "colonialism" was formed as the result of the penetration of agrarian dualism in the traditional closed economy context by the impact of foreigners' interest in trade and capital flows associated with the formation and functioning of colonialism. Both agrarian dualism and colonialism have spatial features that need to be recognized. This will then permit us to present the holistic operational functions of colonialism as the point of departure for the transition into modern growth.

The spatial perspective of agrarian dualism stresses an urban–rural dichotomy. As shown in figure 10.1, the urban sector is composed of a set of hierarchical urban centers linked up by a transportation network. Its dualism is definable in terms of the location pattern of the population, namely, the juxtaposition of a spatially concentrated urban population to the dispersed rural population that surrounds these cities. From an economic standpoint, agrarian dualism depicts the spatial pattern of a division of labor based on agricultural and non-agricultural production. The land space is knitted together by mercantile activities as is typical under commercial capitalism, with capital goods composed of the inventories of the merchant class deployed as working capital. The development of a holistic perspective for the operation of agrarian dualism was the major contribution of the physiocrats during the eighteenth century.

The penetration of such closed agrarianism by foreigners leads to the formation of a colonial system with a spatial feature known as enclaves. Typically, a colonial enclave covers that part of the land space linked up by a transportation network leading to a port city (*A* in figure 10.1). The land space is partitioned into two parts, representing the coexistence of a usually relatively large and backward hinterland of traditional agrarian dualism with a relatively small outward-oriented modern enclave; the latter, by virtue of being an extension of the motherland, is already characterized by the important role of modern science and technology.

The economic life of this enclave is clearly dominated by its virtually exclusive focus on the recovery and export of some primary products, that is, the output of such natural resource-specific products as cash crop agriculture and mineral products shipped to world markets. In exchange, modern factory-produced consumer goods (such as textiles) are shipped into the enclave to induce workers to move from the hinterland into the enclave, as well as capital goods to expand its relative size.

In spite of its external orientation, the enclave retains much of the commercial capital content of agrarian dualism. In addition to internal trade between agricultural and Z-goods or rural non-agricultural activities (see chapter 8), such commercial capital is used primarily to serve the needs of the export trade, for example, via warehousing, transportation and finance, or to process trade-related goods. The colonial import of factory-made textiles often threatens the survival of pre-existing Z-good equivalents. The appearance of domestic modern factories, using industrial capital stock to produce for the domestic market, is a story reserved for a later sub-phase of the transition growth process.

While the above spatial perspective is meant to be representative of the "typical" colonial economy, there exist certain unique features of Japanese colonialism on Taiwan (1895–1945). Given Japan's own needs and Taiwan's deficiency in natural resources, Taiwan's exports to Japan during the colonial period were mainly rice and sugar. In view of its relatively small size and its topology, dominated by the rich agricultural region on the west coast, the customary colonial dichotomy between hinterland and colonial enclave was substantially attenuated. Given that the export cash crop was simultaneously a food crop, the Japanese colonial administration paid a lot of attention to physical and institutional infrastructural investments in the rural areas. This included land reform (1905) and emphasis on irrigation, roads, and electricity, as well as on rice research, extension, farmers' associations and primary education. The west coast of Taiwan especially may be viewed as a well-connected enclave. The linkage between agricultural and non-agricultural or Z-goods activities in the rural areas was unusually strong as a consequence, as were contacts between rural households and urban activities. In short, the colonial heritage of Taiwan was such that it was relatively easy for the agricultural sector to be modernized in line with the inter-sectoral "contact" school of thought, that is, the idea that locational adjacency and interactions with the non-agricultural sector represent an essential precondition for balanced growth as discussed from the theoretical point of view in chapter 3.

The skeleton of a model presenting a holistic perspective on the operation of colonialism is presented in figure 10.2. Succinctly, domestic market duality between agricultural and non-agricultural production and households is shown in juxtaposition to the foreign sector, the world market. The economic life-line of colonialism is centered on primary product exports E that flow from the agricultural sector to the mother country in exchange for imported non-durable consumer goods (M). Notice that in figure 10.2, solid arrows indicate the flow of monetary payments, opposite to the direction of the real flows, marked by dotted arrows.

In addition to supplying primary products to world markets, the agricultural sector also produces food for the domestic market (F in figure 10.2). The domestic non-agricultural production sector is shown primarily as a sector that produces relatively simple industrial goods and services (Z-goods), mainly for the domestic market and involving the use mainly of commercial, rather than industrial, capital.

Monetary incomes generated by the primary product exports (E) are used for two types of imports (M), that of consumer non-durables for households and that of producers' goods required for the expansion of enclave export activities. The domestic labor force P is allocated partly to the agricultural sector (L) and partly to the industrial sector (W), with an overwhelming proportion, typically from 60 percent to 80 percent, allocated to agricultural activities. Moreover, this allocation pattern is typically characterized by previously described agrarian stagnation, with the total population expanding only slowly. However, here again, given Japan's unusual colonial interest in rice and sugar production, agricultural

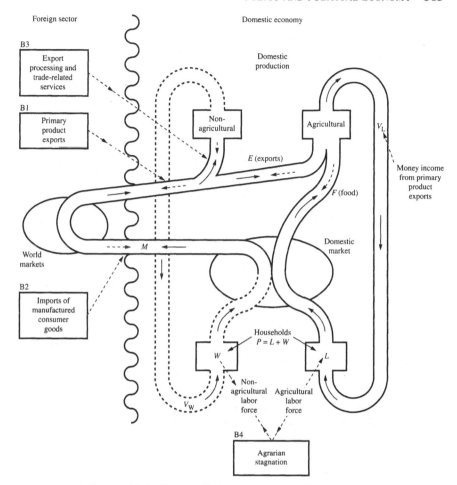

Foreign sector

Domestic economy

B3
Export processing and trade-related services

B1
Primary product exports

B2
Imports of manufactured consumer goods

World markets

Domestic production

Non-agricultural

Agricultural V_L

E (exports)

F (food)

Money income from primary product exports

M

Domestic market

Households
$P = L + W$

W L

Non-agricultural labor force   Agricultural labor force

V_W

B4
Agrarian stagnation

Figure 10.2   Colonialism in operational perspective

output rose an amazing 4 percent annually on Taiwan during most of the colonial era. Moreover, complementary Z-goods production was allowed as long as it did not compete directly with factory-made imports from Japan. While population growth was modest, land was scarce, and Taiwan can be characterized as a typical labor surplus open dualistic economy.

Our holistic operational perspective thus permits us to see colonialism as a system in which production, consumption, labor allocation, as well as imports and exports, form a definite morphological pattern that describes the interaction of three sectors through time. Notice that a number of strategically located boxes (labelled B1, B2, B3, B4) are shown in figure 10.2 to help us emphasize certain salient features of colonialism. Succinctly: B1 represents the reliance on primary product exports (E) directed at world markets, mainly the mother country; B2 represents the importation of manufactured consumer (and some producer) goods (M) for domestic markets; B3 represents minor non-agricultural production for export, in addition to the predominant Z-goods, mostly small-scale domestic market-related goods and services, not shown here; finally, B4 stresses the notion of long-term agrarian stagnation under colonialism.

The operation of colonialism describes a particular pattern of interactions among the three sectors, agriculture, non-agriculture, and the foreign sector. It is through the alternation of this pattern of interactions that we can analyze the metamorphism in the transition process in an evolutionary perspective. The first step that was taken in Taiwan, and elsewhere, at the end of the colonial era was the emergence of a new pattern of interaction, commonly referred to in the literature as the process of import substitution (IS) growth.

We should note that some limited import substitution is likely to already occur during the late colonial era. It is quite likely, for example, that the mother country may decide, on the basis of transport cost and comparative advantage considerations, to place some factories producing non-durable consumer goods in the colony. This is especially true when the domestic market is relatively large, as in colonial India or China. For example, during the 20-year period from 1911 to 1933 on the Chinese mainland, modern textile factories began to appear in the coastal cities to replace some simple domestic Z-goods as well as some of the textile products previously imported from England and Japan. By the time the People's Republic was established in 1949, the 570 million Chinese were clothed largely by domestically produced manufactured goods. Indeed, the exportation of some textiles was already a major component of China's foreign exchange earnings in the 1950s, alongside the still dominant primary product exports.

In this sense, the post-independence IS phase on Taiwan may be seen as the continuation of an historical process and not simply the result of policy change by a newly independent government. The import substitution process is in part a natural consequence of a successful primary product export economy generating higher incomes. Modern factories appeared in China's coastal cities for a rational reason, namely, that it proved cheaper to import capital goods and make use of cheap Chinese labor while saving transport costs. The familiar policy package used by the contemporary LDC to promote IS growth – that is, the over-valued exchange rate and protective tariffs which excluded imported manufactured goods from the domestic markets (see below) – can thus be seen as accommodating or supplementing pre-existing tendencies and accelerating them. Their relative importance depends mainly on country size.

We intend first to discuss the story of the initiation of IS growth as an evolutionary process somewhat independent of government policies. The latter clearly provide an additional boost but play a less dominant promotional role than is ordinarily assumed by most analysts. Indeed, the fact that one can find reasons for the natural appearance of IS growth, independent of policy intervention, is an essential part of our evolutionary or metamorphic approach to transition growth.

10.3.2 Initial sub-phase of transition: import substitution (1950–62)

Import substitution growth constitutes the initial post-colonial sub-phase for virtually all contemporary LDCs emerging from colonial antecedents. In analyzing this important growth phase within an evolutionary perspective, the following issues need to be addressed:

1 the very meaning of "import substitution" as a holistic operational system;
2 its salient features;
3 the relevance of the colonial heritage from an economic standpoint;
4 its relevance from a political standpoint; and
5 the causation of the necessary termination of the IS sub-phase.

Import substitution as a growth type   It should be noted at the outset that import substitution represents a particular growth type that can be identified within a holistic operational perspective as shown in figure 10.3. The fact that IS-growth descends directly from colonialism can be demonstrated by noting that figure 10.3 can be directly derived from figure 10.2 with but slight modifications. This underlines our contention that an evolutionary approach implies changes that preserve a tradition, that is, historical continuity; nature indeed does not "make jumps."

In this growth type total foreign exchange earnings from primary product exports (E) are now diverted from the importation of manufactured non-durable consumer goods (M_C) (and some enclave-destined producer goods) to the importation of manufactured producer goods (M_p) (that carry modern science and technology). The latter build up the capital stock (K) of industries that can produce domestically manufactured consumer goods (C) to gradually replace previously imported consumer non-durables (M_C). The accumulation of an industrial capital stock (financed by domestic savings out of agriculture and non-agriculture, S_a and S_i, and possibly supplemented by foreign savings S_f), serves to attract labor

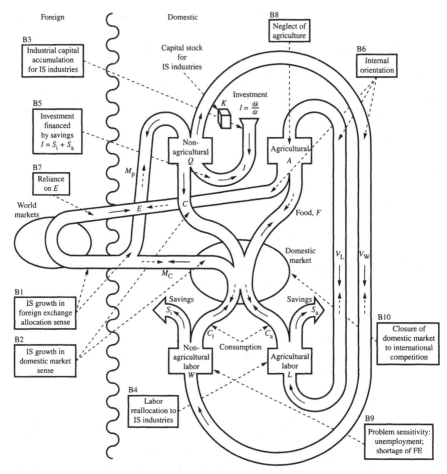

Figure 10.3 Import substitution in operational perspective

released by the agricultural sector in a balanced growth context. This summary sketch indicates quite clearly that import substitution is a growth type involving an integrated system of production, consumption, labor allocation, capital accumulation, finance, and international trade that can only be described within a holistic operational perspective.

The salient features of import substitution growth IS growth has many salient (and unique) features that can be identified with the help of figure 10.3 as indicated in the strategically located boxes (B1, B2, etc.) that can guide our discussion.

There are two meanings to the notion of "substitution," namely, in the "foreign exchange allocation" sense (B1), and in the "domestic market" sense (B2). With respect to B1, the foreign exchange earnings from primary product exports (E) were diverted from the importation of largely manufactured consumer (M_C) to producer goods (M_p). Modern factory produced products first introduced under colonialism helped create a consumption habit which now comes into full bloom.

Import substitution in the domestic market sense (B2) implies that the domestic output of manufactured non-durable consumer goods (C) gradually substitutes for the previously imported goods (M_C) in the domestic market. "Substitution" in this sense has an autarky connotation as foreign products (M_C) are now gradually excluded from the domestic market unless they are judged to be absolutely essential for the modernization of domestic productive capacity. Substitution in both these senses reflects the political culture of anti-colonialism.

The arrival of IS growth clearly signifies the termination of commercial capitalism as industrial capital stock is now being accumulated (B3). Crucial analytical facets relevant to the analysis of a closed dualistic economy remain valid. On the one hand, as shown in B4, there is the reallocation of agricultural labor (L) into the newly formed import substituting industries that can be readily traced via the use of our growth equations (see B3 and chapter 7). On the other hand, agricultural and non-agricultural savings (S_a and S_i) are channelled to finance investments (I) in the import substituting industries (B5). Inter- and intra-sectoral finance relate to some of the more important policy issues in the transition growth process, as we shall see below.

IS growth obviously carries an internal orientation (B6) as can be seen from the stagnation and even decline of total exports (E) as a fraction of GNP, the sum of values added V_L and V_W of the two domestic production sectors. Internal orientation in this sense is thus a special feature of IS growth that contrasts sharply with the later external orientation sub-phase.

Relevance of colonialism to IS growth from an economic standpoint   That IS growth descends directly from colonialism can be seen from B7, emphasizing the continued reliance on primary product exports; B8, the tendency towards the continued relative neglect of the agricultural sector; and B9, highlighting the central problem of the IS era.

A central feature of IS growth is indeed the continued role of primary product exports (E) as the major fuel for growth. This implies that in interactions with the rest of the world, the domestic economy continues to rely on its natural resources endowment rather than its human resources – including its disciplined, if still relatively unskilled, labor force – as the basis of its comparative advantage position. The IS growth phase is as non-conducive to a fuller exploration of the system's human resources potential as was the colonial era.

Given the relative neglect of agriculture (B8) as a consequence of the well-known package of policies favoring the new industrial class, the IS growth phase is typically characterized by structural stagnation as the labor force's absorption into the import substituting industrial activities (W) may barely keep pace with population growth, that is, the critical minimum effort criterion is barely met, resulting in the persistence of the labor surplus condition.

We have earlier on examined this problem of the sluggishness of labor absorption due primarily to agricultural neglect and the fact that the technology employed in the import substituting industrial sector carries insufficient technology intensity, plus a capital using bias, conditions that can well be explained by the fact that the IS phase is non-competitive and does not adequately call on the system's human or technological capabilities. It follows that, typically, throughout the IS phase, unemployment or underemployment, accompanied by high but inefficient industrial growth, remains the key social problem. Moreover, given the continued exclusive reliance on primary product exports and the import intensity of industrialization, the system usually encounters severe foreign exchange (FE) shortages (B9). Sensitivity to these problems, created by the very processes of IS growth, then leads to the emergence of the next phase, an export-oriented phase.

It should be noted that the IS phase in Taiwan was relatively milder and shorter than is typically the case. This is reflected in the relatively strong performance of agriculture, the relatively less severe application of some of the IS policies (for example, early interest rate reform, early shift from quantitative restrictions to tariffs), and the fact that non-agricultural labor absorption (at 3 percent per year) more or less managed to keep up with population growth, thus at least not adding to the pre-existing labor surplus.

Relevance of colonialism to IS growth from a political standpoint   The policy package chosen under this widely accepted initial sub-phase of transition is very much the product of a new political culture emerging in an era of anti-colonialism. On the one hand, both foreign products and foreign investment are generally excluded from domestic markets. On the other hand, the need to create national cohesion, or Kuznetsian nationalism, usually leads to political activism in the form of a variety of growth promotion policies underlining the omnipresence of government and the application of government power in the young sovereign state. Two additional political traits usually become prominent in this era (B10). One constitutes a poorly concealed fear of competition by the new industrial class, usually taking the form of adherence to public or quasi-public industrial activity, along with the private sector's felt need to seek, and obtain, protection, privileged market position and power.

The causation of the termination of the IS sub-phase   While virtually all contemporary LDCs (including Taiwan) initiated their transition process with IS growth, Taiwan (as well as some of the other East Asian "miracle" countries, such as Korea) was conspicuous by the relative mildness (see above) as well as the relatively early termination of this sub-phase. While the phase lasted little more than a decade (1950–62 in Taiwan, 1953–65 in Korea), it has proven a long, protracted process ranging over many decades elsewhere, such as in Latin America.

There is a general tendency for early IS, focused on non-durable consumer goods, to run out of steam once the domestic market for such goods has essentially been exhausted and expands only at the slower pace of per capita income and population increase. At this stage some societies, for example Latin America, persevere with IS but now increasingly of the backward linkage (durables, capital goods, raw material processing) variety. Others move on. The relatively early termination of IS growth in Taiwan or Korea may be seen as an essentially typological phenomenon traced to their small size and, more importantly, to the relative scarcity of natural resources and abundance of cheap labor of good quality. As already mentioned, the continued reliance on primary product exports is a prominent feature of IS growth. When societies are favorably endowed with such exportable natural resources, IS growth can be carried on longer, along with the characteristic "rent-seeking" struggles among various interest groups.

In the case of Taiwan, however, the IS process had to terminate rather more quickly. Once primary product exports can no longer expand without apparent limit, the fuel for the continued importation of producer goods runs out – as does the ability to produce, and possibly export with the help of subsidies, an increasingly high-cost and inefficient output mix. Thus, as the problem of the shortage of foreign exchange and of industrial sector slowdown become increasingly unbearable, a country like Taiwan is actually forced by the very success of its early export-discouraging policies (see 10.3.3 below) to drop the IS strategy.

It should be added that foreign capital, mainly public, can provide an additional way of providing rents and fuelling the prolongation of IS policies. It is a fact, however, that while foreign aid was of substantial importance in Taiwan in the 1950s, as well as in easing the pains of regime change in the early 1960s, it was the simultaneous announcement that such aid would cease altogether by 1965 which provided an additional impetus.

We have here a clear-cut example of our notion of the "conformity of policy evolution." The formation of policy can be seen as a substantially endogenous event caused by the initial conditions plus evolving mode of operation of the system; the IS policies were gradually abandoned in Taiwan for the same reason that an external orientation phase subsequently made its appearance.

10.3.3 Externally oriented (EO) primary export substitution (PES) sub-phase (1962–70)

The EO–PES sub-phase occurred quite naturally in Taiwan for both positive and negative reasons. We have already noted that the shortage of exportable natural resources meant that IS growth could not be financed indefinitely. Moreover, the fact that Taiwan was endowed with surplus labor, the potential of which could only be fully explored in the EO phase, constitutes a positive reason for the switch in regimes. That the EO phase in turn descends directly from the IS sub-phase can be seen with the help of figure 10.4, which turns out to be but a slight morphological modification of figure 10.3.

The salient defining features of the EO-PES sub-phase can be seen as two-fold (see figure 10.4):

E1 enhanced external orientation of the non-agricultural sector;
E2 labor as a vent for surplus sold into world markets in the form of non-agricultural exports.

It should be noted that industrial exports associated with a prolongation of import substitution – sometimes called export promotion in the old Latin American style – does not qualify. Such exports are typically capital intensive and require subsidization. The advent of the true EO sub-phase for Taiwan can be associated with success in transition growth, as seen from the following elements of performance:

E3 rapid growth of GNP;
E4 rapid rate of labor reallocation from agriculture to non-agriculture;
E5 rapid pace of increased external orientation;
E6 eventual termination of the labor surplus condition;
E7 improved income distribution equity.

The story of developmental success is based on the achievement of balanced growth, as defined earlier, but now extended to three sectors, each playing functionally specific, essential, and complementary roles:

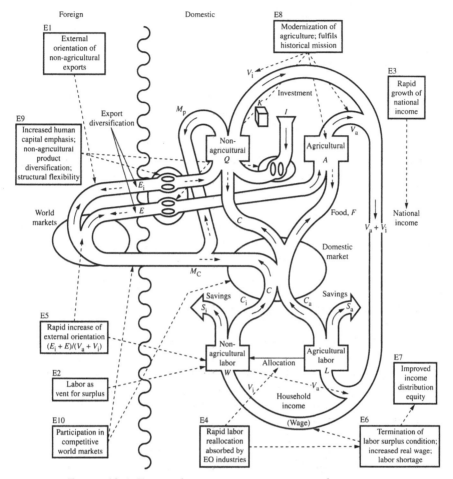

Figure 10.4 External orientation in operational perspective

E8   gradual modernization of agriculture;

E9   continuous modernization of non-agriculture, leading to the maintenance of dynamic structural flexibility;

E10   enhanced participation in competitive international markets.

In what follows, we shall discuss these notions in the order indicated.

The Meaning of EO–PES as a Growth Sub-phase (E1 and E2)   The external orientation sub-phase arrives once the non-agricultural sector begins

to produce goods for the world market (E_i). Labor intensive non-agricultural exports E_i gradually replace the role of traditional agricultural exports E as the major foreign exchange earner. We have referred to this type of EO growth as primary export substitution (PES) growth.

The arrival of the EO–PES sub-phase represents a significant landmark. The competitive exportation of labor-intensive non-durable manufactured goods – previously directed exclusively at the domestic market – implies that, for the first time in the life cycle of the LDC, a way has been found to fully utilize the system's surplus labor. On Taiwan this new pattern was accommodated by liberalization in various markets plus such transitional devices as export processing zones and import duty rebates (see below). Unskilled but high quality labor may be viewed as representing a vent for surplus in exchange for which capital and technology-intensive producer goods can be imported. Human resources characterized by an increasingly unlimited potential thus gradually replace natural resources as the basis of the system's comparative advantage.

The Success of the EO-PES Sub-phase (E3, E4, E5, E6, E7)   The success of the full exploration of the system's unemployed and underemployed human resources during the EO sub-phase can be statistically measured by various performance indicators (that is E3–E7). Thus, the rapidity of per capita income growth (E3) and of structural change (E4) are two familiar indices deployed by Kuznets. The rapid pace of increased external orientation (E5) which signifies the enhanced integration of the domestic economy with that of the rest of the world can be measured by the foreign trade ratio (for example, exports as a fraction of GNP).

Once such a triangular balanced growth process proceeds long enough and fast enough, it is bound to culminate in the drying up of the reservoir of surplus labor as replenished by population and labor force growth. Non-agricultural sector labor absorption in Taiwan during this period exceeded 5 percent annually, almost double that of the IS sub-phase and well ahead of a population growth rate declining towards 2 percent per year. The ultimate termination of the labor surplus condition (E6) clearly represents a significant landmark in the development of the labor surplus economy, with many economic as well as social implications. Most importantly, there results the first sustained increase in unskilled real wages – as labor becomes, for the first time in the system's life cycle, a scarce factor in the marketplace. The implied boost in average incomes, in the distribution of income, and in consumption standards, obviously carries significant welfare implications for the working population.

As rapid EO–PES growth runs its course this also signals a gradual change in perception as to what constitutes the system's basic socio-economic problem. Concerns with unemployment and the foreign exchange shortages of the IS-phase gradually weaken. At the end, the agricultural sector begins to mechanize as signals indicate the advent of labor shortage. Once commercialization is reached, the combination of full employment and higher wages ensures further improvement in income distribution (E7). While Taiwan's performance during the IS sub-phase was better than that of the typical (Latin American) LDC, the primary focus of the so-called East Asian "miracle" is directed to the EO–PES sub-phase of the 1960s.

Further modernization of agriculture after fulfilling its historical mission (E8) In our analysis of the closed dualistic economy, we showed that a major task in the course of transition is the modernization of the traditional agricultural sector. This is accomplished via a set of agricultural/non-agricultural interactions, by means of which modern factory-produced inputs (such as new seeds and fertilizer), as well as incentive consumer goods, are supplied to farmers in exchange for the agricultural surplus, mainly in the form of food supplied to the non-agricultural population. In the case of the open dualistic economy, this interaction can take two alternative forms. In addition to selling their surpluses in the domestic market (F), domestic farmers can also sell into world markets (E). Monetary income from both sources (V_a) can be used to acquire factory-produced incentive consumer goods or modern inputs in the domestic market (C_a).

There are certain features of this "interactions" approach to the agricultural sector's mobilization which deserve to be especially stressed here, namely: (1) commercialization of farmers via product diversification; (2) temporal priority; and (3) abandonment of the typical pro-urban bias in growth promotion policies.

1 *Commercialization.* The heart of the modernization of agriculture always resides in the modernization of farmers themselves, that is, the conversion of traditional risk-averse and "survival oriented" actors into modern economic agents – capitalist farmers – sensitive to inter-sectoral opportunities, market prices, profits and asset accumulation.

In the case of Taiwan the foundations for agricultural mobilization were laid in the IS phase through land reform (consisting of rent reductions, a land-to-the-tillers program, plus distribution of government land) in an effort to convince farmers that they could become masters of their own destiny. Moreover, as was already pointed out, the physical and institutional infrastructure provided to farmers early on, along with the government's reluctance to unduly distort the domestic terms of trade against them, made a substantial contribution.

Nevertheless, the full commercialization process could prosper in earnest only in the early EO phase as farmers began to diversify and learned to send new products (first fruits and vegetables, then mushrooms and asparagus) into world markets.

It should also be noted that the first explosion of non-agricultural exports in Taiwan during the 1960s occurred in food processing. In this way, the continued commercialization of the agricultural sector allowed it to complete its historical mission before atrophying to become a mere appendage of the industrial sector. In the case of Taiwan, such further commercialization was accomplished during the EO–PES sub-phase and was accompanied by a process of product diversification. In spite of the shortage of natural resources, Taiwan's farmers managed for a time to send waves of new products into world markets quite similar to the industrial products sent by the urban entrepreneurial class of Korea.

2 *Temporal priority.* In the course of our analysis of dualism we came to the conclusion that agricultural modernization is a precondition for successful industrialization, that is, as a way of fueling the expansion of the non-agricultural sector via its increased contribution to savings (S_a), generating food surpluses (F), its release of labor, and, in the case of the "open" model, providing foreign exchange resources (E). Accomplishing these various "historical missions" in a balanced growth context must come relatively early in the transition process, that is, before the agricultural sector becomes a mere appendage to the industrial sector – as a result of continuous labor reallocation, the workings of Engel's Law, and the change in the economy's center of gravity as full commercialization point is achieved.

In the case of Taiwan, agricultural output diversification occurred prior to and stimulated non-agricultural output and sector diversification. Moreover, while agricultural productivity increase was formidable, at better than 4.2 percent per year throughout the 1960s, by the time the EO phase ended the agricultural sector was indeed becoming an appendage of the non-agricultural sector in terms of the relative weights of value added (V_a, V_i), of labor force composition (W, L), and of the composition of exports (E, E_i).

3 *Rejection of "pro-urban bias" in growth promotion policies.* The urban-rural dichotomy shown from a spatial perspective in figure 10.1 suggested that the traditional colonial society was already characterized by a distinct pro-urban enclave bias. Indeed, the economic hierarchy of urban centers pictured there coincides with the hierarchy of political power (central, provincial, local governments), implying that spatially dispersed farmers are normally located near the lower end of the power structure. The elite at that time is composed of foreigners

and their domestic collaborators who, together, control the raw material exports-focused enclave. Once IS takes over, the elite, possibly drawn from the same sources, becomes the new industrial class, public or private, usually heavily urban-oriented.

The resulting pro-urban bias is usually pervasive, in terms of infrastructural allocation, terms of trade distortions, etc.[5] Agricultural mobilization, its diversification and commercialization, as well as the survival and growth of Z-goods can, of course, be slowed or even blocked by a pronounced bias of this type. It is obviously severely hampered if the rural population is discriminated against by politically manipulated terms of trade which deprive them of both the means and the incentive to raise agricultural productivity at its source, to diversify, and to engage in rural balanced growth, as between food and Z-goods production. This has traditionally been the pattern during early IS and IS prolongation in most developing countries. While DC governments usually subsidize farmers, LDC governments invariably exploit them. In the case of an open economy, with farmers producing for world markets, the most effective way to implement a mildly pro-urban bias during IS has been to exploit exporting farmers covertly via an overvalued exchange rate. In the case of Taiwan, the elimination of this bias against all exporters (including farmers) was a key policy measure that initiated the EO sub-phase.

The pro-urban bias during IS was, moreover, relatively mild in this instance; in addition, once the system moved into its SES version of EO (see below) and further reassessed its internal orientation, any residual pro-urban bias was effectively removed. Consequently, the aforementioned diversification of agricultural output occurred early in the EO phase. It seems clear that while governments, colonial and early post-colonial, were initially very helpful to Taiwan's rural population in both economic and social infrastructural terms, the removal of residual pro-urban biases made the most important contribution thereafter and permitted the agricultural sector to play its historical role to the hilt.

10.3.4 Externally oriented (EO) secondary export substitution (SES) sub-phase (1970–80)

Once the system's unskilled labor surplus is exhausted, as happened in Taiwan between 1968 and 1970, the non-agricultural sector can be expected to move gradually away from its virtually exclusive concentration on labor intensive output mixes. What we now encounter is: (1) much enhanced emphasis on the development of human capital and creative entrepreneurial response mechanisms; (2) export diversification and dynamic structural flexibility; (3) reaping the full benefits of an increased external exposure.

Encouragement of the creative human potential Such encouragement takes mainly two forms: via an enhanced emphasis on secondary and vocational education to accommodate the skill requirements of an increasingly diversified output mix and via opening up the system to increased participation by an emerging entrepreneurial class.

In 1968, with labor shortage signals beginning to appear, Taiwan shifted from six to nine years of compulsory education and simultaneously undertook a major expansion of the vocational track in its secondary education offerings; by 1972 a remarkable 52 percent of high school students were engaged in vocational education programs emphasizing numeracy and general problem solving abilities in the effort to maintain relevancy for a changing industrial landscape.[6]

With respect to entrepreneurial access, it should be recalled that the arrival of the scientific epoch in the nineteenth century in the West laid emphasis on economic creativity participated in by a broad spectrum of the population, that is, not limited to the cultural elites, quite unlike the elitist scientific discoveries of the sixteenth century period of enlightenment. The multitude of new products that regularly began to appear in catalogues and on television, the literally thousands of models and attributes seen in the exhibition halls and trade centers around the world, are the result of such a broadly shared sense of innovation and experimentation.

The enrichment of human lives as a result of this growing product diversity far exceeds that derived from the "allocative efficiency" stressed by neoclassical Pareto optimality considerations. In the concluding chapter of the *General Theory*, Keynes expressed the view that the loss of "fancy and variety" is perhaps the greatest of all losses suffered by societies which deny their citizens a broad choice in the market place.

Especially the later stages of the EO–SES sub-phase herald the arrival of an economic system based on the exploration of the constantly changing potential of human (as opposed to natural) resources engaged in exploring the system's technological potential in a creative and imaginative way. Such product diversification and process change represent merely a prelude to the full science and technology-oriented sub-phase that arrives later, after 1980 in the case of Taiwan, as the march of scientific and technological progress is accelerated once a society approaches economic maturity.

Export diversification and structural flexibility (E9) With the arrival of the EO–SES sub-phase, exports of manufactured goods (E_i) now not only increase absolutely and in relation to agricultural exports and GNP, but are also characterized by a process of dynamic product diversification – a continuous, healthy GNP metabolism heralding the continuous timely appearance of new products and the equally timely death of the old, rendered obsolete by the dynamics of technology change. This yields a production structure that is characterized by increasing flexibility through time. Indeed the modern growth epoch, characterized by the dynamic march of technology change, rapid growth, and capital accumulation cannot be entered if not accompanied by such continuous structural flexibility, sometimes called the "flying geese" pattern, mimicking the continuous change of comparative advantage internationally. In figure 10.4, the required structural flexibility is demonstrated via a disaggregation of total non-agricultural exports (E_i), accompanied by the disaggregation of investment (I), paving the way for a more technical analysis in the next section.

Benefit of continued external exposure   The product diversification, process change, and structural flexibility associated with the EO-SES sub-phase are very much related to the fact that manufactured goods (E_i) are now directed at the world market and stimulated thereby in a number of ways. Rapid technology change in either dimension undoubtedly could not have occurred in any major way in a closed economy. This is related both to the stimulating importation of ideas with respect to both products and processes which accompany trade and to the fundamental Engel's law which states that higher incomes yield a rising preference for a diversified pattern of consumption.

The markets of the first, as well as the increasingly important markets of the third world, have provided Taiwan (and the other East Asian NICs) with the opportunity to deploy a more and more skilled labor force and a more and more venturesome entrepreneurial class. What we encounter here is another "vent for surplus," this time of creativity which requires the inclusion of new country and product markets to elicit a full-throated response.

Orientation towards enhanced competitive pressures (E10)   A central thesis of this chapter is that the gradual depoliticization of various markets represents a required institutional change if the typical LDC is to move successfully through the various sub-phases of transition growth. The very success of the early external drive of the EO–SES sub-phase naturally breeds the idea that more export orientation is warranted. However, given the heritage of intervention and protection of the IS era which cannot be quickly erased, we usually first encounter a hybrid mixture of markets and governments which, however, tends to increasingly emphasize exports, even if these initially are likely to have to be encouraged by such devices as export processing zones, import duty rebates for exports, etc. It has become abundantly clear that selling in world markets means competing not only with advanced countries but also with other LDC success cases in terms of both quality and price. While the political culture still suggests that governments could and should promote exports through such institutional devices as the application of differential interest rates, tax rates and exchange rates, as well as "moral" and more direct suasion accompanied by export targets as in the case of Korea, it is also becoming increasingly clear that the system's future lies increasingly in unsubsidized participation in world markets in which domestic producers have no choice but to increasingly accept the discipline of international competition. Current controversies on the role of industrial policy in the context of the "East Asian Miracle" study boil down to the extent to which direct export-oriented interventions are required and for how long they need to be maintained. Since it is now generally recognized that most societies experience market failure as well as government failure, it is the pace at which specific interventions which give way to general interventions give way to institutional/organizational interventions, which is really at issue. Clearly an increasingly sharp distinction becomes apparent between selling in protected domestic markets where customers constitute a captive audience and selling in competitive international markets where few favors are given. This distinction is useful in helping us identify the landmark difference in the evolution of government-society relations as depoliticization occurs. Initially Taiwan's foreign sector was liberalized while the domestic market continued to be protected. Later on, this hybrid arrangement began to fall away as the further opening of the domestic market was gradually achieved during the (final) science and technology-oriented sub-phase.

10.3.5 Science and technology-oriented sub-phase (TO) (post-1980)

Consistent with our evolutionary perspective, the TO sub-phase once again descends directly from its EO–SES predecessor and constitutes the final sub-phase in the course of successful transition to economic maturity. Indeed, having transited successfully into the TO sub-phase, it is reasonable to expect Taiwan to be counted in the ranks of the industrially advanced countries by the end of the century.[7]

The holistic operational framework for the TO sub-phase, shown in figure 10.5, can be derived from that of the EO–SES sub-phase (figure 10.4), conveying once again a sense of evolutionary progress. The economy has by now completely lost its "dualistic" characteristic as the agricultural sector (no longer even shown in figure 10.5) has become a mere appendage of non-agricultural activities – as a result of the arrival of labor shortage and the mechanization of agriculture, accompanied by land consolidation and the advent of the cultivating firm. Although, probably misguided, policies aimed at food self-sufficiency via the protection and subsidization of agriculture may now be observed, reflecting the "special" political power of that sector, agriculture has clearly receded into the background in terms of the proportion of national income generated or the percentage of the labor force involved.

The modernizing non-agricultural sector of the Taiwan economy, on the other hand, has become increasingly complex, as illustrated in figure 10.5, containing:

1   a domestic commodity market for consumer goods;
2   a domestic commodity market for capital goods;
3   a financial market;
4   a labor market;
5   a world market for exports;
6   a market for long-run capital movements and transfers; and
7   a foreign exchange market (though not shown in figure 10.5).

The arrival of the TO phase has intrinsically shifted our focus of attention to a set of organization- and institution-oriented issues such as the continued improvement of a system of markets that tends to replace some functions of government as the long run depoliticization process continues and gathers steam, while new institutional requirements for government actions in the realm of science and technology infrastructure come to the fore.

Our holistic operational interpretation of this final sub-phase of transition is based on a disaggregated view of the system of markets referred to above. This is in sharp contrast, for example, to the highly aggregative Keynesian framework. Let us recall that Keynes stressed the interaction of four sectors through a system of markets: (1) the domestic production sector; (2) the domestic household sector; (3) the government sector; and (4) the foreign sector. GNP is produced when labor and capital services are supplied to the production sector which also makes use of imported goods (M). The four components of aggregate demand are exports (E), consumption by households (C), government expenditures (G) and investment expenditures (I). The national income, that is, the sum of values added by labor (V_W) and property income (V_π), is partially diverted to the government as tax payments (T), while the disposable income of

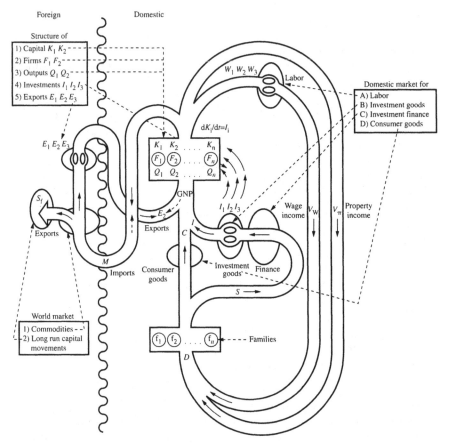

Figure 10.5 Science and technology sub-phase in operational perspective

households (D) is used either as consumption or as savings (S) which flow into the financial market.[8]

In the foreign sector the difference between imports and exports ($S_f = M - E$) may be referred to as "foreign savings" and may be positive or negative. There exists an import surplus when S_f is positive, implying that foreign savings (in the form of long-run private capital inflows and/or foreign aid) are being used to finance domestic investment. Alternatively, when S_f is negative, the export surplus implies that domestic savings are being used to finance investment in foreign countries. It follows that the S_f concept refers to the market governing long-run capital movements (including the unilateral concessional transfer called foreign aid).

In the domestic portion of the economic system what needs to be added is the possibility of monetary expansion, dm/dt, which flows into financial markets and supplements the purchasing power generated by voluntary savings S. In what follows we shall make use of non-Keynesian language by referring to S as loanable funds made available to the financial market as augmented by monetary expansion. We hope to show that an important set of policy issues really relates to this issue of government-sponsored monetary expansion which tends to give LDC growth promotion policies their unique feature as compared with the industrially advanced countries.

This amended Keynesian "macro" framework, though useful, remains deficient as a conceptual tool for describing what really happens in the TO sub-phase in the course of the depoliticization process. Specifically, this calls for a suitable framework that is holistic but disaggregated. For this reason, all the aggregative magnitudes in the framework of figure 10.5 are disaggregated to show the allocation of:

1   capital K into a disaggregated capital structure $(K_1, K_2, ...)$;
2   investment I into a disaggregated investment structure $(I_1, I_2, ...)$;
3   labor W into a disaggregated employment structure $(W_1, W_2, ...)$;
4   output capacity into a disaggregated output structure $(Q_1, Q_2, ...)$; and
5   exports E into a diversified export structure $(E_1, E_2, ...)$.

Macroeconomics in the Keynesian or post-Keynesian tradition can retain an "aggregative view" because in the industrially advanced countries static allocative efficiency can be more or less taken for granted. Not so in the case of the contemporary LDC. Indeed, the very notion of modern economic growth implies, along with Kuznets's famous six characteristics, that the typical LDC is gradually building up an adjusting system of markets to replace the political role of the government. Moreover, what needs yet to be fully constructed is a set of market systems – the commodity, labor, finance and foreign exchange markets – that can accommodate the structural flexibility requirements of the modern mixed economy. For this reason markets in which critical prices are determined, that is, commodity prices, interest, wage and foreign exchange rates, are intrinsically disaggregative in nature, even as, to emphasize their relatedness, they need to be embedded within a holistic framework.[9]

10.4 Growth Promotion Policies in the Course of Transition

This section examines the art of growth promotion policies as practiced during the transition, thus serving as a link between section 10.3 (on the various sub-phases seen in sequential operational perspective) and

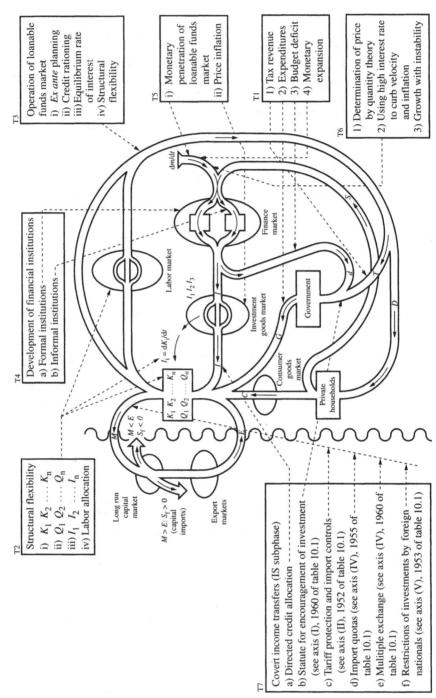

T3
Operation of loanable
funds market
i) *Ex ante* planning
ii) Credit rationing
iii) Equilibrium rate
    of interest
iv) Structural
    flexibility

T5
i) Monetary
   penetration of
   loanable funds
   market
ii) Price inflation

T1
1) Tax revenue
2) Expenditures
3) Budget deficit
4) Monetary
   expansion

T6
1) Determination of price
   by quantity theory
2) Using high interest rate
   to curb velocity
   and inflation
3) Growth with instability

T4
Development of financial institutions
a) Formal institutions
b) Informal institutions

T2
Structural flexibility
i) $K_1\ K_2\ \dots\ K_n$
ii) $Q_1\ Q_2\ \dots\ Q_n$
iii) $I_1\ I_2\ \dots\ I_n$
iv) Labor allocation

T7
Covert income transfers (IS subphase)
a) Directed credit allocation
b) Statute for encouragement of investment
   (see axis (I), 1960 of table 10.1)
c) Tariff protection and import controls
   (see axis (II), 1952 of table 10.1)
d) Import quotas (see axis (IV), 1955 of
   table 10.1)
e) Multiple exchange (see axis (IV), 1960 of
   table 10.1)
f) Restrictions of investments by foreign
   nationals (see axis (V), 1953 of table 10.1)

Figure 10.6 Monetary and fiscal policies of an LDC in transition

section 10.5 (on the actual evolution of policy). For now we shall remain on, for economists, familiar ground by treating policies as exogenous, leaving the causation of their adoption and abandonment to the next section.

The Taiwan policy matrix of table 10.1 is seen to contain ten categories of macro and structural policies. In order to appreciate their relatedness and complexity in a dualistic context, the operational framework of figure 10.5 is modified slightly to generate figure 10.6. As compared with figure 10.5 it is intended to underline several facets that are crucially related to the analysis of growth promotional policies that will be analyzed in this section.

First of all, for the analysis of fiscal policies, figure 10.6 now shows government expenditures (G), revenues (T), as well as the government budget deficit $(F = G - T > 0)$. Notice that the government requires the banks to cover the budget deficit. For the analysis of monetary policies, a key concept therefore is monetary expansion dm/dt, that is, the expansion of the quantity of money (m). Such newly created money is injected into the financial market in such a way as to augment the savings fund (S). Finally, the financial market itself is marked by "dualism" to signify the coexistence of formal financial institutions (for example, commercial banks, trusts, insurance) and "informal" or curb market institutions where borrowing and lending are sustained by kinship, friendship or other informal money-lending arrangements. In the policy analysis which follows, we intend to make use of figure 10.6 where the agricultural sector is omitted.

As a point of departure we first concentrate on monetary expansion as a key policy instrument. Our emphasis on money can be justified on the grounds that, in addition to serving as the standard of value, the medium of exchange, and the unit of account, it represents the most important instrument of social organization in a society that respects property rights. When the quantity of money is caused to change by the command of political power – that is, when monetary expansion is politicized – virtually everyone is affected.

10.4.1 Pervasiveness of monetary policies

Monetary policy centers on the expansion of the monetary stock, that is, the quantity of money. In any contemporary system, DC or LDC, to insist that only one currency can circulate is the primary responsibility of any sovereign government. It is not unusual, moreover, for an LDC government to monopolize the power of monetary expansion. When a fiat (or paper) standard replaces a commodity (such as gold or silver) standard, monetary expansion seems to become costless. Few LDC governments have consequently been able to resist the temptation to indulge in the convenience of money printing to solve economic problems that should have been solved in other more responsible, but less convenient, ways.

The potency of monetary expansion to solve economic problems is due primarily to the fact that in an urban industrial society characterized by production specialization and an advanced division of labor, the population has no choice but to accept money as a medium of exchange and as purchasing power. In the typical LDC, monetary expansion constitutes a political act in terms of creating purchasing power to enable the government itself, or private parties designated by it, to exercise additional command over goods and services in the marketplace. In particular, monetary expansion can be resorted to to solve at least three types of problems that will be touched upon in this section: (1) monetary expansion to enhance governmental "stability" or macro-fiscal solvency by closing the budget gap (section 10.4.2); (2) monetary expansion to promote growth (by raising investment) and close the *ex ante* investment-saving gap (section 10.4.3); and (3) monetary expansion to influence foreign trade in the interest of growth promotion by closing the trade gap (section 10.4.4).

However, in the very act of closing the various gaps in this fashion, the government is likely to destroy anything approaching equilibrium in the level of the interest rate or the foreign exchange rate. Some government activity along these lines is, of course, inevitable, especially during the early IS years, for reasons already referred to. But the persistent and excessive resort to this convenient way of "solving a problem" can become an irresponsible act that will, sooner or later, cause the money-using public to rebel by spending its own money at a faster pace. Such competition for real resources inevitably causes inflation and the frustration of the government's own intentions.

When we examine the monetary experience of transition growth in the case of Taiwan, we should note the atypical way in which the inflation problem was dealt with here when it did occur and, more importantly, the way in which inflation was avoided in the first place.

10.4.2 Monetary expansion and government stability (T1)

In most of the sovereign states born after World War II, the key issue of legitimacy is that the government has to live up to the popular expectation of post-colonial political activism. For example, it must have the capacity to command resources to involve itself in such sector-specific activities, reflected in our policy evolution matrix (see table 10.1), as public sector enterprise and social and economic overhead expansion (VI), agriculture (VII), manpower, education and labor (VIII), eventually the development of science and technology (IX), and, especially early on, economic planning (X), usually connoting an early sense of post-colonial nationalism.

Technically, as indicated in box T1 of figure 10.6, macro-fiscal solvency refers to the gradual building up of a tax capacity (T) to cover the various categories of expenditures (G) and thus avoid the continuous appearance of budget gaps (F). When this fails, either because of the inability or unwillingness to raise taxes, the government is tempted to close the budget gap ($F = G-T$) by monetary expansion (dm/dt).

As far as Taiwan is concerned, in this respect at least, the loss of the mainland to the communists in 1949 proved to be a blessing in disguise. The experience of hyperinflation before 1949 served as a severe warning to the new government on Taiwan to exercise fiscal responsibility. The response, atypical by LDC standards, can be seen from Row I of table 10.1 (on domestic fiscal policies). While US aid inflows helped in the 1950s, Taiwan early on already insisted on either a small budget deficit (1961) or even the achievement of a budget surplus (1964). Any time a small budget deficit reappeared, we may note the immediate convocation of tax reform commissions and concerted efforts to enact new tax laws.

The capacity to tax is, of course, an art that can only be learned gradually. For relatively inexperienced LDCs there always exists the tendency early on to rely on point-specific customs duties that can be collected at ports, requiring minimal administrative capacity. The replacement of customs duties by domestic indirect and direct taxes (the latter requiring the auditing of personal records) as a major source of government revenue usually comes, if at all, at a later stage of transition growth.

In the continued absence of such a domestic capacity to tax, foreign aid can continue to be used to close the budget gap. US aid to Taiwan in the 1950s served precisely this purpose. Such foreign aid, of course, arrived in the form of real goods which were sold in the market, with the monetary proceeds frozen in the form of inactive monetary balances labeled as counterpart funds. The foreign aid program thus reduced the amount of money in circulation and hence contributed to the achievement of macro-fiscal solvency. Later on, foreign aid inflows were negotiated in relation to a number of strategic policy reforms. Finally, as early as 1961 the termination of aid by 1965 was announced, providing a strong fillip for the rapid adoption of the required fiscal and other complementary measures, giving the government time to build up its own fiscal capacity. Such time-constrained use of foreign aid, to reduce the budget deficit and curb inflation in the 1950s, and to reduce the pain attending the package of critical structural reforms (the "19 Points") in the early 1960s, is clearly superior to its frequent role as a long-term, and possibly counter-productive crutch.[10]

10.4.3 Monetary expansion to promote investment and growth

For those brought up in the Keynesian tradition, the idea that investment can be stimulated by an expansionary monetary policy that lowers the interest rate represents a truth that needs no further explanation. However, the simple transfer of this idea to the LDC policy arena is unwarranted on theoretical grounds and can lead to dangerous consequences.

A true follower of Keynes is not likely to concede that monetary expansion, no matter how severe and persistent, must logically lead to inflation because the quantity theory of money is rejected outright. Moreover, the generally prevalent LDC shortage of savings is usually not considered a bottleneck factor leading to higher interest rates.

In the underemployed LDC case, however, these positions are subject to challenge. It is indeed our view that a more relevant theory must be based on the pre-war loanable funds approach. This notion will be developed in four steps:

1   to indicate that the relevant framework of thinking must be based on a holistic but disaggregated framework for the whole economy (as in figure 10.6);
2   to show the idealized operation of a loanable funds market not unduly interfered with by monetary expansion;
3   to show the actual customary penetration of the idealized loanable funds market by monetary expansion;
4   to show the inevitability of inflation to follow.

Let us briefly take up each of these dimensions in turn.

Adherence to a holistic disaggregated framework (T2)   Structural flexibility is absolutely essential to accommodate the dynamics of technology change in a modernizing industrial society (see E9, figure 10.4). We see, from box T2 (figure 10.6), that the flexibility of the capacity output structure $(Q_1, Q_2, \ldots)$ is determined by the capital stock structure $(K_1, K_2, \ldots)$ which, in turn, can be traced to the flexibility of the investment structure $(I_1, I_2, \ldots)$. The role of the labor market, it should be noted, is determined residually. The required "healthy metabolism" of a technologically dynamic society can thus be assured by the flexibility of the finance and labor markets.

We should note that union power, often of considerable influence in LDCs, did not play much of a role in Taiwan until very recently. Nor were minimum wage legislation or public sector wage setting factors in determining the real wage, certainly as long as labor surplus persisted. In sum, there was relatively little institutional intervention in the determination of the real wage, avoiding labor market rigidity and thus promoting the achievement of industrial flexibility.

Principles of operation of the loanable funds market (boxes T3, T4)   According to the loanable funds theory, the operation of the financial market consists of the channelization of the system's savings fund (S) to alternative investment outlets (I_1, I_2,...) via a screening or credit rationing process whereby *ex ante* investment plans prepared by entrepreneurs are compared and ranked. This results in the system's move towards an equilibrium rate of interest.

Entrepreneurs who obtained their purchasing power on credit terms can then go to the market for investment goods to flexibly augment their capital stock. In the course of this process, new purchasing power, aimed at the market for investment goods, is injected into the circulation stream. However, the overall quantity of money is not increased because the saving fund that has been supplied represents voluntary saving. It should be noted that in the financial markets of the industrially advanced economy, credit rationing is intermediated by highly specialized economic agents (such as banks, insurance companies), operating in a variety of institutional markets (for example, stocks, bonds, money markets); in LDCs, on

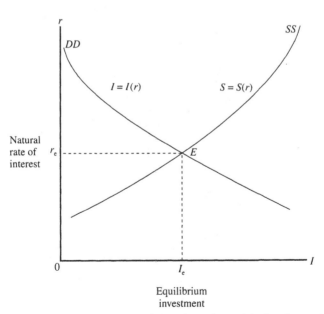

Figure 10.7 Demand and supply in loanable funds market

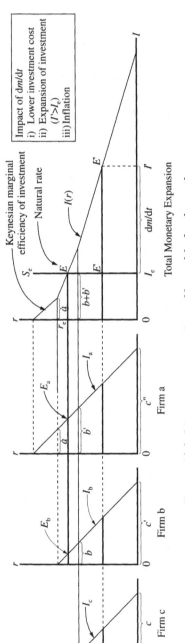

Figure 10.8 Monetary penetration of loanable funds market

the other hand, financial agents and institutions must first be established before the industrial sector can achieve the necessary structural flexibility.

In terms of our evolutionary perspective, the gradual depoliticization of financial markets implies that "formal" financial institutions (with their specialized agents) which serve medium and large-scale borrowers must be developed to replace "informal" (curb, black, or parallel) markets for small-scale borrowers. This customary dual characteristic of LDC financial intermediation markets is indicated in box T4. It is by no means a simple matter to build institutions and develop formal financial markets since they require an increasingly impersonal culture of arms' length trust and creditworthiness to underpin deferred contracts involving interest and debt repayments. Simultaneously, governments are gradually forced to diminish their efforts to control the rate of interest and/or the direction of investment flows through discretionary allocation devices.

The operation of the loanable funds market is shown in figure 10.7, with the real rate of interest (r) shown on the vertical and saving (S) and investment (I) on the horizontal axis. The equilibrium (that is, market clearing) rate of interest is given by r_e where $S_e = I_e$. While it may seem unnecessary to present such an elementary diagram, the truth is that the validity of this simple loanable funds idea has been all but destroyed in the course of the Keynesian revolution. Our attempted rehabilitation of the loanable funds theory will be further elaborated in figure 10.8 to emphasize two additional ideas that are crucial in the loanable funds tradition:

1   We are here concerned with a diversified investment and multiple product world rather than an aggregative theory.
2   The loanable funds theory is directed at the monetary penetration of financial markets, leading to "over investment" as the market rate of interest is depressed below the equilibrium rate (relabeled here as the "natural rate").

Thus, in figure 10.8, the investment demand of three firms (A, B, and C) is shown; their horizontal summation ($I(x)$) represents the investment demand function for the whole economy. (In fact, $I(x)$ is equivalent to the Keynesian marginal efficiency of capital.) When total saving is given, ($S=I$), the natural rate of interest is indicated by r_e while the credit is rationed to firms a and b as indicated by the equilibrium positions E_a and E_b. Notice that while, in the aggregate loanable funds model of figure 10.7, the focus of interest is on the determination of total investment I (similar to the Keynesian focus), our interest in the issue of structural flexibility forces us to examine the structure of investment I_a, I_b, I_c,... as a result of credit rationing in the loanable funds market.

Penetration of the loanable funds market by monetary expansion (T5)   In figure 10.7 the natural rate of interest r_e is indicated at E where voluntary savings S are rationed out to individual borrowers as investment funds (I_1, I_2, . . .) via a competitive process. Monetary expansion dm/dt lowers the natural rate to the level of the market rate at E', while total investment is raised by dm/dt to the level of $S + dm/dt$. In the language of the loanable funds theory, such investment in excess of voluntary savings is referred to as "forced savings" which violates saver sovereignty. That is why savers will try to "fight back" whenever they have the power and opportunity to do so.

While pre-war loanable fund theorists viewed the elastic supply of money by commercial banks as the culprit, the same mechanism of forced saving became too convenient to be resisted by the governments of young sovereign states not yet able to tax but feeling the need to create nation-building infrastructure. The act of monetary expansion through forced savings seems to be capable of killing many birds with one stone: it avoids raising additional tax revenue; it increases investment; it demonstrates the benevolent power of the government by lowering investment costs; it serves to lubricate a government–big business partnership; it obviates the necessity for bureaucratic discretion in the allocation of the investment fund that would have been required if the market rate of interest were lowered in the absence of such monetary expansion (for example, if equilibrium were established at point E' in figure 10.8).

The typical LDC government usually does not see any good reasons not to follow this course because it seems both costless and convenient. To promote growth by forced saving and monetary expansion appears at first glance as a near-perfect policy instrument, especially given the pressures of a synthetic nationalism that does not wish to face the embarrassing question of who will ultimately have to bear the costs.

The pre-war loanable funds theory provided a direct answer to that question by pointing out that such monetary expansion, once actually applied to the investment goods markets, implies an injection of new purchasing power on top of the money stock currently already in circulation. The newly printed purchasing power enables the money-using public to "fight back" in the attempt to restore saver sovereignty. As a consequence, velocity is likely to rise until, in the minds of savers, the artificially lower interest rate is not enough to compensate them for the loss of purchasing power due to inflation. There thus exists a direct and logical linkage between forced savings and the increase in the price level.

Since several of the above mechanisms (the possible divergence between the natural and market rates of interest, the relevance of saving to the rate of interest, and the application of a modified quantity theory) were rejected by doctrinaire Keynesians, one would like to know the theoretical foundation for the current counsel of monetary conservatism to

LDC governments. In the context of the so-called "Washington Consensus" the idea of a "crowding-out effect" – that given large demands and a limited saving capacity, the resulting government borrowing will raise the interest rate and squeeze out private investment – also represents a warning to LDC governments against excessive monetary expansion. Such a crowding-out effect is demonstrated in figure 10.6 as the private sector's demand for loanable funds (I) competes with the public sector's (F).

Inevitability of inflation When the newly created purchasing power is injected into the circulation stream, the price level (p) is determined according to the quantity theory of money ($MV=pQ$), that is, the depression of the market below the natural rate of interest as a result of monetary expansion leads to inflation because of a government/societal conflict as the money-using public is "forced" to save.

Whether or not the velocity of circulation is interest-elastic thus becomes a decisive issue for both theory and policy. From the theoretical point of view, when the demand for money is interest-elastic, a high interest rate makes it more expensive to hold on to liquid assets; hence, the money-using public is likely to suffer the inconvenience of illiquidity. A higher interest rate becomes a cure for inflation.

10.4.4 The monetary experience of Taiwan

Referring to row III of table 10.1, the Taiwan policy matrix, we may note that, before 1975, the relevant story was one of basic monetary conservatism and, after 1975, the story was one of the construction of needed new financial institutions. Notice that the construction of new institutions comes later, a fact that will have to be explained in terms of our evolutionary perspective.

Monetary conservatism As indicated in the policy evolution chart, the Taiwan government successfully turned back inflation twice (once before 1950 and once before 1975) with the help of a high interest rate policy, in spite of the fact that the root cause of the inflationary pressure was different in the each of the two episodes. Around 1949, the problem was one of fiscal insolvency (see box T1, figure 10.6), as the nationalist government had not yet developed sufficient tax capacity. To cure rampaging inflation, government-controlled banks substantially raised interest rates, thus inducing the public to convert liquid money balances into illiquid saving deposits, thereby reducing the velocity of circulation of the total money stock. Inflation was effectively brought under control in this fashion.

Such resort to a high interest rate policy was repeated in the mid-1970s when inflationary pressures were transmitted from the outside into a Taiwan pursuing monetary activism of the type described in T5 and T6 (figure 10.6) according to the loanable funds theory. Early on, the alternation of low and high interest rate policies began to form a pattern, namely, the government would occasionally use low interest rates to stimulate investment and subsequently high interest rates to cure any resulting price inflation. But gradually it became clear that a fundamental cure for inflation was the full renunciation of a low interest policy if macro instability was to be avoided. Indeed, the initiation of the externally oriented (EO) growth phase around 1961 coincided with a decade of prolonged price stability, rare on the contemporary LDC scene. Such monetary and fiscal conservatism represents a lesson that could be noted to advantage by other LDCs.

Institution construction after 1975   Before 1975 the financial markets of Taiwan were characterized by the pronounced "formal–informal" dualism as described in box T4. Side by side with the commercial banks that were owned or tightly controlled by the government, an informal curb market existed for the small-scale informal sector borrower. In an evolutionary perspective, the increased product diversification associated with the externally oriented drive (the EO phase 1962–80) eventually – after 1975 – required the creation of a more efficient, that is, functionally diversified and specialized set of financial institutions. Thus, the government initiated the necessary institutional/organizational changes to accommodate the demand for a more finely differentiated channelization of savings.

The establishment of a bond market (1974) and a money market (1980) also represent prerequisites for further liberalization since these are measures that provide savers with additional institutional alternatives and help reveal the various interest rates that are being determined in these new markets. When this is accomplished, further depoliticization and deregulation of interest rates can occur in rapid sequence (1980–85) as the power to control shifts first to bankers' associations, and then to the broader market. Once this occurs, the informal curb market gradually fades away and financial dualism disappears. In 1985, the prime rate system was introduced in Taiwan as bankers increasingly acquired the capacity to differentiate among the credit standings of various types of borrowers.

The above brief description underlines our basic evolutionary thesis that the depoliticization process (in this case, the liberalization of financial markets) represents a process of gradually substituting market decisions (in this case, by financial institutions and banks) for government discretionary actions (in this case, by the central bank), a process aided by institutional interventions of the government. The recently begun gradual privatization of the so-called government "commercial" banks represents the next logical step in this evolutionary process.

10.4.5 Monetary expansion and the foreign exchange market

Any policy-oriented analysis of transition growth in the open dualistic economy must include consideration of foreign exchange (FE) policies. Once again, we intend to concentrate on a number of key issues which help demonstrate our evolutionary perspective.

The conceptual framework   The purpose of constructing a framework of analysis for dealing with the FE market as represented by figure 10.9 is to show that it represents a logical extension of the domestic system – represented by figure 10.6. The FE market must be viewed as an integral part of an interlocking system containing commodity markets for consumer and investment goods, the financial market, the labor market and the world market for exported goods – reproduced in the lower part of figure 10.9. The three circles shown in the upper part of the diagram contain the key new dimensions to be focused on here, namely:

1   the international commodity market, related to the buying and selling of imported (M) and exported (E) products traded internationally at the world price p_f, in terms of foreign currency – for simplicity, dollars[11];
2   the foreign exchange market, related to the two-way conversion of domestic currency (for example, New Taiwan dollars – NT) into US dollars at the foreign exchange rate e (that is if 40 NT equals \$1, $e=40$ NT);
3   the instruments exercised by the central bank to control the FE market, which include, in addition to the FE rate, the stock of foreign exchange reserves (Z) as well as the power of domestic monetary expansion dm/dt;
4   the domestic price level p, as determined by the quantity theory (see T6 in figure 10.6), that determines the purchasing power parity p_f, when the two prices are given.

Thus, the foreign exchange system is determined by the economic magnitudes of M, E, p_f, Z, e, dm/dt, and p, involving two different currencies (\$ and NT). Notice that the quadruplet (M, E, p, dm/dt) represents a straightforward extension of the lower part of figure 10.9 that focuses on the domestic part of the system. The operation of the FE market can thus be examined from both the traders' and the bankers' vantage point. Let us take them up in sequence.

Both importers and exporters have to participate in all three markets,

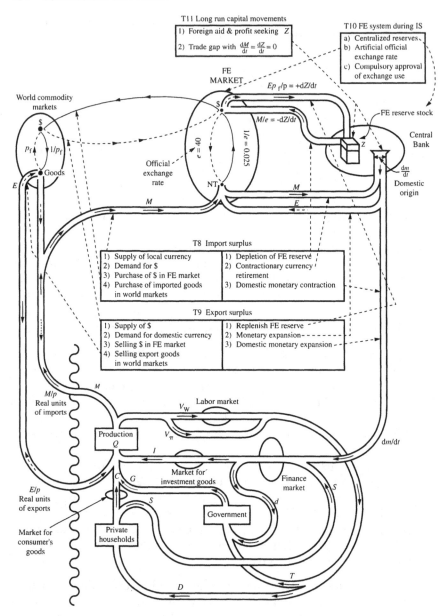

Figure 10.9 Foreign exchange institutions in operational perspective

the domestic commodity market, the international commodity market, and the foreign exchange market. Importers are the suppliers of domestic currency to the FE market (for example, $M=100$ NT), converted into dollars at the given FE rate ($M/e = 100 \times 0.025 = \$2.5$) that allows them to purchase M/ep_f units of imported goods in the product market. When they sell these goods in the domestic market they will be able to obtain $(M/ep_f)p$ units of NTs. If they are to make neither profit or loss, $M=Mp/ep_f$, implying that the equilibrium exchange rate e_e should always be the same as purchasing power parity (that is, $e_e=p/p_f$). Thus, at the left-hand side of box T8 in figure 10.9, the behavior of an importer is summarized as a buyer of dollars as well as a purchaser of imported goods in the foreign market and a seller of imported goods in the domestic market. The behavior of the exporter is summarized, symmetrically, on the left-hand side of box T9, as the condition for an equilibrium exchange rate ($e_e = p/p_f$) can also be readily derived. We shall refer to the case of T8 and T9 as typical for an import surplus and export surplus condition, respectively.

Turning to the same market from the point of view of the bankers, when traders convert their currency this amounts to foreign exchange which can be assumed to be deposited with the central bank, for simplicity's sake. In the case of an import surplus, the buying of foreign exchange from the bank leads to the following result, summarized on the right-hand side of box T8. Denoting Z as the size of the stock of foreign exchange reserves, we have:

1 the depletion of a part of the FE reserves stock ($Me = -dZ/dt$);
2 an equivalent contractionary retirement of NT from circulation;
3 the canceling of a portion of the total monetary expansion dm/dt.

Thus, by the very act of the depletion of the FE reserves, the central bank withdraws a portion of the NT out of circulation and can hold it in the form of an inactive balance in the bank's vault. Thus, when dm/dt injects additional purchasing power via the domestic channel (to fill the saving/investment gap and/or the government's budget gap) a part of this expansionary effect is offset due to such withdrawal of a portion of the money in circulation. In this fashion, the existence of a large FE reserve stock (Z) can be a powerful stop-gap instrument that can help fill the aforementioned three gaps (the government budget gap, the saving-investment gap, and the trade gap) while combatting inflation.

In the case of an export surplus, symmetrical effects are summarized on the right-hand side of box T9. An export surplus will:

1 replenish the foreign exchange reserve stock ($E/e=dZ/dt$);
2 cause additional currency to be injected into the system; and consequently

3   add to the domestic monetary expansion which pre-existed in the effort to fill the domestic budget and/or the savings-investment gap.

In this way the penetration of the foreign exchange market by central bank actions has certain real and monetary effects on the domestic economy that can be analyzed once the FE market is viewed as an integral part of the overall system.

Salient features of Taiwan's FE system prior to 1980   Contemporary LDCs sport a wide variety of foreign exchange related institutions. While it is beyond the scope of this chapter to systematically outline a full classification system, it is helpful to point out the salient features of one success case's FE institutions which, like that of every developing country, are bound to reflect its own particular political-economic culture. Such a description should be useful as a way of demonstrating once again the basic notion of a process of evolutionary institutional change in the direction of simultaneous depoliticization and internationalization.

During the early IS sub-phase the relevant institutional conditions are succinctly summarized in box T10, with respect to three dimensions: (1) a centralized foreign exchange reserve system; (2) the maintenance of an overvalued official exchange rate relative to purchasing power parity; and (3) a compulsory government approval process for all foreign exchange transactions.

A centralized reserve system means that the government, acting through the central bank, has the legal right to monopolize the holding of all foreign exchange reserves. In other words, the foreign exchange earnings of exporters must be sold to the central bank at the official exchange rate e, which can be quite artificial, that is, under- or over-valued relative to purchasing power parity plus capital movement rules. Would-be importers have little choice but to appear at the central bank window if they want to acquire foreign exchange legally.

Since individuals or commercial banks are not allowed to hold foreign exchange, the official foreign exchange rate is not determined by the competitive forces prevailing in the market. Consequently, any even approximately "clean floating" of the FE rate is quite out of the question. Indeed, in Taiwan the FE rate has continued to be viewed until at least 1978 as a policy instrument the central bank can wield in order to promote growth by helping private importers (or exporters) earn unearned profits.

The compulsory sanction of all foreign exchange transactions similarly implies an autarkic orientation with economic as well as political significance. From the economic standpoint all profit-oriented short-run capital movements unrelated to trade are ruled out. Politically, economic contacts between domestic citizens and foreigners – unless specifically sanctioned –

are also effectively ruled out. The unavailability of foreign exchange to travel abroad is as effective as the denial of a passport.

A country's foreign exchange reserve stock Z represents a key asset implying instant international liquidity and constituting the country's first line of defense in case of an emergency so that relatively stable exchange rates can be maintained without resort to quantitative restrictions. In an industrially advanced country such FE stocks are re-enforced by a second line of defense consisting of (the less liquid) claims of domestic citizens against foreigners (or the net claims that indicate the net creditor position of a country against the rest of the world). However, in the case of the developing country operating under a centralized reserve system, few currency dealings with foreigners are allowed. Any long-run capital movement must involve the government as a party to the transaction. Substantial depoliticization of the previously described FE system in the case of Taiwan did not really occur until the late 1970s but has gathered steam since as part and parcel of evolutionary necessity.

We have, up to this point, not explicitly referred to the analytical treatment of long run capital imports and exports in the context of figure 10.9. As indicated in T11, long run capital movements (LRCM) include both unilateral transfers such as foreign aid and profit-seeking private capital flows, both of the portfolio and equity type. To facilitate our effort to treat all flows as part of one system of interrelated markets we shall make the simplifying, if heroic, assumption that the essence of LRCM flows is to accomplish autonomous persistent resource transfers, conceptually unrelated to our short run analysis of figure 10.6 which focused on fiscal and monetary policy-induced variations in foreign exchange reserves and the money supply.

The foreign exchange market in operational perspective   Let us here again emphasize our evolutionary thesis in the context of the gradual withdrawal of political forces from this inter-linked set of markets. The operation of the FE market during the IS phase is shown in figure 10.10. The foreign exchange rate e is measured on the vertical and the amount of internationally traded commodities on the horizontal axis. The foreign price in the commodity market p_f is taken as the numeraire, that is, for simplicity's sake we can define $p_f = 1$. Thus, one dollar's worth of both imports and exports implies one real unit of the traded commodity as measured on the horizontal axis.

When both the domestic (and foreign) prices are given, the demand and supply curves for imports (M) and exports (E) are shown. Notice that the import curve (M) has the shape of a negatively sloped demand curve. This is due to the fact that when e is high, the importer who has the same amount of domestic currency can buy fewer units of imported goods to be sold in the domestic market. For similar reasons, the export curve is positively sloped and looks like a supply curve.

The interaction between demand and supply, as always, determines the market equilibrium exchange rate (for example, $e_e = 25$) and the equilibrium magnitude of trade (for example, $M_e = E_e = \$90$). Notice that the equilibrium exchange rate is approximately the same as the purchasing power parity ($e_e = p/p_f$), which reminds us of the fact that the equilibrium magnitudes are determined under the assumption that the pair of prices (p, p_f) is given.

The equilibrium exchange rate marks off two regimes as shown on the vertical axis. An exchange rate that is higher than e_e leads to a relative export surplus as the domestic currency is undervalued. Conversely, when the exchange rate is lower than e_e, there will be a relative import surplus as the domestic currency is over-valued. In the case of an import surplus, the foreign exchange reserves of the central bank will be depleted (for example, $dZ/dt = -\$150$), accompanied by a monetary contraction due to the retirement of local currency to the amount of $dm/dt = -150$ NT, represented by the area of the shaded rectangle. Symmetrically, for an export surplus the foreign exchange reserve will be increased (for example, $dZ/dt = \$150$), accompanied by an equivalent monetary expansion. The central bank has used its sovereign power of monetary expansion to accumulate, almost effortlessly, an addition to the reserves under its control.

It should be noted that all the essential trade-related concepts indicated in the upper part of figure 10.9 are also involved in figure 10.10 which represents the "minimal model". We shall apply this model to describe the FE market as it is penetrated by the government's FE policies during the earlier import substitution sub-phase.

Operation of the FE market during the IS sub-phase: a backward look Foreign exchange and import duties represent important policy instruments ordinarily thought of as responsible for the promotion of the IS growth type as we described it earlier in relation to figure 10.3. Given our evolutionary perspective, we now have the tools to explain what caused the choices of these FE policies in the first place. Our discussion here will rely on the use of both figure 10.10, which emphasizes the mechanics of policy choice, and figure 10.3, which emphasizes the system's mode of operation during import substitution. A number of critical facets of general relevance to LDCs still engaged in this sub-phase will be treated sequentially.

1   *Windfall profits for the new industrial entrepreneurs.* FE policies in the IS sub-phase center on the notion that political force can be invoked to render imported producer goods (M_p) cheap and thus lower the costs for relatively inexperienced entrepreneurs in the

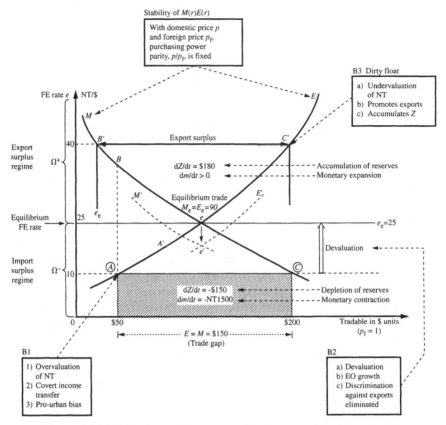

Figure 10.10 Foreign exchange market in operational perspective

import substitution industries. This is accomplished by the overvaluation of the domestic currency so that the official exchange rate lies in the import surplus regime (for example, $e=10$ in figure 10.10).

When compared with the free market rate e_e, which basically reflects purchasing power parity, for every dollar of foreign exchange purchased by these importers/producers, a windfall profit (a profit generated politically, unrelated to entrepreneurial efficiency) is generated as measured by the gap between the equilibrium and the official rate $(e_e - e)$. This "hothouse" atmosphere for the new entrepreneurial class is part of a package to calm its fears of international competition.

2   *Covert income transfers with a pro-urban bias.*   There was little thought given at the time to the fact that the creation of such windfall profits for new industrial entrepreneurs results from covert income transfers that necessarily at the same time discriminate against rural

areas and farmers in particular. The incomes and savings S_a of these farmers are necessarily reduced by the same amount by which these windfall profits augment the incomes, profits, and savings of the industrial entrepreneurial class (S_i) (see figure 10.3). This transfer is covert since farmers as well as the public at large are usually quite unaware of the fact that the official exchange rate can be used for such a purpose. Suspicions to that effect are usually dispelled by the new political culture of synthetic nationalism favoring the urban industrial elite.

3   *Shift from intersectoral to intrasectoral finance for IS industries.*   A direct consequence of these covert income transfers is that the new IS industries, usually large-scale and prematurely capital and technology intensive, are financed increasingly by the savings of the urban entrepreneurial class (S_i) and less by the savings of agricultural households (S_a). Thus, intersectoral finance gradually shifts to intrasectoral finance, that is, via the reinvestment of profits by the entrepreneurial class. In this way "under the table" transfers obviate the necessity of developing an effective intersectoral financial market early on. Or, more realistically, the underdeveloped intersectoral financial market may be seen as a cause of the resort to the covert transfer strategy.

4   *Shortage of foreign exchange.*   The IS period is, of course, characterized by the consciousness of the shortage of foreign exchange as a developmental bottleneck. There are two aspects to this shortage problem that must be distinguished. First of all, since exporters are discriminated against by unfavorable terms of trade, (that is, an overvalued e), traditional primary product exports will not expand as fast. Hence, on the supply side the relative scarcity of export earnings tends to be a permanent feature because there is a diminution, *ceteris paribus*, of the incentive to export. More importantly, the increasing sense of a shortage of foreign exchange due to the overvaluation of the domestic currency implies an excess of demand over supply (that is, of dollars) so that the foreign exchange reserves tend to be dissipated (for example $dZ/dt = -150$ in figure 10.10), unless there are long-term capital inflows, such as foreign aid.

5   *The effort to simultaneously control price and quantity.*   The high degree of politicization of the foreign exchange market during the IS sub-phase can be seen from the fact that monetary authorities attempt to simultaneously control both the price and quantity of foreign exchange. While the e is lowered to benefit importers, the resulting shortage of foreign exchange quite naturally leads to the imposition of quantitative controls on imports as the consequence of the gradual exhaustion of the FE reserves. When and if these reserves are at or near exhaustion, an equilibrium control point will be established, for example at point A in figure 10.10, where the amount of foreign exchange

allocatable to importers (for example, $50) is limited by the amount of foreign exchange earned by exporters. The excess demand (in our example, $200-50=\$150$) must be cut off by quantitative restrictions.

There exists a theoretical possibility that the available foreign exchange (for example, $50) could be allocated to importers via an auctioning process. In that case the foreign exchange rate would be raised to point B (figure 10.10) but the central bank gets the profits, thus violating the very purpose of the creation of windfall profits for importing entrepreneurs. What actually usually happens in the IS era is a combination of a system involving quantitative restrictions, such as import licensing with multiple exchange rates to deal with the problem of FE shortage, giving bureaucrats a maximum sense of control as well as a possible source of additional incomes.

6   *Internal orientation.*   The IS phase is an internally oriented phase because the quantity of international trade ($50), measuring both imports and exports, given the FE shortage, is perpetually limited to an amount which is less than what would have happened under free trade (for example, $M_e = E_e = \$90$). Thus, we see that without an adequate FE reserve stock, an overvalued currency intended to promote imports ends up in restricting both imports and exports. The internal orientation (that is, the decline of the value of trade as a fraction of GNP) is a natural consequence as the capital and import intensity of IS industry expands while the volume of trade is restricted. This tendency is, of course, consistent with the post-colonial political tendency to reduce the scope of international economic relations.

7   *Struggle with devaluation, shortage of FE, and price inflation.*   During IS there is always a struggle involving the intertwining of imports (M), exports (E), the exchange rate (e), the foreign exchange stock (Z), and monetary expansion (dm/dt). In figure 10.10, this can be depicted as an oscillation between points A and A'. When the foreign exchange stock is exhausted, a devaluation of e (from A to A') is likely to encourage exports. The tendency to resort to import restrictions leads to the accumulation of additions to the foreign exchange reserve stock that can be used as an anti-inflationary cushion at a later point in time. Import restrictions can then be partially relaxed, but that may only lead once again to the exhaustion of the FE stock and a new cycle. We shall return below to analyzing such cycling behavior in response to alternative friendly and unfriendly exogenous international shocks.

8   *Termination of IS growth.*   In countries like Taiwan, characterized by a shortage of natural resources and a relatively small domestic market, the above process fortunately proved to be short-lived. As we pointed out earlier, without the requisite natural resources to sustain the continuous expansion of primary product exports, the IS process has to

terminate once virtually all the imports of manufactured non-durable consumer goods have been substituted for. The key measure adopted in the effort to reduce trade restrictions is the devaluation of the domestic currency so that the official rate of exchange e moves closer to the equilibrium level. Such a devaluation (associated with exchange rate unification, if necessary), is a prerequisite for the relaxation of other quantitative control measures (such as import licensing) that will have to follow if markets are indeed to replace bureaucratic discretion in determining both the direction of export expansion as well as the choice of imports.

Taiwan moved towards such an EO regime, as can be seen from row IV of our policy evolution chart (table 10.1). The reader will note the discontinuation of the import licensing system (1958) and the abandonment of the multiple exchange rate system (1960) which suggests a determined departure from the politicized system that existed up to that point. Indeed, these FE-related reforms were part and parcel of the famous 19 points of fiscal and economic reform which characterized Taiwan between 1958 and 1961. For example, a unified exchange rate was established, at $e=40$, in 1960, and maintained at that level until 1972, while the economy operated under conditions of considerable price stability (see row III). In terms of figure 10.3 (box B2), this means that the once overvalued domestic currency was devalued to the point where it approached its purchasing power parity value (e_e), such that the trade gap was no longer a factor affecting domestic monetary expansion.

The relatively short (one decade) duration of the IS phase as well as its relative mildness testifies to the shortage of natural resources and the realization that, through devaluation, the system had to shift to a fuller use of its labor force via a sustained non-traditional export drive. The key contribution of foreign capital, mostly aid, now was to ease the temporary pain of adjustment related to the promulgation of the 19 points – instead of, as in some country cases, serving as a substitute for natural resources in prolonging IS.

Operation of the FE market during the EO and TO sub-phases The arrival of the EO sub-phase in Taiwan's transition growth process thus represented a significant landmark largely because it led to the fuller mobilization of the system's considerable human resource potential. The continued evolution of foreign exchange policies to accommodate this necessity represents a by-product of the changing societal consensus and changing morphological characteristics described in figure 10.6 which, in conjunction with figure 10.10, was found to be useful as a guide to our discussion in this section.

For the first ten years of the EO/PES phase (1962–70), the foreign exchange rate was fixed (at $e=40$) at a realistic level, close to purchasing power parity (p/p_f). In figure 10.10, such an equilibrium is established at point "e" consistent with both price stability and stability of the FE reserves. What marks off this initial EO period most markedly from the IS phase is the move from an overvalued to an equilibrium exchange rate regime. The development of foreign exchange policies since has been characterized by a shift to an export surplus regime, reversing a key characteristic of the IS era.

This shift should be seen as an evolutionary continuation of the previous view of the political role of government, coupled with a break in economic policy. The fundamental belief in government commands was retained in that the foreign exchange rate was viewed as a policy instrument that should be deployed for growth promotion. However, since the economic situation had by now been radically reversed, the social consensus for the government to overvalue the domestic currency in order to benefit importers disappeared. Instead, the pressure now mounted to undervalue the currency in order to benefit exporters which now became the dominant interest group. The undervaluation of the exchange rate indeed became an essential characteristic that was sustained well beyond the exhaustion of the unskilled labor surplus, (the end of the EO–PES sub-phase, around 1970) and into the eighties (1973–86). During this period we may note a dramatic accumulation of foreign exchange reserves.

It is, moreover, obvious that the overall success of external orientation policies was based on achieving the capacity to produce and export a wide range of initially labor-intensive, and subsequently more capital and skill-intensive, manufactured products for world markets. Technically, this regime shift was due to the combination of three factors:

1   A change in the purchasing power parity that affected the equilibrium exchange rate $(e_e=p/p_f)$. (Thus, the relatively greater world-wide inflation that occurred during the 1970s caused e_e to fall, due to the increase of p_f).

2   Gains in the technological flexibility of the export industries causing the E curve to shift to the right (that is, to E'), causing a decrease in the equilibrium exchange rate. Symmetrically, once domestic producers develop the ability to substitute for imports, the M curve shifts down, which would, again, cause the equilibrium exchange rate to fall.

3   A shift to an export surplus regime, if, with a decrease in the equilibrium exchange rate (that is, from e to e'), the official rate remains constant (for example, stopping at e in figure 10.10).

Our analysis should have made it clear that a shift of the real exchange rate to an export surplus regime can happen in spite of the fact that the official exchange rate remains constant. It may thus reflect an endogenous event rather than the arbitrary will of the central bank.

As shown in row IV of the Taiwan policy evolution matrix, the first (reluctant) appreciation of the NT (from $e=40$ to $e=38$) occurred in 1973 and the second in 1976 (to $e=36$). These appreciations give support to our view above that the central bank can now be expected to support the vested interests of exporters by delaying and minimizing appreciation adjustments, the pressure for which has been sustained, as indicated in our policy matrix.

Depoliticization of the FE market in the TO sub-phase The continuing depoliticization of the FE market represents an important facet of the overall change in government/private sector relations during the transition. A key notion along the way was the gradual emergence of the idea of a floating rate in Taiwan as early as 1978. However, between the announcement of a floating system and actual floating there usually exist substantial time and conceptual gaps. Moreover, since there exist very few, if any, truly "clean" floats in the real world, we are really dealing with "dirty" floats, which may become somewhat "less dirty" over time. As one approaches a cleaner float a prerequisite is that the government be ready to renounce the use of the exchange rate as an instrument to promote growth and instead accepts something approaching central bank neutrality. Once the system has arrived at this point, the technical or organizational dimensions of managing a relatively clean float are relatively easily overcome.

As Taiwan, for example, currently prepares itself for this last step, certain steps must still be taken. For one, the central reserve system must be allowed to atrophy further so that private parties are allowed to hold a portion of the foreign exchange reserves. For another, the central bank must get out of the habit of announcing the level of the official exchange rate and leave this to the commercial (increasingly private) banks.

During the 1978–86 period, Taiwan remained within a system of fairly dirty floats but one characterized by a number of special features:

1 The official exchange rate remained undervalued, which, together with a continuing substantial export surplus, resulted in the dramatic accumulation of foreign exchange reserves to the point where Taiwan's reserves are currently the largest or second largest in the world.[12]

2 The rapid accumulation of FE reserves under a system of dirty floats occurred after Taiwan entered the TO phase (post-1980), during which export surpluses have increased rapidly as the industrial sector acquired an enhanced capacity to exhibit structural flexibility.

3   The general public of Taiwan, as well as Taiwan's Central Bank, are not yet fully receptive to the idea that the foreign exchange rate should not be used as a policy instrument to promote exports. As row IV of our policy evolution chart indicates, some of the preconditions for moving towards a relatively clean float have now been met; nevertheless, old paternalistic habits on the part of government, and security concerns on the part of private actors, do not disappear overnight. This is one of the arenas in which more work clearly needs to be done before Taiwan can really join the circle of mature economics. Since 1988, the NT has further appreciated by more than 40 percent. An appreciation of this magnitude testifies to the extent to which it had earlier been delayed by central bank intervention.[13]

Over the long run, the true significance of the Taiwan appreciation experience is that the public will learn that unless the foreign exchange rate is allowed to float more cleanly it will be forced to be adjusted more abruptly, and probably under international pressure. When this is more widely recognized, the depoliticization battle will finally have been won. At that idealized point, not necessarily shared by all developed countries, incidentally, the central bank can be expected to pursue a policy that, except to moderate seasonal fluctuations and/or react to short-term "hot money" flows, means adhering to its basic autonomy and an unwillingness to yield to political pressures either to devalue or to appreciate.

Long-run capital movements   Long-run capital movements can take the form of capital imports (LRCI) or exports (LRCE). In the case of the typical LDC characterized by a shortage of savings, we usually encounter LRCI early on in the transition process; LRCE may follow later. In the case of Taiwan, international capital movements, treated in row IV of our policy evolution chart, involve the following three, largely sequential, types of capital imports:

1   unilateral transfers or foreign aid (1950–65);
2   government official borrowing for infrastructure and large-scale industrial projects (1950–65);
3   private, profit-seeking foreign investment (1965 onwards).

Early on (during IS) here, as elsewhere, private investment was viewed with suspicion as a neo-colonial threat; given the relatively small domestic market, nor was there a long queue of would-be foreign investors in evidence. Thus, early LRCI flows invariably involved two governments, either concessional flows or foreign aid or less concessional government borrowing from bilateral or multilateral donors for infrastructure or large, directly productive public sector activities.

The inflow of private capital became really significant only after 1965, that is, after the termination of foreign economic assistance. It continued, however, to be tightly controlled by the government – that is, admitted only into specific industries and subject to controls on technology, domestic content, profit remittance, etc. Initially, certain sources, such as overseas Chinese and US investors, were favored and others, such as Japan, excluded. Very gradually, initially in 1955, then again in 1965, and most notably in the 1980s, controls over foreign investors were relaxed and the capital market substantially liberalized.

The common attribute of all types of long-run capital imports is, of course, the transfer of foreign resources permitting the appearance of an equivalent import surplus – that is, the transfer of real resources. We can see from the right-hand side of box T8 of figure 10.9 that an import surplus that does not involve LRCI invariably leads to the dissipation of the foreign exchange reserve stock ($-dZ/dt$) and domestic monetary contraction ($-dm/dt$); it may also lead to the possible cancellation of some portion of domestic monetary expansion for reasons unrelated to foreign trade.

It is quite obvious that running a net import surplus cannot go on indefinitely because the system's foreign exchange reserve stock would be depleted sooner or later. The arrival of long-run capital imports, on the other hand, will have a number of beneficial effects. It permits a net inward transfer of real resources (that is, filling the trade gap $M-E > 0$); it reverses the depletion of the stock of foreign exchange reserves; and it effects a contraction of the money supply, or offsets a portion of the monetary expansion which is taking place for other, "domestic", reasons.

If the foreign exchange stock is not drawn down, we thus have:

$$dm/dt = F + (I-S) \qquad \text{monetary contraction of domestic origin}$$
$$dm'/dt = -(M-E) \qquad \text{monetary contraction of foreign origin}$$
$$n = dm/dt - dm'/dt \qquad n \text{ is net monetary expansion}$$
$$n = F + (I-S) - (M-E)$$

In the particular case of foreign aid, the exhaustion of the FE stock can be prevented by such unilateral transfers. In case the saving/investment gap is zero ($I=S$), the above equation reduces to $n=F-(M-E)$, which states that the net monetary expansion can be used to fill the difference between the two gaps – the government budget gap and the import/export gap – to provide the LDC with real resources as the government budget deficit is closed. One can reasonably argue that, in the case of Taiwan, the main purpose of the foreign aid program in the 1950s was to help the government fight inflation, while allowing it time to develop its own tax capacity and, in the early 1960s, to ease the pains of adjustment as the system moved out of its IS and into its EO sub-phase with the help of the 19 point reform program. Undoubtedly the 1961 announcement by the USA that economic aid to Taiwan would be terminated by 1965 had a strong impact on bringing the government budget into balance (by 1964) and ensuring the implementation of the rest of the reform program.

Typically, as an LDC moves out of its IS and into its EO sub-phase, it becomes more willing to admit private foreign investment, both of the portfolio and (especially) the equity type – recognizing the merits not only of such capital inflows but also of the "bundled" technology, managerial, and information resources. Simultaneously, foreign investors now find the LDC a more attractive place to put their capital and participate in its increasingly depoliticized production and export activities. This is clearly what happened in Taiwan between the mid-1960s and mid-1980s. However, as the previously analyzed export surpluses made their appearance and became a persistent feature, not only was there an explosion of the country's foreign exchange reserves but LRCE began to put in an appearance. The current picture of Taiwan as a modest aid donor as well as a major foreign investor, especially in neighboring Southeast Asian countries and mainland China, is part of the natural evolution of the successful system that we have tried to analyze.

Figure 10.10 can be made use of to summarize our analysis of LRCM. Before 1960, that is, during the IS sub-phase, the equilibrium position can be represented by points A and C indicating that the trade gap (\$150) is closed by US aid to replenish the foreign exchange reserves ($dZ/dt = -150$) and to contribute to monetary contraction ($dm/dt = -150$) to combat inflation. After the termination of the foreign aid program in 1965, the LRCM took on the form of profit seeking investments by foreigners. Once export surpluses began to appear consistently, after 1980, the equilibrium position can be represented by points B' and C'. The export surplus ($B'C'$) led to two types of adjustments. On the one hand, it permitted a huge accumulation of foreign exchange reserves. On the other hand, especially towards the latter part of the 1980s, Taiwan became a capital exporter – especially to mainland China and neighboring Southeast Asian countries – all of which is a further indication that Taiwan is getting ready to join the ranks of the industrially advanced countries.

10.4.6 Accommodative policy in an evolutionary context

Our basic premise in this chapter has been that policy change in various critical markets has been consistently accommodative of underlying economic change in the east Asian context, seen as the prototype of successful development, and that these underlying economic changes must themselves be viewed in an evolutionary context. The basic destination of that process is the arrival of modern economic growth which, in addition to the well-known Kuznets criteria, includes institutional/organizational changes permitting the full participation of a society's creative human potential.

These changes have both negative as well as positive connotations. The negative connotations center on the need for a gradual depoliticization of the government's role in the economic arena. The positive connotations reside in the role of government as a source of organizational/institutional change enhancing freedom of choice and diversity of outputs accompanying increasingly complex and competitive markets.

As Kuznets pointed out some time ago, modern economic growth has cultural as well as structural economic origins (including nationalism) eroding feudal divisions, rational egalitarianism (upholding the competitive principle), and secularism – emphasizing this-worldly pursuits. Our presentation of a sequence of operational perspectives from figures 10.2–10.6 to figures 10.9 and 10.10 in this chapter was intended to capture this historical process. The policy evolution matrix of table 10.1 demonstrated, for one economy in transition, the necessary evolution of accommodating policies.

Finally, we shall endeavor to summarize what we have learned, hopefully of transferable value, in this context.

1   First, the asymmetry between the treatment of agriculture and non-agriculture must be recognized. Agriculture's historical mission is to fuel, over time, the expansion of the non-agricultural sector in a balanced growth context. Agriculture, moreover, is likely to be the main foreign exchange earner during the early import substitution sub-phase, an indication of evolutionary continuity with the prior colonial era. However, what needs to be stressed in policy-relevant terms is the importance of the locational dimension in breaking down internal colonial compartmentalization between the sectors by means of early attention to rural infrastructure. It should also be noted that the customary pronounced urban bias of policies can be avoided via the relatively mild application of more overt rather than covert income transfers from agriculture to non-agriculture. Providing agriculture with less unfavorable terms of trade than is typical early on led to a vigorous response by large numbers of dispersed Taiwanese farmers both in terms of domestic productivity change and export diversification. Taiwan's export orientation, it is often forgotten, was initially spearheaded by the agricultural sector.

2   The primary import substitution sub-phase (1950–62) also represents a natural evolution from its colonial antecedents. Growth promoting activism by the newly independent government, building on pre-existing Z-goods and focusing on relatively "easy" consumer goods

home production, consisted of the bureaucratic direction of foreign exchange and savings funds, combined with some early reliance on public sector enterprises taken over from the Japanese. Covert income transfers via exchange rate overvaluation and higher effective protection for non-agriculture meant the relative victimization of agriculture for a time, and of consumers for a longer period. But even during this, seemingly inevitable, import substitution sub-phase of transition, critical human capital accumulation through the continued strong emphasis on previously laid foundations of increased adult literacy took place.

3   Especially in natural resources poor, labor abundant societies, the EO sub-phases evolve naturally out of the prior IS period. The increasing export orientation of the labor intensive non-agricultural sector implies a vent for surplus leading to rapid increases of GNP and improved income distribution equity (counter to the inverse U-shaped hypothesis), even before the labor surplus condition has been eliminated. After the commercialization point we witness enhanced product diversification and structural flexibility.

Accommodating policies means continuing to build the required human infrastructure. During EO-PES this means extending compulsory education to nine years while simultaneously substantially expanding the vocational education component of secondary education. During EO-SES it means substantial government institutional construction in the science and technology area as well as enhanced incentives for tertiary education in the engineering and science-oriented specialties.

4   It should be noted that during both EO sub-phases, the domestic market remained subject to mild versions of both bureaucratic investment allocation guidance and covert income transfer policies. With respect to the international market, however, its separation from the domestic market was accomplished by a series of complementary accommodating policy measures including the early devaluation (and subsequent maintenance at fairly realistic levels) of the exchange rate, the establishment of a number of export processing zones, and the system of import duty rebates for the exported portion of output. The latter may be viewed as transitional devices facilitating the drive for exports while preserving a substantial measure of political interference in domestic markets. This combination of policies demonstrates the gradual evolutionary principle of change.

By the 1970s, moreover, as the Taiwan economy entered the more skill and capital intensive EO-SES sub-phase, government's direction of domestic investment activity and covert income transfers became more nuanced and can be best explained in terms of the loanable

funds framework of thinking. With the investment and output structure becoming increasingly complex, interventions in the domestic
credit markets became less specific, that is, shifted further away from
individual companies or products to broader sectoral or "strategic
industry" categories. Covert income transfer activities continued to
take the form of central bank actions to increase the money supply
(dm/dt) and/or repress the interest rate in the framework of our figure
10.9-related discussion. What is important to recall, however, in the
context of our evolutionary perspective is that one can observe an
increasing societal consensus to respect central bank autonomy. The
concept of "growth with stability" has increasingly become the corner-
stone of policy in the 1970s and 1980s, with tax reforms never allowing
budget deficits to become a serious cause of monetary expansion.

5   Once the successful export drive, first agricultural, then industrial,
convinced Taiwan's entrepreneurs that they could compete successfully in international markets, the next set of accommodating policy
changes focused on additional opening up of the domestic market.
Government could now focus increasingly on creating the necessary
science and technology infrastructure and further enhance the work-
able competitiveness of various interrelated markets, including the
finance and foreign capital markets. For example, the 1970s witnessed
the establishment of a government bond market and a broader money
market, both necessary preconditions for a reasonably full liberalization of the interest rate, with the commercial banks no longer waiting
for central bank commands, but setting their own competitive rates,
using the money market rate for operational guidance. Moreover,
overall levels of protection of domestic industry were gradually being
reduced.

6   Finally, during the TO sub-phase the major accommodating policy
events included a much more pronounced integration with the rest of
the world through further depoliticization and conversion to a reasonably "clean" floating exchange rate system. With Taiwan approaching
economic maturity, tariff protection was severely reduced, including
via the simplification of customs clearing procedures. Foreign institutions were allowed to participate in the stock market and capital
account restrictions both for nationals and foreign investors were
gradually eased. The centralized foreign exchange reserve system and
the compulsory surrender of foreign exchange to the Central Bank
were overhauled in 1987; residents are now allowed to hold and use
foreign exchange.

The gradual depoliticization of government actions in support of the
transition process undoubtedly also carried with it the seeds of
marked democratic change in the political arena. The greater

transparency, communication and information sharing required for overt, as opposed to covert, actions by government undoubtedly implies spill-over for government/society relations in general.

10.5 The Political Economy of Policy from an Evolutionary Perspective

Interpretations of what is meant by the old or new "political economy" dimensions of policy and policy change vary widely, depending on the problem to be addressed and the particular scientific interest of the observer. Some economists and political scientists, for example, focus on the relationship and possible sequencing between economic policy reforms and the presence or absence of democratic political reforms. Others trace out the relevance for various possible outcomes of alternative views of the state, as a rational choice actor using economic agents and/or responding to median voter views in political markets and/or possibly as a predator with its own self-seeking economic or survival agenda. Our own interest has been restricted to trying to understand why some developing societies, such as Taiwan, followed a relatively smooth evolutionary path *en route* to modern economic growth as described in this chapter, while others, for example the Philippines, seem to find it difficult to follow suit. We have endeavored to analyze **what** happened in the successful case; the question of **why** it happened, that is, why the policies chosen generally accommodated, instead of obstructing, the smooth transition through the various sub-phases remains an issue warranting attention.

We, of course, do not claim to be able to answer that question, only to try to render policy and policy change somewhat more endogenous. What we have tried to do in this chapter, beyond examining the policy sequence adopted over the various sub-phases of development, is to emphasize its evolutionary characteristic, that is, the general avoidance of major breaks with the past even as the system shifted from one sub-phase to another. But that recognition still requires further explanation in terms of important differences in the initial conditions which apparently affected subsequent policy choices so markedly in different parts of the developing world over time – witness the contrast between Taiwan and the Philippines, for example.

Three dimensions of such initial conditions strike us as worthy of examination.[14] The first is the extent to which the previously referred to Kuznetsian condition of "nationalism" exists organically at the outset or needs to be synthetically created by a newly independent government. The contrast between Taiwan and the Philippines serves to make the point convincingly. The former sported a relatively homogeneous population, a contiguous territory replete with both physical and institutional infrastructure left behind by the Japanese colonial regime; the latter, in sharp contrast, encompassed a heterogeneous population of many languages, religions and ethnic origins spread over an archipelago of thousands of islands, with both physical and social infrastructures in relatively poor condition. Under such circumstances much more was clearly expected of the government in creating a previously non-existent nationalism in order to pull the various disparate elements together into what may realistically be called an economy for which one set of economic policies become relevant. Consequently the extent of interventionism and covert income transfers was much more pronounced during the early import substitution sub-phase; but once such expansionary growth promoting habits of governments are formed they are likely to harden and persist, rendering the transition to export orientation more difficult. Exaggerated expectations of government's responsibilities and of its ability to meet them help, *ceteris paribus*, to move a system towards a more rigid and elongated period of import substitution and a greater likelihood of stop/go policy oscillation later on. By contrast, in the Taiwan type of situation, the import substitution sub-phase was bound to be briefer, milder and more flexible, and the transition to export orientation thus considerably eased. The temptation to pursue growth activist policies for prolonged periods of time was considerably reduced.

The second dimension of initial conditions we believe to be of critical importance in determining the policy space within which a developing economy can afford to operate is the endowment of natural as opposed to human resources. It is well established that the East Asian labor surplus type of developing economy, represented here by Taiwan, in contrast to, say, the Philippine or Latin American prototype, had relatively high initial levels of literacy and relatively low natural resource endowments. The first dimension, quite conventionally, constituted a strong foundation for the human capital formation which followed, adjusting flexibly to the changing requirements of the economy over the various sub-phases of the transition process. The second dimension, however, constitutes an important political economy link which has not received as much attention to date as we believe is warranted. In our view, it is the absence of a favorable natural resource endowment which can serve to encourage the early adoption of accommodating policy changes keeping a system on a relatively smooth evolutionary path to mature economic growth.

The early import substitution sub-phase is, as has been noted above, characterized by a substantial amount of direct government intervention and the covert redistribution of income flows to certain favored groups, including the new industrial class, organized labor and some of the bureau-crats who hand out the "goodies." The rents which are distributed in this fashion largely emanate from the traditional, natural resource-based exports. The larger these rents, the more difficult it is to give them up and hence the greater the resistance of vested interest groups to the policy changes required if the system is to be able to move into its export-ori-ented sub-phase. Governments acting on behalf of themselves and/or these private interest groups, will be tempted to persist much longer in using the various instruments under their control, that is, the exchange rate, the interest rate, the rate of monetary expansion, as well as the rate of protection, to transfer incomes and micro-manage the allocation of credit in ways we have analyzed in this chapter.

One common sense way of putting the proposition is that the relative abundance of natural resources tends to take the pressure off the decision makers. They are tempted to continue "business as usual" and avoid painful policy change as long as the primary export fuel continues to flow abundantly. Indeed, such a process may be viewed as a political economy extension of the more narrowly defined Dutch disease syndrome, in this case not only keeping the exchange rate overly strong but also having a generally pernicious effect on the decision-making processes of govern-ment. As a result, the system is much less likely to effect the necessary evolutionary shift from land-based, to a labor-based and, subsequently, to a skill and technology-based output and export mix. Even after the EO sub-phase is entered the natural resource rich economy is, moreover, more likely, *ceteris paribus*, to return to import substitution types of policies from time to time, instead of adjusting flexibly to the inevitable advent of temporary exogenous shocks. This phenomenon is likely to yield a stop-go pattern of behavior often associated in the past with Latin America as interventionist episodes alternate with liberalization periods; as a conse-quence, the gradual evolutionary depoliticization process described in this chapter for the natural resources poor East Asian case is severely hampered.

A third and related dimension we need to briefly refer to is tied to a system's relative ability to attract long term foreign capital.[15] Such an abil-ity seems to be highly correlated, certainly in the early stages of develop-ment, with the strength of the natural resource endowment and appears to have a similar political economy impact on the existing policy space. Long-term foreign capital can indeed be viewed, like natural resources, as a source of "under the table" rents whose pursuit can similarly delay or even abort required policy reform.

It should, of course, be understood that additional indigenous natural resources or additional foreign capital inflows need not be viewed as intrinsically or necessarily bad; they can both clearly assist in reducing the short run pain of policy adjustment by providing additional lubrication and the ability to buy off resistant interest groups. It is only in the political economy sense that both are likely to convince policy makers that they can put off painful reforms to another day. As a consequence, policies become obstructive of evolutionary change rather than accommodating it, as in the East Asian case. Delay in the shift to a human capital-focused development pattern can have serious long-term consequences not only for the achievement of full employment and successful entry into modern economic growth, but also for the enhancement of equity and the alleviation of poverty along the way.

CHAPTER 10   POLICY AND POLITICAL ECONOMY IN THE TRANSITION TO MODERN ECONOMIC GROWTH

NOTES

1   Earlier, of course, in Latin America.
2   Kuznets (1966).
3   With respect to the spectacularly successful East Asian cases, most recently in The World Bank's *The East Asian Miracle: Economic Growth and Public Policy* (1993).
4   For a fuller treatment of this *Methodenstreit* in the development literature, see Ranis (1984).
5   See Lipton (1976).
6   For a more extensive discussion of especially the human capital story see Ranis (1995a).
7   See Ranis (1992b) for a number of contributions dealing with this subject on a sector-by-sector basis.
8   The reader will note that G and T are not separately shown in figure 10.4 which consolidates private and public households.
9   It should be noted that such a holistic disaggregative framework is different both from the aggregative (Keynesian) framework in macroeconomics as well as from the disaggregated framework (of the general equilibrium variety) in microeconomics. It is equally irrelevant to what are often called the "microeconomic foundations to macro-theory" due to the fact that the disaggregative holistic framework is being deployed here for a particular purpose, namely to address the issue of the modernization of the LDC's industrial sector in an evolutionary perspective.
10   For more on the political economy implications of this, see section 10.5.
11   It should be noted that if imports and exports are valued in terms of domestic currency, if p denotes the domestic price level, imports and exports are M/p and E/p in real terms respectively, with a value of Mp_f/p and Ep_f/p in terms of international (dollar) prices.

12 There is a special political undertone to the amassing of such a huge cache of foreign exchange reserves in the case of Taiwan. While, ordinarily, such stocks are viewed as liquid (low income earning) assets as a contingency against sudden import surpluses, in this case, they are additionally viewed as a national security nest egg in case of renewed military confrontation with the mainland.

13 It should, in passing, be noted that most of Taiwan's economics profession has opposed even such reluctant appreciations for any number of reasons, including the fear of hot money inflows to Mexico, the need to help small exporters, etc.. Thus, as Keynes predicted, it is a combination of vested ideas and vested interests that often stand in the way of progress.

14 For a fuller exposition as well as empirical test of what is only sketched here, see Ranis and Mahmood (1992).

15 See Ranis (1995b) for an incorporation of this element.

Bibliography

Adelman, I. and Robinson, S. 1989: Income Distribution and Development. In H. Chenery and T.N. Srinivasan (eds), *Handbook of Development Economics*, vol. 2, Amsterdam: North Holland.

Adulavidhya, K., Kurida, Y., Lau, L., Lerttamrab, P. and Yotopoulos, P. 1979: A Microeconomic Analysis of the Agriculture of Thailand, *Food Research Institute Studies*, 17.

Ahluwalia, M.S. 1976a: Income Distribution and Development: Some Stylized Facts, *American Economic Review*, 66.

—— 1976b: Inequality, Poverty, and Development, *Journal of Development Economics*, 3(4).

Ahluwalia, M.S., Carter, G. and Chenery, H.B. 1979: Growth and Poverty in Developing Countries. *World Bank Staff Working Paper* No. 309. Washington, DC: The World Bank.

Ahluwalia, M.S., Nicholas, S., Carter, G. and Chenery, H.B. 1979: Growth and Poverty in Developing Countries, *Journal of Development Economics*, 6.

Ahuja, K. 1978: *Idle Labour in Village India*. Delhi: Manohar.

Anderson, D. and Leiserson, M. 1980: Rural Nonfarm Employment in Developing Countries, *Economic Development and Cultural Change*, 28.

Arrow, K.J. 1962: The Economic Implications of Learning by Doing, *Review of Economic Studies*, 29.

—— 1988: International Economic Association presidential address, New Delhi, India.

Atkinson, A.B. 1970: On the Measurement of Inequality, *Journal of Economic Theory*, 2.

Ayub, M.A. 1977: Income Inequality in a Growth-Theoretic Context: The Case of Pakistan. Unpublished PhD thesis, Yale University.

Bacha, E. 1978: Beyond the Kuznets Curve: Growth and Inequality, *Economia*, 2(2).

Bagachwa, M.S.D. and Stewart, F. 1991: Rural Industries and Rural Linkages in SubSaharan Africa. In F. Stewart, S. Lall, and S. Wangwe (eds), *Alternative Development Strategies in SubSaharan Africa*. London: Macmillan Press.

Baldwin, R.E. 1956: Patterns of Development in Newly Settled Regions, *Manchester School*, 24(2).

Barnum, H. and Squire, L. 1978: An Econometric Application of the Theory of the Farm Household, *Oxford Bulletin of Economics and Statistics*, 43.

Bautista, R.M. 1971: Dynamics of an Agrarian Model with Z-Goods. *Discussion Paper* No. 714, Institute of Economic Development and Research, University of the Philippines.

Behrman, J. and Schneider, R. 1992: Empirical Evidence on the Determinants of and the Impact of Human Capital Investments and Related Policies for Developing Countries, *Indian Economic Review*, 27.

—— 1993: An International Perspective on Pakistan's Human Capital Investments, *Pakistan Development Review*, 32(1).

Berry, A. and Urrutia, M. 1976: *Income Distribution in Colombia*. New Haven: Yale University Press.

Berry, A. and Soligo, R. 1980: *Economic Policy and Income Distribution in Colombia*. Boulder, CO: Westview Press.

Booth, A. and Sundrum, R.M. 1985: *Labour Absorption in Agriculture*. Oxford: Oxford University Press.

Boserup, E. 1965: *The Conditions of Agricultural Growth*. Chicago: Aldine.

Cairncross, A. 1960: International Trade and Economic Development. *Kyklos*, 13(4).

Chenery, H.B. 1960: Patterns of Industrial Growth, *American Economic Review*, 50(4).

Chenery, H.B. and Taylor, L. 1968: Development Patterns among Countries Over Time, *Review of Economics and Statistics*, 50(4).

Chenery, H.B., Ahluwalia, M.S., Bell, C., Duloy, J. and Jolly, R. 1974: *Redistribution with Growth*. London: Oxford University Press.

Clark, J.B. 1899: *The Distribution of Wealth*. London: Macmillan.

Cline, W.R. 1975: Distribution and Development, *Journal of Development Economics*, 1.

Cornia, G.A., Jolly, R. and Stewart, F. 1987: *Adjustment with a Human Face*. Oxford: Oxford University Press.

De Costa, E. 1930: The Cotton Textile Industry. In M. Ghandi (ed.) *The Indian Cotton Textile Industry*. Calcutta: G.N. Mitra Publishing.

Denison, E. 1985: *Trends in American Economic Growth*. Washington, DC: Brookings Institute.

Fei, J.C.H. and Chiang, A. 1966: Maximum Speed Development Through Austerity. In I. Adelman and E. Thorbecke (eds), *The Theory and*

Design of Economic Development. Baltimore, MD: Johns Hopkins University Press.

Fei, J.C.H. and Fields, G. 1978: On Inequality Comparisons, *Econometrica*, 46.

Fei, J.C.H. and Ranis, G. 1965: Innovation Intensity and Factor Bias in the Theory of Growth, *International Economic Review*, 6(2).

—— 1966: Agrarianism, Dualism and Economic Development. In I. Adelman and E. Thorbecke (eds) *The Theory and Design of Economic Development*, Baltimore, MD: Johns Hopkins University Press.

Fei, J.C.H., Ranis, G. and Kuo, S. 1978: Growth and the Family Distribution of Income by Factor Components, *Quarterly Journal of Economics*, 93.

—— 1979: *Growth with Equity: The Taiwan Case*. Oxford: Oxford University Press.

Fields, G.S. 1980: *Poverty, Inequality, and Development*. Cambridge: Cambridge University Press.

—— 1988: Income Distribution and Economic Growth. In G. Ranis and T.P. Schultz (eds), *The State of Development Economics: Progress and Perspectives*. Oxford: Blackwell.

—— 1989a: A Compendium of Data on Inequality and Poverty for the Developing World, Cornell University *mimeo*.

—— 1989b: Poverty, Inequality, and Economic Growth, Cornell University *mimeo*.

Fields, G.S. and Jakubsen, G. 1990: The Inequality-Development Relationship in Developing Countries, Cornell University *mimeo*.

Fisk, E.K. 1962: Planning in a Primitive Economy, *Economic Record*, 38.

Foster, J., Greer, J. and Thorbecke, E. 1984: A Class of Decomposable Poverty Measures, *Econometrica*, 52(3).

Georgescu-Roegen, N. 1960: Economic Theory and Agrarian Economics, *Oxford Economic Papers*, 12.

Griliches, Z. and Jorgenson, D. 1967: The Explanation of Productivity Changes, *Review of Economic Studies*, 34.

Grilli, E. and Yang, M.C. 1988: Primary Commodity Prices, Manufactured Food Prices and the Terms of Trade of Developing Countries: What the Long Run Shows, *World Bank Economic Review*, 2(1).

Grossman, G. and Helpman, E. 1989a: Product Development and International Trade, *Journal of Political Economy*, 97.

—— 1989b: Comparative Advantage and Long-Run Growth, *NBER Working Paper* No. 2809.

—— 1989c: Endogenous Product Cycles, *NBER Working Paper* No. 2913.

—— 1989d: Growth and Welfare in a Small Open Economy, *NBER Working Paper* No. 2970.

—— 1989e: Quality Ladders and Product Cycles, *NBER Working Paper* No. 3201.

—— 1991: *Innovation and Growth in the Global Economy.* Cambridge, MA: MIT Press.

Haberler, G. 1959: *International Trade and Economic Development.* New York: Macmillan.

Haggblade, S., Liedholm, C. and Mead, D. 1986: The Effect of Policy and Policy Reforms on Non-Agricultural Enterprises and Employment in Developing Countries: A Review of Past Experiences. Michigan State University, *Working Paper* No. 27.

Hansen, B. 1969: Employment and Wages in Rural Egypt, *American Economic Review*, 59.

—— 1975: Colonial Economic Development With Unlimited Supply of Land: The Ricardian Case. Department of Economics, Monash University, Melbourne, Australia, *Seminar Paper* No. 40.

Hanson, J. 1971: Employment and Rural Wages in Egypt: A Reinterpretation, *American Economic Review*, 61.

Harrod, R.F. 1960: *Towards a Dynamic Economics.* London: Macmillan.

Hayami, Y. and Kikuchi, M. 1982: *Asian Village Economy at the Crossroads.* Baltimore, MD: Johns Hopkins University Press.

Helleiner, G. 1966: Peasant Agriculture, *Stanford Food Research Institute Studies*, 6(2).

Hendrick, J. and Grossman, E. 1980: *Productivity in the US: Trends and Cycles.* Baltimore, MD: Johns Hopkins University Press.

Hicks, J.R. 1964: *The Theory of Wages.* London: Macmillan.

Ho, S.P.S. 1979: Decentralized Industrialization and Rural Development: Evidence from Taiwan, *Economic Development and Cultural Change*, 28.

Huang, C. 1971: Tenancy Patterns, Productivity, and Rentals in Malaysia, *Economic Development and Cultural Change*, 23(4).

Hymer, S. and Resnick, S. 1969: A Model of an Agrarian Economy with Non-Agricultural Activities, *American Economic Review*, 59(4).

International Labour Office 1977: *The Basic Needs Approach to Development.* Geneva: ILO.

Ishikawa, S. 1975: Peasant Families and the Agrarian Community in the Process of Economic Development. In L. Reynolds (ed.), *Agriculture in Development Theory.* New Haven, CT: Yale University Press.

—— 1981: *Essays on Technology, Employment, and Institutions in Economic Development.* Tokyo: Kino Kuniya.

Jain, S. 1975: *Size Distribution of Income: A Compilation of Data.* Baltimore, MD: Johns Hopkins University Press.

Jorgenson, D.W. 1961: The Development of a Dual Economy, *Economic Journal*, 71.

Jorgenson, D.W. 1966: Testing Alternative Theories of the Development of a Dual Economy. In I. Adelman and E. Thorbecke (eds), *The Theory and Design of Economic Development*, Baltimore, MD: Johns Hopkins University Press.

Kaldor, N. 1956: Alternative Theories of Distribution, *Review of Economic Studies*, 23(2).

—— 1963: Capital Accumulation and Economic Growth. In F. Lutz (ed.), *The Theory of Capital*. London: Macmillan.

Kalecki, M. 1971: *Selected Essays on the Dynamics of the Capitalist Economy*. Cambridge: Cambridge University Press.

Krishna, R. 1973: Unemployment in India, *Indian Journal of Agricultural Economics*, 28(1).

Krugman, P. 1979: Increasing Returns, Monopolistic Competition, and International Trade, *Journal of International Economics*, 9.

—— 1980: Scale Economies, Product Differentiation, and the Pattern of Trade, *American Economic Review*, 70.

—— 1992: Towards a Counter-Counter-Revolution in Development Theory, *mimeo*.

Kuczynski, M. and Meek, R. 1972: *Quesnay's Tableau Economique*. London: Macmillan.

Kuznets, S. 1955: Economic Growth and Income Inequality, *American Economic Review*, 45(1).

—— 1966: *Modern Economic Growth, Rate and Structure*. New Haven, CT: Yale University Press.

—— 1980: Employment Absorption in South Korea, *Philippine Review of Economics and Business*, 25(1–2).

Lal, D. 1985: *The Poverty of Development Economics*. Cambridge, MA: Harvard University Press.

Lau, L., Lin, W. and Yotopoulos, P. 1978: The Linear Logarithmic Expenditure System: An Application to Consumption-Leisure Choice, *Econometrica*, 46.

Leibenstein, H. 1966: Allocative Efficiency versus X-Efficiency, *American Economic Review*, 56.

Lewis, A. 1954: Development with Unlimited Supplies of Labor, *The Manchester School*, 22.

Lindert, P. and Williamson, J. 1983: English workers' living standards during the industrial revolution: a new look, *Economic History Review*, 36.

Lipton, M. 1976: *Why Poor People Stay Poor: Urban Bias in Development*. Cambridge, MA: Harvard University Press.

Liu, P. 1992: Science, Technology and Human Capital Formation. In G. Ranis (ed.), *Taiwan: From Developing to Mature Economy*. Boulder, CO: Westview Press.

Londono, J. 1990: Human Capital and Long-Run Swings in Income Distribution: Columbia 1938–1988, Harvard University, *mimeo*.

Lucas, R.E. 1988: On the Mechanics of Economic Development, *Journal of Monetary Economics*, 22.

—— 1993: Making a Miracle, *Econometrica*, 61(2).

Marx, K. 1890: *Capital: A Critical Analysis of Capitalist Production*. 3rd edn (ed. F. Engels) New York: Humboldt Publishing.

—— 1975: *Collected Works*. Moskva: Progress.

Mehra, S. 1966: Surplus Labour in Indian Agriculture, *Indian Economic Review*, 1.

Minami, R. 1968: The Turning Point in the Japanese Economy, *Quarterly Journal of Economics*, 82.

Mukerji, K. 1959: Trends in Real Wages in Cotton Textile Industry, *Artha Vijnana*, 1(1).

Nicholls, W. 1961: Industrialization, Factor Markets and Agricultural Development, *Journal of Political Economy*, 69.

Nicholls, W. and Tang, A.M. 1958: *Economic Development in the Southern Piedmont, 1860–1950: Its Importance for Agriculture*. Nashville: Vanderbilt University Press.

Otsuka, K.,Ranis, G. and Saxonhouse, G. 1988: *Comparative Technology Choice in Development*. London: Macmillan.

Paauw, D.S. and Fei, J.C.H. 1965: Development Strategies and Planning Issues in South-East Asian Type Economies, *The Philippine Economic Journal*, 4(2).

Pack, H. 1992: Technology Gaps Between Developed and Developing Countries: Are There Dividends for Latecomers? *Mimeo*.

Pack, H. and Westphal, L. 1986: Industrial Strategy and Technical Change: Theory versus Reality, *Journal of Economic Development*, 22.

Papanek, G.F. 1978: Economic Growth, Income Distribution, and the Political Process in Less Developed Countries. In Z. Griliches *et al.* (eds), *Income Distribution and Economic Inequality*. New York: Halsted Press.

—— 1990: Growth, Poverty, and Real Wages in Labor Abundant Countries, paper presented at North-East Development Economics Conference; Economic Growth Center, Yale University.

Papanek, G.F. and Kyn, O. 1987: Flattening the Kuznets Curve: The Consequences for Income Distribution of Development Strategy, Government Intervention, Income and the Rate of Growth. *Pakistan Development Review*, 26.

Paukert, F. 1973: Income Distribution at Different Levels of Development: A Survey of Evidence. *International Labour Review*, 108(2–3).

Pearse, A.S. 1930: *The Cotton Industry of India*. Manchester: Taylor, Garnett, Evans & Co.

Pigou, A.C. 1912: *Wealth and Welfare*. London: MacMillan & Co.

—— 1920: *The Economics of Welfare*. London: MacMillan & Co.

—— 1955: *Income Revisited*. London: MacMillan & Co.

Ranis, G. 1973: Industrial Sector Labor Absorption, *Economic Development and Cultural Change*, April.

—— 1978: Equity with Growth in Taiwan: How Special is the Special Case? *World Development*, 6(3).

—— 1980: Distribución del ingreso y crecimiento en Colombia, *Desarollo y Sociedad*, 3.

—— 1984: Typology in Development Theory: Retrospective and Prospects. In M. Syrquin, L. Taylor, and L.E. Westphal (eds), *Economic Structure and Performance: Essays in Honor of Hollis B. Chenery*. Orlando, FL: Academic Press.

—— 1992: International Migration and Foreign Assistance. Geneva: International Labor Organization.

—— (ed.) 1992b: *Taiwan: From Developing to Mature Economy*. Boulder, CO: Westview Press.

—— 1995a: Another Look at the East Asian Miracle, *World Bank Economic Review*, 9.

—— 1995b: The Comparative Development Experience of Mexico, the Philippines and Taiwan from a Political Economy Perspective, prepared for the Ford Foundation.

Ranis, G. and Fei, J.C.H. 1975: Growth and Employment in the Open Dualistic Economy: The Case of Korea and Taiwan, *Journal of Development Studies*, 12.

Ranis, G. and Fei, J.C.H. 1982: Lewis and the Classicists. In M. Gersovitz, C. Diaz-Alejandro, G. Ranis and M. Rosenzweig (eds), *The Theory and Experiences of Economic Development: Essays in Honor of Sir W. Arthur Lewis*. London: Allen and Unwin.

Ranis, G. and Mahmood, S.A. 1992: *The Political Economy of Development Policy Change*. Cambridge, MA: Blackwell.

Ranis, G. and Stewart, F. 1993: Rural Nonagricultural Activities in Development: Theory and Application, *Journal of Development Economics*, 40.

Resnick, S. 1970: The Decline of Rural Industry Under Export Expansion: A Comparison Among Burma, the Philippines and Thailand, 1870–1938, *Journal of Economic History*, 30.

Ricardo, D. 1963: *Principles of Political Economy and Taxation*. Homewood, IL: Irwin.

Romer, P. 1986: Increasing Returns and Long-Run Growth. *Journal of Political Economy*, 94.

—— 1989: Capital Accumulation in the Theory of Long-Run Growth. In

R. Barro (ed.), *Modern Business Cycle Theory*. Cambridge, MA: Harvard University Press.

—— 1992: "Two Strategies of Economic Development: Using Ideas versus Producing Ideas, *mimeo*.

Rosenzweig, M. 1988: Labor Markets in Low Income Countries. In H. Chenery and T.N. Srinivasan (eds), *Handbook of Development Economics*, vol. 1. Amsterdam: North Holland.

Ruttan, V. 1991: Subsistence Agriculture and Economic Growth. Agricultural Development Council, Seminar on Subsistence and Peasant Economies, East-West Center, Hawaii.

Saith, A. 1983: Development and Distribution: A Critique of the Cross-Country *U*-Hypothesis, *Journal of Development Economics*, 13.

Sanghui, P. 1969: *Surplus Manpower in Agriculture and Economic Development*. New York: Asia Publishing House.

Schumpeter, J.A. 1942: *Capitalism, Socialism, and Democracy*. New York: Harper & Brothers.

Scott, J.C. 1976: *The Moral Economy of the Peasant*. New Haven, CT: Yale University Press.

Scott, M. 1989: *A New View of Economic Growth*. Oxford: Clarendon Press.

—— 1992: Policy Implications of "A New View of Economic Growth," *Economic Journal*, 102.

Sen, A. 1973: *On Economic Inequality*. Oxford: Clarendon Press.

—— 1979: The Welfare Basis of Real Income Comparisons, *Journal of Economic Literature*, 17(1).

—— 1984: *Resources, Values and Development*. Cambridge, MA: Harvard University Press.

—— 1992: *Inequality Reexamined*. New York: Russel Sage Foundation.

Shand, R.T. (ed.) 1986: *Off-Farm Employment in the Development of Rural Asia*. Canberra: NCDS, Australian National University.

Smith, A. 1776: *An Inquiry into the Nature and Causes of the Wealth of Nations*. London: Printed for W. Strahan and T. Cadell.

Solow, R. 1988: Growth Theory and After, *American Economic Review*, 78(3).

Spraos, J. 1980: The Statistical Debate on the Net Barter Terms of Trade Between Primary Commodities and Manufactures, *Economic Journal*, 90.

Srinivasan, T.N. 1977: Development, Poverty and Basic Human Needs: Some Issues. *Food Research Institute Studies*, 16(2).

Strauss, J. 1983: Determinants of Food Consumption in Rural Sierre Leone: Application of the Quadratic Expenditure System to the Consumption-Leisure Component of the Household-Farm Model, *Journal of Development Economics*, 10.

Taylor, L.E. 1991: *Income Distribution, Inflation, and Growth: Lectures on Structuralist Macroeconomic Theory*. Cambridge, MA: MIT Press.

Taylor, L.E., Bacha, E., Cardoso, D. and Lysy, F.J. 1980: *Models of Growth and Distribution for Brazil*. London: Oxford University Press.

Turnham, D. and Jaeger, I. 1971: The Employment Problem in Less Developed Countries: A Review of the Evidence. Paris: OECD Development Centre.

United Nations Development Programme. 1990–1993: *Human Development Reports*. New York: Oxford University Press.

Williamson, J. 1985: *Did British Capitalism Breed Inequality?* London: Allen & Unwin.

—— 1989: Inequality, Poverty, and the Industrial Revolution; Migration and Wage Gaps: An Escape from Poverty?; and Accumulation and Inequality: Making the Connection. Third Simon Kuznets Memorial Lectures; Economic Growth Center, Yale University.

The World Bank. 1993a: *The East Asian Miracle: Economic Growth and Public Policy*. New York: Oxford University Press.

—— 1993b: *World Development Report*. Washington DC: Oxford University Press.

Index